Professional
Beverage
Management

Professional Beverage Management

BOB LIPINSKI

KATHIE LIPINSKI

JOHN WILEY & SONS, INC.

New York • Chichester • Weinheim • Brisbane • Singapore • Toronto

Library of Congress Cataloging-in-Publication Data:

Lipinski, Robert A.
    Professional beverage management / Bob Lipinski, Kathie Lipinski.
      p.   cm.
    Includes bibliographical references and index.
    ISBN 0-471-28737-7
    1. Bars (Drinking establishments)—Management.   2. Alcoholic beverages.
I. Lipinski Kathleen A.   II. Title.
TX950.7.L57   1996   95-49069
647.95'068—dc20

Printed in the United States of America

  2   3   4   5   6   7   8   9   10   01   00   99

We dedicate this book to each other;

For all the storms we have weathered;

For the many blessings in our lives;

And for the love that we share.

Contents

Foreword

The hospitality industry is the world's largest, in terms not only of annual revenues but also number of employees and quite probably the amount of real estate occupied. The beverage industries, of course, are major contributors to the hospitality industry, whether the beverage in question is a fountain drink, a glass of milk or juice with breakfast, a bottle of wine with lunch or dinner, or a mixed drink or beer in the bar.

Given the hospitality industry's huge stake in beverages, there clearly is a need for a comprehensive book that in simple, everyday language tells readers, many of whom are not native speakers of English, everything they need to know about beverages but don't know where to find out. Such a book is *Professional Beverage Management,* by Bob and Kathie Lipinski, two of the most knowledgeable people I've ever met on the sometimes complex, sometimes fascinating, and always commercially important world of beverages.

To be sure, there is no dearth of books on most individual beverages, whether coffee or wine or tea or single-malt scotches. Most of these books are aimed at consumers, and most are either highly technical or hopelessly inane. Few if any writers before Bob and Kathie Lipinski have undertaken the enormous task of research-ing and wring a single book that covers all beverages and should appeal no less to consumers than to restaurateurs, hoteliers, other beverage professionals, and students who aspire to careers in hospitality.

Professional Beverage Management meets the challenge and should be a must for the library of everyone with a more than casual interest in beverages. It takes its place alongside Bob and Kathie Lipinski's earlier volumes, *Professional Guide to Alcoholic Beverages* and *The Complete Beverage Dictionary*, both industry standards.

Paul Gillette

Paul Gillette is publisher and editor of leading newsletters for the food and beverage industies: *Healthy Eating, Taste, California Chef, California Beverage Hotline, The Wine Investor,* and *The Wine Investor's Buyer's Guide.*

Several months after writing this foreword Paul Gillette passed away. Although he will never see the finished work, his thoughts and inspiration will live on. We will miss Paul for he was a pal, buddy, mentor, wine-writing and traveling companion, and a fellow culinarian. But most of all, he was a man we could truly call friend.

Preface

There have been so many, many changes in the hospitality industry during the past two decades that writing a book which adequately covers the fascinating world of wine, beer, and distilled spirits (in addition to low alcoholic and nonalcoholic beverages) while at the same time providing adequate coverage of the controls necessary to run a facility presented a great challenge. The management side of this book takes a hard look at effectively writing a beverage list; wine-by-the glass programs; the often overlooked purchasing function; coverage of cost controls; marketing and merchandising ideas for the 21st century; and finally alcoholic beverage service, which keeps your facility batting 1.000!

The first half of the book discusses the beverages, both alcoholic and nonalcoholic. The second half looks at the management or running of a facility. The reason for this format is simple: "You can't **effectively** sell a product you don't know and the more you know about the product the easier the sale."

The overall objective of this book is to present comprehensive, in-depth information relative to running a facility to those people currently involved or planning to become involved in the beverage industry. Individuals can become knowledgeable about beverage management both through controls as well as through knowledge of the beverages.

Acknowledgments

We would like to thank the many people, wineries, distilleries, breweries, public relations firms, and so on, who directly and indirectly contributed to making this book possible.

Dr. Paul Gillette, editor and publisher of *The Wine Investor;* Carmel J. Tintle of Banfi Vintners; Dr. Frank Brown, Dean of the School of Hotel Administration at St. John's University; Dr. Tom Bloom, Executive Director, Educational Foundation of the National Restaurant Association; Don Sebastiani, CEO of Sebastiani Vineyards; Peter M.F. Sichel, H. Sichel Sohne, Inc. New York; Michaela K. Rodeno, CEO of St. Supéry Vineyards; Donald K. Beaver, National Retail Sales Department; Bradley M. Coleman, National Draft Beer Manager, Miller Brewing Company; Dr. Lucio Caputo, President of the Italian Wine and Food Institute; Augusto Marchini of the Italian Wine Center; Rory P. Callahan; Brian Abbott; Anne Luther; Niki Singer; Marsha J. Palanci; Stefano Girelli of Casa Girelli, Italy; Carol Sullivan, German Wine Information Bureau; Edward L. Pohlman, Libbey Glass Company; Professor Jim Turley, New York Institute of Technology; Plastic Bottle Information Bureau; Champagne News & Information Bureau; Cognac Information Bureau; The Scotch Whisky Information Center; Food & Wines From France; Baron Philippe de Rothschild, Inc.; Joseph Seagram Sons & Co.; M. Shanken Communications; National Restaurant Association; *Nation's Restaurant News;* and Jobson Publications.

A special thanks goes to Melissa Rosati of Van Nostrand Reinhold, who listened to our suggestion of this book and *made it happen.* Also a special thanks to Jackie Martin for her untiring work, time, and effort in making this book possible.

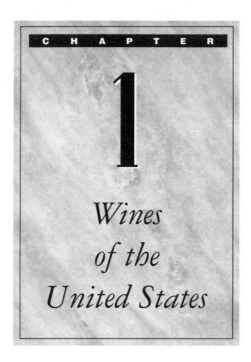

CHAPTER

1

Wines
of the
United States

Since the repeal of Prohibition in 1933, the quality of wine produced in the United States, especially California, has risen so dramatically and to such a high level that winemakers in Europe are seeking advice and technology from the United States. Forty-five states produce wine mostly from grapes, although fruit wines are also produced in some states. (The five states that do not produce wine are Alaska, Nebraska, North Dakota, South Dakota, and Wyoming.) The United States grows more types of grapes and produces more varieties of wine than any other country except Italy. The diversity of tastes and quality is staggering.

▶ WINE LABEL LAWS

Americans are rapidly surpassing their European counterparts in their eagerness to learn more about the wines they purchase. While the U.S. wine industry has developed, matured, and perfected the delicate art of winemaking, it has been able to offer a choice of wines to suit every palate and pocketbook. As Americans have become more adventurous in their wine selections, they look to the label for more information. Some questions generally asked are: What can the label tell the consumer? What makes one wine different from another? What is the dominant grape in the wine? Where is it grown? Federal regulations are quite detailed and the information they require winemakers to display on their labels is sufficient to assist the consumer in making an informed choice. The following labeling regulations became effective on January 1, 1983:

Vintage date. A vintage date on the label indicates that 95 percent or more of the wine is produced from grapes grown in that year. If a vintage date is shown on the label, an *appellation of origin,* other than a country, will be shown as well. The revised European Economic Community (EEC) regulations include a clause which states that wine exported to the United States must contain at least 95 percent of the stated vintage year.

Varietal wine. A wine made wholly or predominantly from a single grape variety, which is named on the label (for example, Cabernet Sauvignon, Pinot Noir, Zinfandel, Baco Noir, Chardonnay, Seyval, Sauvignon Blanc). A varietal designation on the label requires an appellation of origin and means that at least 75 percent of **that** grape variety is used in the wine.

Wines made from *Vitis labrusca* grapes (a species of grapevine native to eastern North America)—such as Concord—are an exception because of the grape's intense flavor. These wines must contain a minimum of 51 percent of that grape variety and it will be so stated on the label. If the label carries no percentage statement, the wine must contain at least 75 percent of the *Vitis labrusca* variety. (*Vitis vinifera* is a European grapevine species considered by many to be the premium grape in winemaking worldwide.)

Wine labels are not required to bear a varietal designation. Other designations such as "red wine," "white wine," and "table wine" are used to identify the wine or the type of grape used or where it was grown. On California wine labels, designations such as "Chablis" or "Burgundy" indicate wines similar in name only to the wines originally made in geographic regions indicated by those names. In this situation, these names are referred to as *generic* wines. Other notable examples of U.S.-produced generic wines are Sauterne, Rhine, Chianti, Champagne, Tokay, Madeira, sherry, and port. There are no federal regulations that stipulate the grape varieties which American-produced "generic" wines may contain.

Some wines, such as Pommard (France), Rüdesheimer (Germany), and Chianti (Italy), are designated with distinctive names that are permissible only on specific wines from a particular site or region within the country of origin.

Alcohol content. A statement of alcohol content in percentage by volume appears on most labels as "alc. ___% vol." or "___ Alc./Vol." or "Alc. ___% to % Vol." As an alternative to listing exact percentage of alcohol, some bottlers prefer to use the label *table wine* for wine that has an alcohol content between 7 and 14 percent. For *table wines,* the law allows a 1.5 percent variation in either direction from the stated percentage as long as the alcohol does not exceed 14 percent. Alcoholic beverages that contain less than 7 percent by volume are called *wine beverages,* and those greater than 14 percent are called *dessert wines.*

Alcohol-by-volume. The alcoholic content of a liquid, usually expressed as a numerical percentage of the volume.

Appellation of origin. An appellation of origin refers to the name of the place where the dominant grapes used in the wine are grown. It can be the name of a country, state, county, or geographical region, also known as a viticultural area. A country, state, or county appellation on the label means that at least 75 percent of the wine is produced from grapes grown there. If two or three states or counties are listed as an appellation of origin and 100 percent of the wine is made from grapes grown in those areas, the label will indicate the percentage from each location. The Bureau of Alcohol, Tobacco, and Firearms (BATF) approved a unique regional appellation known as *Pacific Coast* for wines blended from grapes grown in California, Oregon, and Washington State. This appellation requires a blended wine to list the specific percentages of grapes, in descending order, originating from each of those three states. The Pacific Coast label also allows for vintage dates, which the current American label doesn't.

Viticultural area. A U.S. viticultural area is a delimited, geographical, grape-growing region with soil, climate, history, and geographic features that set it apart from the surrounding areas and make it ideal for grape growing. A viticultural area appellation on the label indicates that 85 percent or more of the wine is produced from grapes grown in the particular area. The growers first proposed this system in 1978 and it became law in 1980. The first "approved viticultural area" was approved in 1983.

Estate bottled. When "estate bottled" appears on a label, it means that 100 percent of the wine comes from grapes grown on land owned or controlled by a winery located in a particular viticultural area. Besides growing the grapes, that winery has also crushed, fermented, finished, aged, processed, and bottled the wine in one continuous operation.

Produced and bottled by. Means that the named winery: (a) fermented not less than 75 percent of such wine at the stated address; or (b) changed the class or *type* of the wine by addition of alcohol, brandy, flavors, colors, or artificial carbonation at the stated address; or (c) produced sparkling wine by secondary fermentation at the stated address. The term is synonymous with *made and bottled by.*

Blended and bottled by. Means that the named winery mixed the wine with other wines of the same class and type at the stated address.

Cellared and bottled by. Means that the named winery, at the stated address, subjected the wine to cellar treatment. The term is synonymous with *vinted and bottled by* and *prepared and bottled by*.

▶ CALIFORNIA

California is the classic wine land. Its long, gentle, sunlit seasons nurture the world's great wine grapes. Its fabled vineyards and wineries combine tradition with modern science to produce wines for every taste, occasion, and pocketbook. Each wine possesses its own merits and characteristics. There are more than 327,000 acres of wine grapes grown in 45 of California's 58 counties.

California's first grapevines were brought from Mexico by the Franciscan Fathers during the 1760s. Among these early grape cuttings was a variety called Criolla (now known as Mission) that, with few exceptions, is no longer planted.

In the opulent gold rush days, vintners started bringing cuttings from the finest grapevines of Europe to be planted in various regions of California. Perhaps the most prominent of these vintners was a Hungarian count, Agoston Haraszthy, often referred to as the "Father of American Viticulture."

The first vineyard was established in 1824 by Joseph Chapman in Los Angeles, and in 1869, George West of Stockton produced this state's first "White Zinfandel."

Wine-Producing Regions

California is divided into wine-producing or viticultural areas whose numbers seem to be increasing on a monthly basis. The most important areas are:

North coast: Napa Valley, Sonoma County, Mendocino County, and Lake County
North-Central coast: Monterey County, Santa Clara, and Livermore
Central Valley: San Joaquin Valley
South-Central coast: San Luis Obispo and Santa Barbara

California's Wineries

Virtually all California wineries produce Cabernet Sauvignon, Merlot, Pinot Noir, Zinfandel, Chardonnay, Sauvignon Blanc (also known as Fumé Blanc), and Johannisberg Riesling. To eliminate repetitiveness, only in those instances where different wines are made, or if the winery limits itself to one type, will the wine type be listed.

ALPHABETICAL LISTING OF WINERIES

Winery Name	Date Established	Winery Name	Date Established
Acacia Winery	1979	Concannon Vineyard	1883
Alexander Valley Vineyards	1963	Conn Creek Winery	1974
Almadén Vineyards	1852	Corbett Canyon Vineyards	1979
Arrowood Vineyards & Winery	1987	Cuvaison Winery	1970
Atlas Peak Vineyards	1987	Delicato Vineyards	1935
Benziger Family Winery	1980	Diamond Creek Vineyards	1972
Beringer Vineyards	1876	Dry Creek Vineyard	1972
Bonny Doon Vineyard	1983	Duckhorn Vineyards	1976
Bouchaine Vineyards	1981	Dunn Vineyards	1982
David Bruce Winery	1964	Emilio-Guglielmo Winery	1925
Buena Vista Winery	1857	Far Niente Winery	1885
Burgess Cellars	1880	Ferrari-Carano Winery	1985
B. V. (Beaulieu Vineyards)	1900	Fetzer Vineyards	1968
Byron Vineyard & Winery	1984	Firestone Vineyard	1974
Davis Bynum Winery	1965	Folie á Deux Winery	1981
Cain Vineyards and Winery	1981	Foppiano Vineyards	1896
Cakebread Cellars	1973	Fortino Winery	1948
Calera Wine Company	1976	Franciscan Vineyards	1972
Callaway Winery & Vineyard	1974	Freemark Abbey Winery	1939
Carneros Creek Winery	1972	Gallo Winery	1933
Caymus Vineyards	1971	Geyser Peak Winery	1880
Chalk Hill Winery	1980	Guimarra Vineyards	1946
Chalone Vineyard	1960	Grgich Hills Cellars	1977
Chappellet Winery	1967	Groth Vineyards & Winery	1982
Château Chevalier Winery	1969	Guenoc Winery	1981
Château Montelena Winery	1882	Gundlach-Bundschu Winery	1858
Château St. Jean Winery	1973	Hacienda Wine Cellars	1973
Christian Brothers Winery	1882	Hanzell Vineyards	1956
Clos du Bois Winery	1976	Heitz Winery	1961
Clos du Val Winery	1972	William Hill Winery	1978
Clos Pegase Winery	1986	Inglenook Vineyards	1879

ALPHABETICAL LISTING OF WINERIES *(continued)*

Winery Name	Date Established	Winery Name	Date Established
Jekel Vineyards	1978	Raymond Vineyard & Cellar	1974
Johnson Turnbull Wine Cellars	1979	Ridge Vineyards & Winery	1962
Jordan Vineyard & Winery	1976	Rutherford Hill Winery	1976
Kalin Cellars	1977	Saintsbury	1981
Karly Winery	1980	Sanford Winery	1981
Robert Keenan Winery	1977	V. Sattui Winery	1885
Kendall-Jackson Vineyards	1982	Sebastiani Vineyards	1904
Kenwood Vineyards	1906	Shafer Vineyards	1979
Charles Krug Winery	1861	Silver Oak Wine Cellars	1972
J. Lohr	1974	Simi Winery	1876
Long Vineyards	1978	Sonoma-Cutrer Vineyards	1973
Lytton Springs Winery	1977	Spottswoode Winery	1982
Louis M. Martini	1922	Stag's Leap Wine Cellars	1972
Paul Masson Winery	1852	Steltzner Vineyards	1983
Matanzas Creek Winery	1978	Robert Stemmler Winery	1977
Mayacamas Vineyards	1889	Sterling Vineyards	1964
Meridian Vineyards	1988	Stonegate, Inc.	1973
Mirassou Vineyards	1854	Stony Hill Vineyard	1953
Robert Mondavi Winery	1966	Rodney Strong Vineyards	1959
Monterey Vineyard	1973	St. Clement Vineyards	1975
Monteviña Winery	1973	St. Supéry Vineyards & Winery	1987
Mount Veeder Winery	1972	Sutter Home Winery	1847
Murphy-Goode Estate Winery	1987	Joseph Swan Vineyards	1969
Newlan Vineyards & Winery	1981	Trefethen Vineyards	1886
Newton Vineyard	1979	Viansa Winery	1987
Niebaum-Coppola Vineyards	1978	Vichon Winery	1980
Parducci Winery	1933	Villa Mt. Eden Winery	1974
Pedrizetti Winery	1938	Wente Brothers Winery	1883
Pedroncelli Winery	1904	Zaca Mesa Winery	1972
Joseph Phelps Vineyards	1973	Z. D. Wines	1969
Martin Ray Winery	1936		

Almadén Vineyards is the oldest winery in operation in the state. The name Almadén translated from the Moorish language means "the mine." It was so named because at that time it was located near the New Almadén Quicksilver Mine. Around 1860, Almadén produced California's first commercial Cabernet Sauvignon, and in 1941 Almadén made the first Grenache rosé.

Beringer Vineyards was established by the brothers Jacob L. and Frederick Beringer from Mainz, Germany. Beringer is noted for its reserve Cabernet Sauvignon.

Bonny Doon Vineyard was established by the Grahm Family. Bonny Doon pioneered the making of Rhône Valley red and white wines in California, along with other interesting wines labeled Vin Gris and Cigar Volant.

Burgess Cellars was originally known as "Rossini Vineyards." Later, in 1943, J. Leland Stewart renamed it the Souverain Winery. In 1949, Stewart of Souverain Vineyards became the first to bottle the Green Hungarian grape variety as a separate *varietal.* In 1972, Tom and Linda Burgess purchased the winery and changed the name.

B. V. (Beaulieu Vineyards) Beaulieu translated means "beautiful place." B. V. was established by Georges de Latour, a native of the Périgord region of France who came to the United States in 1883. In 1938, de Latour traveled to Paris in search of an enologist and hired a young man by the name of André Tchelistcheff, who eventually became the dean of American winemakers.

B. V. Cabernet Sauvignon Georges de Latour Private Reserve, first produced in 1936, is considered to be one of the finest examples of Cabernet Sauvignon made in California.

Cain Vineyards and Winery is noted for a red Meritage wine labeled "Cain Five."

Callaway Winery & Vineyard, which specializes in white wines, was established by Ely Callaway.

Chalone Vineyard, owned by Dick Graf, was known as "F. William Silvear Vineyards" until 1957, when the original owner died.

Château Chevalier Winery was established by Gregory Bissonette. The winery, which features stained glass windows and twin steeples, was originally built by George Chevalier in 1891.

Château Montelena Winery was established by Alfred L. Tubbs, a state senator. In the famous Paris competition held on May 24, 1976, California wines were tasted against their French counterparts, and a 1973 Château Montelena Chardonnay won the competition.

Château St. Jean Winery specializes in white wines, with an emphasis on single-vineyard Chardonnay, late-harvested (wines made from especially ripe grapes that have been picked or harvested later than usual) Johannisberg Riesling, and Gewürztraminer.

Christian Brothers Winery first opened its doors in the city of Martinez. Later, in 1932, the winery moved to its current home in the Napa Valley. The winery originally produced wines under the "Mont La Salle" label until 1937, when the name Christian Brothers replaced it. At one time Christian Brothers produced a red wine labeled "Pinot St. George."

Clos du Val Winery was established by Bernard Portet. He is the son of André Portet, the technical advisor of Château Lafite-Rothschild of Bordeaux, France.

Concannon Vineyard occasionally produces a white wine from a Russian grape variety called "Rkatsiteli," first bottled around 1972. In 1964, Concannon became the first winery to bottle Petite Sirah as a separate varietal.

Corbett Canyon Vineyards was originally known as the Lawrence Winery. The winery became the first to produce a Chardonnay Nouveau, from their 1980 harvest.

Delicato Vineyards, established in 1935, was originally known as the Sam Jasper Winery.

Firestone Vineyard was established by A. Brooks and Kate Firestone of the famous tire and rubber company.

Foppiano Vineyards, originally known as Riverside Farms, was established in Healdsburg by John Foppiano. The winery once sold its premium wines under the label of "Luigi Wines."

Freemark Abbey Winery was established by three owners— Albert "Abbey" Ahern, Charles "Free"man, and "Mark" Foster—hence the name "Freemark Abbey." It is noted for producing a Cabernet Sauvignon, known as "Bosché," named after John Bosché, a San Francisco lawyer.

Gallo Winery was established by Ernest and Julio Gallo. Gallo makes more than 30 percent of all wines produced in the United States. During the winery's expansion, the American Vineyards of Livingston was purchased, making the 130-million-gallon winery the largest in the world. In 1957, proprietary flavored apéritif wines labeled Thunderbird and Gypsy Rose made their debut; in 1960 Ripple followed; in 1964, Hearty Burgundy, and in January 1968, a cream sherry labeled Old Decanter. Since that time other wines such as Paisano, Night Train, Boone's Farm, Madria-Madria Sangría, Tyrolia, Spañada, Polo Brindisi, Carlo Rossi, and Bartles & Jaymes Wine Coolers have been produced.

In addition to producing "jug" wines, Gallo produces an entire line of varietal wines under the Ernest & Julio Gallo label.

Grgich Hills Cellars was established by Miljenko (Mike) Grgich and Austin Hills of San Francisco's Hills Brothers Coffee empire.

Gundlach-Bundschu Winery was established by Jacob Gundlach and his son-in-law, Charles Bundschu. This winery at one time produced an unusual wine labeled "Kleinberger," from a rare clone of the Riesling grape.

Hanzell Vineyards derives its name from a combination of its founders: "zell" for James D. Zellerbach, then ambassador to Italy, and "Hana," his wife's name.

Heitz Winery was established by Joseph and Alice Heitz. The winery was originally known as Leon Brendel's "Only One" Grignolino Vineyards. Heitz's Cabernet Sauvignon with the Martha's Vineyard designation (first produced in 1966) was named after Martha May, a local grape grower, and is considered one of California's finest.

Inglenook Vineyards Inglenook, a Scotch word for fireside, was established by the Finnish Captain Gustave Ferdinand Niebaum. Inglenook occasionally produces Charbono, a full-bodied, varietal red wine.

Charles Krug Winery is the oldest winery in the Napa Valley, owned by Peter Mondavi and Sons since 1943. The letters "C. K." on C. K. Mondavi wine labels stands for Charles Krug, the founder. In 1954, the Charles Krug Winery was the first winery to offer Chenin Blanc as a separate variety.

J. Lohr was established as the Turgeon-Lohr Winery by Bernard Turgeon and Jerome Lohr. The name was changed to J. Lohr after Turgeon sold his half.

Louis M. Martini Winery was originally known as the "E. J. Foley Winery" when it was located in Kingsburg, Fresno. When it moved in 1933 to its current location in the Napa Valley, it took its new name. In 1968, the winery became the first to bottle Merlot as a separate varietal. The winery produces a red wine called Barbera.

Paul Masson Winery claims that it was established in 1852. However, Paul Masson actually came to California in 1878. Masson, who would later marry the daughter of Charles LeFranc, then owner of Almadén Vineyards, was a Frenchman born in Beaune, in the region of Burgundy.

Mayacamas Vineyards was established by John Henry Fischer. The winery once bottled its wines under the label of "Lokoya."

Mirassou is the oldest winemaking family still in continuous operation in the state. For many years, Mirassou Vineyards was in the "jug" wine business (selling private label wines), but in 1966, the family decided to bottle wines under its own name.

Robert Mondavi Winery, in 1966, developed the name *Fumé Blanc* as a means of selling Sauvignon Blanc. The winery also produces a line of lower-priced wines labeled "Woodbridge."

Niebaum-Coppola Vineyards was established by film producer Francis Ford Coppola. The winery specializes in a French-style Cabernet Sauvignon, which is a Cabernet Franc blended wine called "Rubicon."

Pedroncelli Winery was established by John Pedroncelli. In 1958, the winery became the first to produce a "rosé" Zinfandel.

Joseph Phelps Vineyards was originally known as Stonebridge. The winery is best known for its late-harvested Johannisberg Riesling and Gewürztraminer, a German variety called Scheurebe, Syrah, and a red blend labeled "Insignia."

Ridge Vineyards & Winery was originally known as the Montebello Winery. Ridge is noted almost exclusively for red wines such as their extremely full-bodied Cabernet Sauvignon, Petite Sirah, and Zinfandel.

Rutherford Hill Winery, originally known as Souverain of Rutherford, was established by Bernard Skoda.

Sebastiani Vineyards was established by Samuele Sebastiani. In 1972, Sebastiani became the first to produce a Nouveau Gamay Beaujolais.

Simi Winery was established by the brothers Giuseppe and Pietro Simi. "Montepulciano Winery" was the original name of the Simi Winery, which bottled its wines under the label of "Hotel del Monte."

Stag's Leap Wine Cellars was established by Warren and Barbara Winiarski. (This winery has no connection with Stags' Leap Vineyards.) In the famous Paris taste-off held on May 24, 1976, California wines were tasted against their French counterparts, and a 1972 Stag's Leap Wine Cellars Cabernet Sauvignon won first prize.

Sterling Vineyards This chalk white, picturesque, monastery-like winery can be seen for miles at the upper end of the Napa Valley. The only way most tourists can visit this beautiful winery is by means of a cable car. One of the interesting things about this winery is its instructive "self-guided" tours through the crushing and fermenting areas and the aging cellars. Its tasting room is on top of the winery, with a spectacular view of the valley.

Rodney Strong Vineyards In 1959, the Tiburon Vintners of Sonoma County was established. In 1961, the name was changed to Windsor Vineyards, then Sonoma Winery. It was changed to its present name in the 1980s.

Sutter Home Winery was established as the John Thomann Winery and Distillery of Napa Valley. In 1906, its name was changed to Sutter Home Winery, and in January 1947, it was acquired by John and Mario Trinchero. Sutter Home is noted for its white and red Zinfandels.

Trefethen Vineyards was established by the Goodman Brothers. The original name of the winery was "Eschol" after the river in the Bible where Moses and his people found gigantic clusters of grapes. John and Janet Trefethen, the current owners since 1973, produce two proprietary wines labeled "Eschol Red" and "Eschol White."

Wente Brothers Winery was established by Carl Heinrich Wente. Wente produces Johannisberg Riesling (both dry and late-harvest) and was the first winery to bottle Chardonnay (1934) and Sauvignon Blanc (1935) as separate varietals.

Z. D. Wines was established by Gino Zepponi and Norman de Leuze.

The following is a discussion of other wine-producing states.

▶ ARKANSAS

The state of Arkansas has six bonded wineries in operation, a far cry from the 106 original wineries in existence there during the early 1800s.

The best-known wineries are:

Winery Name	Date Established
Post Familie Vineyards	1880
Wiederkehr Winery	1880

▶ HAWAII

There is only one commercial winery in Hawaii, located on the beautiful island of Maui approximately 2,000 feet above sea level on part of a 23-acre ranch; its grapevines were first planted in 1974.

Tedeschi Winery, owned and operated by C. Pardee Erdman and Joanne and Emil Tedeschi, produces an unusual wine made from pineapples, called Maui Blanc. It is produced in two versions, still and sparkling, using the *méthode champenoise.* Tedeschi's first grape harvest was in 1977 when Carnelian grapes were harvested.

▶ IDAHO

Idaho's grape-growing industry began in the 1860s when a Frenchman named Del Sol planted *Vitis vinifera* cuttings from California on a slope outside Lewiston, near the Idaho and Washington border. Del Sol's wines and those of other Idaho growers not only proved to be commercially successful, but won many national awards throughout the years until 1920, when Prohibition dealt its fatal blow to the industry.

With the repeal of Prohibition in 1933, an Idaho farmer named Gregory Eaves started his own winery and bottled his wines under "The Garden of Eaves" label. History is not clear on the cause of the demise of this venture in 1945, but it was the only recorded effort to produce wine in the state until the Symms plantings in 1971. In 1975, Bill Broich founded the Ste. Chapelle Winery, and in 1978, Symms Vineyards merged with Ste. Chapelle Winery (then located in Emmett) and moved to Sunny Slope, 13 miles southwest of Caldwell. Ste. Chapelle produces a Cabernet Sauvignon, Chardonnay, Chenin Blanc, Gewürztraminer, Johannisberg Riesling, and Pinot Noir.

The best-known wineries are:

Winery Name	Date Established
Camas Winery	1983
Ste. Chapelle Winery	1976

▶ ILLINOIS

As far back as 1880, when the U.S. Department of Agriculture published a special report on the progress of viticulture and wine production in the nation, Illinois was one of the grape-growing enterprises of the Midwest. Vineyards around the village of Nauvoo on the Mississippi River were first planted around 1845. In 1847, John Tanner, an industrialist from Switzerland, planted Nauvoo's first vineyard. Nothing happened until 1850, when Alois Rheinberger from Liechtenstein officially opened a winery, producing wines of extraordinary popularity for hundreds of miles in all directions. Fred Baxter eventually purchased the property and opened the Gem City Vineyard Company after overcoming many obstacles, including the Illinois law forbidding the tasting or selling of wines at the winery. (This law was finally changed in 1977.)

The Thompson Winery, founded in 1964 by John Thompson, is one of the leading producers of sparkling wines, labeled Père Marquette. The Lynfred Winery, established in 1975 and owned and operated by Lynn and Fred Koehler, is located in the flatlands west of O'Hare Field in Roselle.

Nowadays wines are made from *Vitis labrusca* and French-American hybrids, although plantings of *Vitis vinifera* are steadily increasing.

The best-known wineries are:

Winery Name	Date Established
Alto Vineyards	1988
Baxter Vineyards	1988
Glunz Family Winery	1993
Lynfred Winery	1975
Thompson Winery	1964

▶ INDIANA

It wasn't until 1971 that the Hoosier State permitted the existence of commercial wineries. One might ask why, since it has a grape-growing history dating back to the early 1800s.

The Ohio River Valley proved favorable for viticulture as early as 1802, when Swiss immigrants led by Jean Jacques Dufour purchased land that is now Switzerland County and established the city of Vevay. Until the late 1820s, Indiana was the foremost grape-growing area in the United States. However, Prohibition destroyed the grape-growing and winemaking industry in Indiana. After Prohibition ended in 1933, wineries slowly began to spring up across the state.

The best-known wineries are:

Winery Name	Date Established
Butler Winery	1983
Château Pomije	1986
Château Thomas Winery	1984
Oliver Wine Company	1972
Scotella Winery	1985

▶ MARYLAND

Maryland's best-known wineries are:

Winery Name	Date Established
Basignani Winery	1986
Berrywine Plantations	1976
Boordy Vineyards	1942
Byrd Vineyards	1976
Catoctin Vineyards	1983
Elk Run Vineyards	1983

Boordy Vineyards was established in 1942 (Maryland's oldest); it was originally owned by Philip and Jocelyn Wagner. Boordy Vineyards was the first U.S. winery to produce a French-American hybrid varietal wine, a 1945 Baco Noir. (French-American hybrids are grape varieties developed from crossing American grapevines with European *Vitis vinifera* grapevines.)

▶ MICHIGAN

St. Julian Winery, located in Paw Paw, the state's oldest winery, was established by Mariano Meconi. Upon the repeal of Prohibition in 1933, Mr. Meconi moved from Windsor, Ontario, Canada, across the river to Detroit, to begin making his wines. Three years later Meconi relocated the winery to its present site to be closer to the grapevines. Meconi was born in Faleria, Italy, a small village north of Rome. He named the winery St. Julian, after the patron saint of Faleria.

The best-known wineries are:

Winery Name	Date Established
Boskydel Vineyard	1976
Leelanau Wine Cellars	1975
L. Mawby Vineyards	1977
St. Julian Winery	1921
Tabor Hill Winery	1970
Warner Vineyards	1938

▶ NEW JERSEY

Grapes were planted in the state more than 200 years ago when the first New Jerseyans cultivated vineyards for the British empire in the mid-1700s. In fact, by 1767, London's Royal Society of Arts had recognized two New Jersey vintners for their success in producing the finest quality wine derived from colonial agriculture.

The best-known wineries are:

Winery Name	Date Established
Alba Vineyard	1983
Amalthea Cellars	1982
Lafollette Vineyard	1986
Renault	1864

The Renault Winery was established by Louis Nicholas Renault, who came to the United States in 1855 as a representative of the ancient champagne house of the Duke of Montebello at Reims. By 1870, Renault had introduced his New Jersey Champagne and had become the largest shipper of sparkling wine in the United States. Renault was the third bonded winery to open in the United States, the first being the California-based Cucamonga Winery, and the second, the Brotherhood Winery in New York State.

▶ NEW YORK STATE

The art of growing fine grapes and producing superior wines in New York State is steeped in a long and proud tradition.

The first settlers in North America discovered huge plantations of wild *Vitis labrusca* grapevines flourishing in the state's fertile valleys. Nurtured by a unique combination of sun, soil, and climate, these native grapevines were ripe with Concord, Delaware, and Niagara grapes. Farsighted wine grape growers and dedicated winemakers attentively cultured the rich native crop. Some growers crossed the native grapevines with the *Vitis vinifera* species to produce hybrid grapes.

Some of the earlier problems of growing *Vitis vinifera* in New York included the following:

1. The grapevines were not winter hardy.
2. The wrong rootstocks were selected.
3. Virus and other "health problems" of the grapevine were not identified.
4. Poor nutrient deficiency of the soil was not identified.

The successful planting of *Vitis vinifera,* without crossing it with native grapes, was accomplished in New York by Dr. Konstantin Frank and Charles Fournier, who in 1961 produced New York's first Chardonnay wine.

New York State is the nation's second-largest producer of grapes and wines (36,000 acres and more than 35 million gallons in 1994). There is a wine for every taste, with white, red, sparkling, sweet dessert wines, and coolers produced from *Vitis labrusca,* French-American hybrids, and *Vitis vinifera* grapes. Wines that carry the New York State appellation, regardless of whether or not they are estate bottled, must have a minimum of 75 percent of their volume derived from grapes grown in New York State.

Wine-Producing Regions

The scenic Finger Lakes, Hudson Valley, Long Island, and Lake Erie regions are the largest wine grape-growing and winemaking areas in the state.

The Finger Lakes region.   The clear, deep waters of the Finger Lakes keep this region's climate temperate while plentiful shale beds (similar to those in Champagne, France) help drain the soil. The slow-warming lakes retard spring growth, protect it against the danger of frost, and keep the grapevines warmer on chilly fall nights. The Finger Lakes vineyards are located approximately 350 miles northwest of New York City along Lakes Canandaigua, Cayuga, Hemlock, Keuka, and Seneca. Although the Finger Lakes received their *appellation* in October 1982, grape growing and winemaking date back to the 1820s.

The Hudson River region.   The Hudson River region is one of the oldest wine-producing areas in North America, with a history that dates from the late 1500s, when immigrant French Huguenots planted grapes on Mohonk Mountain. When Henry Hudson sailed up the river in 1609, he found its banks covered with wild native Catawba and Concord grapevines. From that time wines have been made in the region from these native grapes. In the 1860s, French-American hybrid grapevines were introduced to the area by viticulturist Andrew Jackson Caywood, who developed the Dutchess grape variety. In recent years, growing consumer interest in quality New York State wines has led to a resurgence in vineyard development in this region. The Hudson River Valley received its *appellation* in July 1982.

Long Island.   Grapes were grown on Long Island in colonial times. "Moses the Frenchman" Fournier had extensive vineyards in Cutchogue in the early 1700s and no doubt grew *Vitis vinifera* with the help of the grafting expertise of the local Indians. Just after the American Revolution, the first governor of New York granted Paul Richards a monopoly on the sale of wines produced from his "Little Fief" on the island. Anyone planting grapes there owed him a royalty.

In the 1800s, William Robert Prince experimented extensively with many varieties of grapes in Flushing, Queens. Through his catalog, he even offered a Zinfandel that was occasionally known as "Black St. Peter."

The North Fork strip of Long Island is ideally suited for winemaking and grape growing. The growing season is approximately 210 days a year (the same as in Bordeaux, France, and Napa Valley, California). It is the only grape-growing region in the world surrounded on three sides by water, which provides temperatures that rarely go below zero in the winter and low humidity, the perfect combination for producing excellent wine grapes.

Lake Erie.   Long hours of summer sun, well-drained gravel and shale soils, and the moderating influence of Lake Erie on the local climate combine to make the Erie region one of the finest grape-growing areas in the East. The Lake Erie region received its *appellation* in November 1983.

The Wineries

In 1818, wild grapevines were grown in the Chautauqua region by Deacon Elijah Fay. Dr. Richard Underhill planted the first large vineyard in the Hudson Valley in 1827. In 1829, Reverend William Bostwick, an Episcopalian minister, planted the first grapevines (Catawba and Isabella) at the southern tip of Lake Keuka. In 1839, the first commercial winery in the Hudson Valley was opened by Jean Jacques, named Blooming Grove and later renamed Brotherhood Winery. It is the nation's oldest operating winery. Great Western Winery, which began operating on March 15, 1860 in Hammondsport as the Pleasant Valley Wine Company (changing to its present name in 1865), is the oldest winery in the Finger Lakes region, and became U.S. Bonded Winery No. 1.

In the years following Great Western, other wineries opened in the Finger Lakes region. Gold Seal Vineyards opened in 1865 and was known as the Urbana Wine Company until 1957. Eagle Crest Vineyards, established in 1872, produced wines under the O-Neh-Dah label. The Taylor Wine Company was established in 1880. In 1888 a Swiss couple, John Jacob Widmer and his wife Lysette, established the Widmer Winery; and in 1907, Alexander Bolognesi and family started the Hudson Valley Winery.

The Canandaigua Winery was established in 1945. In the language of the Seneca Indian, Canandaigua means "the chosen place." The winery produces among many others, a wine labeled Virginia Dare, the oldest brand name wine in the United States. In 1957, Mark Miller bought the Andrew Jackson Caywood Vineyards and renamed it Benmarl Vineyards, where the first *nouveau*-style wine on the East Coast was produced. In 1962, Vinifera Wine Cellars was established by Dr. Konstantin Frank, who produced a Johannisberg Riesling *Trockenbeerenauslese* in 1971. In 1970, Bully Hill Winery was founded in Hammondsport by Walter S. Taylor, who opened the first wine museum on his property. In 1973, Long Island saw its first vineyards, planted by Louisa and Alex Hargrave. But the real boom in New York wineries started with the Farm Winery Act of 1976, which essentially made it economically feasible to own and operate a winery producing fewer than 50,000 gallons per year.

ALPHABETICAL LISTING OF WINERIES TO OPEN SINCE 1976

Winery Name	Date Established	Winery Name	Date Established
Bedell Vineyards	1985	Merritt Estate Winery	1976
Bidwell Vineyards	1982	Millbrook Vineyards	1981
The Bridgehampton Winery	1982	Old Brookville Vineyards	1982
Casa Larga Vineyards	1978	Palmer Vineyards	1983
Cascade Mountain Vineyards	1973	Peconic Bay Vineyards	1980
Château Frank	1986	Pindar Vineyards	1980
Clinton Vineyards	1977	Poplar Ridge Vineyards	1981
Four Chimneys Winery	1980	Pugliese Vineyards	1980
Fox Run Vineyards	1990	Southampton Winery	1986
Glenora Winery	1977	Wagner Vineyards	1978
Gristina Vineyards	1988	West Park Wine Cellars	1983
Heron Hills Winery	1977	Hermann J. Wiemer Vineyards	1979
Knapp Vineyards	1982	Woodbury Vineyards	1979
Lenz Winery	1983		

▶ OHIO

The history of winemaking in Ohio began when Moravian missionaries, who had come to work with the Delaware Indians and the French settlers, brought native grapevines to the Marietta and Gallipolis areas. However, it was not until the 1820s and the introduction of the Catawba grape, a domestic variety rugged enough to withstand Ohio's climate, that viticulture in Ohio was to become a reality. It is believed that the Catawba Grape was first discovered in 1802 growing along the Catawba River in North Carolina. The introduction of the Catawba grape to the Ohio River Valley in 1825 from North Carolina was largely due to the efforts of Nicholas Longworth, a New England lawyer who practiced in the Cincinnati area.

Longworth and others in the area saw the potential for the greater Cincinnati area to become a "Rhineland" in America and to produce wine to rival European imports. Soon many acres of grapevines were growing, and by 1845, the annual production was more than 300,000 gallons. From the Catawba, Longworth made a light semisweet wine, which was different from the rather strong American wines of the time. However, as a taste for Ohio wines spread in the 1800s, problems developed. Diseases such as black rot, which causes young grapes to mummify and blacken, and mildew, which infects the leaves and grapes, caused heavy losses in yield and quality. With the manpower shortages accompanying the Civil War, these diseases became permanently established and closed a page in the history of winemaking in southern Ohio.

As the southern vineyards wilted, a new growing area emerged. The Lake Erie Islands had a unique climatic position. The waters surrounding them provided long growing seasons and insulated the grapevines from spreading diseases. These soon-to-be-called "Wine Islands" and the Sandusky area were settled by hard-working German immigrants who brought with them the tradition of winemaking. By the turn of the century, fifteen wineries producing five million gallons operated in and around the wine island area. Grapevines were soon planted along the entire southern shore of Lake Erie. This narrow strip along the lake became known as the Ohio Grape Belt.

Then in 1919 disaster struck with the arrival of Prohibition. Some family businesses survived by making wine for sacramental purposes and others produced juice. But the general grape-oriented economy of the area collapsed.

After Repeal in 1933, a few wineries reemerged, but the industry was generally hampered by disrepair in the vineyards, governmental restrictions, the glut of out-of-state wines, and loss of land already converted to juice varieties.

A turning point came in the 1960s with the planting of French-American hybrid varieties in southern Ohio, encouraged largely by the Ohio State University and Ohio Agricultural Research and Development Center. The success of hybrids in the south encouraged plantings in the northern grape belt. Some vinifera were also planted at this time.

Since 1965, many wineries have been established in the south along Lake Erie and in the west along the lake in the Sandusky Island area. Many of the older, more established operations expanded both plantings and facilities.

The best-known wineries are:

Winery Name	Date Established
Chalet Debonne Vineyards	1971
Harpersfield Vineyard	1986
Markko Vineyard	1968
Meier's Wine Cellars	1895

▶ OREGON

Mrs. Narcissa Prentiss Whitman entered in her diary of September 12, 1836, that in 1825 "grapes were first planted by the Hudson Bay Company at the mouth of the Columbia River, at Fort Vancouver."

The first known wineries in Oregon were established by Peter Britt in the 1850s, followed by Ernst Reuter in 1880, and Adolph Doerner in 1890. Prior to Prohibition, grape growing was sparse and haphazard, with little documentation on the type or variety of grapes grown and no information on the quality of wine produced. Following Prohibition, small wineries, often family owned, started to sprout, encouraging further planting and the start of Oregon's wine industry.

In the mid-1970s, Oregon winemakers drafted and lobbied into legislation consumer-oriented wine labeling regulations whose key provisions were:

1. A vintage date indicates that at least 95 percent of the grapes used are harvested during the year stated.
2. The name of a wine can be varietal, containing at least 90 percent of the grape variety used, with the exception of Cabernet Sauvignon, if the balance is comprised of other red Bordeaux grapes.
3. Wines must carry an appellation of origin on the label and grapes used must be limited to those areas.
4. No Oregon-produced wine may be given a generic name—for example, Chablis, Burgundy, or Rhine.
5. Oregon is noted for the quality of many of its wines including Pinot Noir, Pinot Gris, Müller-Thurgau, Johannisberg Riesling, and Gewürztraminer.

The best-known wineries are:

Winery Name	Date Established
Adams Vineyard	1985
Adelsheim Vineyard	1971
Amity Vineyards	1976
Argyle	1987
Cameron Winery	1984
Château Benoit	1979
Cooper Mountain Vineyards	1987
Domaine Drouhin	1988
Elk Cove Vineyards	1977
Evesham Wood Vineyards	1986
Eyrie Vineyards	1966
Honeywood Winery	1933
Knudsen-Erath Winery	1972
Lange Winery	1987
Oak Knoll Winery	1970
Rex Hill Vineyards	1983
Sokol Blosser	1977
Springhill Cellars	1988
Tualatin Winery	1973

▶ PENNSYLVANIA

The wine history of Pennsylvania covers a span of three centuries, dating back to the seventeenth century when William Penn and other settlers imported French and Spanish grapevines. A tablet placed in Philadelphia's Fairmount Park marks the site of Penn's own vineyard, planted in 1684. A little more than a century later, in 1793, the first commercial vineyards in America were established by Pierre Legaux at Spring Mill, just north of Philadelphia, and in 1818 by Thomas Eichelberger in York County.

None of the early vineyards in the eastern part of the state survived for any length of time. Modern herbicides and pesticides did not exist and many of the present-day grape varieties had not been developed. Low winter temperatures, diseases, and pests all took their toll.

The first vineyard in the western part of the state was planted in the Pittsburgh area in 1793, and grape growing came to Erie County in 1850. In Allegheny County, a religious group known as the Harmony Society also planted vineyards in the 1800s and became well known for its wines. The Harmonists were a celibate group, however, and disappeared around the beginning of the twentieth century.

Grape growing and winemaking flourished during the 1800s and early 1900s. But with the coming of Prohibition after World War I, the last of the state's existing wineries went out of business. Pennsylvania emerged from that era as a tightly controlled monopoly state. It was not until 1968, with the passage of the *Limited Wine Act,* that the modern period began. In recent years the changes have been dramatic; wineries and vineyards continue to spring up across the state.

The best-known wineries are:

Winery Name	Date Established
Allegro Vineyards	1980
Buckingham Valley Vineyards	1966
Bucks Country Winery	1973
The Chaddsford Winery	1982
Mazza Vineyards	1972
Naylor Wine Cellars	1978
Nissley Vineyards	1976
Presque Isle Wine Cellars	1964
Sand Castle Winery	1981

▶ TEXAS

Grape growing in Texas dates back to around 1662, when Spanish padres made sacramental wines from the Mission grapes at the Ysleta Mission near El Paso. Most of the vineyards that were planted by the Mission Fathers contained grapes brought from Spain and neighboring Mexico.

Thomas Volney Munson, a local hybridizer in Denison, developed many grape varieties suitable for planting in the hot, dry Texas sun. He was also instrumental in helping the French to reestablish their vineyards after the devastating effects of the *phylloxera* plague, and because of his work, he was awarded the Legion of Honor in 1888.

Many of the early commercial winemakers preferred the wild grape that flourished in the area and for a while the industry thrived. However, the industry was virtually wiped out when Prohibition became the law of the land in 1919. When repeal came, only one winery remained in Texas—Val Verde Winery, which had survived by selling grapes for home winemaking.

The best-known wineries are:

Winery Name	Date Established
Fall Creek Vineyards	1979
La Buena Vida Winery	1978
Llano Estacado	1976
Pedernales Vineyard	1986
Pheasant Ridge Winery	1982
Schoppaul Hill Winery	1988
Val Verde Vineyards	1883

▶ VIRGINIA

The first glass wine bottle as we know it was actually manufactured in 1608 in Jamestown, Virginia. The making of fine wines is not new to the Commonwealth. More than a century ago Virginia enjoyed an international reputation for producing good Bordeaux-style red wines. The inspiration then and now came from Virginia's original wine pioneer and "father of the American wine industry," Thomas Jefferson. He recognized that Virginia's climate and soils were very similar to those of the European wine regions and insisted that fine wine grapes could be grown there.

Thomas Jefferson's vision is borne out in vineyards that flourish from the Allegheny Mountains to Chesapeake Bay. The state also claims such viticultural areas as Monticello, Shenandoah Valley, Rocky Knob, and the North Fork of the Roanoke, with more on the way.

The best-known wineries are:

Winery Name	Date Established
Barboursville Winery	1978
Burnley Vineyards	1984
Chermont Winery	1981
Ingleside Plantation Vineyards	1980
Lake Anna Winery	1990
Linden Vineyards	1987

Meredyth Winery	1975
Misty Mountain Vineyard	1985
Naked Mountain Vineyard	1981
Oasis Vineyard	1980
Piedmont Vineyards	1973
Prince Michel Vineyard	1983
The Williamsburg Winery	1985

Barboursville Winery, which was originally owned by Governor James Barbour, is a registered Virginia historic landmark. It includes the picturesque ruins of Barbour's mansion, which was designed by Thomas Jefferson, but burned to the ground on Christmas Day, 1884. The current winery was established in 1979 and is owned by Zonin Gambellara of Italy.

► WASHINGTON

Washington is the second-largest producing state (after California) of *Vitis vinifera* grapes, with more than 13,000 acres (1995) planted (Figure 1-1). Most of the *Vitis vinifera* acreage is in the Columbia Valley in the south-central portion of the state. Its vineyards lie just north of the 46 degree latitude, which is the same as that of the Bordeaux and Burgundy regions of France. The grapevine growth pattern is also similar to that of the French regions because of the long summer days (averaging approximately 17 hours of daylight in June) and crisp, cool nights.

This favorable combination in the annual growing cycle provides additional light for *photosynthesis.* Near harvest the sun's rays are less intense, causing warm days but very cool nights. The day and night temperature difference helps to produce balanced grapes— ideal sugar and fruit levels, with good natural acidity and distinctive varietal character.

Washington has three officially recognized major viticultural appellations: Columbia Valley (the state's largest), Yakima Valley (the state's first approved viticultural area since 1983), and the Walla Walla Valley.

The first vineyards were planted in 1872 by Lambert B. Evans in the southern part of the Puget Sound area. Plantings throughout the area continued until the early 1900s when irrigation from the Cascade watershed opened up the Yakima Valley for grape growing. When Prohibition arrived, Washington ceased production of commercial wine, although some sacramental wine was still available.

Washington's wineries center on the Columbia, Yakima, and Snake rivers in the east, Spokane to the northeast, and Seattle to the west.

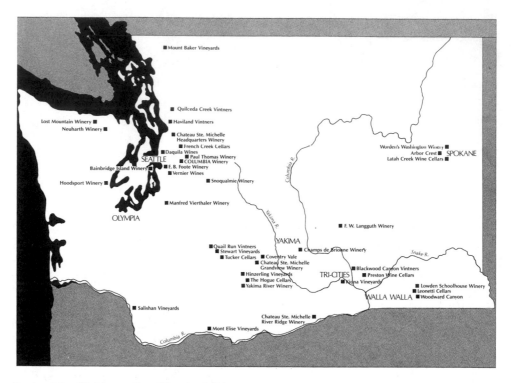

FIGURE 1-1   Washington State Wineries: 1984.

The best-known wineries are:

Winery Name	Date Established
Arbor Crest Winery	1982
Bainbridge Island Vineyards	1982
Bernard Griffin Winery	1983
Blackwood Canyon Vintners	1983
Château Ste. Michelle Winery	1934
Chinook Wines	1985
Columbia Crest Winery	1982
Columbia Winery	1962
Covey Run Vintners	1982

The Hogue Cellars	1982
Hyatt Vineyards	1987
Portteus Vineyard	1987
Preston Wine Cellars	1976
Quail Run Vintners	1982
Quarry Lake Vintners	1985
Quilceda Creek Vintners	1978
Snoqualmie Winery	1983
Staton Hills Winery	1984
Stewart Vineyards	1983
Tefft Cellars	1991
Paul Thomas Winery	1979
Washington Hills Cellars	1989

Château Ste. Michelle Winery (formerly known as the American Wine Growers Winery) in Woodinville was established in 1934. This is Washington's foremost producer of premium *(Vitis vinifera)* table wines. Growing from just over 6,000 cases in 1967 (first crush under the new name), it currently produces approximately nine to ten million cases annually.

▶ WISCONSIN

The best known winery is the Wollersheim Winery, founded in 1857 as the Kehl Winery, by Peter Kehl. When the present owner Robert Wollersheim purchased the winery in 1972, the name was changed to Wollersheim.

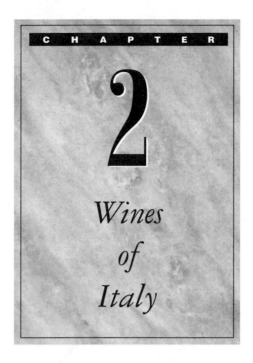

2

Wines
of
Italy

*I*taly *(which is slightly smaller than California) is literally one vast vineyard, stretching from Piedmont in the north to Sicily in the south. Italy is divided into 20 wine-producing regions that are subdivided into almost 100 provinces (Figure 2-1).*

FIGURE 2-1   Italy's twenty wine-producing regions.

Italy has approximately 3.4 million acres of planted vineyards, which produced 1.7 billion gallons of wine in 1994, making it the world's largest wine producer. France is second with 1.4 billion gallons. Italy is the world's largest wine consumer with 19.0 gallons of wine per capita (1994). Italy is also the largest exporter of total wines into the United States (29 million gallons in 1994) and leads all other countries in the exportation of table wines into the United States (24 million gallons in 1994). Italy is the world's largest producer of vermouth and the largest exporter into the United States (1.7 million gallons in 1994). Italy is also the leading exporter of sparkling wines (2.9 million gallons in 1994) and the third largest exporter of fortified wines to the United States (387,000 gallons in 1994). Currently, there are more than 2,000 varieties of Italian wine, an output that no other country can come close to matching.

▶ BRIEF HISTORY

The ancient Greeks brought viticulture to Italy when they established a colony in the countryside south of Naples around 700 B.C., about the same time as the founding of Rome. It is believed that the ancient Greeks found native grapevines already in place which, with additional cuttings, produced wines quite readily.

Viticulture traveled northward from Italy with the conquering Roman armies. Vineyards were established along the Rhône and Gironde rivers in France, the Rhine and Danube rivers in Germany, and on the Iberian peninsula and Adriatic coast.

The Romans have been credited with refining viticulture not only in Italy but throughout most of Europe. Although many of their ancient methods were quite crude, a few remarkable wines were produced as well as some awful concoctions.

One wine from the city of Pompeii had the reputation of causing nasty hangovers, while a wine known as "Troezenian" was said to cause impotence. Another wine known as "Apiana" (from the Latin word *apis,* meaning "a bee"), was so named because bees were attracted to the sweet taste of its Muscat grape. Other ancient Roman wines were Alban, Caecuban, Falernian, Mamertine, Setine, and Sorrentine.

▶ ITALY'S WINE LAWS

DOC Laws

On July 12, 1963, the president of the Republic of Italy, Antonio Segni, signed into law Presidential Decree No. 930, which originated the Italian Wine Laws known as *Denominazione di Origine Controllata* (DOC). On July 15, these laws were published in the *Gazzetta Ufficiale della Republica Italiana,* the official registry of the Italian government.

The basic aim of the wine law was to protect the name of origin and the sources of *musts* (unfermented grape juice) and wines, and to provide measures to prevent fraud and unfair competition. Figure 2-2 shows a comprehensive wine label that incorporates many of the DOC regulations.

These very comprehensive laws cover just about every phase of grape cultivation and wine production and provide strict controls for every step of the process. The following are some of the aspects of wine production that are regulated under these laws:

- Area of production
- Type of soil
- Location of vineyard
- Type of grape variety used
- Pruning and growing techniques
- Allowable yields per acre (tonnage)
- Allowable yield of juice per ton of grapes
- Minimum sugar levels
- Minimum acid and extract levels
- Methods of vinification
- Minimum aging requirements

These laws are quite similar to those of France and Germany. One major exception is that the wines of Italy may not be *chaptalized* (sugar added to the *must*).

An often-used term is *superiore,* which signifies a wine that contains a higher percentage (generally one-half of one degree or more) of alcohol than the minimum regulation required under DOC or DOCG law. Under some laws, additional bottle aging is also a requirement for use of the term. *Classico* is a geographic term applied to DOC or DOCG wines and refers to the central or original area of a production zone. *Riserva* refers to a DOC or DOCG wine with extra barrel aging at the winery. The minimum number of months or years required is solely determined by the individual DOC or DOCG.

Every wine awarded a DOC designation has a set of rules and regulations that apply solely to that wine. A Chianti wine might therefore have completely different rules for production than a Bardolino. As of 1994, more than 250 wines had been granted DOC or DOCG status, which is only approximately 15 percent of the nation's production. The aim of the Italian government is to bring classified wines to more than 50 percent by the year 2000.

DOCG

DOCG stands for *Denominazione di Origine Controllata e Garantita,* a designation given to those wines that are considered to be of a higher quality than DOC wines and made under even stricter guidelines.

Before a wine can apply for the DOCG designation, it must have been admitted to the DOC category for at least five years. The upgrading of DOC to DOCG does not occur automatically, but only when the required amount of producers of a given DOC wine

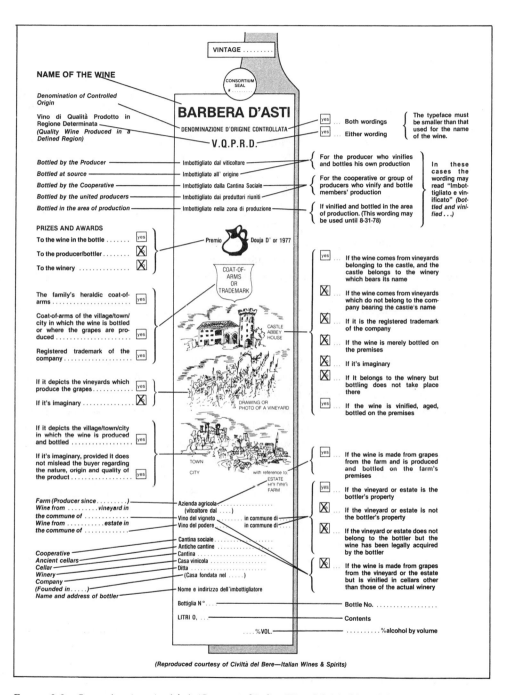

VINTAGE . . . .

CONSORTIUM SEAL #

NAME OF THE WINE

Denomination of Controlled Origin

Vino di Qualità Prodotto in Regione Determinata (Quality Wine Produced in a Defined Region)

BARBERA D'ASTI

DENOMINAZIONE D'ORIGINE CONTROLLATA

V.Q.P.R.D.

yes ... Both wordings
yes ... Either wording

The typeface must be smaller than that used for the name of the wine.

Bottled by the Producer — Imbottigliato dal viticoltore
Bottled at source — Imbottigliato all' origine
Bottled by the Cooperative — Imbottigliato dalla Cantina Sociale
Bottled by the united producers — Imbottigliato dai produttori riuniti
Bottled in the area of production — Imbottigliato nella zona di produzione

For the producer who vinifies and bottles his own production

For the cooperative or group of producers who vinify and bottle members' production

If vinified and bottled in the area of production. (This wording may be used until 8-31-78)

In these cases the wording may read "Imbottigliato e vinificato" (bottled and vinified . . .)

PRIZES AND AWARDS
To the wine in the bottle . . . . [yes]
To the producer/bottler . . . . [X]
To the winery . . . . [X]

Premio   Douja D' or 1977

COAT-OF-ARMS OR TRADEMARK

[yes] If the wine comes from vineyards belonging to the castle, and the castle belongs to the winery which bears its name

[X] If the wine comes from vineyards which do not belong to the company bearing the castle's name

The family's heraldic coat-of-arms . . . . [yes]

Coat-of-arms of the village/town/city in which the wine is bottled or where the grapes are produced . . . . [yes]

Registered trademark of the company . . . . [yes]

CASTLE ABBEY HOUSE

[X] If it is the registered trademark of the company

[X] If the wine is merely bottled on the premises

[X] If it's imaginary

[X] If it belongs to the winery but bottling does not take place there

If it depicts the vineyards which produce the grapes . . . . [yes]
If it's imaginary . . . . [X]

DRAWING OR PHOTO OF A VINEYARD

[yes] If the wine is vinified, aged, bottled on the premises

If it depicts the village/town/city in which the wine is produced and bottled . . . . [yes]

If it's imaginary, provided it does not mislead the buyer regarding the nature, origin and quality of the product . . . . [yes]

TOWN
CITY

with reference to:
ESTATE
HOLDING
FARM

[yes] If the wine is made from grapes from the farm and is produced and bottled on the farm's premises

[yes] If the vineyard or estate is the bottler's property

Farm (Producer since . . . .)
Wine from . . . . vineyard in the commune of . . . .
Wine from . . . . estate in the commune of . . . .

Azienda agricola . . . .
    (viticoltore dal . . . .)
Vino del vigneto . . . . in commune di
Vino del podere . . . . in commune di . . . .

[X] If the vineyard or estate is not the bottler's property

[X] If the vineyard or estate does not belong to the bottler but the wine has been legally acquired by the bottler

Cooperative
Ancient cellars
Cellar
Winery
Company
(Founded in . . . . .)
Name and address of bottler

Cantina sociale . . . .
Antiche cantine . . . .
Cantina . . . .
Casa vinicola . . . .
Ditta . . . .
(Casa fondata nel . . . . .)

Nome e indirizzo dell'imbottigliatore

[X] If the wine is made from grapes from the vineyard or the estate but is vinified in cellars other than those of the actual winery

Bottiglia N° . . .

Bottle No. . . . .

LITRI 0, . . .

Contents

. . . . %VOL.

. . . . %alcohol by volume

(Reproduced courtesy of Civiltà del Bere—Italian Wines & Spirits)

FIGURE 2-2   Comprehensive wine label. (Courtesy of *Italian Wines & Spirits Magazine*)

apply for the designation. In fact, such a choice on the part of the producers can bring about serious economic consequences.

DOCG wines must be sold in containers smaller than five liters in capacity and the container must bear a *state seal* guaranteeing origin and quality. This seal is applied on the bottle neck in such a way that it prevents removal of the wine from the bottle without breaking the seal.

Like DOC wines, all DOCG wines must undergo viticultural and enological controls established by Italian law as well as by their respective production regulations. In addition, before bottling, DOCG wines must be submitted for an *organoleptic* evaluation (evaluation by utilization of the senses: sight, smell, and taste) by a panel of experts appointed by Italy's Ministry of Agriculture and Forestry. Each DOCG wine is tasted by a different panel composed of experts for that particular wine.

All DOCG wines undergo obligatory production controls by agricultural inspectors at harvest time; the controls cover maximum yields, minimum natural alcohol content, and so on. The wines are inspected by fraud prevention authority representatives who examine their chemical, physical, and organoleptic characteristics.

A wine that fails the tasting on its first attempt can be resubmitted, but if it doesn't pass the second time, it is automatically declassified to ordinary table wine *(vino da tavola)*.

On July 1, 1980, Brunello di Montalcino was the first wine to be granted the DOCG status. Since that time, 12 additional wines have been granted DOCG status. Eventually the guarantee is expected to apply to 30 or more wines. The DOCG wines are Albana di Romagna, Asti (a spumante) and Moscato d'Asti, Barbaresco, Barolo, Carmignano, Chianti, Gattinara, Sagrantino di Montefalco, Torgiano Rosso Riserva, Taurasi, Vernaccia di San Gimignano, and Vino Nobile di Montepulciano. Applications for the status have been made and are pending for others.

There are some very good to excellent Italian wines that do not carry the DOC or DOCG designation, because they are either new blends or made from grapes that grow outside of the DOC zone. Some examples are Tignanello, Creso, and Solàia.

Generic, Varietal, and Proprietary Wines

Italy's wines are referred to as *generic* (named for the place of origin), *varietal* (named for the variety of grape from which they are made), and *proprietary* (named by the producer). Soave is a generic wine, Pinot Grigio a varietal wine, and Est! Est!! Est!!! a proprietary wine.

Two wines that often cause confusion are Vino Nobile di Montepulciano and Montepulciano d'Abruzzo. Vino Nobile di Montepulciano, a generic wine, is named for the town of Montepulciano in Tuscany. Montepulciano d'Abruzzo, a varietal wine, is named for the Montepulciano grape variety grown in Abruzzo as well as other regions. Some of Italy's most common proprietary wines (and grapes) are listed below.

Wine Name	Translation
Balestriere	Crossbow Archer
Barbacarlo	Uncle Charles
Buttafuoco	Sparkling Like Fire
Coda di Volpe	Fox Tail
Corvo	Crow
Est! Est!! Est!!!	It is! It is!! It is!!!
Frecciarossa	Red Arrow
Giano	Roman God Janus
Inferno	Hell
Lacryma Christi	Tears of Christ
Lacryma d'Arno	Tears of the Arno River
Piedirosso	Red Feet
Regaleali	Royal Land
Sangue di Giuda	The Blood of Judas
Scacciadiavoli	Chase Away The Devils
Settesoli	Seven Suns
Vin Santo	Wine of the Saints

► ITALY'S WINE-PRODUCING REGIONS

Abruzzo

Abruzzo is located just south of Latium in the south-central part of Italy off the Adriatic Sea. In this region there are only two grape varieties of importance: Trebbiano (a white grape) and Montepulciano (a red grape). These grape varieties produce the region's only DOC wines:

Trebbiano d'Abruzzo (white); minimum 11.5 percent alcohol; received DOC in 1972; best consumed young.

Montepulciano d'Abruzzo (red); minimum 12 percent alcohol; if aged a minimum of two years may be labeled *vecchio* (old); received DOC in 1968; produced in both rosé and red from Montepulciano and Sangiovese grapes. Montepulciano d'Abruzzo is often vinified in a very light, fresh style, similar to a Beaujolais, and should be consumed very young.

Apulia

Apulia stretches from the "spur" to the "heel" of the boot-shaped Italian peninsula. The southwestern shore of the region lies along the Ionian Sea, while its entire eastern shore lies along the Adriatic. Apulia is bordered by Molise to the north and Campania and Basilicata to the west.

For years Apulia was considered by many to be incapable of producing quality table wines due to its intense heat and arid climate. The wines that were produced (mostly reds) were heavy, dark in color, highly alcoholic, and flat tasting (lacking acidity). Therefore, a good percentage of the wines were shipped north to Piedmont where they were blended with other varieties and used to make vermouth.

Within the last few decades, however, modern technology has overtaken the region's vineyards, drastically lowering its total wine production. In place of the heavy alcoholic wines, modern vineyards produce lighter, fresher wines with surprisingly good acidity levels. The producers have sacrificed yield for quality and are making some of Italy's better wines.

Cabernet Franc, Malbec, Chardonnay, and Pinot Bianco are some of the nonlocal grape varieties that have been introduced in the area.

Some of the better-known wines are:

Castel del Monte Bianco (white); minimum 11 percent alcohol; received DOC in 1971; a blend of Pampanuto and other grapes; best consumed young.

Castel del Monte Rosato (rosé) (referred to as "Rivera"): minimum 11 percent alcohol; received DOC in 1971; a blend of Bombino Nero and other grapes; best consumed young.

Castel del Monte Rosso (red): minimum 12 percent alcohol; if 12.5 percent alcohol and aged three years, may be labeled *riserva;* received DOC in 1971; a blend of Bombino Nero and other grapes; best consumed at two to five years old, or if *riserva,* at six to eight years.

Copertino: minimum 12 percent alcohol; if 12.5 percent alcohol and aged two years, may be labeled *riserva;* received DOC in 1977; also produced as *rosato;* made from Negro Amaro, Malvasia Nera, Montepulciano, and Sangiovese grapes; best consumed at five to seven years old.

Primitivo di Manduria: minimum 14 percent alcohol; received DOC in 1974; also produced as *dolce naturale, liquoroso secco,* and *liquoroso dolce naturale;* made from Primitivo grapes; best consumed at five to seven years old.

Salice Salentino Rosso: minimum 12 percent alcohol; if 12.5 percent alcohol and aged two years, may be labeled *riserva;* received DOC in 1976; also produced as a *novella* and *rosato;* a blend of Negro Amaro, Malvasia Nera di Brindisi, and Malvasia Nera di Lecce grapes; best consumed at five to seven years old.

Although not a DOC wine, one of the finest wines of Apulia is Torre Quarto, produced in red, rosé, and white versions. The white is a blend of Bonvino (Bombino Bianco), Trebbiano, and Greco grapes. The red and rosé are blends of Malbec and Uva di Troia grapes and are best if consumed when five to seven years old.

Basilicata

Basilicata is a relatively small, unknown southern wine-producing region best known for its steep, rugged mountains, hot weather, and highly alcoholic red wines.

This inland region is the home of Monte Vulture (Vulture Mountain), an extinct volcano at whose base and on whose slopes grows the famous red Aglianico grape. Aglianico del Vulture is this region's only DOC wine.

Aglianico del Vulture (red): minimum 11.5 percent alcohol; if 12.5 percent alcohol and aged three years, may be labeled *vecchio;* if 12.5 percent alcohol and aged five years, may be labeled *riserva;* received DOC in 1971; best consumed at five to seven years old; if *vecchio* at seven to nine years; if *riserva* at ten to 15 years.

According to legend, the Aglianico grape was brought to Italy by ancient Greek settlers around 800 B.C. Its name is a loose derivative of the ancient Greek grapevine *Ellenico* or *Hellenica.* The Aglianico grape is widely grown throughout much of southern Italy, especially in Basilicata and Campania.

Calabria

Calabria traces its history back more than 2,500 years to the time of Apollo, when it was called "Magna Grecia" by the ancient Greeks who occupied this barren, dry region located at the "toe" of boot-shaped southern Italy.

Some of the better-known wines are:

Cirò Bianco (white): minimum 12 percent alcohol; received DOC in 1969; a blend of Greco Bianco and Trebbiano Toscano grapes; best consumed young.

Cirò Rosato (rosé): minimum 13.5 percent alcohol; received DOC in 1969; a blend of Gaglioppo, Trebbiano Toscano, and Greco Bianco grapes; best consumed young.

Cirò Rosso (red): minimum 13.5 percent alcohol; received DOC in 1969; if aged three years, may be labeled *riserva;* if produced in the heart of Cirò, may be labeled *classico;* a blend of Gaglioppo, Trebbiano Toscano, and Greco Bianco grapes; best consumed at four to six years old; if *riserva,* at seven to nine years.

Campania

When most people think of wines from southern Italy, they immediately think of Naples. Actually, vineyards are not found in the city of Naples but in the outlying areas. Some of Campania's better-known wines are:

Taurasi (red): minimum 12 percent alcohol; received DOCG in 1994; must be aged three years (one year in wood); if aged four years (18 months in wood) and attains 12.5 percent alcohol, may be labeled *riserva;* a blend of Aglianico and other red grapes including Piedirosso, Sangiovese, and Barbera. Taurasi has an unusually long life, sometimes lasting two decades; best consumed at seven to nine years old; if *riserva,* at ten to 15 years.

Greco di Tufo (white): minimum 11.5 percent alcohol; a blend of Greco and Pallagrello (Coda di Volpe) grapes; best consumed at two to four years old.

Fiano di Avellino (white): minimum 11.5 percent alcohol; a blend of Fiano, Greco, Pallagrello (Coda di Volpe), and Trebbiano Toscano grapes; best consumed at two to five years old.

Lacryma Christi del Vesuvio Bianco (white): minimum 11 percent alcohol; received DOC in 1979; a blend of Pallagrello (Coda di Volpe), Greco di Torre, and Biancolella grapes; best consumed young; also produced in a non-DOC semidry version.

Lacryma Christi del Vesuvio Rosso: minimum 12 percent alcohol; best if consumed at three to eight years old.

There are many legends surrounding the Lacryma Christi (tears of Christ) wine. One is that the banished Archangel Lucifer broke off a piece of heaven and let it fall to earth into the Bay of Naples. When Christ saw the loss, he immediately began to weep, and with each tear another grapevine grew.

Emilia-Romagna

A wine-producing region located north of Tuscany in north-central Italy, Emilia-Romagna is famous for its Lambrusco wine.

Most Lambrusco produced in Emilia-Romagna is non-DOC and is available both dry and semidry. Lambrusco is typically *frizzante* (slightly effervescent), although a *spumante* (sparkling) version can be found. The Lambrusco grape produces lively, light-bodied wines that are ruby red in color, with a cherry-strawberry odor and taste. Lambrusco can be red, white, or rosé, and is best when consumed very young.

In Italy, local growers formed what is known as a *consorzio* to help protect and promote their wines. These *consorzios* give member wineries special labels for attachment to the bottle's neck. Each neck label depicts a different scene, insignia, or emblem. The labels on Lambrusco and Sangiovese di Romagna wines, for instance, show a white cock and grapes on a red ground or a man and woman treading grapes.

Some of the better-known wines are:

Lambrusco di Sorbara: minimum 11 percent alcohol; received DOC in 1970; a blend of Lambrusco di Sorbara and Lambrusco Salamino grapes.

Lambrusco Grasparossa di Castelvetro: minimum 10.5 percent alcohol; received DOC in 1970; a blend of Lambrusco Grasparossa and other grapes.

Lambrusco Reggiano: minimum 10.5 percent alcohol; received DOC in 1971; a blend of Lambrusco Marani, Lambrusco Salamino, Lambrusco Montericcio, Lambrusco Maestri, and Ancellotta grapes.

Lambrusco Salamino di Santa Croce: minimum 11 percent alcohol; received DOC in 1970; a blend of Lambrusco Salamino and other grapes.

Albana di Romagna Secco (white): minimum 11.5 percent alcohol; received DOCG in 1987; 100 percent Albana grapes; can be produced *secco* (dry), *amabile* (semidry), *dolce* (sweet), or even utilizing dried grapes *(passito);* best consumed young.

Sangiovese di Romagna (red): minimum 11.5 percent alcohol; received DOC in 1967; if

12 percent alcohol, from a specified area, may be labeled *superiore;* minimum aging six months; if aged two years, may be labeled *riserva;* 100 percent Sangiovese grapes; best consumed at one to two years of age; *riserva* at two to three years. The wine is ruby red with violet reflections; distinctive delicate nose like that of sweet violets. Dry, balanced, berry fruity taste with pleasing bitter aftertaste.

Trebbiano di Romagna (white): minimum 11.5 percent alcohol; received DOC in 1973; 100 percent Trebbiano grapes; best consumed young.

Gutturnio (red): (the name Gutturnio derives from a locally found Roman drinking vessel called a *gutturnium*); minimum 12 percent alcohol; received DOC in 1967; produced in either a still or slightly *frizzante* version; a blend of Barbera and Bonarda grapes; best consumed young.

Friuli-Venezia Giulia

One of the smallest of Italy's wine-producing regions, Friuli-Venezia Giulia borders on Austria and Yugoslavia in the most northeastern region of Italy. Its terrain is predominantly rocky and hilly and the climate is generally quite mild. Pordenone, Gorizia, and Udine are the important wine centers of this region.

Originally known as Julia (after Julius Caesar), many cities of Friuli-Venezia Giulia were in fact founded by the Romans. The fall of the Roman Empire opened the way for successive invasions led by Attila the Hun, the Franks, the Lombards, and the Hungarians. For a time, the area came under the domination of the Byzantine Empire and was finally incorporated into the Venetian Republic around A.D. 1,000.

Of all the grapevines grown in Friuli-Venezia Giulia, none have as fascinating a history as the Tocai. The Tocai grape has been grown for centuries, vinified by the Benedictine monks and enjoyed throughout the ages. Napoléon drank only Tocai during negotiations with the Austrians, which ended in the formation of the Campoformido Treaty.

Another treaty of sorts became associated with Tocai back in the 1950s when the Hungarian government attempted to stop Italian usage of the name, arguing that their "Tokay" was the original. In 1954, after extensive studies by a panel of experts, an International Court in Trieste decided that Hungary did not have exclusive rights to the name Tocai and that the Hungarian grape Furmint (used to make Tokay), is a different grape variety entirely. According to the panel's findings, these grapevines actually originated in Italy. It is believed that Italian missionaries to the court of King Steven the Saint brought them to Hungary in the eleventh century.

There are six delimited zones within the Friuli region; from smallest to largest, they are: Latisana, Aquileia, Isonzo, Collio, Colli Orientali del Friuli, and Grave del Friuli. The five most important of these wine-producing zones are: Grave del Friuli, Colli Orientali del Friuli, Collio, Isonzo, and Aquileia.

Some of the better-known wines of these zones are:

Grave del Friuli.   This area produces sound red and white wines, which were mostly granted the DOC designation in 1970.

The white wines are all dry and should be consumed young.

Chardonnay
Pinot Bianco
Pinot Grigio
Riesling Renano (Johannisberg Riesling)
Sauvignon Blanc
Tocai Friulano
Traminer Aromatico (Gewürztraminer)
Verduzzo Friulano

The red wines are all dry and should be consumed at two to four years old.

Cabernet Franc
Cabernet Sauvignon
Merlot
Pinot Noir
Refosco

Colli Orientali del Friuli.   This area produces mostly white wines, many of which received the DOC designation in 1970. The white wines are all dry (except for Picolit) and should be consumed young.

Some of the better-known wines are:

Chardonnay
Malvasia Istriana
Pinot Bianco
Pinot Grigio
Ribolla Gialla
Sauvignon Blanc
Riesling Renano (Johannisberg Riesling)
Tocai
Traminer Aromatico (Gewürztraminer)
Verduzzo

Picolit: minimum 15 percent alcohol; if aged two years, may be labeled *riserva;* made from 100 percent Picolit grapes (technically known as Picolit Giallo).

Picolit grapevines thrived in Friuli during the late 1700s, and by the mid-nineteenth century produced the most prestigious wines of Italy, bottles of which graced the tables of royalty throughout England, France, Russia, and Austria.

Unfortunately, in later years the grapevine produced very few grapes, and was thought to have a genetic disease called *floral abortion.* Modern research conducted by Dr. Giovanni Cargnello at the Conegliano Institute, however, discovered that the Picolit grape variety is not self-pollinating *(hermaphroditic),* because it is purely female.

Picolit, a brightly golden-colored dessert wine, is produced in dry, semidry, and sweet versions (without the help of *Botrytis cinerea,* known in Italy as *muffa nobile*). The sweet version is made from dried grapes (called *passito*). Picolit commands extremely high prices; the dry and semidry types are best consumed when three to eight years old; the sweet version is best consumed when seven to 12 years old.

Some of the red wines are:

Refosco dal Peduncolo Rosso: minimum 12 percent alcohol; received DOC in 1975; a blend of Refosco and other red grapes; if aged two years, may be labeled *riserva;* best consumed at two to four years old; *riserva* at three to five years.

Merlot: minimum 12 percent alcohol; best consumed when two to five years old.

Cabernet Sauvignon: minimum 11 percent alcohol; if aged two years, may be labeled *riserva;* best consumed at three to five years old; *riserva* at four to six years.

Pinot Noir: minimum 11 percent alcohol; a blend of Pinot Noir and other red grapes; if aged two years, may be labeled *riserva;* best consumed at two to four years old; *riserva* at three to five years.

Schioppettino: minimum 11 percent alcohol; best when two to three years old.

Collio. This area produces excellent dry red and white wines, which are recognized by their varietal character. The white wines, which are all dry and 100 percent varietals, should be consumed young.

Some of the better-known wines are:

Chardonnay
Malvasia Istriana
Müller-Thurgau
Picolit
Pinot Bianco
Pinot Grigio
Ribolla Gialla
Riesling Italico
Riesling Renano (Johannisberg Riesling)
Sauvignon Blanc
Tocai Friulano
Traminer Aromatico (Gewürztraminer)

The red wines are all dry and should be consumed when two to four years old.

Cabernet Franc
Cabernet Sauvignon
Merlot
Pinot Noir

Isonzo.   This area produces red and white wines, many of which received the DOC designation in 1974. The white wines, which are all dry and 100 percent varietals, should be consumed young.

Some of the better-known wines are:

Malvasia Istriana
Pinot Bianco
Pinot Grigio
Riesling Italico
Riesling Renano (Johannisberg Riesling)
Sauvignon Blanc
Tocai Friulano
Traminer Aromatico (Gewürztraminer)
Verduzzo Friulano

The red wines are all dry and should be consumed when two to four years old.

Cabernet (Franc or Sauvignon)
Merlot

Aquileia.   This area produces red and white wines, many of which received the DOC designation in 1975. The white wines are all dry and should be consumed young.

Some of the better-known wines are.

Chardonnay
Pinot Bianco
Pinot Grigio
Riesling Renano (Johannisberg Riesling)
Sauvignon Blanc
Tocai Friulano
Traminer Aromatico (Gewürztraminer)
Verduzzo Friulano

The red wines are all dry and should be consumed when two to four years old.

Cabernet Franc
Cabernet Sauvignon
Merlot
Refosco dal Peduncolo

Latium

Latium, whose regional capital is Rome, is located in the central part of Italy. It is bordered in the north by Umbria and Tuscany; in the south by Molise and Campania; in the east by Abruzzo; and in the west by the Tyrrhenian Sea.

The production of wine in Latium is approximately 90 percent white, with the remaining 10 percent mostly devoted to non-DOC reds. Some of the best wines of this region are in fact not DOC wines and are bottled under the name of Castelli Romani.

Some of the better-known wines are:

Colli Albani (white): minimum 11 percent alcohol; received DOC in 1970; if 11.5 percent alcohol, may be labeled *superiore;* also produced as a *spumante;* a blend of Malvasia, Trebbiano, and other grapes; best consumed young.

Marino (white): minimum 11 percent alcohol; received DOC in 1970; if 11.5 percent alcohol, may be labeled *superiore;* also produced as a *spumante;* a blend of Malvasia Bianca, Trebbiano, and other grapes; best consumed young.

Trebbiano di Aprilia (white): minimum 11 percent alcohol; received DOC in 1966; a blend of Trebbiano Giallo and Trebbiano Toscano grapes; best consumed young.

Est! Est!! Est!!! di Montefiascone (dry or semidry white): minimum 11 percent alcohol; received DOC in 1966; a blend of Trebbiano Toscano, Malvasia Bianca, and other grapes; best consumed young.

In the year 1110, Bavarian Bishop Baron Johannes Fugger of Augsburg was traveling to Rome for the coronation of Emperor Henry V. The nobleman, a connoisseur of good food and wine, sent his faithful servant Martino ahead to find suitable quarters for food, drink, and lodging. He was instructed to chalk the word *est* (it is) at the entrance of every inn where the wine was especially good, and *non est* (it is not) on all others. The servant was so enthusiastic about the wine of Montefiascone that he wrote *Est! Est!! Est!!!* on the door of a local inn. The baron agreed with his servant's choice, so much so in fact that he remained in Montefiascone.

Upon his death, the baron agreed to give all his money to the local church in exchange for a small favor. Each year, on the anniversary of his death in August, a barrel of Est! Est!! Est!!! was to be poured over his grave so he could once again savor that glorious wine. That tradition was carried on for centuries until Cardinal Barberigo, who became Montefiascone's bishop, thought it better to donate the wine to the poor rather than wasting it on the baron, who was dead.

The story is commemorated in this ancient town at the church of San Flaviano, where on a tombstone is this inscription, in Latin; translated, it reads:

It is, It is, It is,
and though too much it is,
my master Johannes Fugger,
dead is.

Frascati.   The Frascati zone production is made up of the territories of Frascati, Grotta-ferrata, and Monteporzio Catone, and in part, Rome and Montecompatri. Only vineyards with appropriate slopes and exposure and with terrains of volcanic origin that are rich in potassium, phosphorus, and microelements and poor in nitrogen and limestone are considered suitable. The soils must be crumbly, permeable, and dry but not arid.

Frascati is produced on the slopes of the Alban hills in the Castelli Romani district, approximately 12.5 miles south of Rome, and covering approximately 5,000 acres.

Frascati received its DOC in 1966. It has a minimum of 11 percent alcohol and if 11.5 percent alcohol, may be labeled *superiore.* It is a blend of Malvasia Bianca di Candia and Trebbiano Toscano, with small amounts of other white grapes, including Malvasia del Lazio, Greco, Bellone, Bonvino, and Chardonnay. The dry version is labeled *secco* or occasionally *asciutto* and can contain a maximum of 1 percent sugar. The *amabile* contains from 1 to 3 percent sugar, and *dolce* or *cannellino* (sweet), from 3 to 6 percent sugar. The last two types are generally made from grapes affected by the "noble rot." Frascati can also be produced as a *spumante* or *vino novello* (similar to Beaujolais Nouveau). Frascati is pale straw in color with a clean, fresh, fruity aroma. It is soft and fruity tasting with a dry finish and a lingering, faint almond aftertaste. It is best consumed within three years after the vintage.

Liguria
Liguria, the second-smallest wine-producing region (Valle d'Aosta is the smallest), is located along a narrow strip of land on the Italian Riviera.

One of the better-known wines is:

Cinque Terre, a white wine named after the five communes in which it is produced; minimum 11 percent alcohol; received DOC in 1973; a blend of Bosco, Albarola, and Vermentino grapes; best consumed young.

Lombardy
The region of Lombardy, located in the center of northern Italy, borders on Switzerland to the north, Veneto and Trentino to the east, Emilia-Romagna to the south, and Piedmont to the west. Three of Italy's largest freshwater lakes—Maggiore, Como, and Garda—are in Lombardy. The Po, Italy's longest river, flows through this region's premier agricultural zone, the Po River Valley.

There are three major areas of wine production in Lombardy: Oltrepò Pavese, Valtellina, and Brescia, which includes the area south of Lake Iseo and the Lake Garda district. Two smaller areas of production also contribute to the regional output: the Colli Morenici Mantovani del Garda, the hills just south of Lake Garda in the province of Mantua; and the area north of Bergamo, in central Lombardy.

Some of the better-known wines of these areas are:

Oltrepò Pavese.   Oltrepò Pavese was once part of Piedmont and is also referred to as "Vecchio Piemonte," or Old Piedmont. This area has for the past century been Milan's chief supplier of Barbera and Bonarda wines.

The Barbera and Bonarda (known locally as Croatina) red grape varieties, the principal ones of the area, are grown exclusively in hillside vineyards. Increasing amounts of vineyard space, however, are being devoted to such white varieties as Riesling Italico, Riesling Renano, Moscato Bianco, Pinot Grigio, Chardonnay, and Müller-Thurgau. Pinot Noir and Uva Rara (both red) are also grown.

The better-known DOC wines produced in the Oltrepò Pavese area are:

Barbacarlo (red): minimum 12 percent alcohol; received DOC in 1975; a blend of Barbera and Bonarda grapes; best consumed when three to six years old.

Buttafuoco (red): minimum 12 percent alcohol; received DOC in 1975; a blend of Barbera and Bonarda grapes; best consumed young.

Riesling (white): minimum 11 percent alcohol; also produced as a *spumante;* received DOC in 1970; a blend of Riesling Renano and Riesling Italico grapes; best consumed young.

Sangue di Giuda (red): minimum 12 percent alcohol; received DOC in 1975; a blend of Barbera and Bonarda grapes; best consumed young.

Frecciarossa (brand name): a single-vineyard producer, Dr. Odero, bottles four different wines, all under the umbrella name Château Frecciarossa—La Vigne Blanche (dry) and Sillery (semidry), are white; Saint George is a rosé; Grand Cru is red.

Valtellina.   A grape-growing district situated in the Adda River Valley in the northern province of Sondrio, near Switzerland (about 60 miles northeast of Milan), is one of the few places where the Nebbiolo grape thrives. This grape, a well-known Piedmont variety, is called *Chiavennasca* in Lombardy and has been grown there since the fifth century A.D.

Nebbiolo is the principal variety of the area and is grown in the terraced vineyards that scale the steep, rugged north bank of the valley. Here the grapes receive optimum exposure to the sun, as well as all the other microclimatic conditions needed to flourish. Among the varieties grown are Rossola Nera, Brugnola, Pignola Valtellinese, Merlot, and Pinot Noir.

The area's two DOC wines, Valtellina and Valtellina Superiore, are produced from the Nebbiolo grape. The bottle label of Valtellina Superiore will usually carry the name of the designated area where the wine was produced. DOC law recognizes only four such geographic subdistricts for Valtellina Superiore: Sassella, Grumello, Valgella, and Inferno.

Valtellina (red): minimum 11 percent alcohol; received DOC in 1968; must be aged one year; a blend of Chiavennasca (Nebbiolo), Merlot, Pinot Noir, Rossola Nera, Pignola Valtellinese, and Brugnola grapes; best consumed when three to five years old.

Valtellina Superiore and Riserva: minimum 12 percent alcohol and aged two years for *superiore* and four years for *riserva;* a blend of Chiavennasca (Nebbiolo), Merlot, Pinot Noir, Rossola Nera, Pignola Valtellinese, and Brugnola grapes; best consumed when three to five years old.

Sfurzat (red): minimum 14.5 percent alcohol; produced from the same grapes as Valtellina, except that it is made from partly dried grapes that have been allowed to dry on racks from the harvest until December; must be aged three years; deep, vinous, and sometimes slightly reminiscent of port; best consumed when seven to 12 years old.

Grumello, Inferno, Sassella, and Valgella (reds): produced from the same grapes as Valtellina Superiore; received DOC in 1968; all are Valtellina Superiores, so they must be aged two years or more; if aged four years, may be labeled *riserva;* individual characteristics (color, bouquet, taste) of each wine are slightly different; best consumed when five to seven years old.

One of the finest producers of Valtellina Superiore is Nino Negri, who labels his wines Castel Chiuro and Castel Chiuro Riserva.

Brescia.   Wine production in the province of Brescia can be roughly divided into three areas: the Lake Garda district, the hills of Lake Iseo in the DOC zone known as Franciacorta, and the hills around the provincial capital of Brescia.

Four DOC wines are made in this district: Lugana, Tocai di San Martino della Battaglia, Riviera del Garda Bresciano Chiaretto, and Riviera del Garda Bresciano Rosso.

Nowadays many grapevines are grown in the Lake Garda district: Gropello, Barbera, Sangiovese, Marzemino, Nebbiolo, Cabernet Franc, Trebbiano, Tocai Friulano, Pinot Noir, Pinot Bianco, and Riesling.

Lugana (white): minimum 11.5 percent alcohol; received DOC in 1968; also produced as a *spumante;* a blend of Trebbiano di Lugana and other grapes; best consumed young.

Riviera del Garda Bresciano Chiaretto (dry rosé): minimum 11.5 percent alcohol; received DOC in 1967; a blend of Gropello, Sangiovese, Barbera, and Marzemino grapes; best consumed young.

The DOC appellation of Franciacorta applies to four wines produced in the hills south of Lake Iseo near the town of Cortefranca in central Lombardy: Franciacorta Pinot Spumante, Franciacorta Rosato Spumante, Franciacorta Pinot Bianco, and Franciacorta Rosso. The grapevines grown in the area include Barbera, Cabernet Franc, Chardonnay, Merlot, Nebbiolo, Pinot Bianco, Pinot Grigio, and Pinot Noir.

Mantua.   The Etruscans are thought to have been the first to have introduced the grapevine into this region, although grape seeds dating back to the Neolithic Age have been discovered there as well. Five centuries after the Etruscans, Virgil sang the praises of "Retico" (Rhaetian), forerunner of the Colli Morenici wines. Augustus Octavian (27 B.C.– A.D. 14), grandnephew of Julius Caesar and first emperor of Rome, was said to be especially fond of "Retico." By the Middle Ages, producers were already exporting their wines to Germany as well as supplying the Papal courts with the local rosé.

The province of Mantua also produces the DOC Colli Morenici Mantovani del Garda. Three wines—a white, a rosé, and a red—carry this appellation.

Many grapevines are planted in the area, including Molinara (Rossanella), Rondinella, Negrara, Sangiovese, Lambrusco, Merlot, Trebbiano Giallo, Trebbiano Toscano, Trebbiano di Soave, Trebbiano del Mantovani, Pinot Bianco, Riesling Italico, and Tocai Friulano.

Marches

The region of Marches is located in the north-central part of Italy, with its entire east coast on the Adriatic Sea. It is bordered to the west by Umbria, to the south by Abruzzo, and to the north by Emilia-Romagna and Tuscany.

In parts of Marches and Abruzzo, the peasant growers make a wine that they call *vino cotto*. It is actually a cooked wine, where the liquid content is reduced to 40 percent of its original volume. Fresh juice is then added, allowed to ferment, and aged for two years, producing a heavy, sweet wine of 18 to 20 percent alcohol. Unfortunately, its production has severely dwindled in recent years.

Some of the better-known wines are:

Rosso Piceno (red): minimum 11.5 percent alcohol; if 12 percent alcohol, it may be labeled *superiore;* received DOC in 1968; minimum of one year of wood aging; a blend of Sangiovese, Montepulciano, Trebbiano, and Passerina (white) grapes; ruby-red color with floral hints of plums, ripe fruit, and licorice; best consumed young.

Rosso Cònero (red): minimum 11.5 percent alcohol; received DOC in 1967; a blend of Montepulciano and Sangiovese grapes; best consumed young.

Verdicchio di Matelica (white): minimum 12 percent alcohol; received DOC in 1967; also produced as a *spumante;* a blend of Verdicchio, with the possible addition of Trebbiano Toscano and Malvasia Toscana grapes; best consumed young.

Verdicchio dei Castelli di Jesi (white): minimum 11.5 percent alcohol; received DOC in 1968; also produced as a *spumante;* a blend of Verdicchio, with the possible addition of Trebbiano Toscano and Malvasia Toscana grapes; best consumed young.

Verdicchio is occasionally bottled in the traditional "amphora-shaped" bottles that were used to bring wine from Greece to the Italian peninsula in ancient times. It is one of the oldest wine bottle shapes in the world, predating the Bordeaux bottle.

One of the most popular brands of Verdicchio in the United States is from the firm of Fazi-Battaglia, featuring a *cartogio,* or tiny scroll, attached to the neck of the bottle that provides information about the wine. The *consorzio's* neck label on bottles of Verdicchio depicts a heraldic lion.

Molise

Molise is Italy's youngest wine-producing region. It was originally a part of Abruzzo, but a change in the laws of 1963 made it a separate region. Molise is bordered to the north by

Abruzzo, to the west by Latium and Campania, and to the south by Apulia. Its east coast border is the Adriatic Sea.

In 1983, these wines gained DOC status: Biferno Bianco, Biferno Rosso, Biferno Rosato, Pentro di Isernia Rosato, Pentro di Isernia Bianco, and Pentro di Isernia Rosso.

Piedmont

Piedmont is in northwestern Italy, bordered by France to the west and Switzerland to the north. The Ligurian Apennines and the Alps surround Piedmont to the south, west, and north.

The Nebbiolo grape.   Piedmont has been producing good to excellent wines for more than a century and has used the most underrated wine grape in the world, the Nebbiolo. Originally called *Vitis vinifera Pedemontana* (the grapevine of Piedmont), the grape is referred to as *Nubiola, Nebiola, Nibiol,* and *Nebiolum* in documents dating back to the Middle Ages. Its present name and spelling, officially sanctioned in 1962, is derived from the word *nebbia* (fog). Some say that it was given this name because of the persistent fog found in the area of cultivation, while others believe that it alludes to the thick bloom that forms on the grape skins, making them look as if they were surrounded by tiny patches of fog.

In Vercelli and Novara, the Nebbiolo is called Spanna. The Nebbiolo in fact is not one grape but a family of grapes whose variations probably occurred through mutation. Two subvarieties, Michet and Lampia, are both widely planted throughout the area.

The Nebbiolo produces wines that are usually rough and tannic when young but with age evolve into wines of extraordinary power, depth, and complexity. When blended with other varieties, the Nebbiolo grape gives the resultant wine body and substance.

Grown only in certain parts of Piedmont and Lombardy, the Nebbiolo grapevine is extremely sensitive to microclimatic conditions. It is particularly affected by slight variations in soil conditions. These variations explain in part why separate DOC appellations have been granted to Nebbiolo wines (for example, Barolo and Barbaresco) produced in adjoining zones of production. Nebbiolo grapes require fairly warm summers and rather cool and damp autumns, particularly in late October and early November when the grapes reach maturity.

Another characteristic of Piedmont is the practice of growing different grape varieties on the same slope: For instance, Barbera will be planted to a certain altitude, followed progressively by varieties that require more sun, such as Dolcetto, Moscato, or Nebbiolo. This explains how one area can produce wines with different denominations: for example, Nebbiolo d'Alba, Dolcetto d'Alba, and Barbera d'Alba.

Wine production.   Piedmont produces the greatest number of superb red wines in Italy. Piedmont has many DOC appellations, as well as some DOCG wines, including Barolo, Barbaresco, Gattinara, and Asti (a spumante) and Moscato d'Asti (both Asti wines). Grape varieties that mature early or have built-in resistance to the cold, damp Piedmont autumns tend to prevail in the region. Nebbiolo is the region's best-known grape variety, although Barbera is the most prolific. The grapevines are generally grown on hillsides to give them optimum exposure to the light and warmth of the sun.

The production of DOCG, DOC, and non-DOC wines is concentrated in the southern part of Piedmont in the provinces of Cuneo, Asti, and Alessandria. This area of exclusively hilly vineyards accounts for 90 percent of the total regional output. Other areas of production are the hills between the towns of Novara and Vercelli and the zone around the regional capital of Turin. As the fame of Piedmont's fine wine has spread throughout the world, exports abroad have increased accordingly.

Piedmont today. Winemakers in this area are beginning to use newer or lighter methods of vinification for a host of reasons. For some the concern is strictly economic; they are paying exorbitant interest on bank loans and need a quick turnover of wines to pay off their debts. Others feel that most wine drinkers do not want to wait 20-plus years for a bottle of wine to mature.

In years past the practice was to ferment red wines on the skins, allowing them to sit one or more months after zero Brix (sugar) was reached. The wine then picked up additional grape tannins (phenolics) and a concentration of flavor. This also necessitated several years of barrel aging, several years more of bottle aging, and then more years of cellar aging before the wines became drinkable. Some producers are replacing this method with shorter skin contact time and less barrel aging. Some growers and producers are trying to force DOC authorities to cut the minimum aging (barrel) requirement because they feel the traditional methods produce wines that are lacking fruit and are actually dried out before they become ready to drink.

Barolo. Barolo is frequently referred to as "il vino dei re e il re dei vini" (the wine of kings and the king of wines). This renowned, full-bodied, dry red wine is produced all over the DOCG area of Barolo, particularly in Serralunga d'Alba, Castiglione Falletto, and La Morra (traditionally the best communes within the DOCG area of production for Barolo), the area centering around the town of Barolo in the Langhe Hills just southeast of Alba.

The Barolo vineyards of Piedmont consist of 3,000 acres with an annual yield of approximately 400,000 to 600,000 cases. Barolo must be produced from 100 percent Nebbiolo grape or its subvarieties Lampia and Michet.

Barolo must be aged at least three years (two of which are in wood) and have a minimum alcohol content of 13 percent. When aged five years (four in wood), it may be labeled *riserva.*

Barolo received its DOCG status in 1981. The Barolo *consorzio* features on its neck label a golden lion or a helmeted head on a blue background, according to the particular district it comes from.

Barolo is garnet red in color with orange highlights and has an intense fragrance with a characteristic scent of withered flowers, violets, licorice, spices, and the classic earthy bouquet and taste often found in well-aged Barolos. It has a dry, full-bodied and well-balanced taste that is harmonious and velvety. This powerful, robust, tannic, full-bodied dry red wine requires considerable aging before it can be fully enjoyed. Barolo is best consumed within 15 years after the vintage.

Barbaresco.   Barbaresco is often referred to as Barolo's "younger brother" or the "queen of Piedmont's wines." While not quite as powerful, Barbaresco does share Barolo's robust and austere qualities.

Barbaresco's DOCG (granted in 1981) states that it must be produced from 100 percent Nebbiolo grapes grown in vineyards located in the towns of Barbaresco, Neive, Treiso, and Alba, all in the southern province of Cuneo.

Barbaresco is garnet red with characteristically orange highlights and has an intense bouquet reminiscent of violets, spices, and wild cherries, and sweet fragrances in general, like vanilla. It is dry, robust, and full-bodied, yet it nevertheless exhibits a surprising gentleness.

Barbaresco must have an alcoholic content of no less than 12.5 percent and be aged for a minimum of two years (one of them in wood); when aged four years (three in wood), it may be labeled *riserva.*

The Barbaresco *consorzio* features on its neck label the ancient tower of Barbaresco, in gold, on a blue background.

Gattinara.   The city of Gattinara has a precise date of birth, which is March 30, 1242, exactly 250 years before Columbus discovered America. On March 10, 1872, Victor Emmanuel II established the first experimental enological station in Gattinara, headed by Professor Ingegnere G. B. Cerletti, to study the production and quality of Gattinara wine.

Gattinara's DOCG, which was granted in 1988, states that Gattinara must be made from 90 to 100 percent Nebbiolo (known locally as *Spanna*), with the remaining Bonarda and Vespolina grapes grown exclusively within the territory known as Gattinara. The wine must attain a minimum of 12.5 percent alcohol and be aged three years (one in wood). If it attains 13 percent alcohol and is aged four years (two in wood), it may be labeled *riserva.* This dry, full-bodied wine is garnet-red in color with a balanced flavor and a typically bitter aftertaste. It is best consumed when six to ten years old.

The Gattinara *consorzio* features on its neck label towers standing among the vineyards.

The Barbera grape and its wines.   Barbera is Piedmont's most prolific grape variety, accounting for 50 percent of the region's total acreage. Barbera is a particularly vigorous, resilient grapevine with consistently abundant yields and an easy adaptability to a variety of growing conditions. It is widely planted throughout Italy, from Piedmont—where the climate is temperate and is said to produce the best Barbera wines—to Campania, Sicily, and Sardinia, where the Mediterranean climate produces wines with a different, distinctive style.

The Barbera d'Asti *consorzio* features on its neck label blue grapes superimposed on the old city's tall part-Roman, part-Medieval tower.

Piedmont Barberas are generally full-bodied and slightly tannic, with a high natural amount of acidity; they are best enjoyed with food. Of the four DOC Barberas, Barbera d'Asti is generally recognized as being the most full-bodied. These dry red wines are best consumed at four to six years of age.

Barbera d'Alba: minimum 12 percent alcohol; received DOC in 1970; aged one year minimum; if 12.5 percent alcohol and aged one year in oak or chestnut barrels, may be labeled *superiore;* 100 percent Barbera grapes.

Barbera d'Asti: minimum 12 percent alcohol; received DOC in 1970; aged one year minimum; if 13 percent alcohol and aged three years, may be labeled *superiore;* 100 percent Barbera grapes.

Barbera dei Colli Tortonesi: minimum 11.5 percent alcohol; received DOC in 1973; if 12.5 percent alcohol and aged two years, may be labeled *superiore;* a blend of Barbera with the addition of Freisa, Bonarda, and Dolcetto grapes.

Barbera del Monferrato: minimum 12 percent alcohol; received DOC in 1970; if 12.5 percent alcohol and aged two years, may be labeled *superiore;* a blend of Barbera, Freisa, Grignolino, and Dolcetto grapes.

Dolcetto, Grignolino, and Freisa.   Dolcetto, Grignolino, and Freisa are all dry red varietals produced in the northeastern part of Piedmont. Like all DOC varietals, the labels of these wines must indicate the specific area of production. The nature of the soil, exposure to sunlight, altitude, and other important factors account for discernible differences in wines produced from the same grape varieties grown in different areas. Dolcetto, Grignolino, and Freisa differ from the more famous Piedmont wines like Barolo in that they are lighter, are intended to be drunk young, and usually have a high level of acidity.

The name *Dolcetto* could be roughly translated to mean "little sweet one." The name, however, is misleading: Dolcetto is a dry red wine with a pleasing bitter aftertaste.

Dolcetto is produced in the Langhe Hills just south of the town of Alba. The Dolcetto grapevine is indigenous to the area and was subject to local government regulations as early as 1593. It is Piedmont's most widely planted grapevine after Barbera. Inherently a little weak, it is not an easy grapevine to grow; it requires much pruning and thrives only in the *calcareous* soil (containing high levels of calcium carbonate and often magnesium carbonate) characteristic of the Langhe area.

Dolcetto is considered the everyday wine of the locals, who drink it with most of their meals. There are seven DOC Dolcettos; some of the better-known ones are:

Dolcetto d'Acqui: minimum 11.5 percent alcohol; received DOC in 1972; if 12.5 percent alcohol and aged one year, may be labeled *superiore;* 100 percent Dolcetto grapes.

Dolcetto d'Asti: minimum 11.5 percent alcohol; received DOC in 1974; if 12.5 percent alcohol and aged one year, may be labeled *superiore;* 100 percent Dolcetto grapes.

Dolcetto d'Alba: minimum 11.5 percent alcohol; received DOC in 1974; if 12.5 percent alcohol and aged one year, may be labeled *superiore;* 100 percent Dolcetto grapes.

The *Grignolino* grapevine is indigenous to the Asti area of southern Piedmont and its presence there can be traced back to 1252. Small and inconsistent in yield, it is a difficult grapevine to tend and thrives only in certain types of light, sandy soil.

The relative scarcity of this dry, somewhat bitter wine has only served to enhance its desirability, elevating it to almost legendary status. There are only two DOC zones of production for Grignolino—Alessandria and Asti, both in southern Piedmont. The name of one of these two places must appear on the label of every bottle of Grignolino DOC. The best-known Grignolino is:

Grignolino d'Asti: minimum 11 percent alcohol; received DOC in 1973; a blend of Grignolino and Freisa grapes; best consumed young.

The *Freisa* grape produces two styles of wine: a dry and a slightly sweet one *(amabile).* The *amabile,* which is often *frizzante,* is the better known of the two and is considered an ideal accompaniment to desserts. The best-known Freisa wine is:

Freisa d'Asti: minimum 11 percent alcohol; received DOC in 1972; if 12.5 percent alcohol and aged for one year, may be labeled *superiore;* also made *frizzante* and as a *spumante;* 100 percent Freisa grapes.

Freisa d'Asti features on its neck label black grapes superimposed on a yellow tower in Asti.

Nebbiolo d'Alba. This wine is produced from 100 percent Nebbiolo grapes grown in the sandy soil of the steep, rugged Roero Hills. Situated just north of the town of Alba in the southern province of Cuneo, this area is also close to Turin, which has traditionally been a major market for its wine.

Perhaps the softest of the Nebbiolo family of wines, Nebbiolo d'Alba requires less aging than Barolo and Barbaresco, and is not as costly. Classy and elegant, this ruby red wine has a delicate bouquet reminiscent of violets and raspberries, and a full, velvety, pleasantly bitter taste.

Nebbiolo d'Alba: a minimum of 12 percent alcohol; received DOC in 1970; dry, sweet, and *spumante* versions produced; the dry version is best consumed when three to six years old.

Other red wines. Other well-known Piedmont wines include Boca, Brachetto d'Acqui, Bramaterra, Carema, Fara, Ghemme, Lessona, Roero, and Sizzano.

Boca: minimum 12 percent alcohol; received DOC in 1969; minimum three years aging (two in wood); a blend of Nebbiolo, Vespolina, and Bonarda grapes; best consumed at five to nine years old.

Brachetto d'Acqui: minimum 11.5 percent alcohol; received DOC in 1969; dry or *amabile spumante* versions produced; a blend of Brachetto, Aleatico, and Moscato Nero grapes; best consumed young.

Bramaterra: minimum 12 percent alcohol; received DOC in 1979; minimum three years aging (18 months in wood); if aged two years in wood, may be labeled *riserva;* a blend of Nebbiolo, Croatina, Bonarda, and Vespolina grapes; best consumed at five to nine years old.

Carema: minimum 12 percent alcohol; received DOC in 1967; minimum four years aging (two in barrel); 100 percent Nebbiolo grapes; best consumed when six to ten years old.

Fara: minimum 12 percent alcohol; received DOC in 1969; minimum three years aging (two in barrel); a blend of Nebbiolo, Vespolina, and Bonarda Novarese grapes; best consumed when five to eight years old.

Ghemme: minimum 12 percent alcohol; received DOC in 1969; minimum four years aging (three in barrel); a blend of Nebbiolo, Vespolina, and Bonarda Novarese grapes; best consumed when six to nine years old.

Lessona: minimum 12 percent alcohol; received DOC in 1977; minimum two years aging (one in barrel); a blend of Nebbiolo, Vespolina, and Bonarda grapes; best consumed at five to eight years old.

Roero: minimum 11.5 percent alcohol; received DOC in 1985; minimum eight months aging; a blend of Nebbiolo and Arneis (white) grapes; best consumed at four to six years old.

Sizzano: minimum 12 percent alcohol; received DOC in 1969; minimum three years aging (two in barrel); a blend of Nebbiolo, Vespolina, and Bonarda Novarese grapes; best consumed at five to eight years old.

Moscato Bianco.   Believed to have originated in the eastern basin of the Mediterranean, the Moscato Bianco grape is widely planted throughout Italy. The wine it produces is generally vinified to be sweet and is particularly renowned for its fragrant aroma. In some parts of Italy, most notably Sicily, Moscato Bianco grapes are partially dried, then pressed to produce an exquisite dessert wine called Moscato Passito. The Moscato Bianco grapevine has been an integral part of Piedmont's viticulture for centuries.

Moscato Bianco is the principal grape of several related Piedmont DOC and DOCG wines, including Moscato Naturale d'Asti, Moscato d'Asti, and Asti (a spumante). (See Chapter 6 for information on Asti.) Together these wines account for almost 50 percent of the total regional DOCG and DOC production. Asti (a spumante) in particular enjoys a very fine reputation and is, in fact, Piedmont's most exported DOCG wine. Moscato d'Asti, though not as well known, shares many of the same characteristics:

Moscato d'Asti (sweet): minimum of 11 percent alcohol; received its DOCG status in 1994; made from 100 percent Moscato Bianco grapes; best consumed very young.

The Moscato d'Asti *consorzio* features on its neck label a blue helmeted head on a gold background, or San Secundo, the patron saint of Asti, mounted in red, on a blue background.

Gavi (or Cortese di Gavi).   Cortese is the traditional white wine grape of Piedmont; it produces wines of particular refinement. Once widely grown throughout southern Piedmont, its area of production is limited to the Colli Tortonesi, Monferrato, and Novi Ligure zones of Alessandria. An extremely resilient grapevine, it thrives in vineyards that have good exposure to the sun.

Wines made from Cortese grape may be labeled *Cortese, Cortese di Gavi, Gavi,* or *Gavi di Gavi.* Gavi di Gavi is only allowed to come from vineyards in the commune of Gavi, which have a reputation for being the best sites.

Gavi: minimum 10.5 percent alcohol; received DOC in 1974; 100 percent Cortese grapes. There is no minimum aging requirement under DOC. Gavi is pale gold in color with a green hue. It has a pleasant, full and distinct aroma, with a persistent floral fragrance of lemon, lily of the valley, sour apples, and tropical fruit. Gavi is dry, fruity, fresh, and well-balanced. *Frizzante* and *spumante* versions are authorized under DOC; best consumed three years after the vintage.

Sardinia

Sardinia, the second-largest island in the Mediterranean, for centuries has been a little-known wine-producing region, even to most Italians from the mainland and Sicily. It is located across the Tyrrhenian Sea, just west of Rome. Its largest winery (which actually is a wine cooperative) is Sella & Mosca, established more than 80 years ago.

Viticulture in Sardinia has undergone tremendous changes thanks to extremely effective efforts on the part of regional authorities, cooperatives, and private producers. Sardinia's goal is to update production methods for the DOC wine varieties, as well as for the range of high-quality non-DOC wines.

Some of the better-known wines are:

Cannonau di Sardegna (dry or sweet white): minimum 13.5 percent alcohol; received DOC in 1972; a blend of Cannonau and other grapes.

Vermentino de Sardegna (dry white): minimum 10.5 percent alcohol; received DOC in 1989; also produced as a *spumante;* a blend of Vermentino and other grapes; best consumed young.

Vernaccia di Oristano (dry or sweet white): minimum 15 percent alcohol; received DOC in 1971; if 15.5 percent alcohol and aged three years, may be labeled *superiore;* if aged four years, may be labeled *riserva;* can also be produced as a *liquoroso;* 100 percent Vernaccia grapes; best consumed when two to six years old.

Sicily

Sicily is one of the world's oldest winemaking regions. The Greeks founded a colony in the eighth century B.C. on the eastern end of the island and established commercial supremacy in the Mediterranean that was rivaled only by the Carthaginians.

Since the end of World War II, the Sicilian wine industry has seen an intensive modernization of the ancient traditional methods of viticulture and vinification. The Regional Institute of Wines & Vines was established in 1991 to review and improve Sicily's wine industry. The wineries and vinification methods were also carefully reviewed and large sums of money invested to introduce the latest equipment. The result of the institute's research provided Sicily's growers and vintners with guidelines that helped develop a modern, flourishing industry. Growers were advised to concentrate on planting specific grape varieties, giving preference to the native Catarratto (which accounts for more than 50 percent of total grape production), Damaschino, Grecanico (Dorato), Grillo, Inzolia, and experimenting with other Italian varieties such as Trebbiano Toscano, Nebbiolo, and Sangiovese. Other grapes include Chardonnay, Sauvignon Blanc, Pinot Blanc, Müller-Thurgau, Cabernet Sauvignon, and Pinot Noir, which all appear to thrive in the Sicilian soil.

Some Sicilian wines tend to have a higher alcoholic content due to the fact that they receive a great deal of sunshine throughout the year. The heat of the sun can often bake the grapes or cause them to become "sunburnt"; the effect is most noticeable in white wines. Direct sun causes a higher sugar content, darker color white wine (due to a high concentration of coloring matter in the skins), and a heaviness in taste. Wines produced from grapes with very high sugar levels also tend to be "flat," lacking a sufficient acid backbone to support the high sugar and alcohol levels.

Credit must be given to the skills of Sicilian winemakers who, in spite of difficult working conditions, have produced wines that display lightness of body, freshness of taste, and a good balance between fruit and acidity.

Some of the better-known wines are:

Alcamo or *Bianco di Alcamo* (white): minimum 11.5 percent alcohol; received DOC in 1972; a blend of Catarratto Bianco, Damaschino, Grecanico (Dorato), and Trebbiano Toscano grapes; best consumed young.

Cerasuolo di Vittoria (red): minimum 13 percent alcohol; received DOC in 1973; a blend of Frappato, Nero d'Avola (Calabrese), and other grapes; best consumed young.

Etna wines were written about centuries ago, especially in Homer's "Ulysses," where Ulysses gave Polyphemus, the cyclops, a wine called Etna to get him drunk so that he could be disarmed.

Etna Bianco: minimum 11.5 percent alcohol; received DOC in 1968; if 12 percent alcohol, may be labeled *superiore;* a blend of Carricante, Catarratto, and other grapes; best consumed young.

Etna Rosato or *Rosso* (rosé or red): minimum 12.5 percent alcohol; received DOC in 1968; a blend of Nerello Mascalese and other grapes; both rosé and red are best consumed young.

There are some very good to excellent Sicilian wines that do not carry the DOC designation because they are either new blends or are made from grapes that are grown outside of the DOC zone. Some notable wines are:

Corvo winery was founded on the estate of Edoardo Alliata di Villafranca, duke of Salaparuta, in 1824, in the small town of Casteldaccia. It produces Rosso, Duca Enrico,

Bianco, Colomba Platino (dry white), Bianca di Valguarnera, and Spumante Brut and Demisec.

Regaleali winery has been owned since 1835 by Count Giuseppe Tasca. It produces four unique wines considered to be among the finest of Sicily—Bianco, Nozze d'Oro, Rosato, Rosso,—and a specially aged (two years in wood, one year in glass) limited reserve called Rosso del Conte, which is 14 percent alcohol.

Segesta: originally called Egesta by the Greeks and renamed Segesta by the Romans; produced by Diego Rallo (of Marsala fame) as a dry red or dry white wine.

Other non-DOC wines include: Bonifato, Canicatti, Cavisa, Donnafugata, Draceno, Drepano, Faro, Porto Palo, Rapitalà, Saturno, Settesoli, Solunto, Steri, and Terre di Ginestra.

Trentino-Alto Adige

Trentino-Alto Adige, bordered by Austria and Switzerland, was part of the Austro-Hungarian Empire until it was annexed to Italy by the Treaty of Versailles after World War I.

This area, like Friuli-Venezia Giulia, has a dual cultural heritage, but here the mix is German and Italian. While the whole region is officially bilingual, the Germanic influence is most apparent in the Alto Adige to the north. The southern part of the area, Trentino, takes its name from the town of Trento, which rose to fame in 1545 when the Council of Trent was held there to discuss the Reformation of the Church.

Geographically and climatically, Trentino-Alto Adige has all the requirements for producing top-quality wine. The region is roughly on the same latitude as Burgundy and northern Bordeaux, where France's finest wines are made. The high Alps create a natural wind block to protect the grapevines from the harsh cold weather of central Europe. The Adige River, flowing south through the length of the region, has created a wide fertile valley whose center supports some of Italy's best fruit orchards, while vineyards terrace every inch of its slopes. The foothills of the Dolomites provide perfect altitudes and soil types for grape growing. In fact, the Adige River Valley has often been referred to as one big natural vineyard.

Some of the better-known dry red wines are:

Cabernet Sauvignon del Trentino: minimum 11 percent alcohol; received DOC in 1971; if aged two years and attains 11.5 percent alcohol, may be labeled *riserva;* a blend of Cabernet Sauvignon and Cabernet Franc grapes; best consumed when four to seven years old.

Marzemino del Trentino: 11 percent alcohol; received DOC in 1971; must be aged a minimum of one year; if aged two years and attains 11.5 percent alcohol, may be labeled *riserva;* minimum 90 percent Marzemino grapes; best consumed when three to five years old. Marzemino is ruby-red in color with a delicate, "plumy" fragrant and intense aroma of violets, and a dry, full-bodied taste, and is meant for early consumption.

Lagrein del Trentino: minimum 11 percent alcohol; received DOC in 1971; if aged two years and attains 11.5 percent alcohol, may be labeled *riserva;* 100 percent Lagrein grapes; best consumed young.

Merlot del Trentino: minimum 11 percent alcohol; received DOC in 1971; must be aged a minimum of one year; if aged two years and attains 11.5 percent alcohol, may be labeled *riserva;* minimum 90 percent Merlot grapes; best consumed young.

Caldaro or Lago di Caldaro (known as Kalterersee in Germany): minimum 10.5 percent alcohol; received DOC in 1970; a blend of Schiava Grossa, Pinot Noir, Lagrein, and other grapes; best consumed when three to five years old.

Santa Maddalena: minimum 11.5 percent alcohol; received DOC in 1971; a blend of Schiava Grossa and other grapes; best consumed when three to five years old.

Teroldego Rotaliano: minimum 11.5 percent alcohol; received DOC in 1971; if attains 12 percent alcohol, may be labeled *superiore;* if aged two years, may be labeled *riserva;* made from 100 percent Teroldego grapes; best consumed young.

Some of the better-known dry white wines are (these wines should all be consumed young):

Pinot del Trentino: minimum 11 percent alcohol; received DOC in 1971; also produced as a *spumante;* a blend of Pinot Bianco and Pinot Grigio grapes.

Riesling del Trentino: minimum 11 percent alcohol; received DOC in 1971; 100 percent Riesling grapes.

Traminer Aromatico (Gewürztraminer) del Trentino: minimum 12 percent alcohol; received DOC in 1971; 100 percent Traminer grapes.

Tuscany

Tuscany, which is located in central Italy, north of Latium, is the home of such great native red wines as Chianti, Brunello di Montalcino, Carmignano, and Vino Nobile di Montepulciano. With the influx of imported grapevines, great red wines such as Tignanello, Cabreo di Bitùrica, Sassicaia, Cabernet Sauvignon, Cabernet Franc, Merlot, and others have appeared on the international wine scene. Some very fine white wines are produced in Tuscany, including Vernaccia di San Gimignano, Galestro, Vin Santo, as well as those made from Pinot Grigio, Chardonnay, and Sauvignon Blanc grapes.

Banfi Vintners.   One of the most adventurous viticultural endeavors ever undertaken in Italy was the development (in 1978) of 7,100 acres of virgin land into one of the most technologically advanced vineyards in the world. The land, located in Montalcino, was originally primarily forests and pastures; it has since been planted with more than a million grapevines (Figure 2-3).

The wines of Tuscany.   There are many wines produced in Tuscany that have gained DOC status, five which have been awarded the DOCG.

Some of the better-known ones are listed below.

White wines   *Moscadello di Montalcino:* one of the most distinguished ancient wines of Tuscany; received DOC in 1985; minimum 10.5 percent alcohol; if produced in *frizzante* or *liquoroso* versions, must attain 12 percent alcohol; a blend of Moscato Bianco and other

FIGURE 2-3 Militarily precise rows of grapevines at Banfi vineyards. (Courtesy Banfi Vintners, Montalcino, Italy)

white grapes; slightly sparkling, straw colored, with an intense aromatic bouquet and the sweet and distinctive characteristic flavor of the Moscato grape; best consumed young.

Vernaccia di San Gimignano (dry): the first wine granted DOC status (1966) and later raised to DOCG; minimum 11.5 percent alcohol; if aged a minimum of one year (four months in glass), may be labeled *riserva;* only Bordeaux-shaped bottles may be used; a blend of Vernaccia di San Gimignano and other white, nonaromatic varieties; best consumed young. Vernaccia di San Gimignano is a dry white wine with considerable body and acidity and an aromatic odor and slightly bitter taste. The blue seal of the *consorzio* Vernaccia di San Gimignano shows a lion rampant on a crest.

Red wines   Brunello di Montalcino is a picturesque and very hilly section of Tuscany situated approximately 25 miles southeast of Siena and Chianti Classico, approximately 1,600 feet above sea level. It is bordered by the Orcia River to the south and the Ombrone River to the west.

In 1967, the producers of Brunello wines voluntarily formed a *consorzio* to establish a uniform price structure and quality control system. Their seal is a southern European evergreen oak with hollylike leaves, on a green background. Brunello and Barolo are among the longest-lived of all Italian wines. Most Brunello wines are best consumed when nine to 12 years old, and the *riservas* at 12 to 15 years; if produced in great years, a life of 25 years is not uncommon for *riservas*.

Brunello: received DOC in 1966; first wine to receive DOCG status, 1980; minimum 12.5 percent alcohol; must be aged minimum of four years (three years in oak barrels and one year in glass); if aged five years (four years in oak barrels and one year in glass), may be labeled *riserva;* 100 percent Sangiovese Grosso grapes (also called Brunello grapes).

Rosso di Montalcino: received DOC in 1983; produced by the same vineyards as the world-famous Brunello di Montalcino; 100 percent Brunello grapes (also called Sangiovese Grosso); can be made from very young grapevines not considered mature enough for Brunello di Montalcino or a Brunello wine aged for a shorter period of time than required under DOCG laws (one year minimum aging, not necessarily in oak barrels); full-bodied, fragrant; best consumed when four to six years old.

Chianti.   Geographically and historically, Chianti is an area lying between Florence and Siena, encompassing approximately 1.2 million acres and including the towns of Arezzo, Pistoia, and Pisa in the region of Tuscany. In the heart of this area in the hills between Florence and Siena lies Chianti Classico (approximately 175,000 acres), the largest of the seven Chianti zones. The historic center of this area belonged to an ancient military league formed in 1270 called the *lega del Chianti*. Although its primary purpose was the defense of both its land and people, it was probably the first organization in the world to establish a wine quality law.

The grapevine has been a dominant feature in Tuscany and fossilized evidence suggests that the grapevine flourished before the appearance of prehistoric man. The first references to wine production in the Chianti area date back to the Etruscan civilization.

Chianti Classico is the oldest classified wine region in the world. Grapevines were already growing in Tuscany and central Italy when the Etruscans settled there in about the tenth century B.C. and, as early as the ninth century B.C., produced wine. Since then, the history of the area has been tumultuous, complex, and illustrious.

Chianti was originally known as Vermiglio in the latter part of the fourteenth century. While today's Chianti is red, documents of the fourteenth century (tracing its origin to 1260) call a local white wine Chianti. Baron Ricasoli, descendant of Baron Bettino Ricasoli, has in his possession a document dated June 18, 1696, that is believed to be the certificate of origin for Chianti wine.

In the eighteenth century, Chianti was produced from Sangiovese, Canaiolo Nero, Mammolo, Marzemino, and Roverusto grapes. No mention was made of the Trebbiano Toscano or Malvasia del Chianti (also known as Malvasia Toscana) grapes in connection with Chianti. These white grapes were vinified separately for a white style of Chianti. In

1835, Baron Bettino Ricasoli (1809–1880), developed and defined the grape variety formula for Chianti, which consisted of a blend of Sangiovese, Canaiolo Nero, and Malvasia del Chianti grapes.

These words were written in 1874 by Bettino Ricasoli to Professor Studiati of Pisa University when he sent samples of Brolio Chianti resulting from his long years of research: "From Sangioveto the wine takes the main component of its bouquet as well as its vigorous quality; Canaiolo Nero softens the tone of the first without taking anything from its bouquet and Malvasia del Chianti, which could be omitted in those wines intended for aging, tends to slightly dilute the product resulting from the first two, making it lighter and more suitable for everyday drinking."

A technique (known as *governo Toscano*) used in making Chianti during Ricasoli's time was to induce a secondary fermentation by the addition of 5 to 10 percent *must* pressed from selected grapes partly dried on straw mats known as *cannici*. This secondary fermentation took place immediately after the first racking of the wine before December 31. This process produced wines meant for early consumption. Most of the wines made by the *governo* technique were, and still are, bottled in squat bottles covered with straw, called *fiaschi*.

It is interesting to note that when the DOC law for Chianti was drawn up and finally instituted on August 30, 1967, the producers decided not to register a white wine, but asked to be allowed to include white grapes in the blend for red Chianti.

DOCG regulations specify two slightly different regulations, one for Chianti and another for Chianti Classico: Chianti calls for a blend of 75 to 90 percent Sangiovese, 5 to 10 percent Canaiolo Nero, and 5 to 10 percent white grapes (Malvasia del Chianti and/or Trebbiano Toscano).

Chianti Classico can be made from 100 percent Sangiovese grapes, with an option to include up to 15 percent of other approved grapes, including Canaiolo Nero, Colorino, and non-traditional grape varieties such as Cabernet Sauvignon, Merlot, Cabernet Franc, and others. The DOCG also eliminates the use of white grapes in the blend.

Chianti must be aged a minimum of five months and Chianti Classico, seven; however, it cannot be sold prior to June 1 after the harvest. Chianti must attain a minimum of 11.5 percent alcohol, Chianti Classico 12 percent. Chianti *riserva* must attain 12 percent alcohol, and Chianti Classico *riserva* 12.5 percent alcohol. Both Chianti *riserva* and Chianti Classico *riserva* mandate a minimum aging of three years, two of which must be in wood.

Since 1932, Chianti has been produced in an area encompassing five provinces: Arezzo, Florence, Pisa, Pistoia, and Siena, which are subdivided into seven areas. These are listed below, with descriptions of their *consorzio's* neck labels:

Chianti Classico: The label shows a black rooster or cock *(consorzio del Marchio Storico)*; this was the crest of the thirteenth-century Chianti Defense League; first used on May 14, 1924.

Chianti Montalbano: The label shows the Tower of Montalbano.

Chianti Rufina: The label of this *consorzio* (founded in 1927) shows a *putto* (chubby baby cherub).

Chianti Colli Fiorentini (also known as Putto): The label of this *consorzio* (founded in 1927) shows the infant Bacchus, naked and entwined in a grapevine with clusters of purple grapes, a detail from Della Robbia's painting, *Hospital of the Innocents.*

Chianti Colli Senesi: The label depicts Romulus and Remus with the she-wolf.

Chianti Colli Aretini: The neck label shows a *chimera.*

Chianti Colline Pisane: The label shows a centaur or, more commonly, the Leaning Tower of Pisa.

Chianti has a brilliant, intense ruby red color with overtones of dried plums, ripe raspberries, black cherry, and an underlying aroma of black tea. Its taste is dry and well defined with an elegant flavor of blackberries, plums, and anise. Chianti is best consumed when five to eight years old; *riserva* when eight to 12 years old and, if produced in a great year, when it is as much as 20 years old.

There are many producers of Chianti; among them are Antinori, Banfi Vintners, Ruffino, Nozzole, Brolio, Monsanto, Badia a Coltibuono, Castello di Gabbiano, Melini, Rocca della Macìe, and Castellare.

Carmignano.   A DOCG wine made from essentially the same grape blend as Chianti (Sangiovese and Canaiolo Nero), except that white grapes may be left out of the blend. Also, the maximum percentage of other red grapes Cabernet Sauvignon and Cabernet Franc is increased to 15 percent. Carmignano must attain a minimum of 12.5 percent alcohol and be aged 20 months; if aged three years, it may be labeled *riserva.*

Vino Nobile di Montepulciano is produced in a small area surrounding the town of Montepulciano, in the province of Siena. This wine was famous in the fourteenth and fifteenth centuries and was a favorite of Pope Paul III. Its name, "vino nobile," is derived from the fact that it was produced exclusively for the titled families who lived in the area.

Vino Nobile di Montepulciano was granted its DOCG status in 1982. It must be aged a minimum of two years and if aged three years may be labeled *riserva.* It must have a minimum of 12.5 percent alcohol and be made from a blend of Prugnolo Gentile (Sangiovese Grosso), Canaiolo Nero, Malvasia del Chianti, and several other grape varieties. This dry wine is best consumed when three to five years old; the *riserva* is best when six to eight years old.

The Vino Nobile di Montepulciano *consorzio* features on its neck label a griffin rampant on a white background within a red circle.

There are some very good to excellent Tuscan wines that do not carry the DOC or DOCG designation, because either they are new blends or are made from grapes grown outside of the DOC zone. Some notable Tuscan wines are:

Bianco Toscano: made from a small percentage of Malvasia and Trebbiano, the white grapes grown in Tuscany that are used in making Chianti and other wines. During the past two decades Chianti producers have begun using a higher proportion of black grapes in their wines, thereby increasing the percentage of white grapes available for other purposes. As a result, more and more producers are vinifying the Trebbiano and Malvasia grapes to produce a fragrant, dry white table wine. The wine is usually labeled Bianco Toscano, or sold under a brand name; it is best consumed young.

Galestro: first produced by Antinori, Frescobaldi, Ricasoli, and Ruffino in 1979. The original idea was to find use for the Trebbiano grapes whose use in Chianti was on the decline. This delicate, light white wine takes its name from the ancient rocks of its native Tuscany. It owes its distinctive aroma to the presence of Trebbiano Toscano, Chardonnay, Vernaccia di San Gimignano, Malvasia del Chianti, Riesling Renano, and Pinot Bianco grapes.

Vin Santo.   This unfortified dessert wine is produced in several regions of Italy, each claiming that theirs is the true area of origin. Vin Santo Toscano is made from the ripest Malvasia del Chianti grapes (although Trebbiano Toscano, Grechetto, or even red grapes can be utilized), which are tied together and either hung from the beams of a well-ventilated room or dried on straw mats. This process results in the evaporation of a high percentage of the grapes' water content, at the same time increasing the percentage of sugar. The higher the sugar content of the grape, the higher the resulting alcoholic content and the richer the final product.

The grapes are crushed during the winter and the *must* placed into oak barrels for a period of about two years. The barrels are filled to three-quarters capacity, closed with a cork or wooden bung, and placed in the winery's attic, exposed to heat, where the wine is left to slowly ferment. This helps give Vin Santo its characteristic amber-brown color and contributes to the complexity of its aroma. Another characteristic of this special aging process is the development of a sort of "cooked" or *maderized* taste in the wine.

Vin Santo has an intensely golden-yellow to amber color with a distinctive and unmistakable nutty bouquet, with overtones of cream, apricots, and various types of nuts (hazelnut, pecan, or walnut). Its taste is extremely rich, with a somewhat nutty-creamy, tangy taste reminiscent of dried apricots, which is similar to that of an amontillado sherry, bual Madeira, dry Marsala, or tawny port.

Its alcoholic content is usually somewhere between 15 to 18 percent. The dry version is an excellent apéritif, served chilled from the refrigerator, while the sweeter Vin Santo is best enjoyed at room temperature after dinner. Vin Santo is best consumed when ten to 15 years old and often has a life of more than 20 years.

Other non-DOC wines are listed below:

Solàia: produced by Villa Antinori, is a blend of Cabernet Sauvignon and Cabernet Franc grapes.

Tavernelle: produced by Banfi Vintners.

Tignanello: produced by Villa Antinori (first produced in 1971), is a blend of Sangiovese and Cabernet Sauvignon grapes.

Vini dei Capitolare.   The term means "title of relevance or merit," which indicates a particular typology and can only be utilized by estates that belong to the Authority for Protection of the Wines of the Hills of Central Tuscany.

Capitolare is a classification of high-quality wines that utilize nontraditional Tuscan grapes. The wines were first introduced into Italy in 1982 and into the U.S. market in 1986.

Capitolare regulates vineyard location, techniques of viticulture, and altitude. It forbids the inclusion of wines produced from grapes other than those grown in the zones singled out as having ideal soil and altitude for each of the four grape varieties. The four categories are:

Capitolare del Muschio: white wine, from 100 percent Chardonnay grapes.
Capitolare di Bitùrica: red wine, basically Sangiovese with a minimum of 30 percent Cabernet Sauvignon grapes.
Capitolare di Cardìsco: red wine, from 100 percent Sangiovese grapes.
Capitolare del Selvànte: white wine, from 100 percent Sauvignon Blanc grapes.

Umbria

One of Italy's landlocked regions, Umbria is surrounded by Tuscany, Latium, and the Marches. It is known as the "green heart of Italy" because it lies in the center of the peninsula and is rich in woods and pastures. The hillsides and gentle inclines of the Umbrian landscape are carpeted with olive trees and grapevines; the region's major freshwater lake—Trasimeno, which gives its name to one of the area's DOC wines—is surrounded by vineyards. The Tiber River flows from north to south through the eastern part of the region, creating the Upper Tiber Valley, a major viticultural zone of Umbria. Perugia, the region's capital city, stands on a hilltop just east of Lake Trasimeno. Other major cities of Umbria are Assisi, Spoleto, Todi, Gubbio, Norcia, Spello, and Montefalco. The smaller towns of Orvieto and Torgiano have lent their names to the DOC and DOCG wines of the region.

Umbria's major wine-producing areas include the Colli Altotiberini to the north; the Colli del Trasimeno to the west; Torgiano, near Assisi; and the well-known Orvieto zone in the southwest.

Some of the better-known wines are:

Orvieto.   Orvieto is named for the medieval city of the same name built by the Etruscans (pre-dating Rome) upon the top of a sheer cliff overlooking the Tiber River. This fortressed city, repeatedly invaded during the centuries, remains a splendid masterpiece.

The city of Orvieto is well known for its magnificent cathedral, originally commissioned in 1492 to Bernardino di Betto, known as "Il Pinturicchio." As part of his contract, he demanded part of his payment in Orvieto wine. His contract, however, was rescinded after a year, for having consumed too much gold, paint, and wine!

Orvieto wine is produced in the Paglia and Upper Tiber valleys as well as throughout the province of Terni, in the classico zone, just 75 miles northeast of Rome.

This well-known white wine is produced in both *secco* and *abboccato* (semisweet) varieties. Although not well known in the United States, Orvieto *abboccato* has been produced for centuries. Its golden color and delicate sweetness made it one of Italy's most esteemed wines during the Renaissance. Orvieto *abboccato* achieves its semisweet taste from grapes that have been attacked by *Botrytis cinerea.* Just as the grapes begin to become affected, they are harvested and left to continue to develop the *Botrytis* in open trays.

After World War II, popular taste shifted to dry wines, and production of Orvieto *secco* was stepped up considerably, with many producers investing in expensive equipment and the best technology for making dry white wine.

In 1970, special emphasis was placed on upgrading the image of Orvieto by replacing its traditional squat bottles (called *pulcianella* or *toscanello*) with the more familiar Bordeaux-shaped green bottles.

Orvieto received its DOC in 1971 and must have a minimum of 11.5 percent alcohol. It is made from a blend of Procanico (also known as Trebbiano Toscano), Verdello, Grechetto, Drupeggio, and Malvasia Toscana grapes.

Orvieto *secco,* a straw-colored wine, has a delightfully fruity aroma, which is melonlike with odors of kiwi, lime, and almonds. It is light-bodied, with a dry, delicately fruity taste of bitter orange and lemon, and a lingering aftertaste of almonds. It is best consumed within three years after the vintage.

The Orvieto Classico *consorzio* (formed in 1934) features on its neck label the cathedral of the town of Orvieto.

Torgiano.   Torgiano, named after a small medieval town, is a contraction of two words—Torre di Giano (tower of Giano). It is said that this medieval town was the home of the two-faced (one face looking forward and one backward) Roman god, Janus.

The DOC area in which this wine is produced is in the province of Perugia. The most famous winery in Umbria is Cantine Lungarotti, which pioneered the growing of Cabernet Sauvignon and Chardonnay grapes. Torgiano is produced in both white and red varieties.

Torgiano Rosso: minimum 12 percent alcohol; a blend of Sangiovese, Canaiolo Nero, Trebbiano Toscano, Ciliegiolo, and Montepulciano grapes; best consumed when two to six years old. Torgiano Rosso Riserva (DOCG) utilizes essentially the same grape blend as the Torgiano Rosso. It must attain a minimum of 12.5 percent alcohol and be aged at least three years. It is best consumed when six to 12 years old.

Torgiano Bianco: minimum 11.5 percent alcohol; a blend of Trebbiano Toscano, Grechetto, Malvasia Toscana, Malvasia di Candia, and Verdello grapes; best consumed young.

Sagrantino di Montefalco.   A DOCG wine with a minimum of 13 percent alcohol, made from 100 percent Sagrantino grapes. It must be aged a minimum of 30 months, of which at least 12 are in wooden barrels. It is ruby-red in color tending to garnet, with a well balanced, rich flavor.

Sagrantino is a red grape variety of obscure origins, indigenous to Umbria. Although most Sagrantino is a dry wine, some producers continue to make the more traditional *passito* wine, which vaguely resembles Recioto della Valpolicella.

Veneto

Veneto takes its name from its capital, Venice, once one of the most powerful sea nations in all of history. There are three distinct Veneto wine zones: the Verona area, famous for Soave, Valpolicella, Amarone, and Bardolino; the Euganean hills between Vicenza and Padua, where table wines are made; and the areas of Treviso and Conegliano, which lie about 40 miles due north of Venice. The latter are best known for excellent varietal wines, especially Tocai, Merlot, and Cabernet Sauvignon.

Some of the better known wines of these areas are:

Treviso.   One of the seven provinces that make up the region of Veneto is also known as the Marca Trevigiana. It borders on the Dolomite Mountains to the north, the region of Friuli-Venezia Giulia to the east, the province of Venice, 25 miles to the south, and Padua to the west. The Piave River, one of Italy's most important waterways, flows south through the province to the Adriatic.

A wide range of both native and imported grape varieties are grown in the area. Of the total wine production, 60 percent is red and 40 percent is white. Most of the wine produced in the province of Treviso comes from six grape varieties. Three are white: Prosecco, Verduzzo, and Tocai Italico; and three are red: Merlot, Cabernet, and Raboso. Other varieties grown are Verdiso, Pinot Bianco, Pinot Grigio, Pinot Noir, Riesling Italico, and Sauvignon Blanc. One of the most important of Treviso's DOC wines is:

Prosecco di Conegliano-Valdobbiadene (a spumante): received a DOC in 1969 and contains a minimum of 10.5 percent alcohol. If it attains 11 percent alcohol, it may be labeled *superiore.* It is made from 100 percent Prosecco grapes; best consumed young.

Verona.   A picturesque wine-producing town located in the northeast region of Veneto that rests on the river Adige near Lake Garda, just 50 miles west of the romantic and canal-latticed city of Venice. Verona is famous for the production of Soave, Valpolicella, Amarone, and Bardolino.

All of the following white wines are dry and should be consumed young:

Bianco di Custoza: received DOC in 1971; minimum 11 percent alcohol; no aging requirements; also produced as a *spumante;* a blend of Trebbiano Toscano, Garganega, Tocai Friulano, Cortese, Riesling Italico, Chardonnay, Pinot Bianco, and Malvasia Toscana.

Gambellara: received DOC in 1970; minimum 10.5 percent alcohol; if 11.5 percent alcohol, may be labeled *superiore;* a blend of Garganega and Trebbiano grapes.

Merlot del Piave: received DOC in 1971; minimum 11 percent alcohol, if 12.5 percent alcohol and aged two years, may be labeled *vecchio;* blend of Merlot and other red grapes.

Verduzzo del Piave: received DOC in 1971; minimum 11 percent alcohol, if 12.5 percent alcohol and aged two years, may be labeled *riserva;* 100 percent Verduzzo grapes.

Soave. This wine is produced in the territories of the communes of Soave, Monteforte, San Martino, and others in the province of Verona. The DOC Soave zone consists of approximately 15,250 acres with an annual yield of approximately 5,200,000 cases. Soave, which received its DOC in 1968, must attain a minimum of 10.5 percent alcohol; if 11.5 percent alcohol and aged eight months, it may be labeled *superiore.* If it is labeled *classico,* it must come from a strictly delimited area of production. Soave is made from a grape blend of Garganega, Trebbiano di Soave (Nostrano), Trebbiano Toscano, Chardonnay, Sauvignon Blanc, and Pinot Bianco grapes. Soave can also be made into a *spumante* under DOC.

Soave is straw yellow in color, tending at times to be greenish. Its aroma is very fruity with a delicate odor of apple, pear, honeydew melon, and almond. It is dry, light-bodied, and balanced, with a slightly bitter-almond aftertaste. Soave is best consumed within three years after the vintage.

There is also a Recioto di Soave (12 percent alcohol), made from partially dried grapes. It is sweet to the taste, with overtones of pears, apricots, and bananas, and is best enjoyed after dinner.

The *consorzio* of Soave features a Roman arena at Verona on its neck label.

Other dry Veronese wines are:

Bardolino. A dry, light-bodied red wine, produced in the northeastern region of Veneto. From the Brenner-Verona highway, the classico zone of Bardolino can be seen in the rolling hills between the Adige and Lake Garda. Bardolino is produced in the area to the southeast of Lake Garda, including all or parts of the communal territories of Bardolino, Garda, and others, in the province of Verona.

The name Bardolino was first utilized during the beginning of this century. Prior to that it was called Garda wine, although Bardolino wine is quite old.

Bardolino, a DOC wine since 1968, contains a minimum of 10.5 percent alcohol. If 11.5 percent and aged one year, it may be labeled *superiore.* Bardolino Classico must come from a strictly delimited area of production. Under DOC, there is also a Bardolino Spumante. Bardolino is a blend of Corvina Veronese, Rondinella, Molinara, Negrara, and other grape varieties.

Bardolino is bright ruby-red in color, tending at times to be cherry red. It has a light and delicate aroma, reminiscent of raspberries and cherries. It has a dry, spicy cherry and fruity taste, with a good balance, subtle, and at times a lightly spritzy flavor. It is best served chilled, 55 to 60 degrees Fahrenheit. It should be consumed within three years after vintage.

There is also a very light Bardolino, resembling a rosé, called Bardolino Chiaretto.

Bardolino bottled by December 31 of the year of the harvest can be identified on the label as *novello* (nouveau). The *consorzio* of Bardolino features a Roman arena at Verona on its neck label.

Valpolicella. This wine is produced in the territories of the communes of Marano, Negrar, and others in the Verona province. The area of Valpolicella, which received its DOC in 1968, consists of 13,800 acres. Valpolicella must attain a minimum of 11 percent alcohol; if 12 percent alcohol and aged one year, it may be labeled *superiore.* If labeled *classico,* it must come from a strictly delimited area of production. Valpolicella is made from a blend of Corvina, Rondinella, Molinara, and other grapes.

Valpolicella's color is ruby-red of medium intensity, tending to garnet with aging. Its bouquet is appealing, delicate, and characteristic of spice and ripe cherries, which at times recalls the scent of bitter almonds. The taste is dry, velvety, medium-bodied, bitterish, and balanced, with flavors of raisins and berries. Valpolicella is best consumed within four years after the vintage.

The *consorzio* of Valpolicella features a Roman arena at Verona on its neck label.

Amarone. When one thinks of great Italian red wines, wines like Barolo, Barbaresco, Chianti Riserva, and Brunello di Montalcino all come to mind. But what about Amarone, that rich, mouth-filling wine that sends warmth and vigor to the body and taste buds? For some unknown reason, Amarone is not mentioned in the same context as other great red wines.

Amarone della Valpolicella. Amarone is produced on hilly portions of the Valpolicella Classico Zone in the northeastern part of Veneto, bordered on the west by the Adige River.

The word *amarone,* from the Veronese dialect, means bone dry almost to the point of bitterness. The grapes used are the same as those in Valpolicella: Corvina Veronese, Rondinella, Molinara, Rossignola, Negrara, Sangiovese, and Barbera. Amarone, however, unlike Valpolicella, is made exclusively from the best grapes, which are located at the top and outside perimeter of the clusters. The grapes used for Amarone are grown on three-foot-high trellises in the hills of Valpolicella that rise one to two thousand feet above sea level. The best grapes, which have received the most direct sunshine, are called *recie* or *orecchie* (ears); hence the formerly used name Recioto della Valpolicella Amarone (*recioto* is a word from the old Veronese dialect of the area).

In the picking process, more than 50 percent of the grapes are immediately rejected because they are not ripe enough. In addition, the bunches that are selected are those whose grapes are sufficiently spaced to allow air to circulate between them in the eventual drying process (this limits the formation of *grey mold*). These grapes, whose sugar levels are the highest because of the amount of sunlight they receive, are picked and then arranged on flat drawers that easily fit into racks, which allow a good circulation of air. It is very important that they be kept in a dry, cool, well-ventilated room. In years past, bamboo, straw mats, or trellises were used to dry the grapes. Each mat is clearly marked with the day the grapes were picked and the part of the vineyard from which they originated. The grapes are cleaned and turned about every 20 days and are constantly inspected during the three- to four-month drying period. This drying period causes a 30 percent loss of juice, resulting in grapes low in juice but extremely high in sugar and varietal character. The best Amarones produced depend on the formation of *Botrytis cinerea,* which releases gluconic acid during the drying process. Enzymatic action also changes the properties (internally) of the acids and sugar balance. The dried grapes, which resemble shriveled raisins, are pressed just after Christmas and fermented slowly for approximately 45 days with the skins and stems intact. The wine is aged for a minimum of two years (DOC regulation) in wood, but it is not uncommon for Amarone to be aged for five years or more in barrels prior to bottling and further bottle aging.

The resultant wine is, not surprisingly, highly alcoholic; a minimum of 14 percent under DOC law. However, most Amarones are higher in alcohol, sometimes even as high as 17 percent alcohol. When produced in the heart of the DOC production zone the wine may be labeled *classico.* Amarone received its DOC status on August 21, 1968 and was formerly known as *Recioto della Valpolicella Amarone.*

Amarone can be described as having a remarkably beautiful, darkish ruby red color, with a lush, persistent spicy bouquet of sweet cherry, almost port-like; a moderately robust, strong, concentrated, complex flavor of fruit, reminiscent of raisins, with considerable finesse; velvety rich, with a dry, warming spicy taste, and slightly bitter. The aftertaste is warming and quite dry, with sensations of rich spicy fruit. Amarone is suitable for long aging, often decades.

The *consorzio* of Amarone features the Roman arena at Verona on its neck label.

Legend has it that in April 1320, Federico della Scala, who was the lord of the Valpolicella county in 1325, went to the square of Marano Castle, where he knighted the first members of the "order of the ancient *recioto."* This order was re-established in April 1969 with the objective of spreading the fame of recioto throughout the world. In April of each year all knights meet for a banquet wearing the impressive ancient fourteenth-century costumes. During the festivities, they also knight new members.

Recioto della Valpolicella.   A wine type, which is labeled Recioto della Valpolicella; Recioto della Valpolicella Spumante; Recioto della Valpolicella Liquoroso; or simply Recioto. Reciotos without the suffix Amarone are *amabile* and contain more than 1 percent residual sugar (the maximum that Amarone can have under DOC regulations). The *liquoroso* designation is for a very sweet dessert wine (with a minimum of 16 percent alcohol). There is also a *spumante,* which is *amabile,* with a remarkable amount of body and finesse.

To produce an *amabile* or *spumante,* the fermentation is halted before all of the sugar is metabolized, and the wine is immediately filtered to eliminate the yeast. The *spumante* is made by inducing a secondary fermentation, which creates effervescence (less carbonation, however, than in traditional champagne).

Some very fine producers of Veronese wines are Allegrini, Bertani, Bolla, Fabiano, Lamberti, Masi, Santa Sofia, Sartori, Tedeschi, and Tommasi.

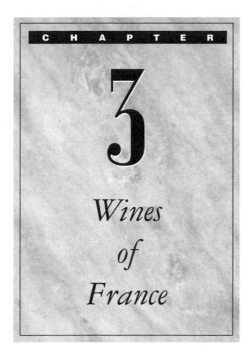

3

Wines
of
France

For many, the wines of France evoke pictures of lush vineyards filled with ripe grapes, huge fermentation tanks, and rows of barrels filled with some of the world's finest wines—but this description fits every wine-producing country in the world. A formidable public relations campaign and excellent public image obviously enhance France's reputation as a great wine-producing country; however, that reputation is solidly based on centuries of winemaking experience and the country's climate and soil, which are ideal for growing the world's great wine grapes.

▶ **FRENCH WINE LAWS**

On July 30, 1935, a French law established the Institut National des Appellations d'Origine (INAO) for wines and distilled spirits, and decrees governing each wine appellation were laid down by the minister of agriculture.

Under the *appellation d'origine contrôlée* (AOC), wines and distilled spirits must conform to certain conditions regarding area of production, root stocks, output per hectare (2.471 acres), minimum alcoholic strength, processes of grape growing, and winemaking or distillation. Only wines meeting the specified requirements can be sold under the appellation, and shipments must be documented. Controls are provided for checking vintage returns, plantings within the delimited area, dressing the grapevine stock, output, aging, and so on.

Conceived to guarantee the authenticity of wines released under an appellation, the AOC system is also a guarantee of taste and quality, insuring that all wines from a delimited area will be similar, while different from those of other areas. As of 1995, there are approximately 250 AOC wines.

There are other designations under this system: The letters *VDQS* that appear on some wine labels were first used on December 18, 1949 and stand for *vins délimités de qualite supérieur,* denoting wines that are just slightly below the AOC designation in quality. Wines designated as *vins de pays,* simple regional country wines, are below VDQS wines in quality. *Vins ordinaires* include almost 70 percent of all French wines and are not controlled by the government. They are simple wines made locally for everyday consumption.

In 1936, many of France's wine districts were officially given their AOC designation. They included Sauternes and Barsac (September 11); Saint-Émilion, Saint-Estéphe, Saint-Julien, and Pauillac (November 14); and Pomerol (December 8). On March 4, 1937, the wines of Graves were officially granted their AOC designation, and on August 10, 1954, the designation was granted to the wines of Margaux.

▶ **SHIPPERS WINES**

Some of the finest wines in the world are the red and white wines of France's six wine-producing regions (Figure 3-1), which are under the auspices of the AOC. Because of their status, these wines are also higher in price, and an intelligent purchase generally takes a basic knowledge of wine. But there is another possibility, and that is to choose what are known as French country wines—simple wines made for easy daily consumption, without all the fuss often associated with higher-priced wines. Some of the wines that are often used as "house" or "pouring" wines are:

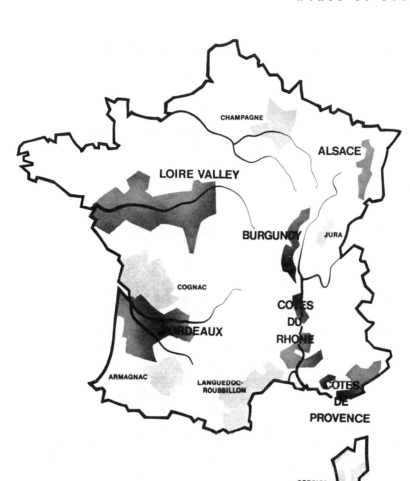

FIGURE 3-1   Map of France's major wine-producing regions.

B.&.G.	French Rabbit	Partager
Boucheron	Rene Junot	Père Patriarche
Canteval	Le Jardinet	Remy Pannier
Chantefleur	Musette	Valbon
Dourthe	Papillon	

► FRANCE'S WINE-PRODUCING REGIONS

France (which is roughly the size of Texas) is divided into six wine-producing regions:

- Alsace: produces white and red dry wines.
- Bordeaux: produces red and white dry wines as well as some sweet wines.
- Burgundy: produces red and white dry wines.
- Champagne: produces sparkling wines.
- Loire Valley: produces white and rosé dry wines.
- Rhône Valley: produces red, white, and rosé dry wines.

There are many other fine wine-producing areas in France, but they are too numerous to cover.

Alsace

This storybook region, which is dotted with picturesque villages, occupies a narrow strip of land between Strasbourg and Mulhouse. It is less than two miles wide and about 60 miles long, with an area of approximately 30,000 acres. It is nestled between the Vosges Mountains and the Rhine River, just east of Champagne and Burgundy (Figure 3-2).

Alsace is a region that has a very marked history, surrounded in turmoil. From the beginning of the 1600s to 1870, conditions were less than ideal: wars, famine, and *phylloxera* (*phylloxera* is an aphidlike pest which lives on grapevines, eating their roots, eventually killing the vine) all took their toll on the vineyards. After the defeat of France in the Franco-Prussian War (1870–1871), Alsace was ceded to Germany and remained under German rule until the Armistice of 1918, which ended the First World War. In 1925, the Alsace growers association officially agreed to concentrate on planting only "noble" varietals, setting the precedent for an emphasis on quality, rather than quantity.

During the Second World War, Alsace was again annexed to Germany until General George S. Patton liberated it in 1945. The Alsace growers in the 120 villages where the principal activity is winemaking had to almost completely replant their damaged vineyards. They then resumed their efforts to recapture lost markets and establish themselves firmly on the wine map of France, rather than Germany.

Alsace produces one-fifth of all of France's white wines entitled to the AOC designation. Because it is located so far north, there is generally insufficient sunshine to fully ripen the red grapes. Therefore, better than 90 percent of all wines are white.

Bottling and labeling regulations.   Effective July 5, 1972, all Alsatian wines must be bottled in tall, elegant "flute" bottles. It also is compulsory for wines sold under the Alsace appellation to have been bottled in Alsace and not shipped in barrels.

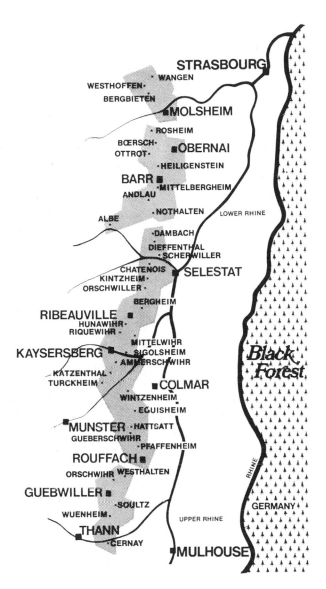

FIGURE 3-2   Map of Alsace.

The labels on Alsatian wines usually indicate the grape variety used and provide the shipper or grower's postal address. When the name of the vineyard is stated on the label, 100 percent of the grapes used must come from that vineyard. The labeling terms *réserve personnelle, cuvée,* or *réserve* indicate quality level: wines so designated are considered to be among the finest that a house produces. *Appellation contrôlée, grand cru,* and *crémant d'Alsace* may also appear on labels.

On October 3, 1962, the wines of Alsace were given their *appellation contrôlée.* To help promote the wines of Alsace, a wine brotherhood, Confrérie Saint-Etienne, was formed in the fourteenth century. It still meets every year at the Château de Kientzheim near Colmar for a festival and special promotional meeting.

In June 1975, wine legislation created the *grand cru* appellation in Alsace. For a vineyard to qualify as *grand cru,* it must demonstrate every year that its wines are of excellent quality and consistently show the personality of its soil and *microclimate* (the climate of a small distinct growing area). The *grand cru* appellation has been awarded to 47 vineyards at this time, but the list is not final. These vineyards are on the slopes with excellent drainage and sun exposure. All wines must be tasted by an INAO panel each year before receiving the *grand cru* appellation. Sometimes the panel will decree that a wine not be released until it has been aged an additional year. The *grand cru* wines are at this time a very small percentage of Alsatian exports to the United States.

The wines of Alsace.   By long-standing tradition, the wines of Alsace have usually been named after a single grape variety. They are vinified completely dry (except for 1 percent of late harvest wines), unlike the majority of their German counterparts. Due to the abundance of fruit in many Alsatian wines, some mistakenly call them semisweet, confusing the fruit in a dry wine with the residual sugar found in a semisweet or sweet wine.

Alsace is the only major French wine region that identifies its wine by the name of the grape. AOC regulations for Alsace wine mandate that any wine called by the varietal name be made 100 percent from that grape.

Some of the better-known wines of Alsace are described below.

Edelzwicker is made from a blend of noble grape varieties.

Gewürztraminer is a quintessentially Alsatian wine. Twenty percent of the Alsatian vineyards are planted with this grape, and very few if any countries produce a wine of equal distinction. It is delicious, spicy, and fruity, with a pungent flavor and a highly perfumed and flowery bouquet that is strongly reminiscent of grapefruit. Once tasted, Gewürztraminer can always be identified again and again in a blind tasting—it is that distinctive. It is not always popular; one tends to either love it or hate it.

Muscat d'Alsace is planted in only 3 percent of Alsace's vineyards. The wine has an intense bouquet of sweet, ripe grapes, although the wine itself is dry with a delicate, lingering aftertaste.

Pinot Blanc (Clevner is the local name for Pinot Blanc) is more structured and fuller-bodied than the Sylvaner, but is still very crisp, fresh, and supple, with a floral bouquet.

Riesling is the most elegant grape of Alsace and one of the world's most noble white wine grapes. In Alsace, it is planted in 20 percent of the vineyards. The Riesling of Alsace is always Johannisberg Riesling, the aristocrat of Rieslings, which is the perfect grape for northern climates. Its yield is never high, it matures late and will continue to ripen in cool weather. A very adaptable grapevine, it can be found in various terrains, producing a different wine in each. In a Riesling of Alsace one should find a well-defined floral bouquet with fine steely nuances in the nose. On the palate there should be firm fruit, framed by good, crisp acidity. The wine should fill the mouth, but not be heavy in body, and a combination of subtle flavors should linger.

Sylvaner is one of the most widely planted grape varieties in Alsace, accounting for about 20 percent of the vineyards. The wine is very crisp, fruity, and usually light.

Pinot Gris (also called Tokay d'Alsace), is not to be confused with Hungarian Tokay; with that in mind, the European Economic Community (EEC) banned the use of the name Tokay in France. The grapevine, which accounts for only 5 percent of the production of Alsace, produces wines that are well-balanced and full-bodied. Pinot Gris can be fruity, but that sensation on the palate is often followed by a luscious, slightly smoky, absolutely dry finish.

Pinot Noir is planted in Alsace, although it comprises only a small percentage. Traditionally it was used to produce rosé wines called Pinot Noir or Rosé d'Alsace. If the producer wishes, this grape can produce a more robust and typical Pinot Noir. The production of this type of wine is on the increase and imports to the United States have risen dramatically, although it still contributes little to the total Alsace imports.

Crémant d'Alsace is an AOC sparkling wine made by the *méthode champenoise.* It is fresh, fruity, and appealing. Much Crémant d'Alsace is made from the Pinot Blanc grape, but some is made from Johannisberg Riesling, with the name of the grape variety often added under the Crémant d'Alsace name.

Vendanges tardives and *récolte tardives* are late-harvested wines made from Johannisberg Riesling, Gewürztraminer, Pinot Gris, or Muscat grapes. In years of abundant sunshine the grapes are left to ripen on the vine, resulting in much higher levels of natural sugar. During vinification almost all of this sugar is fermented into alcohol, creating a wine that is rich, fills the mouth, and has an extraordinary depth of flavor. Wine laws passed on April 1, 1983 officially recognize the *vendanges tardives* classification. These laws established the minimum sugar level and allowable grape varieties and require that the wine be aged a minimum of 18 months prior to release.

Sélection de Grains Nobles are even more rare and more sweet than the *vendanges tardives.* They were recognized as a classification in the wine laws of 1983 and are subject to the same restrictions as the *vendanges tardives,* with even higher minimum levels of natural sugar and alcohol. Only produced in truly great years from individually selected grapes affected by the "noble rot" *(Botrytis cinerea), sélection de grains nobles* wines are pure nectar, highly concentrated, with a lingering flavor. Produced in very small quantities, these wines are very difficult to obtain in the United States.

Major producers of Alsatian wines are:

Léon Beyer	Muré-Clos Saint Landelin
Dopff "Au Moulin"	Schlumberger
Dopff & Irion	Pierre Sparr
Hugel et Fils	Trimbach
Klipfel	Willm
Gustav Lorentz	Zind-Humbrecht

Bordeaux

Bordeaux, located approximately 300 miles southwest of Paris, is known worldwide for its incomparable red, equally fine dry white, and superb sweet white wines. Wine production in Bordeaux is far easier to learn about than Burgundy; its *châteaux* are larger, have been in the same hands for several generations, and are owned by fewer *vignerons*.

Appellation contrôlée wines. The Bordeaux appellation vineyard area covers approximately 260,000 acres, which accounts for 2 percent of the world's wine production. There are 54 appellations within Bordeaux, encompassing dry white, sweet white, rosé, sparkling (since 1994), and world-renowned red wines. Bordeaux is the largest AOC wine-producing region, producing approximately 25 percent of all of France's AOC wines. Bordeaux's production of AOC wines is approximately 80 percent red and 20 percent white.

The more precise the designation on a Bordeaux label, the more distinguished the wine. If the wine is labeled *appellation Bordeaux contrôlée,* the wine is of the lowest standard permitted. The next higher designation would be *appellation Bordeaux supérieur contrôlée;* higher yet is a specific area designation, such as *appellation Médoc contrôlée.* The most specific designation short of a *château* name would be, for instance, *appellation Pauillac contrôlée;* this appears only on wines of the highest quality.

Bordeaux is divided into many districts, most of which are called *communes.* The four most important communes, which make up the Médoc district, are located on the west side of the Gironde River. The Médoc produces predominantly dry red wines, with only a few white wines, which by law must be sold under the simple Bordeaux appellation. The communes from north to south are *Saint-Estèphe, Pauillac, Saint-Julien,* and *Margaux.* On the right bank of the Dordogne River are the districts *Saint-Émilion* and Pomerol, both of which produce only dry red wines. South of Médoc, along the Garonne River, in the capital of Bordeaux, lies the Graves district, where dry red and white wines are produced. Thirty miles southwest of the city of Bordeaux lies the district of Sauternes, noted for its extremely sweet white wines and a few dry white wines as well.

Only five grape varieties may be used to make red wine in Bordeaux.

Cabernet Sauvignon: predominant variety in the Médoc, sometimes accounting for as much as 90 percent of blend; known locally in Graves as Vidure.

Merlot: predominant variety in Saint-Émilion and especially Pomerol, sometimes accounting for as much as 90 percent of a blend.

Cabernet Franc: used in small amounts as a blending grape; known as Bouchet in Saint-Émilion and Pomerol; and Breton in Touraine.

Malbec: used in small amounts as a blending grape; known as Pressac in Saint-Émilion, and as Cot or Auxerrois in southwestern France.

Petit Verdot: used in small amounts as a blending grape.

Graves and Sauternes are the only districts in Bordeaux that produce white wines. Only three grape varieties are permitted: Sémillon, Sauvignon Blanc, and Muscadelle.

Médoc.   This is the largest and most important wine district of Bordeaux and possibly the greatest producer of red wines in the world. Its four most important vineyards are Château Lafite-Rothschild, Château Mouton-Rothschild, Château Latour, and Château Margaux.

The famous 1855 classification.   The Bordeaux Wine Classification of April 18, 1855, was established under the sponsorship of Emperor Napoléon III (Second Empire), who wanted to showcase the classification at the 1855 Paris Exposition (World's Fair). This classification applies to the wines of the Médoc (with the exception of Château Haut-Brion, in Graves) and the wines of Sauternes and Barsac.

In the Médoc, the classification divides the 62 great vineyards into five categories, known as *crus* or "growths," according to their recognized quality in 1855, based on the prices obtainable for their wine at that time (a first-growth or *premier cru* vineyard, for instance, is of the highest quality, and a fifth growth or *cinquième cru,* the lowest).

The 1855 classification has been in effect for so long partly because the soil content and climate (for example) of any given vineyard has not changed dramatically. However, some owners currently produce far better-quality wines than they did in 1855, and their wines deserve to be elevated to a higher classification. Others, unfortunately, produce somewhat lower-quality wines that should be lowered or even declassified from the 1855 ratings.

In 1953, a classification of the wines of Graves was begun by the INAO, who completed the task in 1959. On October 7, 1954, the INAO laid down a classification for Saint-Émilion that divided the 76 great vineyards into two classes: *premier grand cru* and *grand cru* classe. The *premier grand cru* classe is subdivided into *a* and *b* classifications. Château Ausone and Cheval Blanc are the only two vineyards considered worthy of an *a* classification. Ten vineyards were classified as *b*. Provision was made in the decree for a revision of the classification every ten years—and in fact eight of the ten vineyards were given the *grand cru* status *a* on November 17, 1969, with additional changes taking place on May 23, 1986.

The error of trying to grade vineyards first, second, or third growth, and so forth, which tends to handicap certain wines, especially in a publicity-conscious age, was not made with the Graves and Saint-Émilion classifications.

There is no official classification of the wines of the Pomerol region, though Château Pétrus would undoubtedly rate *grand cru* status if 1855 standards were applied.

The following is a list of red wines as they were classified in 1855.

Château	*Commune*
First growth (premier cru)	
Château Lafite-Rothschild	Pauillac
Château Latour	Pauillac
Château Margaux	Margaux
Château Haut-Brion	Graves
Château Mouton-Rothschild	Pauillac
Second growth (deuxième cru)	
Château Cos d'Estournel	Saint-Estèphe
Château Rausan-Ségla	Margaux
Château Rauzan-Gassies	Margaux
Château Léoville-Las Cases	Saint-Julien
Château Léoville-Poyferré	Saint-Julien
Château Léoville-Barton	Saint-Julien
Château Durfort-Vivens	Margaux
Château Lascombes	Margaux
Château Gruaud-Larose	Margaux
Château Brane-Cantenac	Cantenac-Margaux
Château Pichon-Longueville	Pauillac
Château Pichon-Lalande	Pauillac
Château Ducru-Beaucaillou	Saint-Julien
Château Montrose	Saint-Estèphe
Third growth (troisième cru)	
Château Kirwan	Cantenac-Margaux
Château d'Issan	Cantenac-Margaux
Château Lagrange	Saint-Julien
Château Langoa-Barton	Saint-Julien

Château Giscours	Labarde (Margaux)
Château Malescot-Saint-Exupèry	Margaux
Château Cantenac-Brown	Cantenac-Margaux
Château Boyd-Cantenac	Margaux
Château Palmer	Cantenac-Margaux
Château La Lagune	Ludon
Château Calon-Ségur	Saint-Estèphe
Château Ferrière	Margaux
Château Marquis-d'Alesme-Becker	Margaux

Fourth growth (quatrième cru)

Château Saint-Pierre-Sevaistre	Saint-Julien
Château Saint-Pierre-Bontemps	Saint-Julien
Château Talbot	Saint-Julien
Château Branaire-Ducru	Saint-Julien
Château Duhart-Milon-Rothschild	Pauillac
Château Pouget	Cantenac-Margaux
Château La Tour-Carnet	Saint-Laurent
Château Lafon-Rochet	Saint-Estèphe
Château Beychevelle	Saint-Julien
Château Prieuré-Lichine	Cantenac-Margaux
Château Marquis-de-Terme	Margaux

Fifth growth (cinquième cru)

Château Pontet-Canet	Pauillac
Château Batailley	Pauillac
Château Haut-Batailley	Pauillac
Château Grand-Puy-Lacoste	Pauillac
Château Grand-Puy-Ducasse	Pauillac
Château Lynch-Bages	Pauillac
Château Lynch-Moussas	Pauillac
Château Dauzac	Labarde (Margaux)
Château d'Armailhac	Pauillac
Château du Tertre	Arsac
Château Haut-Bages Libéral	Pauillac

Château	*Commune*
Fifth growth (cinquième cru) *(continued)*	
Château Pédesclaux	Pauillac
Château Belgrave	Saint-Laurent
Château Camensac	Saint-Laurent
Château Cos Labory	Saint-Estèphe
Château Clerc-Milon	Pauillac
Château Croizet-Bages	Pauillac
Château Cantemerle	Macau

Château Lafite-Rothschild.   The name Château Lafite-Rothschild evokes visions of grand *châteaux* and centuries-old winemaking methods; in fact, this *château* produces one of the finest red wines in the world, and has a fascinating history.

In 1716, the Marquis Alexander de Ségur acquired Château Latour, Château Mouton-Rothschild, and Château Lafite-Rothschild through a marriage to Marie-Thérèse de Clauzel. In addition to these three properties, he also owned Château Calon-Ségur and Château Phélan-Ségur. Although he certainly didn't realize it at the time, he had taken possession of the three finest vineyards in the world. During the Revolution, however, the properties were split up and Ségur retained only Calon and Phélan. He is said to have been fond of saying, when talking about his empire, "I make wine at Lafite and Latour, but my heart is at Calon"; but one can be sure that his heart would skip more than a beat if he saw the astronomical prices these first-growth wines fetch.

It wasn't until 1787 that Lafite was vintage dated; in 1797, it was *château* or *estate* bottled for the first time, although that was an isolated experiment, and full *château* bottling did not resume until as late as 1907 (1906 vintage). The 1795 vintage of Château Lafite-Rothschild was blended with Hermitage (a red wine from the Rhône Valley) to give it strength. It was almost standard practice to blend Bordeaux wines with those from the Rhône Valley or even Spain that contained high alcohol. The blended Lafite wine was labeled Lafite-Hermitaged.

On August 8, 1868, Baron James Rothschild purchased Lafite for a record $3 million. By then the famous classification of 1855 had taken place and Lafite-Rothschild was unanimously voted a first-growth vineyard.

During the years 1885 to 1906, *château* bottling was not permitted because grapevines that had been devastated earlier (1876 to 1885) by the *phylloxera* root-louse had to be replanted.

At one time Lafite produced a white wine (the grapes were later uprooted) for the personal use of Baron Elie de Rothschild. The last vintage of this wine (1959) fetched $230 per bottle at auction in August 1978.

In 1962, Lafite's owners acquired Château Duhart-Milon, a fourth-growth vineyard producing a red Bordeaux, and later added Château Clarke, of Listrac, and Château La Cardonne, in the Bas-Médoc region.

Carruades de Lafite (last produced in 1966) was the so-called "second" wine of Lafite. It was replaced in 1974 by Moulin des Carruades, formerly the "third" wine of Lafite, and in 1985, the name Carruades de Lafite was once again reinstated.

Nowadays the wines produced by Lafite, along with those of Château Mouton-Rothschild and Château Pétrus, command the highest prices of any red Bordeaux wines, often more than $100 per bottle.

An interesting aside to the Lafite-Rothschild story is that, in 1882, Baron Edmond de Rothschild (son of James) decided to give financial assistance to some Russian Jews in the development of winemaking in Palestine, where Israel's present winemaking industry originated. Carmel Vineyards is the result of the Rothschild family's financial and technological expertise and shrewd marketing strategies.

In 1820, Château Mouton-Rothschild was known as Château Brane-Mouton and remained so until Baron Nathaniel de Rothschild purchased it on May 11, 1853. Since 1853, Mouton-Rothschild has been owned by members of successive generations of Rothschilds: first Nathaniel, then James, Henri, and, since October 22, 1922, Philippe.

In 1924, Mouton was *château* bottled for the first time. It was with the 1934 vintage that Mouton's labels first mentioned the number of bottles produced in that year. The letters RC occasionally appear on labels, meaning that the wine is reserved for the *château* and normally not released to the public.

Baron Philippe signs his name on the bottle's label, which led one enterprising individual in Venezuela and another in Los Angeles to superimpose the signature onto a French bank check (these attempts failed miserably and led to their arrest). Baron Philippe uses a slightly different signature for business and personal matters. It is the letter *R* that makes the difference, and it is speculated that this was the reason why he changed his traditional signature on the label from "Philippe de Rothschild" to "Baron Philippe" in 1979.

One of the most fascinating aspects of Château Mouton-Rothschild bottles is the art work on the label. Every year Baron Philippe de Rothschild commissions a famous artist to design the upper portion of Mouton's label. The tradition began in 1927 (with the 1924 vintage), but the practice did not become regular until 1945. (See Appendix C for a complete list.)

In 1933, Philippe de Rothschild acquired Château Mouton-d'Armailhacq, a fifth-growth vineyard producing a red Bordeaux wine. In 1956, the name was changed to Château Mouton-Baron Philippe, and in 1975, to Château Mouton-Baronne Philippe. Finally, in 1979, Baron Philippe again changed the name to Château Mouton-Baronne Pauline, to honor his late wife Pauline, who died in 1976. In order to give the wine a stronger identity, its name was again changed (1991) to Château d'Armailhac.

In 1962, the world-famous wine library of Château Mouton-Rothschild first opened its doors to the public. In 1970, Baron Philippe purchased Château Clerc-Milon, a fifth-growth Pauillac vineyard. On June 22, 1973, Château Mouton-Rothschild was officially granted *grand cru* status by Monsieur Jacques Chirac, then France's minister of agriculture. Before this reclassification (from second- to first-growth status) Château Mouton-Rothschild had this world-famous slogan: "First I am not, Second I do not deign to be, I am Mouton." In 1973, the slogan was changed to: "First I am; Second I was; Mouton does not change."

Mouton's "second" wine, called Le Second Vin, debuted with the 1993 vintage. Mouton also produced a regional red, white, and rosé wine labeled Mouton-Cadet, which is produced in huge quantities. Before 1933, the wine was called Carruades de Mouton-Rothschild.

Château Latour is noted for extremely dark, hard, full-bodied wines that need decades of aging before becoming even remotely drinkable. It is one of the longest-lived wines in the world and, unfortunately, many people drink it before its time. Latour has the uncanny ability to produce good wines even in mediocre vintages (e.g., 1963, 1965, 1968, and 1974). Latour is generally blended with a high percentage of Cabernet Sauvignon, which gives it its longevity.

The Latour label depicts an ancient tower which, according to records, was originally used to guard against pirates during the second half of the Hundred Years War. A lion is perched on top, ready to strike its enemies.

Since 1966, Château Latour has produced a "second" wine called Les Forts de Latour, made from vineyards whose grapevines are not considered mature enough for Latour.

Château Margaux, originally known as Château Lamothe or Château LaMotte, is the only classified wine that uses its commune name as its vineyard name.

In 1977, the Mentzelopoulos family, owners of a French supermarket chain, purchased Château Margaux from the Ginestet family. Unfortunately, the Ginestets' had been slowly bringing Château Margaux down in quality and reputation due to financial problems.

Although basically a red wine producer, Château Margaux has produced an excellent dry white wine since 1847, made exclusively from the Sauvignon Blanc grape. It is labeled "Le Pavillon Blanc de Château Margaux" and is entitled to be sold under the appellation *Bordeaux Blanc Contrôlée*. Château Margaux has produced, beginning with the 1912 vintage, a *second* red wine labeled "Le Pavillon Rouge."

Graves.   The name of this district is derived from the gravelly soil, found there; it produces both dry red and white wines. The most important vineyard in this district is Château Haut-Brion, the producer of one of the finest red wines in the world. Less well known is its superb white dry wine, labeled Château Haut-Brion Blanc.

Although only one Graves wine (Château Haut-Brion) was classified in 1855, there are many fine vineyards in this district which, if classified today, would certainly rank quite high. Graves produces very good dry white wines from Sémillon (about 70 percent of total plantings), Sauvignon Blanc, and Muscadelle grapes. The vineyards listed below are the most well known in Graves. They are mainly red wine vineyards; an asterisk indicates that the vineyard also produces white wine.

- Château Bouscaut*
- Château Carbonnieux*
- Château Chantegrive*
- Domaine de Chevalier*
- Château Couhins*
- Château de Fieuzal*
- Château Haut-Bailly
- Château Haut-Brion*
- Château La Louvière*
- Château La Mission Haut-Brion
- Château La Tour-Haut-Brion
- Château Laville-Haut-Brion (only makes white wine)
- Château La Tour-Martillac*
- Château Malartic-Lagravière*
- Château Oliver*
- Château Pape-Clément*
- Château Smith-Haut-Lafitte*

Pessac-Léognan. On September 9, 1987, an *appellation contrôlée* was established, which applies only to those red and white wines that are produced in the northern ten communes of Graves, located southwest of the city of Bordeaux. It was recognized that these ten communes consistently produced superior quality wines than those further south. The red wines must contain a minimum of 25 percent Cabernet Sauvignon, and the white wines, a minimum of 25 percent Sauvignon Blanc.

Pomerol and Saint-Émilion. Although the wines of Pomerol were never officially classified, several of them would rank with the finest from Médoc. The wines of Saint-Émilion were classified on October 7, 1954. The classification was not designed to be fixed, but rather to be revised every ten years.

Most Pomerols and Saint-Émilions (both make only red wine) are made with a predominance of the Merlot grape, which yields a softer wine than those made with a higher proportion of Cabernet Sauvignon grapes. This is not to say that Pomerols and Saint-Émilions lack staying power or aging ability; for the most part they mature slightly faster than their counterparts from the Médoc. The use of the Merlot grape in making Pomerols and Saint-Émilions is important: the Merlot ripens earlier than the Cabernet Sauvignon grape and therefore often escapes early frosts or severe late fall weather while Cabernet

Sauvignon grapes are still ripening on the grapevines. The 1967 vintage, for example, was only fair in the Médoc district because of early autumn rains, but was exceptional in Pomerol and Saint-Émilion.

Among the best-known vineyards in Pomerol are:

- Château Pétrus
- Château Petit-Village
- Châtcau Trotanoy
- Château l'Évangile
- Château Nenin
- Château Gazin
- Château la Fleur
- Château la Fleur Pétrus
- Vieux Château-Certan
- Château la Pointe

To help promote the wines of Pomerol, a wine brotherhood was estabished, known as the La Confrérie des Hospitaliers de Pomerol.

Among the best-known vineyards in Saint-Émilion are:

- Château Cheval Blanc
- Château Ausone
- Château Beauséjour Duffau-Lagarrosse
- Château Beau-Séjour Bécot
- Château Belair
- Château Canon
- Château Figeac
- Château la Gaffelière
- Château Magdelaine
- Château Pavie
- Clos Fourtet
- Château Simard
- Château Trottevieille
- Château la Conseillante
- Château Monbousquet

Although almost all of the vineyards of the Médoc use *château* in their name, in Saint-Émilion, *clos* (enclosure or field) is used instead in some vineyard names and the meaning is the same.

To help promote the wines of Saint-Émilion, on July 8, 1199, John Lackland established a wine brotherhood known as the Jurade de Saint-Émilion.

Côtes de Bordeaux. Wines from the Côtes are the hidden treasures of Bordeaux and are among the oldest "crus" of the Bordeaux wine district. "Côte" means a vineyard planted on a slope. The Côtes de Bordeaux are produced on the slopes along the right banks of the region's three rivers: the Garonne, the Dordogne, and their confluence, the Gironde. The soil of these steep slopes forms a perfect geological unity, heavy with clay and lime. The exposure is west-southwest, providing plenty of sunshine especially in late autumn, when the sun's rays strike the slope at nearly right angles. The wines that result from such a microclimate are ripe, richly colored, with good fruit.

The Côtes produce both red and white wines, with the reds accounting for 15 percent of the total output of Bordeaux AOC. This appellation includes the Côtes de Bourg, Premières Côtes de Blaye, Premières Côtes de Bordeaux, Côtes de Castillon, and Côtes de Francs.

The wines are produced on small family vineyards, most covering no less than 20 acres, with meticulous care and attention by growers who pass on land, experience, and their love of the wine from generation to generation. Grapes used for the red wines are Cabernet Sauvignon, Merlot, and Malbec, in varying proportions. In most cases the wine is made and bottled on the estate. About 25 percent of the production is exported and the percentage is increasing.

Côtes de Bourg. The Bourg-Sur-Gironde region, about 20 miles north of the city of Bordeaux, extends along the right bank of the Dordogne just above its confluence with the Garonne. The terrain of steep slopes and deep valleys has given it the nickname of "Gironde Switzerland."

Grapevines cover 70 percent of the district, which produce AOC Côtes de Bourg. This is one of the smallest wine districts in Bordeaux and one of the oldest, with grapevines having been grown here since the first century A.D. The appellation is limited to wines grown on the high ground, clay-lime soil above the limestone mother-rock. Ninety percent of the production is red wines that are deeply colored, full-bodied, and firm, and that, with their robust character, age well.

Premières Côtes de Bordeaux. This wine district covers a strip of land some 37 miles long and three miles wide along the right bank of the Garonne, from Bordeaux to Saint-Macaire. The soil is clay and lime with occasional surface gravel and a limestone subsoil that provides perfect drainage. Quarries dug into the limestone are often used as storage and aging caves. Both red and white wines are produced here with the red mostly in the north where southern exposure yields long hours of sunshine. A Renaissance château in Cadillac known as the Dukes of Epernon is the home of the famous wine fraternity, the "Connétablie de Guyenne."

The appellation covers more than 36 communes, of which 14 produce red wine. It is a traditional grape-growing district where family properties are the rule. The wine is normally made and bottled on the estate.

Drunk young, these reds are rich, very fruity, and fresh. They age well, becoming rounded and smooth on the palate, with a more complex bouquet. They are firm, generous, full-bodied wines.

Premières Côtes de Blaye.   The Blaye district extends north of Bourg along the right bank of the Gironde opposite the Médoc. Along the river, hills of chalk and clay are planted with red grapes. They merge into a vast, sandy plateau where whites are produced.

The district of Blaye is the main producer of the red Premières Côtes de Blaye, which is grown on clay and chalk or gravel, rather than alluvial soil of the river valley. The appellation accounts for approximately 25 percent of the red Côtes.

The wines have a characteristic taste derived from the Blaye chalk. They have an attractive red color, a clean flavor, fine bouquet, and are fruity and supple. They retain their freshness and may be drunk young, but also age well, acquiring a fine bouquet as they mature.

Côtes de Castillon, Côtes de Francs.   This little-known district is located on the right bank of the Dordogne with Saint-Émilion to the west and Bergerac to the east. The grapevines are grown on steep clay-lime slopes, or on soil with varying amounts of clay at the foot of the slopes. The subsoil is almost always a hard limestone, formerly used for buildings. Outside the little city of Castillon, General Talbot died in battle in 1453, which closed the Hundred Years War.

Some nine communes share the AOC Bordeaux Côtes de Castillon, and red appellation wines account for 24 percent of red Côtes wine.

The wines are deeply colored, full-bodied, and very individual in character. The typical "rustic character" of the Côtes wines combines well with the suppleness given by the dominant Merlot grape. These wines age exceptionally well and are increasingly sought out by wine lovers.

Other important wine-producing districts of Bordeaux are: Moulis, Listrac, Côtes de Fronsac, and Entre-Deux-Mers (translated means "between the two seas"); Garonne and Dordogne.

Regional, proprietary, shippers, unclassified and cru bourgeois wines.   Although the wines classified in 1855 are the finest available from Bordeaux, they are also the most expensive and, for many, are not affordable. One could certainly not drink them every day; generally they are reserved for special occasions.

In addition to *château*-bottled wines, there are many wines that are bought, aged, bottled, and shipped by cooperatives and shippers under one of the names listed below. Careful shoppers look for these lower-priced shippers' wines, which are of good to excellent quality:

B & G	Cruse	J. P. Moueix
Calvet	Ginestet	Sichel
Cordier	Alexis Lichine	

Some *proprietary wines* are Mouton-Cadet, Lacour Pavillon, Grand Marque, and Maitre d'Estournel.

Regional wines are simply labeled with the name of the commune or district that produces them: Médoc, Saint-Émilion, Graves, Bordeaux, and so on.

Some *unclassified* and *cru bourgeois* wines are:

Château Chasse-Spleen	Château Lanessan
Château Coufran	Château La Rose-Trintaudon
Château Fombrauge	Château Meyney
Château Fourcas-Hosten	Château de Pez
Château Gloria	Château Phélan-Ségur
Château Greysac	Château Trimoulet

Sauternes.   Sauternes (which takes its name from the Sauternes district where it is produced) are, along with German *trockenbeerenauslese,* the sweetest wines in the world and among the most expensive. Sauternes is produced from three white grape varieties: Sémillon, Sauvignon Blanc, and Muscadelle. It appears that Sémillon, with its thin skin, is more susceptible to *Botrytis* than either Sauvignon Blanc or Muscadelle.

Sauternes are made by a beneficial mold called the "noble rot" (technically, *Botrytis cinerea*). *Botrytis cinerea* is a mold present as spores at all times in most vineyards. Depending on the grape variety, the time of year, and climatic conditions, it can greatly enhance or severely damage the grapes in a vineyard.

Affected berries may resemble dark, purplish-brown, desiccated, cracked raisins, but retain much more natural fruit acid than raisins, and do not have the caramelized taste of a raisin.

The grapes that have been attacked by the "noble rot" are extremely overripe and may be hand-picked individually after the ripeness has been determined. From each bunch of grapes the pickers might select one or two berries for use. The same vineyard might have to be picked over several times in order to obtain all the affected grapes. It is said that it takes one picker one full day to pick enough grapes to produce one bottle of this sweet wine. Obviously, the result is an extremely high cost of production.

Wines made from these grapes are yellow to gold-amber in color with a distinctive honeylike, raisiny character. They are extremely sweet (about 7 percent residual sugar) and have an unusually long bottle life, lasting easily five to ten years, and if from an excellent vintage, as long as 50 years or more.

The five communes entitled to be called Sauternes are: *Sauternes, Barsac, Preignac, Far-*

gues, and *Bommes.* (Only wines from the commune of Barsac are entitled to the Barsac *appellation contrôlée;* however, a decree of 1936 gave this commune the right to the illustrious Sauternes appellation as well.) The Sauternes appellation requires a minimum alcoholic content of 13 percent; and the practice of *chaptalization* **is** permitted.

To help promote the sweet wines of Sauternes, a wine brotherhood, La Commanderie du Bontemps de Sauternes et Barsac, was established.

The sweet wines of Sauternes and Barsac were among those ranked by the 1855 classification; the vineyards are listed below by classification:

Château	*Commune*
First "great" growth (grand premier cru)	
Château Y'Quem	Sauternes
First growth (premier cru)	
Château Climens	Barsac
Château Coutet	Barsac
Château Guiraud	Sauternes
Clos Haut-Peyraguey	Bommes
Château Lafaurie-Peyraguey	Bommes
Château La Tour Blanche	Bommes
Château Rabaud-Promis	Bommes
Château Rayne-Vigneau	Bommes
Château Rieussec	Fargues
Château Sigalas-Rabaud	Bommes
Château Suduiraut	Preignac
Second growth (deuxième cru)	
Château d'Arche	Sauternes
Château Broustet	Barsac
Château Caillou	Barsac
Château Doisy-Daëne	Barsac
Château Doisy-Dubroca	Barsac
Château Doisy-Védrines	Barsac
Château Filhot	Sauternes

Château Lamothe	Sauternes
Château Lamothe-Guignard	Sauternes
Château de Malle	Preignac
Château de Myrat	Barsac
Château Nairac	Barsac
Château Romer-du-Hayot	Fargues
Château Suau	Barsac

Burgundy

Burgundy's four wine-producing districts—Saône-et-Loire, Côte d'Or, Rhône, and Yonne—are known around the world for the wines they produce.

When the Roman legions came to Gaul, they brought a knowledge of viticulture that inspired the Burgundians to grow and treasure their grapevines. The name of the region comes from a migrant people, the *Burgondiones*, who settled there around A.D. 450.

The fourteenth and fifteenth centuries were auspicious times for Burgundy thanks to the four Valois Dukes of the West—Philip the Bold, John the Fearless, Philip the Good, and Charles the Bold—who made the duchy so powerful that the kings of France and the princes of Europe were intimidated.

On July 31, 1394, Philip the Bold, Duke of Burgundy, issued an edict, banishing the *"evil and disloyal"* Gamay grape from his kingdom (the areas around Dijon, Beaune, and Chalon), in favor of the bigger and fruitier Pinot Noir grape, which was in demand at that time.

Bit by bit, by marriage and war, the dukes acquired a territory that extended from the North Sea to the Mediterranean and included part of Holland, Belgium, and a piece of Northern Italy.

Under the last duke, Charles the Bold, Burgundy started to disintegrate. Charles died in 1477 while fighting to establish an independent Burgundy with its capital located in Nancy, Lorraine. Louis XI succeeded in grabbing the duchy, but Charles' daughter, Marie de Bourgogne, was a tough adversary. Many revolts against the king by the Burgundians ensued, but peace finally came. Five years after her father's death, Marie was thrown from a horse while hunting and killed. The territory was then annexed to the French crown.

By the Middle Ages, Christianity was firmly established. The religious orders dispensed charity, provided the only hospitals and schools, and ran "hospices" (rest places) for travelers, both rich and poor. Burgundian viticulture survived because of the monks. For nearly 1,300 years, almost all of the biggest and best vineyards in Burgundy were owned and operated by the Benedictines and Cistercians. Slowly and patiently they improved the quality of their grapevines.

Research carried out first at the Benedictine Abbey of Cluny and later at Citeaux, run by the Cistercians, gave rise to the methods of grape growing and winemaking in Burgundy that exist to this day.

According to manuscripts that date from the thirteenth century, Burgundy was governed by the Prince of Conde. A network of canals was built that links the Loire, the Seine, and the Saône Rivers. The wine trade developed and expanded. On the advice of his doctor, Louis XIV drank, and thereby promoted, the wines of the Côte d'Or. When Mâcon grape grower Claude Brosse took his harvest to Versailles, the king also gave it his royal patronage. At the beginning of the eighteenth century the first wine firms were founded in Beaune, soon followed by others in Nuits-Saint-Georges and Dijon.

Throughout its turbulent history, Burgundy's boundaries contracted and expanded according to the fortunes of war. The French Revolution abruptly changed Burgundy's viticulture, as the large estates owned by the nobility and the church were seized and sold. Properties were broken up into small lots and purchasers subdivided these lots into thousands of small patches which they sold to the peasants. Further fragmentation was continued by the French laws of inheritance and a comparatively small volume of wine was made by an enormous number of producers. Ownership of a Burgundian vineyard, no matter how minuscule, was and still is a badge of prestige.

At the time when the land was divided (and subdivided), the unit of measurement was a *journal,* being anywhere from one-third to five-sixths of an acre. This explains why there are often more than 40 different individual owners of one vineyard.

Many of these small vineyards sell their grapes to shippers; others make their own wine or sell it in *hogsheads* (barrels holding approximately 60 gallons) to shippers who mature it and then sell it. About 75 percent of the wine sold by shippers is made by small independent proprietors. No big shipper has the time to deal with a multitude of growers. Intermediaries known as *courtiers* (brokers), who work on commission, handle most of the sales of the small growers' wines to the shippers. They know what the shipper wants and try to match what is available to his needs.

Many cooperatives have been formed to deal with the problems of the small producer. Twenty-nine cooperative wineries make 24 percent of the total wine production in Burgundy (this number is low compared to other French wine-producing areas). They are located in the areas of Beaujolais, Mâcon, and Chablis.

Approximately 80 percent of the Burgundy wine produced is red; most of it is from the Côte de Nuits. The other 20 percent is white, mostly from the Côte de Beaune.

Burgundy is the northernmost great red wine-producing region in the world, located approximately 200 miles southeast of Paris, and is the easiest to understand of France's wine-producing regions, in terms of the grape varieties permitted, under law, to be grown there. There are five: *Pinot Noir* for red wines; *Chardonnay, Aligoté,* and *Pinot Blanc* for white wines (including Chablis); and *Gamay Noir* for Beaujolais (Figure 3-3).

HOW TO READ A WINE LABEL

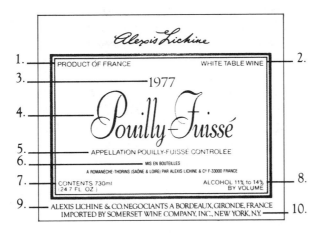

READING A BURGUNDY WINE LABEL

1. The wine is a product of France

2. The color of the wine

3. Vintage

4. It is either the name of the grape, vineyard or specific place-name where the vineyard is located.

5. Appellation (d'Origine) Controlée: controlled place-name of origin. These words represent certification that the wine comes from the regulated place-name indicated on the label.

6. "Mis en Bouteilles à" or "put in bottles at . . ." The name of the property where the wine was bottled.

7. The net contents of the bottle

8. The alcoholic percentage by volume

9. The name and address of the shipper

10. The name and address of the importer

FIGURE 3-3 Reading a Burgundy wine label.

Chablis. This grape-growing area takes its name from the charming village of Chablis, which is nestled by the side of the Serein River.

Chablis is 75 miles north of the Côte d'Or in Burgundy on a horizontal parallel that runs north of Seattle, Washington. Frost is always a danger in the northern climates and the Serein River compounds the problem. When a frost arrives it sinks into the river bottom and hovers for days, searing the delicate grapevines on the river's banks.

Chablis is known worldwide; its chalky soil gives it its clean taste. Fruitiness and bouquet are contributed by the Chardonnay grape. Chablis is an extremely dry, crisp wine with refreshing acidity.

By law there are four Chablis: *grand cru, premier cru, chablis,* and *petit chablis. Grand cru* Chablis must have a minimum alcoholic content of 11 percent; *premier cru,* 10.5 percent; *chablis,* 10 percent; and *petit chablis,* 9.5 percent alcohol. *Chaptalization* is not only permitted but is practiced yearly. Chablis received its AOC designation in 1938, which specifies that only the Chardonnay grape (known locally as Aubaine or Beaunois) may be used to produce it.

The most elegant Chablis is the *grand cru.* There are seven, all from one stretch of hillside at the end of the village:

Blanchot	Les Clos	Vaudésir
Bougros	Preuses	
Grenouilles	Valmur	

At the other end of that same hill and facing it across the narrow river are the vineyards from which the *premier cru* Chablis is produced. Until much-needed changes in the law took place in 1967, there were more than 30 vineyards entitled to be called *premier cru.* These have been narrowed down to 11:

Beauroy	Mélinots	Vaillons
Côte de Léchet	Montmains	Vaucoupin
Fourchaume	Mont de Milieu	Vosgros
Les Fourneaux	Montée de Tonnerre	

Simple *chablis* and the lightest wine, *petit chablis,* are produced from vineyards farther from the village. *Chablis* is the largest category, covering more than 3,000 acres of vineyards. *Petit chablis* is rarely exported to the United States.

Les Piliers Chablisiens is the wine brotherhood, founded in 1953, which is responsible for promoting the wines of Chablis.

Some of the better-known producers and shippers of Chablis are:

Albert Bichot et Cie
Joseph Drouhin
Louis Jadot
Patrick de Ladoucette
Henri Laroche

J. Moreau et Fils
Albert Pic et Fils
A. Régnard et Fils
William Fèvre

The Côte d'Or. The Côte d'Or (Golden Slope) is 25 to 30 miles long and only about one mile wide at its widest point. The greatest vineyards in Burgundy are in this district, which is traditionally divided into two wine-producing areas: Côte de Nuits in the north and Côte de Beaune in the south.

Soil content is one factor critical to the development of a wine's qualities. The soil of the Côte de Nuits is a mixture of clay, silica, and limestone; that of the Côte de Beaune is high in limestone or its near relation, chalk.

By law, the red wines of the Côte d'Or are made exclusively from the Pinot Noir grape. The Pinot Noir seems to like warmth spread throughout the day, rather than cool mornings and hot afternoons.

The Côte de Nuits stretches for about 12 miles, from the town of Fixin in the north to Nuits-Saint-Georges in the south. There are 29 *appellation contrôlée* wines produced in this region. The communes named Gevrey-Chambertin, Morey-Saint-Denis, Vougeot, Vosne-Romanée, Nuits-Saint-Georges, Aloxe-Corton, Pommard, and Volnay have world-renowned vineyards. Only three white wines are entitled to the *appellation contrôlée* designation in the Côte de Nuits: Musigny Blanc, Nuits-Saint-Georges Blanc, and Clos Blanc de Vougeot.

All of the *grand cru* and the most important *premier crus* wines of this area are listed below, under the names of the communes that produce them.

FIXIN	
Grand cru	*Premier cru*
None	Les Hervelets
	La Perrière
	Clos du Chapitre
	Les Meix-Bas
	Les Arvelets
	Clos Napoléon

GEVREY-CHAMBERTIN

Grand cru	Premier cru
Chambertin	Clos Saint Jacques
Ruchottes-Chambertin	Les Varoilles
Clos de Bèze	
Charmes-Chambertin	
Chapelle-Chambertin	
Griotte-Chambertin	
Latricières-Chambertin	
Mazis-Chambertin	

MOREY-SAINT-DENIS

Grand cru	Premier cru
Clos de Tart	Clos des Lambrays
Clos Saint-Denis	Clos des Ormes
Clos de la Roche	Monts-Luisants
Bonnes Mares (Part)	

VOSNE-ROMANÉE

Grand cru	Premier cru
Richebourg	Les Suchots
La Romanée	Malconsorts
Romanée-Conti	Les Chaumes
La Tâche	La Grande Rue
Romanée Saint-Vivant	Les Beaumonts

FLAGEY-ECHÉZEAUX

Grand cru	Premier cru
Les Echézeaux	None
Grands Echézeaux	

CHAMBOLLE-MUSIGNY	
Grand cru	*Premier cru*
Musigny	Les Charmes
Bonnes Mares (Part)	Les Amoureuses

VOUGEOT	
Grand cru	*Premier cru*
Clos de Vougeot	Clos Blanc de Vougeot
	Les Cras

NUITS-SAINT-GEORGES	
Grand cru	*Premier cru*
None	Les Saint-Georges
	Les Cailles
	Les Porets
	Les Vaucrains
	Pruliers

The southern half of the Côte d'Or, the Côte de Beaune, extends approximately 15 miles, from Nuits-Saint-Georges in the north to Santenay in the south. It is wider, longer, and has nearly twice the amount of land of its northern neighbor. During the early Middle Ages, the city of Beaune was wealthy and important; rings of battlements built around it as protection from marauding enemies still stand. Some of the city's distinguished wine shippers use the fortresses as wine cellars.

Just six miles south of the city is the Côte de Meursault, an area scarred by old quarries. It is one of the few hills where the soil is perfectly suited to the Chardonnay grapevine from which fine white wines are produced in the communes of Meursault, Puligny-Montrachet, and Chassagne-Montrachet.

The Côte de Beaune is known for its outstanding white wines, although there are also some very fine red wines produced. One vineyard in particular, Corton (from the village of Aloxe-Corton), is the only *grand cru* red wine vineyard in the Côte de Beaune.

All of the *grand cru* and the most important *premier cru* wines produced in this area are listed below, under the names of the communes that produce them.

ALOXE-CORTON

Grand cru	Premier cru
Le Corton	Les Chaillots
Corton-Charlemagne	Les Fournières
	Les Guérets

PERNAND-VERGELESSES

Grand cru	Premier cru
None	Ile des Vergelesses
	Les Basses Vergelesses
	Les Fichots
	Creux de la Net

SAVIGNY-LES-BEAUNE

Grand cru	Premier cru
None	La Dominode
	Les Jarrons

BEAUNE

Grand cru	Premier cru
None	Les Grèves
	Les Fèves
	Les Marconnets
	Les Teurons
	Les Clos des Mouches
	Les Bressandes

POMMARD

Grand cru	*Premier cru*
None	Les Epenots
	Les Rugiens
	Les Arvelets
	Clos de la Commaraine

SANTENAY

Grand cru	*Premier cru*
None	Les Gravières
	La Comme
	Le Clos-de-Tavannes
	Beauregard

MONTHÉLIE

Grand cru	*Premier cru*
None	Le Château-Gaillard
	Les Riottes
	La Taupine

AUXEY-DURESSES

Grand cru	*Premier cru*
None	Les Duresses
	Clos du Val
	Les Grands Champs

MEURSAULT	
Grand cru	*Premier cru*
None	La Goutte d'Or
	Les Charmes
	Les Genevrières
	Les Perrières

PULIGNY-MONTRACHET	
Grand cru	*Premier cru*
Montrachet	Clos du Cailleret
Chevalier-Montrachet	Les Combettes
Bâtard-Montrachet	Les Pucelles
Bienvenues-Bâtard-Montrachet	

CHASSAGNE-MONTRACHET	
Grand cru	*Premier cru*
Montrachet	Clos Saint-Jean
Bâtard-Montrachet	Morgeot
Criots-Bâtard-Montrachet	La Boudriotte
	La Maltroie
	Les Grandes Ruchottes

VOLNAY	
Grand cru	*Premier cru*
None	Caillerets
	Champans
	Clos des Chênes
	Les Santenots

Côte Chalonnaise is a long, low line of hills that extends southward from the Côte de Beaune for about 20 miles. The grape varieties from which its classified red, white, and rosé wines are made are the same as those grown in the Côte d'Or, but the wines of the Côte Chalonnaise are somewhat lighter in body and mature faster. The most important villages in this appellation are Bouzeron, Givry, Mercurey, Montagny, and Rully.

The Mâconnais region takes its name from Mâcon, a rather pretty town on the river Saône. The local red wine is fruity and very pleasant when young; but the predominant wine here (approximately 70 percent of total production) is white. The region's slopes are covered with vineyards that produce light, dry white wines, such as the world-renowned Pouilly-Fuissé. Other white wines, in ascending order of quality, are Mâcon Blanc, Mâcon Supérieur, Mâcon-Villages, Saint-Véran, and Pouilly-Vinzelles.

In 1951, the Confrérie des Vignerons de Saint-Vincent was formed; it is the wine brotherhood responsible for promoting the wines of Mâcon in southern Burgundy. A celebration is held every January 22, on the birthday of Saint Vincent, Burgundy's patron saint.

The small village of Chardonnay is nestled among the vineyards, just three miles from the celebrated Romanesque church of Tournus; this, supposedly, is where the grape got its name.

Some reputable producers and shippers of Burgundy are:

Albert Bichot	Domaine Lamarche
Jean-Claude Boisset	Leroy
Bonneau du Martray	Louis Jadot
Bouchard Aîné et Fils	Louis Latour
Bouchard Père et Fils	La Reine Pedauque
Domaine Camus	Domaine Leflaive
Champy	Marcilly
Chanson Père et Fils	Prince de Mérode
Clair-Dau	Moillard
Domaine de La Romanée-Conti	Mommessin
Joseph Drouhin	Patriarche Père et Fils
Drouhin-Laroze	Pierre Ponnelle
Dufouleur Frères	Jacques Prieuer
Domaine Dujac	Prosper Mafoux
Joseph Faiveley	Ropiteau Frères
Pierre Gelin	Armand Rousseau
Domaine Jacques Germain	Roland Thévenin
Henri Gouges	Tollot-Beaut
Heritier-Guyot	Domaine des Varoilles
Hospices de Beaune	Comte Georges de Vogüé

Beaujolais

The Beaujolais region is the southernmost district in Burgundy, just south of the vine-yards of Mâcon. To the west is the mountain chain of the Monts du Beaujolais; to the east, the river Saône; and to the south, the region ends just slightly north of Lyon. This is a large and very productive region just over 40 miles long, with a total of 55,000 acres, which produce the light, fruity red wine that takes its name from the region. Beaujolais comes from *Beaujeu,* the name of a little town that was the seat of the province in the twelfth century, until the village of Villefranche was built nearer to the Saône and became the province's capital.

The production of *nouveau* or *primeur* wines began in Beaujolais in the early 1900s. Certain bottlers in Lyon would buy wines either before or during harvest. These new wines, destined to be drunk young, were stored in wood barrels before fermentation occurred. Small holes were drilled in the barrel and stuffed with straw; this both prevented explosions that could result from the accumulation of carbonic gas and allowed the wine to breathe. The barrels were then loaded on horse-drawn carts headed for bottlers in Lyon. The people of Lyon began to realize that some wines had qualities that recommended them for drinking very soon after harvest. Soon the word—and the wine—traveled throughout France.

Beaujolais, produced and consumed in considerable quantities for centuries in the Saône River Valley just above Lyon, is more popular in the United States than the wines of any other French region. A good percentage of Beaujolais is never even bottled, but goes to market in the barrels from which it is drawn in the restaurants of Paris and Lyon. It is the most popular *vin ordinaire* of France (Figure 3-4). In this region in years past, the wine was served free at outdoor restaurants in small bottles known as *pots* (with a capacity of approximately 17 ounces), to demonstrate the quality of the new wine.

Good Beaujolais should have the fresh, full, fruity nose reminiscent of berries, which is part of its Gamay Noir heritage. On the palate one should taste cherries, strawberries, raspberries, and an overwhelming freshness. Beaujolais should be young, lively, and joyous. It is the grapiest of all European wines, flowery yet quaffable.

In a prolific year, the region may produce six or seven million cases of wine. Less than 1 percent of this yield will be white, usually without the bouquet or the breed of a good white Burgundy. The red wines produced in Beaujolais could legally be called Burgundies if the producers adhered to the requirements of the appropriate *Appellation Contrôlée* laws, among them that only the Pinot Noir grape be used.

Beaujolais is divided into two areas: the Haut-Beaujolais in the north and the Bas-Beaujolais in the south. One of the special features of Beaujolais is that just south of the town of Pouilly-Fuissé, the soil suddenly becomes granitelike and is composed of manganese, porphyry, and schist or diorite (also granitelike). These elements are not suitable for the Pinot Noir grape. Consequently, growers in the south have slowly switched to using Gamay Noir as the primary grape in making the jubilantly light and cherry-colored

FIGURE 3-4   Annual Beaujolais Nouveau celebration. (Courtesy *Food & Wines from France*)

Beaujolais. The calcareous soil of the Bas-Beaujolais is composed mainly of clay and chalk, or limestone.

The table below indicates the alcohol content requirements for red Beaujolais wines under the *Appellation Contrôlée* laws (*cru* wines are listed separately).

Wine	Minimum required strength
Beaujolais	unfermented 9 percent
Beaujolais-Supérieur	unfermented 10 percent
Beaujolais-Villages	unfermented 10 percent
Cru	
Saint-Amour	unfermented 10 percent
Moulin-à-Vent	unfermented 10 percent
Morgon	unfermented 10 percent
Juliénas	unfermented 10 percent
Fleurie	unfermented 10 percent
Chiroubles	unfermented 10 percent

Wine	Minimum required strength
Cru *(continued)*	
Chénas	unfermented 10 percent
Régnié	unfermented 10 percent
Brouilly	unfermented 10 percent
Côte de Brouilly	unfermented 10.5 percent

If the wine does not meet these standards, it will be declassified to a lower level or simply sold as *vin rouge* (red wine). A Beaujolais wine at 10 percent alcohol or above, produced from a vineyard that meets yield per acre and other requirements, may be sold as Beaujolais Supérieur.

Wines labeled Beaujolais or Beaujolais Supérieur are lighter wines probably from one of the 59 communes in the Bas-Beaujolais area. Beaujolais with less than 10 percent alcohol is generally unstable for travel and rarely reaches the United States. The next-highest grade is Beaujolais-Villages, produced in 39 communes located in the northernmost section of the Haut-Beaujolais area. If Beaujolais-Villages is made from vineyards whose yield per acre is too high, it will be dropped in class. Beaujolais-Villages is a little fuller-bodied than the wines from the south, but still rich and charming.

Ten communes that are all located in the northern part of the region, each of which is entitled to its own appellation, produce the *cru.* These *cru* wines do not use the word *Beaujolais* on their labels, but are sold under the name of the commune that produces them. *Cru* vineyards are limited in yield per acre and their wines must contain a minimum of 10 to 10.5 percent alcohol.

The northernmost of these communes is *Saint-Amour,* whose grapes have ripened in the full sunlight of hill slopes. The rich red wine is tinged with violet and is less fruity than its nine neighbors. Saint-Amour has a spicy aroma, with hints of kirsch. In parts of Saint-Amour the soil contains some limestone, which produces the delightful Beaujolais Blanc (white)—a drier and more delicate wine than Mâcon Blanc, and with slightly less body. Beaujolais Blanc is made from a blend of Chardonnay and Aligoté.

South of this is the commune of *Juliénas,* supposedly named after Julius Caesar. The wine produced here is sometimes harsh in its youth, but softens with one to two years of bottle aging. In a normal year, the fresh fruity wine of Juliénas is more assertive and longer-lasting than those of Saint-Amour.

Below Juliénas is *Chénas,* named after the oak trees *(chéne)* that at one time covered all of the Beaujolais area. The Chénas wines, along with those of Moulin-à-Vent, Juliénas, and Morgon, are the sturdiest of the *crus.*

The commune of *Moulin-à-Vent* (south of Chénas) produces the best-known and probably the finest of all Beaujolais wine. A nearby seventeenth century windmill *(moulin-à-*

vent)—still standing (minus its sails)—is the source of its name. The character and taste of the wine are due to the granitelike quality of the local soil. Moulin-à-Vent is a dark-colored, full-bodied wine that takes a long time to mature; it lasts up to four or five years, but peaks in about three years.

Close by is the commune of *Fleurie,* probably so named because the wine it produces is known for its delicate and flowery bouquet. Fleurie is light in both color and body, with a silky flavor, lasting up to three years.

Below Fleurie are the communes of *Chiroubles* and *Morgon.* Chiroubles makes robust wines with a distinctive berry flavor. However, they mature quickly and should be drunk within a year or two after harvest. Morgon produces a full-bodied but not coarse wine that usually requires nearly a year in the barrel and another year in the bottle before it is ready to drink. It takes three years for Morgon to actually reach its prime.

Régnié is located near the communes of Brouilly and Morgon, which produces distinctive and appealing fruity wines reminiscent of strawberries. Régnié officially received its AOC designation in 1988.

The two southernmost communes are *Brouilly* and *Côte de Brouilly.* Brouilly is the largest producer of the ten *cru* communes, producing wines with a distinct flavor of black and red currants. However, the wines from the sloping vineyards of Côte de Brouilly, which possess a deeper color and somewhat livelier style than Brouilly, are considered to be better than those of Brouilly.

The wines of these ten communes, from lightest to fullest in body, are: Fleurie, Chiroubles, Juliénas, Saint-Amour, Chénas, Brouilly, Régnié, Côte de Brouilly, Moulin-à-Vent, and Morgon.

Beaujolais Nouveau, also known as *Beaujolais Primeur,* is the "new" Beaujolais that is rushed through fermentation, then sold only a matter of weeks after harvest. Nouveau is at its best when it first appears on the market. After one year it is tired and, with few exceptions, should be forgotten.

Beginning in 1967, the official date of first release or sale of the *nouveaus* was November 15. However, since 1985, the official date is the third Thursday in the month of November, regardless of the specific date.

Some important Beaujolais shippers and producers are:

Paul Beaudet	Louis Jadot
B. & G.	Le Marquisat
Bouchard Père et Fils	Mommessin
Château de La Chaize	Père Patriarche
David & Foillard	Piat
Joseph Drouhin	Louis Tete
Georges Duboeuf	

The Compagnons du Beaujolais, formed in 1947, is the wine brotherhood of Beaujolais.

The Loire Valley

The river Loire has a double distinction: It is the longest river in France (625 miles) and the longest of all the world's great rivers (from its source in the Massif Central until it flows into the Atlantic, near Nantes) that nurture wine grapes along their banks.

The Loire Valley produces mostly dry white wines (75 percent of the total production); the rest are rosé and red wines. Like Alsace, the region lies very far north and doesn't receive sufficient sunshine to fully ripen red grapes.

Most of the wines of the Loire Valley are sold under district or village appellations, such as *Anjou, Pouilly Fumé, Saumur,* and *Vouvray.* There is one notable exception—Muscadet, which is sold under its grape varietal name. Technically speaking, the Muscadet grape is actually the Melon de Bourgogne, which was transplanted from Burgundy by order of King Louis XIV in 1639, and again in 1709. In 1709, a severe frost decimated the vineyards around Nantes. A search for a grapevine that would withstand the killing winter frosts resulted in the importation (from Burgundy)—of a hardier grape, Melon de Bourgogne, later renamed Muscadet.

The best-known wines of the Loire Valley are described below:

Pouilly Fumé is a dry, full-bodied white wine made from the Sauvignon Blanc grape in the village of Pouilly-Sur-Loire. Its name comes from the bloom of yeast on the grape's surface that looks grey (fumé: smoked).

Sancerre, also made from the Sauvignon Blanc grape, is bone dry, with striking acidity, but lacks the richness and full-bodied quality of Pouilly Fumé.

Vouvray is made from Chenin Blanc grapes, also known locally in the district of Anjou as *Pineau de la Loire,* or *Blanc d'Anjou.* The taste of Vouvray can range from bone dry to semisweet and even sweet. There is also a delightful sparkling version produced in limited quantities.

Saumur, a delightfully dry white wine made from Chenin Blanc grapes, is sometimes made into a sparkling wine via the *méthode champenoise.*

Bourgueil, stretches along the right bank of the Loire for nearly ten miles and produces almost exclusively red wine from the Cabernet Franc grape. These usually are fine to drink in about two years, but in great years can be enjoyed up to eight years.

Chinon is located on the southern bank of the Loire and both banks of its tributary, the Vienne. Chinon is best known for its red wine, with a tiny production of white and rosé. The red comes from the Cabernet Franc, while the white is made from the Chenin Blanc grape.

Montlouis, across from Vouvray, also produces wines exclusively from the Chenin Blanc grape. Sparkling wines are also produced.

Touraine produces white wine from the Sauvignon Blanc grape, and red and rosé wines utilizing mostly Gamay grapes.

Rosé d'Anjou (made from mostly Cabernet Franc and Groslot grapes) is produced in the northern part of the valley. It is light and delightful, with a fresh and almost floral aroma and flavor. A hint of sweetness in its taste allows it to be enjoyed by most everyone, including those who prefer dry wines.

Directly south of Anjou lies the district of *Coteaux du Layon,* whose wines are among the Loire Valley's sweetest and most distinguished. The two finest appellations are the *Quarts-de-Chaume* and *Bonnezeaux.* These wines are made from Chenin Blanc grapes that have been affected by the "noble rot." They have good acidity and balance and an elegant, lingering finish. These are wines that can be aged for ten to 20 years.

Muscadet, produced in the far western part of the valley, is a bone-dry, steely, clean, light white wine, usually high in acidity.

The Rhône Valley

Located below Burgundy in the southeast section of France, Rhône Valley's wine production is more than 90 percent red, with some fine whites and even rosé wines. It is the second-largest AOC wine-producing region (Bordeaux is the largest). The Rhône Valley, which is the southernmost of France's six major fine wine regions, received its AOC status in 1937.

The vineyards—totaling nearly 150,000 acres—stretch along both sides of the Rhône river for about 125 miles, beginning in the south around the famous papal stronghold of Avignon, and extending north to the outskirts of the city of Lyon. In the south the grapevines work hard to survive in chalky, stone-covered soil; in the northern area they scale palisades towering over the river.

Rhône wines are robust and full-bodied, with plenty of bouquet and taste. They are too heavy to be drunk in the summer, but are perfect for cold winter nights. They are higher in alcohol (a minimum 11 percent) than red Burgundies or Bordeaux because of their location.

The red wines of the northern Rhône improve with age, sometimes lasting as long as ten to 15 years, while the whites reach their peak between two and four years of age. In the northern region lies the famous village of *Côte Rôtie (roasted slope),* whose wine must be made with a minimum of 80 percent Syrah grapes, with the other 20 percent being Viognier. Côte Rôtie is only permitted (under AOC) to produce red wines. Côte Rôtie wines are full-bodied and are usually at their best between six to eight years of age.

Côte Rôtie is also home of the famous hillside vineyards of *Brune et Blonde.* At one time during the Middle Ages, these hills were owned by an aristocratic nobleman named Maugiron, who inhabited the château of Ampuis. According to legend, he gave the vineyards on these hills to his two daughters for their dowries. His two daughters, although different as day and night, were nevertheless ravishing beauties. One possessed blonde hair while the other had long jet-black hair. Upon his death, the color of his daughters' hair determined the wine's future name—Côte Blonde (blonde-haired daughter) and Côte Brune (dark-haired daughter).

Southward of Côte Rôtie is the village of *Condrieu,* which produces white wines solely from the Viognier grape. These wines are best when they are two to three years old.

South of Condrieu is Château Grillet, the smallest vineyard (six acres) in France, which was granted its *appellation contrôlée* designation in 1936. Château Grillet produces only white wines from 100 percent Viognier grape, and due to its small output, the wines are extremely rare and quite expensive.

Further south are the vineyards of the village of *Saint-Joseph,* whose wines were awarded their AOC designation in June 1956. Saint-Joseph produces red, white, and rosé wines. The red wine is made solely from the Syrah grape, which yields a somewhat full-bodied wine. The white wines, also full-bodied, are produced from the Roussanne and Marsanne grapes. Saint-Joseph red wines are best when four to six years old; and the white and rosé wines, two to four years old.

The next southern village is that of *Hermitage,* which produces the fullest and biggest of all the Rhône red wines. These wines are often able to age for eight to ten years and sometimes (depending on the vintage) as long as 15 years. Red Hermitage is produced from 100 percent Syrah grapes, while the white Hermitage, which has a smell of hazelnuts, is produced from a blend of Roussanne and Marsanne grapes. Red Hermitage wines are best when ten to 12 years old, and white Hermitage wines, when three to four years old. The wines from the vineyards of *Crozes-Hermitage* made from Syrah (red grape) and Marsanne and Roussanne (white grape) are lighter than those of Hermitage and should be drunk when they are younger.

Hermitage or *hermit* was a name supposedly given to Henri Gaspard de Stérimberg, a valiant knight in Pope Innocent III's Crusade. As the story goes, upon his return in 1225, he spent his remaining years (30) at the top of a hill as a hermit, dedicating his life to viticulture.

Cornas, the next village, is famous for a red wine produced from the Syrah grape, which is difficult to find due to its small production. Its wines can age for more than 15 years, although most are drinkable in eight to ten years.

The southernmost wine-producing area in the northern half of the Rhône is the village of *Saint-Péray.* Its white wine, made predominantly from the Marsanne grape, is one of the lightest of all Rhône whites. Since 1929, some of its production also goes into the making of *brut* and *demisec méthode champenoise* sparkling wines. Saint-Péray is best when it is two to three years old.

The northernmost village in the southern half of the Rhône is *Gigondas.* The red wines, produced from the Grenache, Syrah, Cinsaut, and Mourvèdre grapes, are some of the most powerful wines of the Rhône. The minimum alcohol content is 12.5 percent for the red wines, which will occasionally last more than 20 years, but are best when seven to nine years old. A small quantity of rosé wine is made, but is rarely exported to the United States.

The village of *Châteauneuf-du-Pape* was the summer residence of the papacy from 1309 to 1377, beginning with Archbishop Bertrand de Goth, who had succeeded to the papacy as Pope Clement V. On June 28, 1929, Châteauneuf-du-Pape became the first wine in France to be granted its AOC. By law, Châteauneuf-du-Pape wines must attain a minimum alcoholic content of 12.5 percent, and although they can be made from a blend of up to 13 grape varieties, they are usually blends of 65 percent Grenache and 35 percent Syrah grapes. The 13 grapes that are allowed to be used by law are: Bourboulenc, Cinsaut, Clairette, Counoise, Grenache, Mourvèdre, Muscardin, Picardin, Picpoul, Roussanne, Syrah, Terret Noir, and Vaccarèse. Châteauneuf-du-Pape produces predominantly red wines which are light to full-bodied depending on the year and producer. The lighter ones should be consumed at about five years of age, and the heavier ones at about ten. A small percentage of white Châteauneuf-du-Pape is produced from a blend of Grenache Blanc, Clairette, Roussanne, and Bourboulenc grape varieties. The white version is rich and full-bodied, with a fine bouquet, loaded with fruit.

Lirac produces red, white, and rosé wines. The grape varieties grown are Grenache, Mourvèdre, Cinsaut, and Syrah for the red and rosé wines, and Clairette, Ugni Blanc, and Bourboulenc for the white wines. Most of the wines of Lirac should be consumed fairly young.

The village of *Tavel,* certainly best known for its rosé wines, is located on the right bank of the Rhône River. These rosés are soft and plump, with just the right amount of taste and fullness. They are quite dry and have a light, bright crimson color. They are produced from a blend of Grenache, Cinsaut, Clairette, Picpoul, and Bourboulenc grapes.

The Côtes-du-Rhône-Villages *appellation contrôlée* was established in August 1967 for 17 villages in the southern half of the Rhône. The red, white (dry or naturally sweet), and rosé wines of this area can be marketed either under the name of the village where they were produced or under the name of Côtes-du-Rhône-Villages if the wine is a blend of wines from several villages. Most wines labeled Côtes-du-Rhône-Villages are usually fruity, a bit fuller than Beaujolais, and should be consumed very young.

The southernmost vineyard of the entire Rhône is *Beaumes-de-Venise,* which produces a sweet white wine. A fortified wine is made exclusively from Muscat grapes that are allowed to hang on the grapevines until overripe, then pressed and made into wine using traditional methods.

There are many reputable producers and shippers in the Rhône, including:

Max Chapoutier	Domaine de Mont-Redon
Château de Beaucastel	Marcel Guigal
Château Fortia	Paul Jaboulet Aîné
Château La Nerte	La Bernardine
Domaine de Cabrieres	Les Cedres
Domaine de la Serriere	

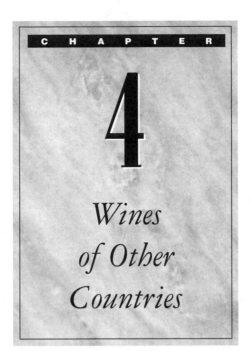

4

Wines of Other Countries

*A*t one time, if you wanted a fine
bottle of wine, you would simply have had to select from the wines of France, Germany,
Italy, or California. Nowadays, although these are still considered the leading
wine-producing areas, many countries are producing wines close or equal
to the quality level of these world leaders.

Modern technology has spread globally; with it, the production of world-class wines has surfaced in countries thought not to have the capacity to produce anything better than an inexpensive "jug wine." As these countries' wines enter the American wine market, shelf space will become more and more critical in the attempt to satisfy Americans' ever-growing awareness of fine quality wines.

▶ AUSTRALIA

Australia's wine history is a mere 200 years old. Captain Arthur Phillips, the first governor of New South Wales, introduced grapevines on January 26, 1788, when he arrived at Sydney Harbor with a fleet of 11 ships. He brought with him grapevine cuttings from Rio de Janeiro. Also in the late 1700s, the Hunter Valley was discovered by a royal Navy expedition led by Captain John Hunter. James Busby, a native of England, arrived in Australia in 1824 and began planting numerous types of grapevines in hopes of finding the most suitable ones for making wine. He toiled many years until 1828, when he established Australia's first vineyard, located in New South Wales, which he named *Kirkton.* Not too long after, in 1851, Joseph E. Seppelt, an immigrant from Germany, established his vineyards in the Barossa Valley of Southern Australia.

Australia, which is slightly smaller than the United States, has more than 500 wineries, although most of them are quite small. Basically, the same grape varieties flourish in Australia that grow in Europe and California: Cabernet Sauvignon, Merlot, Pinot Noir, Chardonnay, Sauvignon Blanc, and Sémillon. Australia's most interesting grape variety (by far) is Syrah, generally referred to as *Shiraz.* Syrah is a black-skinned grape, which produces dark, full-bodied, long-lived wines, with fruit flavors of wild blackberries, plums, and cassis. It is often incorrectly called *Hermitage,* which in actuality is the name of a great red wine-producing village in the Rhône Valley, as well as the local name for the Cinsaut grape variety in South Africa.

Australia is divided into three major grape-growing states: New South Wales, South Australia, and Victoria. Wine is also produced (to a lesser degree) in Queensland, Tasmania, and Western Australia.

New South Wales

This wine-producing state, located west of Sydney, is the second largest in terms of production after South Australia. The grape-growing areas are *Canberra District, Hastings Valley, Hunter Valley* (both Lower and Upper), *Mudgee,* and *Riverina.* The better-known wineries are [(date) indicates the year the winery was founded]:

Arrowfield (1969)	Huntington Estate (1969)
Brokenwood (1970)	Lake's Folly (1963)
Cassegrain (1980)	Lindemans (1870)

McWilliams (1880)

Tyrrell (1858)

Rosemount Estates (1969)

Wyndham Estate (1828)

Rothbury Estate (1968)

South Australia

South Australia was established on December 28, 1836 by His Majesty King William IV. South Australia's grape-growing areas are *Adelaide* (Hills and Surrounds), *Barossa Valley, Clare Valley, Coonawarra, Padthaway,* and *Southern Vales.* The better-known wineries are [(date) indicates the year the winery was founded]:

Barossa Valley Cooperative (1931)
  Kaiserstuhl label, translated
  means "kings seat," named after
  a German wine region
d'Arenberg (1928)
Elderton (1921)
Hardy's (1921)
Kingston Estate (1979)
Leasingham (1894)
Leo Buring (1945) by Leo Buring
McLarens (1984)
Mountadam Vineyards (1984)
Normans (1853)

Orlando (1847)
Penfolds (1844) by Dr. Christopher
  Rawson Penfold
Peter Lehmann (1980)
Lindemans (1938)
Reynella (1838)
Ryecroft (1985)
Seppelt (1955)
St. Halletts (1918)
Wolf Blass (1973) by Wolf Blass
Wynns (1913) by Samuel Wynns
Yalumba (1847) by Samuel Smith of
  Dorsetshire

Victoria

Victoria's grape-growing areas are *Bendigo, Central Goulburn, Geelong, Great Western, Macedon, Mornington Peninsula, Murray River, North Goulburn River, Northeastern Victoria, Pyrenees,* and *Yarra Valley.* The better-known wineries are [(date) indicates the year the winery was founded]:

Brown Brothers (1889)
Château Tahbilk (1860)
Lindemans (1969)
Mitchelton (1969)
Seppelt (1886)
Taltarni (1972)—local Aboriginal dialect for "red soil"

Wine Laws

Varietal designation (1994).   A varietal wine requires that at least 85 percent of that grape variety be used in the wine.

Viticultural area (1994).   A viticultural area appellation on the label indicates that 85 percent or more of the wine is produced from grapes grown in that particular area.

Chaptalization.   The wines of Australia may not be *chaptalized* (sugar added to the *must*); however, they may be acidified (adding acid to *must* or wine).

▶ AUSTRIA

Austria's wineries are located mainly in four provinces: *Lower Austria, Burgenland, Styria,* and *Vienna.*

Lower Austria produces approximately two-thirds of the country's wines, including Grüner Veltliner, a white grape variety that is not only the largest planted grape variety, but also Austria's leading white wine. Other white grapes such as Müller-Thurgau, Rheinriesling, Weissburgunder, and Gewürztraminer are grown in this province. Blaufränkisch, a grape that yields a particularly fruity wine with a glowing ruby red color, is also grown. Eight important regions are located in Lower Austria: *Krems, Langenlois, Klosterneuburg, Wachau, Falkenstein, Retz, Gumpoldskirchen,* and *Vöslau.* Wachau, considered the wine paradise of Lower Austria, is noted for its Schluck, a dry white wine made from the Sylvaner grape.

Burgenland, Austria's second-largest wine-producing area, is famed for its beeren-auslese, a sweet white wine made from Johannisberg Riesling, Furmint, and Muscat Ottonel grapes.

Grape growing in the province of Vienna extends into Austria's capital city, which is flanked by grapevine-clad hillsides that produce fine white wines. *Grinzing, Nussberg, Nussdorf,* and *Neustift* are the best-known villages near the city of Vienna. Further south of Vienna, around Baden, lies the district of the *Südbahn,* where wines are made from the late-harvested Grüner Veltliner, Johannisberg Riesling, and Gewürztraminer grapes.

Styria, in the southernmost area of Austria, produces mostly white wines, which are consumed locally.

Like other great wine-producing countries, Austria regulates and rigidly controls grape growing and ensures high quality standards. Its wine laws, which were enacted in 1961, include legally prescribed designations for different wines. The key provisions are described in the following:

Wines that have no faults in appearance, aroma, taste, and are characteristic of their type, can qualify as "quality wines." This is the highest rating. The grower must provide a written statement verifying the geographical origin of the wine. Wines that fulfill these conditions must also pass a two-part official test. First, the wine must undergo a basic laboratory test and meet certain legal standards. Second, it must pass a taste test, which is conducted by a committee of at least six members of impartial institutions. Each committee member examines the wine in a blind sample and gives his or her judgment in writing. To pass, the wine must receive at least five favorable judgments. Only wines that successfully meet all of these requirements qualify for the Austrian Wine Quality Seal, which features a government control number. Special attention is paid to residual sugar content, which is strictly specified by law. An ordinary table wine *(normalwein)*, for example, uses grapes whose minimum sugar content is below 15 degrees on the Klosterneuburg Mostwaage Scale (KMW) equivalent to less than 18.75 Brix. (For more information, see Appendix A.)

A quality wine *(Qualitätswein)* must meet the following criteria:

1. The juice of the grape must have a minimum original sugar content of 15 degrees KMW (18.75 Brix).
2. The wine cannot be fortified.
3. The grapes must have been grown in one region and produced from grapevines designated for that region. The grapes used must be listed in the quality grape register.
4. At least 85 percent of the grapes used in any wine must be of the grape variety and vintage given on the label.
5. The wine must be typical of wines from the particular grapevine from which it was produced, especially if the label carries such designation.
6. The wine must be harmonious in color, bouquet, and taste, and free from flaws.

A quality wine must be sold under a geographic designation: the wine province, region, district, or village where it was produced.

Kabinett wines must meet the above conditions for quality wines. In addition, its *must* has to attain a minimum of 17 degrees KMW (21.25 Brix), and cannot be enriched by the addition of sugar, grape juice, concentrated grape juice, or *must.*

Spätlese wines are produced from grapes that are fully ripened and gathered later than the ordinary harvest time for that particular grape variety. The juice must have a minimum sugar content of 19 degrees KMW (23.75 Brix).

Auslese wines are produced from grapes that are carefully hand picked to select only those that are fully ripened. Their sugar content must be at least 21 degrees KMW (26.25 Brix).

Beerenauslese is an *auslese* wine made from overripe grapes affected by the "noble rot" *(Botrytis cinerea).* Sugar content for this wine must be at least 25 degrees KMW (31.25 Brix).

Trockenbeerenauslese are *auslese* wines with an even higher sugar content—a minimum of 30 degrees KMW (37.5 Brix)—and are made from raisinlike dehydrated grapes. Although 30 degrees KMW is the specified minimum sugar content, the choicest and rarest of these wines can have an even higher sugar content of their musts—35, 40, or even 50 degrees KMW. These rarities can legally be called *essenz* or *trockenbeerenauslese-essenz* and are served in cognac glasses so that their glorious bouquet can be fully enjoyed.

Eiswein is produced exclusively from frozen grapes, which can be harvested as late as mid-January in a great year, and must have a minimum sugar content of 25 degrees KMW (31.25 Brix).

Many different grape varieties are used to produce Austria's fine white wines, which account for approximately 85 percent of total production. The most important varieties, and the wines produced from them, are:

Grüner Veltliner: This most commonly used grape is grown extensively in areas of Lower Austria and Vienna. An Austrian specialty, the wine is effervescent and light, with a greenish gold color and a spicy-fruity taste of green apples, pepper, and herbs.

Müller-Thurgau: An early ripening grape, it produces a mild, aromatic, pleasant wine with a slight Muscat flavor. The wine is best consumed young.

Rheinriesling (Johannisberg Riesling): This top-quality grape yields an outstanding wine characterized by a unique, delicate bouquet. Maturing slowly, the wine reaches its peak after being aged two to four years.

Neuburger: The wine made from this grape is another Austrian specialty—a full-bodied, mild wine with a particularly fine bouquet.

Weissburgunder (Pinot Blanc): The wines from this premium grape are characterized by their robustness and aromatic bouquet.

Gewürztraminer: These wines have a rich, spicy flavor, pronounced aroma, and a deep golden color.

Muscat Ottonel: Wines made from this grape are distinguished by an exceptionally strong but pleasant Muscat aroma; they are produced primarily in Rust and Neusiedler.

Welschriesling: Best grown in light soil and a warm climate, this grape produces a spicy wine which varies in color from pale yellow to gold.

Zierfandler and *Rotgipfler:* These are two specialties of the Baden vineyards in Lower Austria. They are usually blended to produce wines that are outstanding in quality. Aging brings out their full body and superior bouquet.

The majority of Austria's red wines are produced from four grape varieties:

Blaufränkisch: This is a popular grape yielding a dry, fruity wine which ranges in color from light to deep ruby red.

Blauer Portugieser: This grape produces mild wines with a delicate spicy flavor, characterized by a deep red color.

St. Laurent: These grapes are used for high-quality table wines that are deep red in color and have a fine bouquet.

Blauburgunder: This grape yields a wine that is dry and rich in body. Mild and spicy, it is noted for its velvety elegance.

► BULGARIA

Bulgaria, though not commonly thought of as being a very important wine-producing country, is actually among the top ten in total production. The bulk of production (about 80 percent) goes to Eastern European countries, with the rest exported to Canada, Great Britain, Japan, the Scandinavian countries, Germany, and the United States.

Bulgaria, located in southeastern Europe, is divided into 13 wine-producing areas, each varying in size and overall production. The best white wines come from Shumen in the northeast; the best reds come from Suhindol in the north-central area.

Bulgaria's wine laws, although currently quite confusing, do recognize such terms as *reserve,* indicating aging in barrels for at least two years for whites and three years for reds.

Traditional European grape varieties—Cabernet Sauvignon, Merlot, Johannisberg Riesling, and Chardonnay—grow side by side with native red grapes such as Gamza, Red Misket, and Mavrud, and white grapes such as Dimiat, Muscat Ottonel, and Rkatsiteli.

► CHILE

Chile, a wine-producing country since 1548, has its viticultural roots in Europe, when Spanish Conquistadors brought with them grapevines that flourished in the climate and soil of Chile. The first grapevines were brought to Chile from Peru through the Atacama Desert in 1548 by Father Francisco de Carabantes, a Jesuit priest. These grapevines were first planted in the province of Copiapó, about 500 miles north of Santiago. Unfortunately, the initial grapevines that were planted were the lowly Mission Grape (locally called País), a variety often used in California during the early and mid-1800s.

In 1851, Don Silvestre Ochagavía, a Chilean scholar (of Basque ancestry), often referred to as the "Father of Chilean Viticulture," contracted the services of M. Bertrand, a French viticulturist, to help establish Chile's wine industry. Bertrand is also credited with importing grapevine cuttings from France, which he planted in the fertile Central Valley.

Chile is approximately 2,650 miles long and about 150 miles wide, although most of Chile is a mere 100 miles in width. Chile is 292,257 square miles in size, making it slightly larger than the state of Texas. It is bordered on the north by Peru and Bolivia, on the east by Argentina, and on the west by the Pacific Ocean. Chile's vineyards lie along a narrow zone from Coquimbo in the north to Valdivia in the south, a distance of more than 900 miles.

Chile has a total of 148,000 acres planted with grapevines, with an annual yield of approximately 106 million gallons (44.5 million cases). Chile exports approximately 1.3 million cases of wine to the United States. The per capita consumption of wine in Chile is approximately 7.9 gallons (all 1992 figures).

Chile has three large viticultural regions: The largest in area is the southern region, which contains the provinces of *Concepción,* the *Bío-Bío Valley, Linares,* the banks of the

Maule River, and *Nuble.* Production here is mainly red wines with a small quantity of white wines. It is also planted heavily with the País grape, a local name for the Mission grape.

The second largest viticultural region, and by far the most important, is the *Central Valley,* which lies between the Aconcagua River, north of the capital Santiago and the Maule River, below Talca in the south (32 to 36 degrees south latitude). The climate of the Central Valley is quite similar to that of Bordeaux, France, and Northern California's Napa and Sonoma Valleys. The vineyards, which bask in the sun, are cooled by the breezes of the Pacific Ocean, and are protected from storms by the Andes Mountains. This grape-growing region includes the provinces of *Aconcagua, Casablanca, Colchagua, Curicó, O'Higgins, Rapel, Santiago, Talca,* and *Valparaiso.* These provinces, which receive an annual rainfall of less than 20 inches, are irrigated by waters from the Cachapoal, Lontué, Maipo, and Maule Rivers, fed by Andean glaciers. Due to the irrigation, grape varieties such as Cabernet Sauvignon, Cabernet Franc, Merlot, Malbec, Petit Verdot, Pinot Noir, Chardonnay, Sémillon, and Sauvignon Blanc can flourish.

The third principal viticultural region is farther north, near Coquimbo in the Aconcagua Valley and along the banks of the Aconcagua River, as well as up to the rim of the Atacama Desert. Here the Muscat of Alexandria grape flourishes, producing wines with high alcohol, which is often the base of many of Chile's fortified wines and brandy. The most noted brandy is Pisco, made from a blend of Muscat of Alexandria and/or Mission grapes, and is produced in this northern region.

It is contended that *phylloxera* has been unable to penetrate Chile due to several factors: Chile is bordered on the west by the Pacific Ocean; on the east by the Andes Mountains, where some peaks rise to more than 23,000 feet above sea level; on the south by Antarctica; and on the north by the Atacama Desert. These factors present a strong argument for *phylloxera*'s inability to invade Chile. In addition to the absence of *phylloxera,* Chile is also virtually unaffected by mildew, both powdery and downy (mildew is a fungal disease that causes direct yield losses by premature defoliating and rotting of grapevine leaves). *Botrytis cinerea,* however, is present in the vineyards, and fungicides must be applied to control its infestation. In the winemaking process, both *amelioration* (the addition of water to juice or wine to adjust the acid level) and *chaptalization* are forbidden by Chilean law.

Chile's viticultural climatic zones, expressed in *degrees of heat summation,* range from the cool region II, in the south, to region V, in the hot northern desert.

In Chile, which has an opposite growing season to that of the Northern Hemisphere, *bud break* (when the first tiny floral cluster emerges) generally occurs around the first week in September. Harvest usually commences at the beginning of March and lasts until the first or second week in April.

▶ GERMANY

Wine is so highly regarded in Germany that the state not only controls labeling but also establishes quality standards. It also maintains institutions that constantly devise methods of viticulture and vinification to constantly improve Germany's wines.

German wines are confusing to Americans because their names are difficult to pronounce and the labels are difficult to decipher. Most of the wine in Germany is produced by 100,000 small landholders whose average vineyard size is only two acres. Therefore, many of the small growers belong to cooperative organizations through which they make and market their wines.

On July 14, 1971, the German government put into effect a wine law that has made Germany's wines among the most carefully regulated in the world. It is the fifth in a series of wine laws, its predecessors dating back to 1892, 1901, 1909, and 1930. Although the German wine law is too complicated to examine here in all its aspects, its regulations governing the labeling and categorizing of wine (as well as brandy) are important, and they are described below.

Chaptalization

A limited amount of sugar, set by law, can be added to the *must* prior to or during fermentation when a lack of natural sugar exists. *Chaptalization* is only permitted for *Tafelwein, Landwein,* and Q.b.A. wines. The *Prädikat* (higher quality) grades of wine are never permitted to be *chaptalized.*

Süssreserve

Prior to fermentation, a portion of the unfermented grape juice, which is high in natural sugar, is filtered and held under refrigeration until after fermentation is complete. At this point, a small amount of this sugar-rich juice, called *süssreserve,* is then added back to the wine to add a sweet flavor. Under law, this technique is permitted in making of all German wines, including the *Qualitätswein* category: *Kabinett, Spätlese, Auslese,* and even *Beerenauslese.* However, the *süssreserve* must be of the same category as the wine being sweetened— *Spätlese* süssreserve for *Spätlese* wine, for example.

Öechsle is the term used in Germany and Switzerland to measure the level of sugar present in the *must.*

Labeling

The very precise German labeling laws require that wine labels carry a great deal of vital information. All wine labels indicate the grape variety or varieties used, the district and village name in which they were grown, the vineyard name, the name of the vineyard's owner, and the vintage (Figure 4-1).

A wine must contain at least 85 percent of the grape variety listed on its label. No more than two grape varieties can be used.

The German Wine Label

① RHEINHESSEN
② 1991
③ Winzerdorf Rebberg
④ Riesling halbtrocken ⑤
⑥ Qualitätswein b.A.
⑦ A.P. Nr. 516 987 92
Alc. 10 % vol.   0,75 l
⑧ Erzeugerabfüllung Winzer Bacchus, Winzerdorf

Example of a German Wine Label

Geographic origin, grape variety, the degree of ripeness at harvest and the wine maker's individual style determine a wine's taste. And German wine labels provide all the information you need to select the right wine.

What it Means

① The specified growing region: one of the 13 designated regions in Germany.
② The year in which the grapes were harvested.
③ The town and the vineyard from which the grapes come. (In this case, a hypothetical example.)
④ The grape variety.
⑤ The taste or style of the wine. In this case, medium dry. If it were trocken, it would be dry. If there is no indication the wine usually offers a harmonious balance of sweetness and acidity.
⑥ The quality level of the wine, indicating ripeness of the grapes at harvest.
⑦ The official testing number: proof that the wine has passed chemical and sensory testing required for all German Quality Wines.
⑧ Wines bottled and produced by the grower or a cooperative of growers may be labelled "Erzeugerabfüllung". Estates and growers can use "Gutsabfüllung" as an alternative. Other wineries and bottlers are identified as "Abfüller".

FIGURE 4-1 (a–b)   A German wine label. (Courtesy German Wine Information Bureau, New York)

Labels must carry any of the following:

the name of the *Gebiet,* or region (a region is a division of one of Germany's 13 vineyard areas);
the name of the district, *Bereich,* into which regions are further divided;
the name of the subdistrict, *Grosslage,* into which districts are still further divided;
and, finally, the name of an individual vineyard, or *Lage.*

These designated areas are always preceded or followed by the name of the local village, for example, Bereich Johannisberg. Labels may show a subregion, village, or vineyard name provided that a minimum of 85 percent of the wine originates from such smaller geographical areas inside the specified region.

Almost all German wines use combination names, of which the first word is the town or district name and the second is the specific vineyard name. Thus, there are wines called Niersteiner Auflangen, Niersteiner Rehbach, Niersteiner Heiligenbaum, and so on.

There are approximately 2,600 individual vineyard sites registered in Germany. As the supply from each vineyard is limited and the multitude of names can be confusing, most wines shipped are labeled by *Bereich:* Bereich Nierstein, Bereich Bernkastel, and so on. They are also labeled with proprietary names such as:

Affenthaler	(monkey or ape wine)
Drachenblut	(dragon's blood)
Goldtröpfchen	(golden drop)
Liebfraumilch	(milk of the blessed mother)
Moselblümchen	(little flower of the Mosel)
Zeller Schwarze Katz	(black cat)

As a further safeguard, the wine law requires that for every harvest, all producers of Q.b.A. and *Prädikat* wines submit two bottles of their wine to an official government panel. The wines are then analyzed and tasted by this panel, which assigns the passing wines an *A.P.* (Amtliche Prüfungsnummer) number that must appear on its label (see below). If the wine fails this examination, the producer can appeal the decision, make necessary corrections to the wine, and resubmit it. If the wine fails a second time, it cannot be sold to the public. The tasting panel can also declassify the wine, assigning it to a lower category. For example, a *spätlese* can be downgraded to a *kabinett* wine.

The A.P. number system is best explained by use of an example. A. P. number 3677030295, for instance, can be broken down as follows:

    3 = The approving authority's number.

  677 = The number identifying the place of business of the bottler.

  030 = The bottler's code or identification number.

    2 = The running approval number of the applicant (*not,* as it might seem, the month in which the wine was bottled).

  95 = The year in which the wine was submitted for approval (not necessarily the year of harvest).

Three basic categories of German wines were created under the 1971 law; later, the law was amended to include the following four:

Deutscher Tafelwein: a very ordinary table wine that is not normally exported.

Deutscher Landwein: a step above *Tafelwein* in quality, but less than ten percent is exported.

Qualitätswein Bestimmter Anbaugebiete (or simply Q.b.A.): a label classification for "quality" table wines that meet certain requirements for alcohol content, region of origin (must come from one of 13 specified wine regions), and grape variety, and is subject to examination by authorities. Qualitätswein wines may be *chaptalized.*

Qualitätswein mit Prädikat (Q.m.P.): traditionally includes Germany's finest and most expensive wines. None of these can be *chaptalized. Prädikat* wines must come from a specific area or *Bereich.* This category has six subdivisions that correlate the successively higher levels of sugar produced by the German custom of late and selective picking. (The drawback to this custom is that the riper the grapes—and thus the higher the sugar level—the smaller the quantity of wine produced, as selectivity increases with lateness of harvest.) The *Qualitätswein mit Prädikat* subdivisions are:

Kabinett: the most basic of Qualitätswein Mit Prädikat grade of wines, which indicates the wine in question is a quality wine that must be sold under a geographic designation: the wine province, region, district, or village where it was produced. These wines are dry, generally the lightest, and may not be *chaptalized.*

Spätlese: a term that means "late-picking" or "late-harvesting" of the grapes. The official date for the end of the normal harvest, which is set by wine commissioners of each village, usually takes place at least seven days after the normal harvest.

Auslese: a wine made from particularly ripe, selected late harvested bunches of grapes. Auslese wines are especially full, rich, and somewhat sweet; however, they may not be *chaptalized.* Auslese wines are generally sweeter and more expensive than *spätlese* wines.

Beerenauslese (sometimes abbreviated as BA): "berry selection" wines made from extremely overripe grapes, picked individually and produced in very small quantities only in best vintages. Out of each bunch of grapes, the pickers might only select one or two berries to use. Obviously the result is an extremely high production cost. In addition, the grapes generally have been attacked by the mold *Botrytis cinerea* (known in Germany as *edelfäule*). The resultant wine is intensely sweet and can generally age for several decades.

Trockenbeerenauslese (sometimes abbreviated as TBA): a wine made entirely from late-picked, individually selected grapes (resembling raisins) that have been allowed to dry and shrivel on the grapevine after they've been attacked by *Botrytis cinerea.* These grapes, which are extremely high in sugar, produce one of the sweetest and rarest wines in the world, extremely rich and luscious-tasting.

Eiswein: the name reserved for wine made from grapes of the BA or TBA category, harvested frozen. These frozen grapes produce a wine that is both sweeter and more concentrated than the average *Prädikat* wine. Since 1982, German rules require that the frozen grapes must contain about 30 percent grape sugar.

The practice of making wine from grapes naturally frozen on the grapevine has long been a part of the wine culture of Germany and Austria. With the Rhine and Mosel's best vineyards lying just about as far north as grapes can ripen, working with frozen grapes is not only a tradition but sometimes a necessity as well. German winemakers have built their reputations by manipulating nature, allowing the grapes to hang on the grapevine past normal harvesting time to further ripen.

The adversary that the vintner faces late in the growing season is cold weather—the chance of an early frost or hard freeze. If the grapes are spared a freezing cold and can sufficiently dry before harvest, wines of incredible lusciousness and complexity can be produced. But if nature wins the battle and a hard freeze hits the vineyards, the winemaker has but one outside chance—to pick and crush the frozen grapes, hopefully producing the rare and unique *eiswein.* Although this was once a rare product (made only every second or third decade), *eiswein* is nowadays produced somewhat more frequently because new, colder vineyard sites are allowed to yield frozen grapes.

Trocken and Halbtrocken Wines

The designations *trocken* and *halbtrocken* were put into effect by the wine authority of the Common Market in Brussels on August 1, 1977. The reason for these designations was that some people prefer wines drier than most of the German wines on the market. The terms *trocken* (dry) and *halbtrocken* (semidry) wines, which have no connection whatsoever with the *Trockenbeerenauslese* wines, attempt to lure dry white wine drinkers over to the less sweet white wines of Germany.

Contrary to popular belief, the Johannisberg Riesling grape is not the preferred variety for use because its high acid level (often more than 1 percent) gives the wine an unbalanced character. German winemakers usually prefer not to allow contact between the grape skins and the *must,* because additional acids from the skins will increase the already high acidity level. Instead, varieties such as Müller-Thurgau, Sylvaner, Weissburgunder (Pinot Blanc), Kerner, and Gutedel, which are lower in acidity, are used. The *trocken* and *halbtrocken* wine categories are described below.

Trocken: these wines contain a maximum of 9 grams per liter of residual sugar (which can also be expressed as 0.9 grams per 100 milliliters, or 0.9 percent residual sugar). The sugar level cannot exceed the acidity level by more than two grams. For example, if a wine has five grams of acidity, its maximum sugar level can only be seven grams per liter.

Halbtrocken: these wines contain a maximum of 18 grams per liter of residual sugar (which can also be expressed as 1.8 grams per 100 milliliters, or 1.8 percent residual sugar). The variance here can be ten grams per liter. For example, if the wine contains five grams per liter of acidity, the maximum sugar level can only be 15 grams per liter.

Germany's Wine-Producing Regions

In all grape-growing regions, the quality of wine is dependent upon climate, grape variety, soil, viticulture, and vinification techniques. As Germany is the northernmost great wine-producing country in the world (most of the vineyards are on the same latitude, 50 degree north, as Newfoundland), the success of its wine demands a delicate coordination of climate and grape variety. The best-quality grape varieties mature slowly and produce only a moderate quantity of wine. German grape growers have learned to balance quantity with quality. The state and members of the wine trade work together as an effective control force overseeing this delicate balance.

Although Germany produces predominantly white wine (about 90 percent), a relatively small quantity of red wine is made in Germany, mainly in Ahr, Pfalz, Württemberg, and Baden, usually from the Spätburgunder (Pinot Noir) grape.

The principal grape varieties grown in Germany are *Johannisberg Riesling, Sylvaner,* and *Müller-Thurgau,* although Müller-Thurgau is the most planted grape variety (in acreage) in Germany. Other grape varieties include *Albalonga, Bacchus, Gewürztraminer, Gutedel, Kerner, Ortega, Perle, Portugieser, Rieslaner, Spätburgunder, Weissburgunder,* and, since June 1991, *Chardonnay.*

The tiny Johannisberg Riesling grape, considered the noblest of all, matures slowly and produces a relatively small amount of wine. Both the Sylvaner and the Müller-Thur-gau have larger berries which mature more rapidly and produce a greater, but by no means large, quantity of wine. Most of the high-quality wine in Germany is produced from these three grape varieties, with the Johannisberg Riesling predominating in the Mosel and Rheingau regions, and parts of Rheinhessen.

Due to Germany's cold climate, harvest is delayed as long as possible and usually does not take place until late October. By then, the grapevine has gathered enough summer sun to produce a good balance of sugar and acidity, the hallmark of German wine. German vintners maintain that 100 days of sun between May and October make for a good wine, and 120 days, a great wine.

Germany's 13 grape-growing regions are: *Ahr, Baden, Franken, Hessische Bergstrasse, Mittelrhein, Mosel-Saar-Ruwer, Nahe, Pfalz, Rheingau, Rheinhessen, Württemberg, Sachsen,* and *Saale-Unstrut.* Most of the high-quality wines of Germany are grown in the Mosel-Saar-Ruwer, Pfalz, Rheingau, Rheinhessen, Franken, and Nahe vineyard regions.

Mosel-Saar-Ruwer.   The grapes of this region, which have been producing wine for more than 2,000 years, are grown mainly on slate ground covering the exceedingly steep hillsides of the valleys watered by the Mosel River and its tributaries, the Saar and Ruwer. Wines here are made primarily from the Johannisberg Riesling grape. They are the light-est of the German wines, being fragrant and flowery, refreshing and clean, with an almost peachy taste. These wines have a low alcoholic content and are best drunk in their youth while they still have all of their charm. Mosel-Saar-Ruwer wines often have a *spritzig* qual-ity: They are characterized by a little natural sparkle. Some of the towns on the Mosel River from which these wines come are Piesport, Bernkastel, Wehlen, Graach, Tritten-heim, Zeltingen, Brauneberg, and Zell; on the Saar River, Ockfen, Serrig, Ayl, and Wiltingen; and on the Ruwer River, Waldrach, Kasel, Avelsbach, and Eitelsbach. The wines made on the Saar and Ruwer in outstanding years can be as good, if not better, than the Mosel wines, combining crispness with bouquet and flavor, yet somewhat lighter in body.

Rheingau.   This is one of Germany's smallest grape-growing regions and it usually pro-duces the greatest of all German wines. It is almost all one large hillside, facing south and protected against the northern climate by the Taunus mountain chain. The wines made in this area are noble indeed, combining elegance with style and delicacy, with substance and fruit. The Johannisberg Riesling is the predominant grape variety planted in the Rhein-gau. Some of Germany's better-known winemaking estates, such as Schloss Johannisberg, Steinberg, and Schloss Vollrads, are in this area. The main Rheingau villages in which wines are made are Rüdesheim, Johannisberg, Rauenthal, Kiedrich, Erbach, Hattenheim, Oestrich, Hallgarten, Eltville, Geisenheim, and Hochheim. For many years the wines from Hochheim, which contains five vineyards between Mainz and Wiesbaden, were referred to, mainly by the British, as *Hock;* earlier, the British called them *Rhenish* wines.

Rheinhessen. Most of Germany's wine that is exported is made in this region; it produces even larger quantities than Mosel-Saar-Ruwer and Rheingau. Its wines, which benefit from a warmer climate, are softer, rounder, and a little fuller than the aristocratic wines of the Rheingau. The main grape varieties of Rheinhessen are the Sylvaner and Müller-Thurgau, which produce very soft, sometimes fairly sweet wines with a delicate bouquet. Because this is a large area, Rheinhessen's wines vary a great deal in their characteristics. In good years, some of the finest, if not *the* finest, *Prädikat* wines of Germany are made here. Some towns with well-known vineyards are Nierstein, Oppenheim, Bodenheim, Nackenheim, Bingen, Worms, and Guntersblum. It is in Rheinhessen that most of the better Liebfraumilch wine is produced.

Liebfraumilch was at one time produced from a blend of grapes grown in Rheingau, Rheinhessen, Pfalz, and Nahe. However, with changes in the German wine law (1990), vintners are no longer allowed to blend grapes from the four regions for Liebfraumilch. Only one of four regions can be shown as a source for Liebfraumilch—Rheingau, Rheinhessen, Pfalz, or Nahe—and the region must be stated on the label. No single vineyard site, district, or grape variety designations are allowed on the label. The word *Liebfraumilch* cannot be shown in type larger than that used to identify the region. The law further specifies that all Liebfraumilch must be made at least 70 percent from one of the following grape varieties: Johannisberg Riesling, Sylvaner, Müller-Thurgau, or Kerner. Additionally, the wine law restricts residual sugar to a range of 1.8 to 4.5 percent. It is estimated that 60 percent of all wines from Germany are exported under the Liebfraumilch appellation.

Pfalz (formerly known as Rheinpfalz and often referred to as Palatinate). This is a very large wine-producing region, located along the Rhine River to the east, France to the south and southwest, the Mosel-Saar-Ruwer to the west, and the Rheinhessen to the north. The majority of the high-quality wines here are made from the Sylvaner and Müller-Thurgau grapes, with a small portion of Johannisberg Riesling. Climate and soil combine to aid in the production of the common wine of the German *Weinstube* or local pub, as well as of some of Germany's most outstanding wines. Wines from the villages of Forst and Deidesheim are among the finest of Pfalz, being fuller and sweeter than Mosels, Rheingaus, and even Rheinhessens. Other major Pfalz winemaking towns are Wachenheim, Ruppertsberg, Duerkheim, and Ungstein.

Nahe. This region is planted with Johannisberg Riesling, Sylvaner, and Müller-Thurgau grapes, and produces wines of varying taste and quality, some of which are not unlike Rheingau wines. Other wines, however, are heavier and earthier in taste. Though not much wine from this region is shipped to the United States, it does deserve mention. Some of the better-known villages in this region are Schloss Böckelheim, Bad Kreuznach, Niederhausen, Langenlonsheim, and Rüdesheim (not to be confused with the town of the same name in Rheingau).

Franken (also spelled *Franconia*).   The wines of Franken, which are made under the close scrutiny of the Frankischer Weinbauverband (Franken Wine Association), which was founded in 1836, are pleasant, combining dryness with a certain mellowness but lacking somewhat in the varied aromas and bouquets of other German wines. Most Franken wines are made from Müller-Thurgau, Sylvaner, and Johannisberg Riesling grapes.

This is the only region from which wine is exported in a *bocksbeutel,* the distinctive, round flagon-style bottle first introduced in 1728.

Other regions.   The regions described above are those in which Germany's highest-quality wines are produced. These regions produce less outstanding wines:

Ahr: This northernmost region is noted for its excellent red wines, produced from the Spätburgunder and Portugieser.

Baden: A large grape-growing region in the southwest, which lies along the Rhine River, known for its full-flavored wines. Baden is marked by the Kaiserstuhl, an extinct volcano whose soil helps produce wines that are powerful and aromatic. The predominant grape varieties are Müller-Thurgau, Pinot Gris, Weissburgunder, and Gewürztraminer.

Württemberg: This region is separated from Baden by the famed Black Forest. Thousands of Württemberg's small growers produce pleasant red and white wines, mostly from Trollinger, Schwarzriesling, Spätburgunder, Portugieser, Johannisberg Riesling, and Müller-Thurgau.

Hessische Bergstrasse: This is a very small region whose wines are produced primarily for local consumption. Johannisberg Riesling and Müller-Thurgau are the primary grape varieties planted here.

Mittelrhein (also referred to as *Middle Rhine*):   Mittelrhein is located along the Rhine River in the northwestern part of Germany. The region is famous for its spectacular vineyards on the steep Rhine slopes. Its wines, almost exclusively white, are hearty and stylish. Major grape varieties are Johannisberg Riesling, Müller-Thurgau, and Kerner.

Saale-Unstrut: A small grape-growing region located in the northernmost of Germany's regions. Müller-Thurgau, Sylvaner, and Weissburgunder grape varieties are widely planted here.

Sachsen: This is the easternmost of Germany's grape-growing regions. Müller-Thurgau, Weissburgunder, and Gewürztraminer grape varieties are widely planted here.

Most German wines are bottled in the traditional slender, swan-necked *schlegelflasche.* Although not mandated by law, Rhine wines are usually found in brown bottles, while wines from the Mosel region are found in green ones.

▶ HUNGARY

When one thinks of the wines of Hungary, the rich, naturally sweet, world-renowned Tokay wines immediately come to mind. However, most Hungarian wines (approximately 95 percent) are table wines whose variety and volume are constantly increasing.

The most popular is *Egri Bikavér,* which comes from the town of Eger. It is a deep, rich, robust, dry red wine often referred to as "bull's blood," made primarily from the Kadarka grape. Other wines include Egri Léanyka, Debröi Hárslevelü, Merlot, Cabernet Sauvignon, and Pinot Noir.

Tokay, by far the most popular dessert wine, comes from the region of Tokaji-Hegyalja in the northeast corner of the country. Tokay is made from the Furmint, Hárslevelü, and Muscat Lunel grapes, which are harvested at various degrees of ripeness. Tokay wines range from bone dry to exquisitely sweet. The sweet Tokays are identified by a number on the label (usually one to six), which indicates the amount of juice from raisined grapes *(aszú)* that has been added to the wine.

Tokaji Szamorodni indicates a simple Tokay wine not necessarily made with the addition of *aszú* berries. Tokaji Száraz is a dry wine and Tokaji Édes is sweet.

▶ PORTUGAL

The best-known Portuguese wines are the delicious, fruity, refreshing rosé wines and wonderful port wines. But Portugal has quite a bit more to offer than just rosés and port. In fact, some of the greatest wine buys are the red *reservas* and *garrafeiras* from the fine wine houses of Portugal (both terms denote an outstanding wine from an exceptional harvest, which has been given additional barrel aging). These wines are full-bodied and robust, with all the bouquet, flavor, taste, grace, and charm of some of the finest French Bordeaux, Burgundies, Rhône Valley reds, or Italian Barolo and Barbaresco.

Portugal is roughly half the size of California, with a total population slightly less than that of New York City. It appears to be one of the last untapped great wine regions of the world. Many Portuguese winemakers still produce red wines in the "old style," with plenty of wood aging. Their white wines, on the other hand, have the freshness, lightness, and fruitiness of some of the best in the world. Some of the more important wine-producing regions are:

Vinho Verde (literally green wine), the world's largest demarcated grape-growing region, is located in the northwest corner of Portugal. Although one-half of the production is red wine, which is consumed locally, only the whites, which are exported to the United States, will be discussed. Vinho Verde is made from a blend of Arinto, Baga, and Loureiro grape varieties. These wines are often quite young, most of them bottled only four months after harvest, and are not meant to be stored away for prolonged aging. Their charm lies in their youthfulness, "spritzy" character, and absolutely clean, crisp, refreshing taste.

Aliança, Arealva, Aveleda, Casal Garcia, Gatão, Gazela, Lancer's, Mesa do Presidente, and Ouro do Minho are some of the brand names available in the United States.

The Dão, a large grape-growing region (demarcated in 1908), some 120 miles north of Lisbon, is where most of the more popular red wines that are available in the United States originate. Its lovely reds and whites are found in the traditional Burgundy-shaped bottles. The Dão reds are the softest of all Portuguese reds, meant to be drunk within a few years. These rich-tasting ruby-colored wines are made principally from the Alfrocheiro, Bastardo, and Touriga Naçional grape varieties, which tend to produce full-bodied and extremely fruity wines. The Dão white wines, made from Assario Branco, Barcelo, and Encruzado grape varieties, are well made, always dry, with a considerable amount of body and earthiness. Like most other dry whites of the world, they should be consumed young.

The region of *Bucelas,* demarcated in 1911, produces white wines made primarily from the Arinto grape. They are well balanced due to the cool sea breeze and climate, which actually prevent the grapes from becoming overripe. They retain a high level of natural acidity, yielding wines that are clean, crisp, and very refreshing.

Bairrada is, without a doubt, one of the finest red-wine-producing regions of Portugal. Its deep, dark, very rich tasting (almost portlike) wines have a fine fruit-acid structure. While the reds are big and hearty, the whites are very light and often sparkling. The grape varieties for reds include Baga, Periquita, and Tinta Pinheira. For white wines they include Bical and Rabo de Ovelha.

The *Colares* region is probably one of the most difficult places in the world to grow grapes. The principal grapevine, *Ramisco,* must be planted in clay, 15 feet below the surface of the sandy soil of the wind-blasted shores of the Atlantic Ocean. Cone-shaped holes, several yards across, are dug down through the sand by workers who wear baskets over their heads to allow them to breathe in the event of a cave-in. After planting, the grapevines are covered with sand. When the grapevine breaks the sand's surface, bamboo palisades and stone walls have to be built around to protect it against constant ocean gales. This is why so precious little wine is produced in this region and why it is so expensive. It is, however, well worth searching out.

The region of *Algarve* produces red wines that are light-bodied and quite fruity, from Negra Mole and Periquita grape varieties.

Moscatel de Setúbal, produced from the Muscat grape, is certainly one of the greatest dessert wines in the world—so great in fact, that it has been known to last more than 50 years.

Other wine-producing regions include Carcavelos, Ribatejo, Douro, and Madeira. (Douro and Madeira are covered in Chapter 6, Apéritifs and Fortified Wines.)

The Portuguese government has strict laws that govern the labels and seals on its wine exports. A *selo de garantia* (seal of guarantee) bearing the name of the region of origin and a registration number is the formal government stamp of approval. Found around the cork or on the bottle, it assures the buyer that the wine has met standards set by the regional governing bodies. The bottle's label also indicates (when applicable) the wine's region of origin. It also shows the name of the shipper or bottler and may include the wine's alcoholic content, vintage, and brand name.

▶ SOUTH AFRICA

Grapevines were first planted at the Cape of Good Hope in the early 1650s by a Dutchman, Jan Van Riebeeck, who also made the first wine on February 2, 1659. The first distillation of wine (brandy), however, didn't occur until about 1672. In 1679, Simon van der Stel founded the town of Stellenbosch, one of the centers of today's South African wine industry.

In 1685, the Huguenots came from France bringing with them the secrets of making the great wines of Bordeaux, Burgundy, and the Rhône Valley. Within 30 years the wines of the Cape were known throughout the vast empire of the Dutch East India Company, from Europe to the Far East. Even the practical British, after they made the Cape their own in 1806, went so far as to reduce import duties to stimulate and improve Cape wine production.

In its early years, the Cape produced heavy, sweet wines, mostly from the Muscat grape. The most famous of these was Constantia, although it is still debated whether or not this legendary wine was fortified. Constantia became the toast of fashionable Europe in the eighteenth century and was found in the cellars of men of history such as Napoléon, Bismarck, the Duke of Wellington, and Louis XVI.

The wine lands of the Cape of Good Hope lie between 32 and 35 degrees south latitude on the southwest corner of the continent, and therefore enjoy a typical Mediterranean climate. The Cape wine area is divided into three main regions: the *coastal region,* the *Boburg region,* and the *Brede River Valley* region. These three regions are divided into 16 areas of production. As in Bordeaux, many smaller districts have also been defined in recognition of important local variations in soil and climate. These districts, sometimes only a few square miles in size, produce wines of great distinction and character.

The coastal region includes the following five grape-growing areas: *Stellenbosch, Constantia, Durbanville, Paarl,* and *Swartland.* Here the cool Atlantic spring rains, followed by a sunny summer and cooling Indian Ocean winds, create an ideal grape-growing climate. This area produces some of South Africa's finest red and white wines, including Cabernet

Sauvignon, Shiraz, Cinsaut, Pinotage, Chenin Blanc, Clairette Blanche, and Johannisberg Riesling.

A little inland is the Boburg region, a valley sheltered by high mountains. The Tulbagh area in this region is famous for its Johannisberg Riesling and Gewürztraminer.

The Brede River Valley region has a varied topography; in its sandy valleys, between mountain ranges, grapes grow well and produce superb dry wines.

South Africa's *Wines of Origin* legislation (amended in 1990) is based essentially on that of the traditional European wine countries and is thus similar to the French *appellation contrôlée* laws. Some of its provisions are described below.

The addition of sugar *(chaptalization)* is strictly prohibited. The use of sulfur dioxide is limited to a maximum of 200 parts per million.

An official certificate issued by the South African Wine and Distilled Spirits Board certifies the grape variety from which a wine is made, its vintage, and the area of origin. This certificate is attached to the neck of the bottle.

Wine that is classified as a "Wine of Origin" must originate 100 percent from a particular area. Estate wines must be made on a registered estate, from grapes grown on that estate. The highest classification is *Wine of Origin Superior* (WOS), awarded only to wines of exceptional quality.

Some of the major South African wines from the Cape are:

Die Bergkelder
Fleur du Cap
Grunberger
KWV (Kooperative Wijnbouwers Vereniging)
Lanzerac
Meerendal
Oude Libertas
Oude Meester Winery
Tasheimer
Zonnebloem

Most of the grape varieties planted in South Africa are of European ancestry: Chardonnay, Sauvignon Blanc, Chenin Blanc, Gewürztraminer, Cabernet Sauvignon, Pinot Noir, and Merlot. However, there are some local varieties such as Pinotage, Cinsaut, Steen, and Tinta Barocca.

► SPAIN

Although Spain is most famous for its sherry wines, the majority of wines produced in Spain are red, white, and rosé table wines.

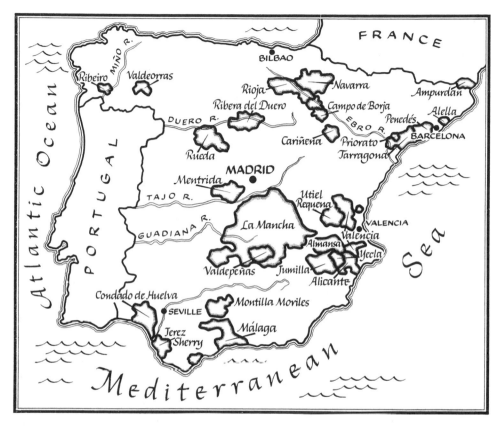

FIGURE 4-2   Map of the wine regions of Spain. (Courtesy of Bozell, Jacobs, Kenyon and Eckhardt Public Relations, New York)

Spain, only slightly larger in area than the state of California, has 4.5 million acres of vineyards, more than any other country. The average yearly production is about 800 million gallons, placing Spain among the top five wine-producing countries worldwide.

The quality and integrity of the wines produced in Spain are assured by a central national system of control regulated by the *Instituto Nacional de Denominaciónes de Origen* (INDO), which was established in 1972.

Forty-one (1995) grape-growing regions have been defined by the INDO (Figure 4-2); wines produced in these regions carry the *denominación de origen* (DO) designation. Each *DO* has its own *Consejo Regulador* or Control Board, which oversees and controls the standards required for each delimited winemaking region. These regulations are similar to France's *appellation contrôlée* system. More than half of Spain's vineyards are covered by this comprehensive quality control system, which monitors the entire industry from the embryonic stage of grape growing to the finished bottle of wine. Since 1991, the wines of Rioja have been granted the *DOC* (Denominación de Origen Calificada), Spain's highest designation for wines.

The two wine regions of Spain that export the most table wine to the United States are Rioja and Catalonia.

Rioja

Rioja encompasses some 110,000 acres of vineyards in the northeastern part of Spain, in an 80-mile stretch of land along the Ebro River, not far from the western Pyrenees and only 200 miles south of Bordeaux, France. There are two major population centers in Rioja—Haro and Logroño. The town of Haro is the traditional center of the wine district and still retains its sixteenth-century appearance. The colorful and modern city of Logroño is the provincial capital and the business and financial hub. The majority of Rioja wineries or *bodegas* are to be found along the roads that run between Logroño and Haro.

The average elevation of Rioja's vineyards is more than 1,500 feet above sea level. These heights produce lighter wines than those made from grapes grown in lower and warmer sections of the country. Most of the vineyards are situated on either side of the Ebro River, which flows east from the Pyrenees toward the Mediterranean.

Seven tributaries cross the Rioja region and one of them that lies toward the western end is called the "Rio Oja." Actually, the name Rio, which means "river," is joined with Oja. Rio Oja is actually the name of a mountain stream that flows into the River Ebro, some 165 miles northeast of Madrid.

Rioja is divided into three viticultural subzones: *Rioja Alta, Rioja Alavesa,* and *Rioja Baja.* Rioja Baja is in the southeastern portion of the *DOC.* The wines from Rioja Baja are heartier, full-bodied, with higher alcohol and lower acid than those produced in the other two subzones. Rioja Alavesa, to the west, north of the Ebro River, is higher in altitude, cooler, and wetter. Rioja Alavesa produces wines that are light and delicate, with excellent flavor and color, but not usually possessing sufficient body, alcohol, and acid to permit beneficial aging. Rioja Alta, the largest of the three subzones located in the hilly western part of Spain south of the Ebro River, enjoys a mild continental climate. Its wines are elegant and fruity in style with good acidity, which age well.

The premier red wine grape of Rioja is the Tempranillo (planted in up to 30 percent of the vineyards); it is comparable in quality to the Cabernet Sauvignon grape, although it is not related to that particular variety. It is the Tempranillo that gives Rioja's reds a deep color and fine acid balance. Other grapes used for reds are the Graciano, Cariñena, and Garnacha Tinta (Grenache). The Garnacha, which gives the wine body, acidity, and alcoholic strength, is planted in approximately 40 percent of Rioja's vineyards.

The white wines of Rioja are made from the Macabeo (Viura), Garnacha Blanca (Grenache), and Malvasia grapes.

Following fermentation (often in wood), the red wines are racked into 225-liter (59-gallon) oak barrels called *bordelesas,* where they are aged.

The reservas must be aged a minimum of three years (of which at least one year must be in barrel) in oak barrels called *bordelesas*. *Gran reservas* must be aged a minimum of two years in barrels and three in bottles.

Although not mandated by law, it is customary for the red wines of Rioja to be aged in white American oak barrels. The whites are fermented and are usually aged in stainless steel (in years past it was customary to age them in oak barrels for two or more years). A general emphasis on wood aging, as well as the qualities inherent in the grapes themselves, gives Rioja wines their unique character and taste.

Red Rioja wines that are labeled Tinto are generally full-bodied, with a dark color and lots of tannin; they are shipped in Burgundy-style bottles. Riojas labeled *clarete* are generally lighter in color and body and are shipped in Bordeaux-type bottles.

In 1560, Rioja vintners formed an association to regulate and guarantee the quality and origin of their exported wines. The governing body for wine production in Rioja is the *Consejo Regulador de la Denominación de Rioja,* which was established in 1925.

Some of the better-known wineries of Rioja are:

Alavesas	Marqués de Cáceres
Bodegas Berberana	Marqués de Murrieta
Bodegas Beronia	Marqués de Riscal
Bodegas Bilbainas	Montecillo
Bodegas Lan	Muerza
Bodegas Olarra	Muga
Bodegas Palacio	Federico Paternina
Bodegas Rioja Santiago	Ramon Bilbao
C.U.N.E. (Compañia Vinícola del Norte De España)	La Rioja Alta
Pedro Domecq	Carlos Serres
Franco-Españolas	Unidas
R. López de Heredia	Camp Viejo

Catalonia

Catalonia is located in the northeast region of Spain where the best-known appellation of origin is Penedès. Penedès, located south of Barcelona, has been producing wine for more than 2,500 years. It is still one of the most important wine-producing areas in Spain with more than 60,000 acres of grapevines planted, 35,000 of which qualify for *DO* Penedès. Not only does Penedès produce fine table wines, it is one of the world's biggest producers of *méthode champenoise* sparkling wines.

Perhaps the best-known producer of Catalonian wines is the Torres Winery. The Torres vineyards are situated in the Mediterranean region of Catalonia, 20 miles west of Barcelona around the city of Vilafranca del Penedès, the capital of the grape-growing district of Penedès.

► SWITZERLAND

Switzerland produces great quantities of table wine, but imports more wine than it produces. Most Swiss wines come from four famous grape-growing areas: *Valais* (the valley of the Rhône); *Lake Geneva; Ticino;* and *Seeland* (the lake area, Neuchâtel, Bienne, and Morat lakes). In addition, there are many small vineyards all over Switzerland, along the Rhine from Chur to Basel, and on Lake Zurich.

By far the greatest quantity of Swiss wine available in the United States is white wine, predominantly Neuchâtel (made from Chasselas grape) and Dézaley, although occasionally rosés and reds can be found.

Valais

One of the most famous wine districts in Switzerland is Valais, a deep, sheltered valley at the headwaters of the Rhône River, where carefully grown and terraced vineyards step up the mountainsides, reaching very high altitudes (the Visperterminen vineyard, the highest in Europe, is at 4,000 feet). The high Alps shield Valais from winds and storms, giving it one of Switzerland's most temperate climates in summer, although the winters are bitterly cold. Since Valais is the most arid section of Switzerland, the grapevines are irrigated with water taken from mountainside canals fed by the melting glaciers. The rich lowlands of Valais are famous for their lush fruits, especially the pears that are used to make Switzerland's celebrated pear brandy. Winemakers of the Valais district produce delicate white wines and Dôle, a full-bodied red wine.

Lake Geneva

The Lake Geneva area is divided into two grape-growing districts—Geneva and Vaud (which is itself divided into three areas).

In the Geneva district, at the easternmost tip of Lake Geneva and north of the city, is the area of Mandement, where Perlana, a fruity, sparkling white wine is made from Chasselas grapes. The Chasselas grape, known locally as *Fendant,* produces some of the most popular wines in Switzerland. The Geneva district also produces specialty wines made from the Johannisberg Riesling, Sylvaner, Aligoté, and Chardonnay grapes. Light rosés are also made from the Gamay grape.

Vaud's three grape-growing areas are *Chablais,* which is upstream from where the Rhône enters Lake Geneva; *Lavaux,* bordering the lakefront east of Lausanne; and *La Côte,* located between Lausanne and Geneva. Nearly all of Vaud's wines are white wines made from the Chasselas grape, known locally as *Dorin.* Charming, fragrant reds, labeled Salvagnins, are also produced throughout Vaud from a blend of Pinot Noir and Gamay grapes.

Seeland

The limestone-rich terrain of the slopes surrounding Lakes Neuchâtel, Bienne, and Morat produces mostly white wines, often with a light sparkle. The vineyards of Neuchâtel are the source of a light-colored, intriguingly fragrant red wine, and one of Switzerland's celebrated rosés, Oeil de Perdrix; both are made from the Pinot Noir grape.

Ticino

In the shadow of the St. Gotthard mountains, on the southern slopes of the Alps, is the Italian-speaking region of Ticino, which produces mostly red wines, most notably Merlot del Ticino.

▶ TUNISIA

Tunisia is located in North Africa, between Libya to the east, and Algeria to the south and west.

Under Islamic rule in the seventh century A.D., grape growing was limited to table grapes, and wine consumption was forbidden. The wine industry was revived during the French Protectorate (1881–1956), at which time mainly blended wines were produced.

Tunisian vineyards, which cover an area of more than 85,000 acres, are located in the northeastern regions of the country, and are being revived and improved for the production of high-quality wines.

Tunisia produces an average of 25 to 30 million gallons of wine per year, a fifth of which is classified under selected and controlled categories: *vins d'appellation contrôlée* (AOC), *vins supérieurs* (VS), and *vins délimités de qualité supérieur* (VDQS). Classified wines must conform with various legal and technical criteria including chemical analyses, bacteriological and organic tests, and tastings by qualified enologists.

To maintain high standards, the growing of hybrids is forbidden, as is irrigation of the vineyards. This explains both the low grape yields and their high quality. *Chaptalization* and watering of the wines are also severely prohibited.

The Tunisian vineyards are planted with traditional grapevine stocks that have adapted to the Mediterranean climate, including: Carignan, Cinsaut, Alicante Bouschet, Alicante Grenache, Clairette, Beldi, Pedro Ximénez, Muscat of Alexandria, Mourvèdre, Cabernet Sauvignon, and Pinot Noir.

▶ YUGOSLAVIA

Only during the past three decades have the Yugoslavs been in a position to develop a world market for their wines. During the 1950s and 1960s, Yugoslavia established markets in most of Europe: around 1950 the first bottles of the Yugoslavian wine Ljutomer Riesling reached the shores of Great Britain.

All Yugoslavian wines entering the United States are labeled as they are on the home market—by grape variety and region. The unfamiliarity of some of the Yugoslav grape and place names undoubtedly causes confusion. Fortunately, many of the classic grapes have been given the same or similar names in Yugoslavia as they have in the United States and Europe; for example, one can speak of a Cabernet Sauvignon from Istria or a Rizling from Fruska Gora. A wine such as Opolo from Dalmatia is a fresh, fruity, deeply colored rosé. Dalmatia is the Adriatic coastal region of Yugoslavia, the two most famous Dalmatian cities being Dubrovnik and Split. One variety of white grape that prospers in Yugoslavia is the Sipon. The wine of the same name, from Maribor, is a very pleasing and unique wine, but its name will certainly not, because of its unfamiliarity, command immediate recognition on a wine list.

The 45 degree east and west parallel that goes through the north of Yugoslavia also cuts across such celebrated wine regions as the Piedmont region of Italy and the Rhône Valley and Bordeaux region of France. The climate in Yugoslavia ranges from Alpine to Continental to Mediterranean. The topography and soil content are equally varied, of natural combinations contributing to a rich diversity of high-quality wines.

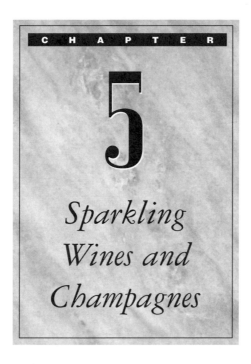

Sparkling
Wines and
Champagnes

*S*parkling wines, the most elegant of all alcoholic

beverages, for centuries have been served to royalty and heads of state, at New Year

celebrations and at weddings, births, and other important occasions. "Bubbly," as

sparkling wine has come to be known, is the most labor-intensive of all wines, yet its

prices scarcely reach those of Bordeaux, Burgundy, and other high-priced wines;

its popularity and price seem to grow each year.

▶ BUREAU OF ALCOHOL, TOBACCO, AND FIREARMS (BATF) REGULATIONS

A sparkling wine is defined as an effervescent wine containing more than 0.392 grams of carbon dioxide (CO_2) per 100 milliliters of wine, resulting solely from the secondary fermentation of the wine within a closed container.

▶ FRENCH CHAMPAGNE

History

The Roman chalk quarries of the French Champagne region date from the Roman-Gallo period of the third century A.D. when Reims was the capital of Northern Gaul. Excavations made by slaves consisted of large pits that were shaped like pyramids (growing wider as one descended). They were often more than 100 feet deep; large pulley-type hoists were employed to lift out the huge and heavy blocks of chalk, which were dried and used for building houses and ramparts. In this way, a maximum yield of raw material was obtained with little damage to the ground's surface. Excavations were begun near the groundwater level; once completed, they were filled with debris and rubbish and covered by earth.

It was not until centuries later that the people of Champagne rediscovered these pits and for years worked to enlarge and connect them, forming the basis of the unique chalk caves that consist of hundreds of miles of tunnels, housing well into hundreds of millions of bottles of champagne (Figure 5-1). One of the chief characteristics of the Champagne region is the chalky subsoil (known as *Belemnita quadrata,* which evolved during subterranean earthquakes millions of years ago) in areas where vineyards are planted. The grapevines thrive in this fractured subsoil, which ensures natural and regular drainage but does not take all of the moisture from the topsoil. This chalky soil has the advantage of storing the heat of the sun and reflecting it back onto the underside of the grapevines at night. This speeds the growth of the grapevines and the ripening of the grapes, by moderating the microclimate and aiding in fruit maturity. Therefore, the vintage may be earlier there than in other areas.

The word *champagne* is of Latin derivation *(campagna),* from the time when Julius Caesar's Roman legions arrived unexpectedly in the rolling wooded hills northeast of what is now Paris. Caesar and his men drilled and battled in an open field they called a *campus;* corrupted by the less than elegant soldiers, the word became *champagne.* This name was given to the ancient French region and is also used for the sparkling wine produced in the region's 84,000 acres (as of 1992) of vineyards (60,000 are planted in grapevines) in some 250 different *crus* or villages clustered around the cities of Reims and Epernay.

It was not until the mid-sixteenth century that Dom Pierre Pérignon (January 1638–September 1715), a blind (during his latter years) Benedictine monk, during his

FIGURE 5-1 A view of the ancient Henriot cellars in Reims where millions of bottles of champagne age to maturity and perfection under ideal conditions. In the background, with Roman arches over their entrances, are the great rooms quarried out of the chalk. They remain today as they were left by the Romans. (Courtesy Henriot Champagne Cellars, France)

tenure as chief cellar master at Hautvillers (1668–1715) perfected the technique for making champagne by blending grapes and wines from various vineyards to achieve a consistent and harmonious balance. He used an oil-soaked hemp rag, an ill-fitting wooden plug, or the bark of a tree as a temporary bottle stopper. He did not, however, discover, invent, or create the wine that is known as champagne. In 1668, Dom Pérignon bottled the first bottle of champagne.

Geography

The Champagne region is 90 miles northeast of Paris. A law passed on July 22, 1927 demarcated a zone of that region, which by virtue of its natural characteristics is capable of supporting the vineyards whose product has the exclusive right to be called champagne. The French insist that no other wine can legally be called champagne regardless of how it is made, how it tastes, or how beautifully it bubbles; and there are treaties and trade agreements to support them. The Treaty of Paris in 1883; The Treaty of Madrid (1891), which states that "all goods imported or exported under false appellation are subject to seizure." The Hague Conference (later often called "The Hague Tribunal") in the Netherlands 1899; The Treaty of Brussels 1900; The Hague Conference 1907; The Treaty in Washington 1911; The Treaty of Versailles (May 6, 1919) forced nations defeated in World War I to accept the victor's appellation laws and trade names. In 1927 at the Hague Tribunal, in 1934 in London, in 1946 in Madrid, and on July 18, 1949, again in Madrid, there were international conferences of all of the wine-producing countries of the world whose purpose was to limit place names on wine labels. Finally, a document known as the "Agreement of Lisbon" was ratified by 12 countries on October 31, 1958: France, Cuba, Czechoslovakia, Greece, Hungary, Israel, Italy, Morocco, Portugal, Spain, Romania, and Turkey. Ratification constituted an agreement to protect product appellations that derive from geographical origin. The governing body is the Office International du Vin (OIV), an organization in which almost all the leading wine-producing countries are represented. The only notable nonsigners of the agreement are Russia and the United States. Why not the United States? Some claim that the United States simply chose not to attend the relevant conferences; others contend that during Prohibition (1920–1933) the United States had no interest in the matter, and still others speculate that the United States simply refused to sign the agreement.

On December 16, 1960, Mr. Justice Danckwerts of the High Court of England issued a judgment ending the use by the Costa Brava Wine Company of the name "Spanish champagne" for a sparkling wine it produced. In 1973, under a Franco-Spanish agreement, Spanish sparkling wine producers could not use the word *champagne* on their labels after 1978, and could not use it in advertising or promotion after 1983. These sparkling wines are instead marketed under the name "Cava." Also, according to a 1973 agreement, Japanese producers cannot use the word *champagne* for their sparkling wines. In addition, legitimate French champagne producers can seek redress for infringements on their rights by foreign wineries that produce or sell sparkling wines labeled "champagne" on Japanese territory.

Largely as a result of the concern of champagne producers about competition from Cava (Spain), a European Common Market (ECM) regulation of November 1985 has rendered illegal the use of the term *méthode champenoise* for any wines made outside the Champagne region. The ruling took effect September 1, 1994.

In the United States, Federal Administration Act wine regulations are enforced by the Bureau of Alcohol, Tobacco, and Firearms (BATF) of the Department of the Treasury.

These regulations require that sparkling wine labels must provide an appellation of origin such as "American," "California," "New York State," "in direct conjunction with, and in lettering substantially as conspicuous as" the word *champagne*. Violations of this regulation are brought to the attention of the BATF. In the United States, the term *champagne* has been legal to use (as long as a geographic origin is on the label) since U.S. District Court Judge Frank S. Dietrich ruled (April 7, 1911) on the trial of A. Finke's Widow for selling champagne.

Countries that have either signed the international trade agreement or simply abide by its definition call their sparkling wines by names other than *champagne*. In Italy sparkling wine is known as *spumante;* in France, *mousseux*; in Bulgaria, *champanski*; in Germany and Austria, *schaumwein* or *sekt*; in Spain, *espumosa* or *cava*; in Yugoslavia, *sampanjac*; in Hungary, *pezsgo*; in Portugal and Brazil, *espumante*; and in South Africa, *cap classique* (the local producers call themselves *méthode cap classique association—MCCA*). In England, in a famous 1960 test case, the courts ruled that the British could no longer market any product called "champagne" unless it was true Champagne (made in Champagne, France). Therefore, in England sparkling wine is called *moussec*.

Grape Varieties

In making champagne only three varieties of grapes may be used: Chardonnay (white), Pinot Noir (red), and Meunier (red). The grapes are usually picked before they reach full maturity and sugar content, generally at 17 to 19 Brix (Figure 5-2). At this point they are extremely high in natural grape acidity, which gives champagne its refreshingly clean, crisp taste. The classic champagne blend consists of approximately 70 percent red grapes and 30 percent white grapes. The juice of the red grapes is fermented without the skins, which would otherwise color the wine, making it unsuitable for champagne, more than 98 percent of which is white. If only white grapes are utilized, the sparkling wine is known as *blanc de blancs,* and if only black grapes are utilized, it is known as *blanc de noirs.*

The traditional champagne wine press is quite shallow, with a capacity of 4,000 kilograms (8,800 pounds) of grapes, yielding a total of 2,550 liters (673 gallons) of juice. The shallowness allows the grapes to be spread out in a thin layer, which reduces skin contact, and thus limits color extraction. According to champagne law (1992) grapes are pressed twice, resulting in two different grades of juice. The first pressing yields 2,050 liters, which is called *jus de cuvée*; the second pressing yields 500 liters, which is called *jus de première taille.*

When the grapes have been harvested, pressed, and fermented, the winemaker begins to assemble his *cuvée* or blend. He might, for instance, have Chardonnay wine from many different vineyards, sometimes as many as 30 to 50. From these he chooses wines that display certain desirable characteristics for the final blend; the same is true for the red wines. The next step is to develop a blend of all three wines that captures the particular style of that champagne house. The winemaker has to take into consideration the bottlings of the last 15 to 20 years and attempt to achieve a sameness of taste, so that this year's bottle will taste like last year's bottle and also next year's bottle. He must consider what the blended

FIGURE 5-2   A *vendangeuse* harvesting grapes for champagne in a Moet & Chandon vineyard. (Courtesy of Moët & Chandon, Epernay, France)

wine will taste like after it has undergone secondary fermentation, when it contains bubbles (Figures 5-3 and 5-4). This can drastically change the wine's appearance and taste.

▶ MAKING SPARKLING WINES AND CHAMPAGNES

Sparkling wines are made in a multitude of ways, from the cheapest—an overnight "charge" of carbon dioxide (CO_2)—to the most costly, *méthode champenoise.*

Artificial Carbonation

Perhaps the quickest and cheapest method of making wines sparkle is similar to the way sodas are made to "fizz"—that is, by pumping them full of carbon dioxide. With this method the bubbles are not an integral part of the wine and do not last long after it is poured. Sparkling wines made via this method are easy to spot. Their bubbles are very large and the wine froths up very quickly for a few moments and then appears to go flat.

The Bulk or Charmat Method

The next method is known as "bulk fermentation" or the "Charmat" method, after its inventor Eugène Charmat, a French wine scientist who developed the process in 1910 to save both the time and money involved in the classic method of producing sparkling wines. The original Charmat process (which is still, with some modifications, used today) requires three tanks. *Still* wine (wine without carbonation) is run into the first tank and heated for 12 to 16 hours, then immediately cooled. This wine is then pumped into a second tank, where yeast and sugar are added; it then ferments for 15 to 20 days. The wine is then pumped into the third tank, where it is clarified by cooling the tank to about 30 degrees Fahrenheit; this also aids in tartrate stabilization. Finally, the wine is filtered and bottled under pressure. This method usually produces sparkling wines within one month and is the least expensive of the higher-quality methods. Because all of the fermentation takes place in temperature-controlled stainless-steel pressurized tanks, bottle breakage is

FIGURE 5-3 Laboratory analysis of wine destined to be made into champagne. (Courtesy Champagne News & Information Bureau, New York)

FIGURE 5-4 Cellarmasters blend wine from different vineyards with reserve wines from previous harvests to produce nonvintage champagnes that typify a house style. (Courtesy Moët & Chandon, Epernay, France)

virtually nonexistent. Cooler fermentation allows for greater retention of fresh grapy flavors and the fermentation can be halted at any point by simply chilling the wine.

Asti is a white, sweet sparkling wine produced in the southern area of Langhe (province of Cuneo) and Monferrato (province of Asti and Alessandria), in the region of Piedmont. The production area was delimited on March 7, 1924, when Asti Spumante was classified as a "typical wine." In 1994, Asti Spumante was granted its DOCG and with it came a name change to *Asti* with the suffix *Spumante* eliminated.

In Italy all of the Asti (a spumante) is made in a modified Charmat method, which is favored over the *méthode champenoise.* One of the earlier problems associated with using the classic method to produce Asti was that the Moscato grape's fresh aroma was lost. Another problem was that it was difficult to maintain the presence of residual sugars, which are necessary for consistent sweetness. When the classic method is used, all of the sugars are metabolized during the secondary fermentation, and the desired sweetness is accomplished later, with the final *dosage* (sugar syrup).

The grapes are pressed and the juice (prior to fermentation) is clarified in special centrifuges and filters to clarify it and to remove solids. The juice is then put in thermally insulated containers and chilled to 28.4 degrees Fahrenheit and kept at that temperature until needed.

The juice ferments until it reaches an alcoholic content of approximately 5 percent. The temperature is then dropped below 32 degrees Fahrenheit to stop fermentation, while at the same time, the wine is pumped into containers that are constructed to prevent the escape of carbon dioxide.

After this has been accomplished, the temperature is increased and fermentation continues until the alcoholic content reaches somewhere between 7.0 and 9.5 percent. Then the wine is bottled. This can be accomplished in less than one month.

For Asti, under the Italian DOCG regulations, the minimum residual sugar after the secondary fermentation must be 7.5 to 9.0 grams per 100 milliliters. This presented a major problem to Italian winemaker Carlo Gancia (he produced the first bottle of *spumante* in 1865), who experimented with the *méthode champenoise.* At that time countless bottles would explode—often 20 to 30 percent of the entire production. When, in 1910, the Charmat process was discovered, it was immediately put to use in the making of Asti. The process, which has been greatly modified and advanced, utilizes such techniques as refrigeration, pasteurization, and sterile filtration and bottling.

Asti is light straw-yellow or golden-yellow in color with a delicate, musky, and spicy aroma that is reminiscent of orange blossoms, peaches, pears, and apricots. Also present is the seductive scent of wild honey, linden leaves, acacia blossoms, wisteria, and sage. It is sweet and harmonious, tasting very much of the Moscato grape, with balanced acidity and a long and lingering aftertaste.

The Asti *consorzio* (founded on December 17, 1932), known as *consorzio per la tutela dell'Asti,* features on its neck label San Secondo, the patron saint of Asti, mounted on horseback in blue, on a gold background.

Méthode Champenoise (Champagne Method)

The most costly of all procedures, which produces the finest-quality sparkling wines and champagnes, is called *méthode champenoise.* It was pioneered in France during the nineteenth century, and is the only method that can legally be used to produce French champagne. The base wine or *cuvée* (blend) must be delicate in flavor, low in alcohol (because there is a 1- to 2-percent increase in alcohol after the secondary fermentation), and relatively high in acidity. If the level of alcohol in the base wine was 12 or 12.5 percent (prior to secondary fermentation), the finished sparkling wine would contain about 14 percent alcohol, smell "hot," and taste harsh and out of balance, due to the presence of carbonation. (Under AOC regulations, 13 percent alcohol is the maximum legal concentration.) This base wine is placed in a champagne bottle, to which is added a measured amount of sugar, known as *liqueur de tirage* (approximately four grams per liter, which yields one atmosphere of pressure) and yeast that is dissolved in wine. Too much sugar can result in bursting bottles or a "hot" (high-alcohol) sparkling wine. The formula relative to the precise quantity of sugar to add was developed in 1837 by André François.

Errors are costly and at this stage of development it is important to choose a yeast that agglomerates readily—that is, clumps up and forms particles large enough to settle out of the wine, rather than remaining in suspension. The yeast used in the secondary fermentation is not the same type as that used in primary alcohol fermentation. Special strains are used that are suitably matched to the base wine and can reproduce in a stoppered bottle. (However, there are several factors that inhibit secondary fermentation: ethyl alcohol concentration levels are already high; increasing production of CO_2; and nutrients required for yeast growth are generally depleted.) The bottles are secured with either a metal crown cap or a cork held in place by an *agrafe* (metal clip). They are stacked horizontally to distribute the yeast lengthwise, exposing a greater surface area. Each stack contains about 1,000 bottles; thin strips of wood called laths *(lattes)* are placed between each row of bottles, making the stacks quite firm.

While this aging takes place, the bottles are periodically inspected for breaks or leaks and the center bottles (which are the warmest due to the heat given off during fermentation) are interchanged with the outer ones to ensure uniformity of fermentation. The bottles remain in cool (50 to 55 degrees Fahrenheit), dark cellars for the secondary fermentation, which normally takes about 45 days to complete. Five to six atmospheres of pressure or about 110 pounds per square inch of CO_2 is formed. During this time, the cell walls of the yeast crack open, allowing the protoplasm present to metabolize the sugar, converting it to more or less equal parts of alcohol and inert carbon dioxide gas. The finished sparkling wine usually contains 11.5 to 12.5 percent alcohol. Since the CO_2 cannot escape, it is absorbed into the wine over a period of time. After the fermentation in the bottle is complete, the wine is left to age in a cellar. Under AOC regulations, the minimum duration of aging for a nonvintage champagne is one year; for vintage champagne it is three years (vintage champagnes must also come from 100 percent of the harvest date on the label). Most champagnes are aged from three to nine years on the yeast.

During secondary fermentation, sugar metabolism and production of CO_2 proceed quickly (about six weeks), but after about eight to ten months, a process known as yeast *autolysis* begins. This is a process whereby the yeast cells in the aging champagne break down, and release vitamins (such as A, C, D, and E), proteins, peptides, volatile aromas, and amino acids, which contribute to the formation of tiny bubbles and add to the complexity and elegance of the wine. The dead yeast are often referred to as *ghosts* because yeast cells, which are surrounded by a very rigid, thick, and chemically resistant wall persists long after the cell has died. When the sparkling wine has aged sufficiently, the bottles are placed on their sides in racks called *pupîtres*—specially constructed, hinged "A-frame" racks, drilled with large angled holes (invented in 1818 by Antoine Müller, an employee of the champagne house of Veuve Clicquot), for ten to 12 days, during which time the sediment in the bottle settles (Figure 5-5).

Riddling begins at this point: Experienced riddlers usually place a white paint mark on the bottom of the bottle (punt) at 6 o'clock position and rotate the bottles clockwise in one-eighth to one-quarter turns. While rotating the bottles the riddlers gently shake them and increase the angle at which they lie to a more vertical position, which moves the sediment that was formed during the secondary fermentation down to the bottle's neck. An experienced riddler can turn 10,000 bottles per hour and as many as 50,000 bottles per day (Figure 5-6). Riddling is done on a daily basis for approximately six weeks (see the later section on encapsulated yeasts). When all of the sediment is collected at the neck of the bottles, a process known as *dégorgement,* or disgorgement, takes place.

The bottles are then chilled to about 35 degrees Fahrenheit, after which the neck of the bottle is immersed to a depth of one inch in an extremely cold (−20 degrees Fahrenheit) circulating, propylene glycol brine solution or "bath," which freezes the neck of the bottle and the sediment in it within 15 minutes. (Calcium chloride prevents the water from freezing.) The bottle is immediately turned upright, the cap is removed, and the pressure in the bottle literally blows out this semi-frozen slush, which contains all the wine's sediment (Figures 5-7 and 5-8). Because the bottle was cooled off before disgorg-

FIGURE 5-5 Bottles of sparkling wine made via *méthode champenoise* showing various stages of the sediment gradually being worked toward the neck of the bottle for eventual *dégorgement.* (Photo by Bob Lipinski)

FIGURE 5-6 The time-honored method of *remuage* (hand-riddling). (Courtesy Champagne News & Information Bureau, New York)

ing, there is only a loss of about one atmosphere of pressure during this process, and still plenty of bubble left in the bottle. The bottle is then topped with a shipping *dosage (liqueur d'expédition),* which consists of an older champagne in which cane sugar has been dissolved. Occasionally grape brandy is added to increase the alcoholic strength of very sweet champagnes. This sugar addition determines the relative degree of dryness or sweetness in the wine. Finally, the bottle is corked, secured with a wire hood, and returned to the aging cellar to rest for two to four months (one month minimum under AOC) while the *dosage* is absorbed by the wine.

Until the 1840s, champagne was a sweet to very sweet wine. This changed in 1848, when Mr. Burne, a London wine merchant, persuaded the champagne house of Perrier-Jouët to ship him some *undosaged* 1846 vintage champagne. Unfortunately, Mr. Burne's customers found the champagne to be undrinkable. In 1850, Mr. Burne approached the champagne house of Roederer to produce a *brut* champagne, but they flatly refused. After a few more years of trying, several champagne houses agreed and sent him cases of 1865 *brut* champagne, which the French referred to as *English cuvée.*

FIGURE 5-7 The traditional, somewhat daring hand method of "disgorgement." (Courtesy Moët & Chandon, Epernay, France)

French champagne makers follow the European Common Market guidelines for the dosage (Figure 5-9):

Designation	*Common Market Standard*
Extra brut*	less than 6 grams of sugar per liter
Brut	less than 15 grams of sugar per liter (most brut champagnes have 8-10 grams per liter)
Extra Dry	12–20 grams per liter
Sec	17–35 grams per liter
Demisec	33–50 grams per liter
Doux	more than 50 grams per liter

*Synonyms include brut de brut, brut nondosage, brut sauvage, brut zéro, dosage zéro, pas dosé, natural, naturale, sans sucre, and ultra brut; these are synonyms of extra brut only.

FIGURE 5-8   Bollinger R.D. is disgorged by hand to remove the natural sediment on which it has been aging for at least seven years. (Courtesy Niki Singer, Inc., New York)

After the final aging, the sparkling wine is ready for labeling and eventual shipping. Most sparkling wines are traditionally fermented in 375-milliliter, 750-milliliter, magnum (1.5 liters), and double magnum (3 liters) bottles. Other sizes, both larger and smaller, are hand-filled from 750-milliliter bottles. The hand-filling of other size bottles does not violate the AOC regulations relative to méthode champenoise; in fact, this is common practice in Champagne, France, where the regulations originate.

Many of the large bottles—Jeroboam (3 liters), Methuselah (6 liters), Salmanazar (9 liters), Balthazar (12 liters), and Nebuchadnezzar (15 liters), for instance—have Old Testament names, which were given to them during the 1850s and 1860s by the British négociants.

Sparkling wines made in this manner are entitled to indicate so on their labels, displaying either the words *méthode champenoise* or "fermented in *this* bottle." A three-layer cork, usually two discs of natural solid cork and one layer particle cork, must be used, and the word *champagne* must be stamped on every cork used for this wine.

How To Read A Champagne Label

SIZE

Many wine lovers argue that champagne fermented in magnums tastes better. Whatever the evidence, magnums are more festive and practical for crowds — they're BIG!

Here are the main choices:

- *Bottle* — 750ml (Serves 6 flutes)
- *Magnum* — 1.5 liter (Serves 12 flutes)

DRY, DRIER, DRIEST

The amount of sugar used in the dosage determines how dry a finished champagne will taste. Here are the main choices:

- *Brut* — no sweetness
- *Extra Dry* — slightly sweet
- *Sec* — noticeably sweet

(Yes! Brut is *drier* than Extra Dry.)

BRAND

Here's where the champagne producers have done us a favor. They generally stay true to their chosen style through the use of artful blending (whereas still wines are subject to that harvest's characteristics). So once you've found a style you like in a particular brand (e.g., delicate, robust, etc.), you can rely on finding what pleased you again . . . and again.

VINTAGE DATE

A vintage wine is one which contains 95% or more of wines of the year stated. As a rule, there is no quality connotation to a vintage American sparkling wine. Like many wineries, Domaine Chandon does not vintage date its bubblies, blending as much as 30% of reserve wines from previous years to maintain a consistent style.

ALCOHOL CONTENT

Like most table wines, most champagnes contain 12% alcohol by volume. Because people tend to sip wine with foods, it is often referred to as the "beverage of moderation."

VITICULTURAL REGION

This simply tells you that 85% or more of the wine was produced from grapes grown in that designated region.

TYPE

There are three grape varieties which make up the majority of fine champagnes: Pinot Noir, Chardonnay and Pinot Blanc. Champagne vintners are notorious for giving us confusing nomenclature, but here are some simple guidelines:

- *Blanc de Noirs* are generally made from the Pinot Noir grape (dark skin, light juice) and often have an attractive tinge of color.
- *Blanc de Blancs* are made from Chardonnay (light skin, light juice) or other white grapes.
- *Reserve* usually connotes lengthy aging. Chandon Reserve is aged a minimum of four years, for example.

CHAMPAGNE OR SPARKLING WINE?

Where French appellation (wine labeling) law applies, sparkling wine can only be called champagne if it is produced in the Champagne region of France. Here in the U.S., these laws do not apply, so it's up to each producer to decide how to describe his wine. Domaine Chandon sparkling wines are so named out of respect for its parent, Champagne Moët and Chandon. (Note: For simplicity and consistency, the term champagne is used here to mean *any* bubbly wine.)

METHOD OF FERMENTATION

Careful: you get what you paid for.

- *Méthode Champenoise* — A trustworthy signpost. It's the traditional and most expensive process, whereby the bubbly goes through its second fermentation in the same bottle you buy. If you want the best quality, look for it.
- *Charmat* — Also called the "bulk" process, charmat bubblies are fermented in large tanks and often produce champagnes with large, lazy bubbles that disappear too quickly.
- *Fermented in the Bottle* — This phrase indicates that the "transfer" process was used. The bubbly undergoes its second fermentation in a bottle, but unlike the méthode champenoise, the wine is emptied from that bottle, filtered and re-bottled. Many agree it loses some flavor in transit.

FIGURE 5-9   How to read a sparkling wine label. (Courtesy Domaine Chandon, Yountville, California)

Although champagne is an AOC wine, there is no legal obligation to carry the phrase *appellation contrôlée* on the label.

In addition to the degree of dryness, the year of the harvest if the champagne is a vintage bottling, and whether the wine is a rosé or blanc de blancs, the label will provide a registration number, preceded by two initials:

- N.M.—produced by a *négociant-manipulant* (shipper-producer)
- R.M.—produced by a *récoltant-manipulant* (grape grower)
- C.M.—produced by a *coopérative-manipulant* (cooperative-producer)
- M.A.—private label *marque d'acheteur* (buyer's own brand)

The Transfer Method

This last method was developed in Germany in the 1930s and is a modification of the *méthode champenoise.* In fact, the two methods are identical, except that the transfer method does not employ the riddling technique. Instead, when the wine has been sufficiently aged, the bottles are moved to a large tank in which pressure is used to remove the corks, suck the wine out of the bottles, and then chill it to below 32 degrees Fahrenheit. After being filtered, the wine is transferred to clean bottles, and the final dosage is added. This does appear to be an easier and certainly cheaper way of making high-quality sparkling wines. However, during the filtering process it has been found that the filtration can strip the subtlety that the winemaker has worked so hard to create. The reverse is also true—if the winemaker starts off with a mediocre wine, the filtering can improve the wine by clearing it of "off" flavors. Sparkling wines made in this manner are labeled "fermented in *the* bottle."

▶ ROSÉ CHAMPAGNES

History: Fact or Fancy?

The supposed origin of rosé champagne is part of its romantic charm. One story claims that it was created to match the satin slippers and long dresses of the bridesmaids at a fashionable French wedding; another suggests that it was blended to honor the coronation of a queen. It is more likely that pink or rosé champagne was an accident of nature. During an exceptional growing year in the Champagne region, the grapevines received more than the usual limited amount of sunshine. This caused some of the pigment in the red grape skins to migrate to the pulp of the fruit, giving the resultant wine a pink or rosé tinge.

Rosé champagne, which has a much longer history than do *blanc de blancs,* is often seen as the quintessential wine of the gay and frivolous late Victorian and Edwardian ages. In the nineteenth century, for instance, it was synonymous with wild and dissolute living. But it is a serious wine and one of the most difficult and complex to produce.

It was not until the end of the seventeenth century, a period in which great efforts were made to improve French wines, that champagne's tendency to sparkle was analyzed and exploited. Before then the wines of Champagne, although much appreciated, were still, delicate red wines that did not keep well or stand up to travel. In the nineteenth century, the common name for pink or rosé champagne was *oeil de perdrix* (eye of the partridge).

The Production of Pink or Rosé Champagne

Rosé champagne is perhaps the most difficult wine in the world to produce. Of the four basic ways in which rosé champagne can be made, the first is illegal in France. The pink color of a rosé champagne was once obtained by artificial coloring; for instance, *cochineal* (the juice of scarlet-colored berries) was often added to "white" champagne. Other methods included the addition of elderberry juice boiled in cream of tartar (tartaric acid)—known as *teinture de fismes*—or red vegetable dyes or anything else that could produce a red color.

The first legal method used in making rosé champagne is seldom used nowadays. Again, champagne is traditionally produced 70 percent from red grapes (Pinot Noir and Meunier) and 30 percent from white grapes (Chardonnay). If the winemaker decides that he wants to make a rosé wine, he will simply leave the skins of the red grapes in contact with the fermenting grape juice or *must* for anywhere from four to 12 hours. During this time both the high acid content of the grapes and the initial stage of alcohol production will draw out some pigmentation from the grape skins, giving the *must* a slight rosé color. (Grape tannins will also be given off during this time.) This method is avoided in making the more traditional golden-colored champagnes. One of the most basic problems with the method is that it is difficult to control the stability of the color it produces and its eventual development in the sparkling wine. The rosé color has been known to fade in the bottle or turn to a pale tawny or onionskin color. This method is seldom utilized.

Another legal method of rosé champagne making, one that is more universally accepted and practiced, is the addition of still red wine (also made in the Champagne region, mostly from Bouzy, but occasionally from Ambonnay, Verzenay, or Trepail, in the Montagne de Reims). The red wine added in a proportion of 10 to 15 percent in relation to the white champagne gives the sparkling wine the right degree of color. The addition of red wine takes place prior to the secondary fermentation in the bottle.

In either of the above legal methods, the desired color may not "develop" after three to five years in the bottle, since, as stated earlier, the effect of pigmentation is not wholly predictable and could precipitate out at a later date as sediment. It has occasionally been known for the final champagne to emerge yellow, blue, orange, or brown. During this aging period the wine could also take on a pale tawny color, which is why the second method is preferable to deriving the rosé color solely from skin contact.

A final method that is seldom employed is exactly the same (employing the addition of red Bouzy wine) as the method described above, except that the red wine is added *after* the secondary fermentation, when the *liqueur d'expédition* (shipping dosage) is added. The problem with this method is that the red wine never has a chance to "marry" with the existing champagne; therefore, an "off" flavor usually develops.

The Risk of Producing Rosé Champagne

As it is so risky to make this special champagne, most firms producing a rosé do so in limited quantity and only in the finest vintage years when exceptionally mature grapes are available. When one understands the commercial courage needed to produce a rosé champagne (a firm can lose its entire rosé *cuvée* if the color or taste is incorrect), one can also appreciate why production is so small and why it is more expensive than the more common golden champagnes.

Rosé champagne could very easily be made in a *demisec* style. Instead, it is almost always a *brut* champagne, which is much drier than the more traditional golden champagnes. Rosé champagne usually has more tannin and tartness than golden champagne and has a greater aging potential. Rosé champagnes have a characteristic aroma of raspberries and black currants—the light scents that give rosés their charm.

Rosé Champagne Producers

Rosé champagne accounts for approximately 1 percent of the total production of champagne. Some of the better nonvintage and vintage rosé champagnes on the market are:

Ayala	Lanson
Besserat de Bellefon	Laurent-Perrier
Billecart-Salmon	Moët & Chandon
Bollinger	Mumm
Charbaut	Perrier-Jouët
De Castellane	Philipponnat
Deutz	Piper-Heidsieck
Nicolas Feuilliatte	Pommery
Gosset	Louis Roederer
Charles Heidsieck	Pol Roger
Heidsieck Monopole	Ruinart
Henriot	Taittinger
Jacquesson	Veuve Clicquot
Krug	

Some examples of *prestige cuvées* rosé champagnes are:

Charbaut Certificate	Krug
Dom Pérignon	Perrier-Jouët
Roederer Cristal	Pol Roger Cuvée de Réserve
Dom Ruinart	Taittinger Comtes de Champagne

Riddling Machines

The vibrating or automatic riddling racks used to shake bottles in preparation for *dégorgement* was pioneered in 1966, by the late Adolf Heck of Korbel Champagne Cellars of Sonoma, California. There have been many variations on this automated system; one very successful one is called a *gyropalette,* or "very large machine" (VLM) for short. Older models stood approximately 4 feet high, wasted 13 feet of airspace, and were capable of riddling 504 bottles at once. The newer machine, which stands 17 feet high, once described as a "cubist gyroscope," can riddle 4,032 bottles at once! It can also be programmed to turn and/or tilt three times in 24 hours. A bottle of sparkling wine can be machine riddled in 12 days (three movements a day) as opposed to the approximately 30 days of a traditional hand-riddling cycle (Figure 5-10).

FIGURE 5-10 Domaine Chandon's giant riddling machine mechanically turns 4,032 bottles of sparkling wine at once. (Courtesy Domaine Chandon, Yountville, California)

Encapsulated Yeasts

During the past two decades, the research laboratory at Moët & Chandon has been trying different techniques to facilitate the process of *remuage*. Since 1980, Moët has been researching, in conjunction with INRA (Institut National de la Recherche Agronomique), a technology that consists of enclosing yeasts responsible for the second fermentation in "beads" of alginate, a natural polymer extracted from marine algae. Thus, while activating the second fermentation in exactly the same way as yeasts in their free state, the encapsulated yeasts remain enclosed in these beads even after *autolysis* (the self-destruction of the cells). During autolysis the molecules that contribute to the flavor and aroma of the wine pass in solution into the champagne, leaving the yeast cells imprisoned in the beads. As these beads have a density that is higher than that of the wine, they settle easily by gravity (rather than floating freely), collecting in the neck of the bottle without the need to use the traditional *pupîtres*, or racks. They are then disgorged by the conventional method.

Classically, *remuage*, or riddling, serves to eliminate the dead yeast (lees) contained in a bottle of champagne before shipment in a straightforward mechanical operation.

With yeast encapsulation, there are millions of cells in the bottle which create a distinct cloudiness and then leave a very fine deposit which also has to be eliminated by means of *remuage*. Because the yeasts are trapped in beads, the wine remains perfectly limpid throughout the bottle fermentation. With encapsulated yeasts, the usual large number of yeasts is contained in a few hundred beads, each having an average diameter of a few millimeters (approximately one-tenth of an inch; see Figure 5-11).

Moët & Chandon has studied the selection of yeasts, the qualities of seaweeds used to produce the encapsulating "beads," and methods for preparing the "beads" in laboratory conditions, with a view to producing wine of a quality similar to that obtained by the classical method. Research undertaken in collaboration with the CIVC (Comite Interprofessionel du Vin de Champagne) enables them to say at this stage that, in the method employing encapsulated yeast, the second fermentation takes place normally; and the panel of specialists has found that the organoleptic properties of champagne that has been produced by this method and that has been aged for up to two years on the *lees* are indistinguishable from those of champagne containing yeasts in the free state.

It should be noted, however, that the use of this technique will have virtually no effect on the length of time during which the wines develop and age in the cellars, which will remain approximately three years for nonvintage champagne and between five and seven years for vintage *cuvées*.

According to Richard Geoffroy, Moët & Chandon's chief enologist, the first champagnes made by this revolutionary process will probably be sold toward the end of the 1990s.

FIGURE 5-11   The calcium alginate beads in a bottle of champagne, after the second fermentation (in the bottle) has taken place. The photo illustrates how much easier it is to move the alginate beads to the neck of the bottle as compared to traditional yeast. (Photo courtesy of Moët & Chandon, Epernay, France)

Champagne Houses

There are more than 100 champagne houses; some of the most popular are:

Bollinger.   On February 6, 1829, the house of Bollinger was founded by Jacques Bollinger of Württemberg. Bollinger is known for making a super-prestige champagne called R.D. (*récemment dégorgé,* or recently disgorged), first produced with the 1955 vintage and disgorged on January 18, 1968.

Heidsieck & Co.   The firm of Heidsieck was founded in 1785, by Florens-Louis Heidsieck, and became Heidsieck & Co. in 1794.

Florens-Louis Heidsieck, who was childless, brought three of his nephews into the business: Henri-Louis Waldbaum in 1795, Charles-Henri Heidsieck in 1805, and Christian Heidsieck in 1808.

Charles-Camille Heidsieck (son of Charles-Henri), born in 1822, entered the champagne business in 1845 and founded his own company, Charles Heidsieck, in 1851.

In 1834, Henri-Louis Waldbaum founded Waldbaum Heidsieck, but it wasn't until 1923 that the name was changed to Heidsieck Monopole.

Christian Heidsieck formed his own company and incorporated under the name Heidsieck. Christian died the year after, but his widow continued the business and in 1837, married her brother-in-law, Henri Piper. At that time, the firm was named H. Piper & Co. and traded the brand name Heidsieck, and in 1845, the brand became Piper-Heidsieck.

Henriot.   This champagne house was founded in 1808 by Nicolas-Simon Henriot. In 1969, Henriot produced for Baron Philippe de Rothschild of Château Mouton-Rothschild, a high-quality champagne reserved for the baron and his friends. It was called *Réserve Baron Philippe de Rothschild* and since that time has been released to the general public in limited quantity.

Lanson Père & Fils.   This house was originally known as Delamotte Père & Fils when founded in 1760 by François Delamotte. In 1828 Delamotte took Jean-Baptiste Lanson as a partner, and upon Delamotte's death in 1838, the firm's name was changed to Lanson.

Laurent-Perrier.   The Laurent family founded this house on December 12, 1812. Eugène Laurent, who had married Mathilde Émile Perrier, died in 1887 and the firm's name was changed to Laurent-Perrier.

Moët & Chandon.   The year 1743 marked the birth of Moët & Chandon and also of Thomas Jefferson, third president of the United States (1743–1826), who would later become extremely fond of this champagne. Moët was originally founded by Claude Louis Nicolas (of Dutch heritage) in 1743. In 1832, Claude's daughter Adélaïde, married Pierre-Gabriel Chandon de Briailles and the name was changed to Moët & Chandon.

The cellars of Moët & Chandon, which consist of more than 18 miles of connecting underground caves (approximately 120 feet deep) that were dug in the beginning of the eighteenth century, are the world's largest (Figure 5-12).

The most popular super-prestige champagne is *Dom Pérignon,* which is produced by Moët & Chandon. The name originally belonged to another champagne house—Mercier—but was never used by it. When Paul Chandon-Moët married Mercier's daughter, Francine Durant-Mercier in 1927, Moët received the rights to the Dom Pérignon name. In 1936, the first vintage (1921) of Dom Pérignon champagne was sold in the United States. However, it was not until 1949 that the first vintage (1943) of Dom Pérignon was introduced on the French market.

Moët & Chandon also produces sparkling wines in other countries. Other company production facilities using the Chandon name are Domaine Chandon in California, Proviar in Argentina, Provifin in Brazil, and Chandon Munich in West Germany.

Mumm.   In 1827, Mumm was originally founded by two German immigrants, Peter-Arnold de Mumm and Frederick Giesler. In 1852, Georg Hermann, Peter's son, took over

FIGURE 5-12   Moët & Chandon's cellars, in which millions of bottles of Moët champagne, in various stages of development, are stored. (Courtesy Moët & Chandon, Epernay, France)

running the business. In 1873, G. H. Mumm (as it was then called) developed the famous *Cordon Rouge* brand, which was inspired by the red ribbon *(cordon rouge)* of the French Legion of Honor. The bottle was originally wrapped in red silk ribbons and was first exported to the United States in 1882. During World War I, the business was confiscated because the Mumms had not sought naturalization. In 1920, it was sold to a group of investors headed by René Lalou, who became president, a post he retained until his death in 1973 at the age of 96. In 1966, in recognition of Lalou's contribution, Mumm introduced a prestigious *tête de cuvée* called *René Lalou,* a 1961 vintage bearing his signature.

In 1930, Mumm introduced Crémant de Cramant, a 100 percent Chardonnay champagne from the village of Cramant, whose light effervescence is the result of lower-than-normal pressure in the bottle.

Perrier-Jouët. This house was established in 1811 by Pierre-Nicolas Marie Perrier, who married Adèle Jouët. At the height of art nouveau during the turn of the century (1902), Emile Gallé, the renowned French artist and glass decorator, created the famous flower design of the Perrier-Jouët bottle. The decorative bottle, which disappeared during World War I, was rediscovered in 1963 and inspired Perrier-Jouët to develop its prestige cuvée, *Fleur de Champagne,* beginning with the 1964 harvest.

Louis Roederer. This house was founded in 1760 by M. Dubois under the name of Dubois Père & Fils. It wasn't until 1827 that Louis Roederer joined the firm and changed its name. Roederer was the favorite champagne of Czar Alexander II (1818–1881) of Russia. Louis Roederer created the famous *Cristal* (then a sweet champagne) in the 1860s, which was presented in a clear crystal bottle made exclusively for the Russian Imperial Court. Roederer registered the label on May 13, 1876, and registered the bottle's design the following year. The Cristal bottle was exclusively for the Imperial table until 1917, when the Bolshevik Revolution made it available to the world.

Pol Roger. Founded in 1849 by Pol Roger, this house's champagne was the favorite of Winston Churchill, who, during his tenure as prime minister, reportedly consumed some 500 cases.

In tribute to the great friendship between the Pol Roger family and Winston Churchill, the labels of the champagne sent to England after his death in 1965 were bordered in black. In 1975, that practice ended with the introduction of the *cuvée de prestige, Cuvée Sir Winston,* which is Pol Roger's permanent tribute to the great statesman.

Pommery & Greno. This house, founded in 1836 by Narcisse Greno, was joined by Louis-Alexandré Pommery in 1856. One of Madame Pommery's (Louis-Alexandré Pommery's widow) greatest achievements was the premier of the Pommery Nature 1874, inaugurating the firm's first commercially produced *brut* champagne.

Ruinart Père & Fils. On September 1, 1729, Nicolas Ruinart founded the oldest existing champagne house. Dom Thierry Ruinart (1657–1709), Nicolas's uncle, was a good friend of Dom Pérignon during the late 1600s and early 1700s.

Taittinger. Founded in 1930 by Pierre Charles Taittinger, this house was built upon the foundations of the venerable house of Forest-Fourneaux, itself established in 1734. The Taittinger trademark bears the likeness of Thibaut IV (1201–1253), the Count of Champagne. Legend has it that, on his return from the Crusades in 1240, the count brought back the first Chardonnay grapevine from Cyprus, making the development of champagne possible. Their *Comtes de Champagne Blanc de Blancs* was first produced in 1952.

Super-Prestige Champagnes

In the Champagne region of France, vineyards are rated according to the quality level of the grapes they produce. This official designation, called a "growth," or *cru,* can range from 80 (the least distinguished) to 100 percent. Vineyards that produce the best grapes because of the right consistency and drainage of the soil, the most ideal exposure to the sun, and other viticultural and climatic conditions, are rated 100 percent. The prices of grapes at harvest time are fixed in relation to the classification of each *cru* in this scale.

Just about every champagne house produces its version of a super-prestige (highest quality) champagne, or *tête de cuvée.* Below is a list of champagne producers and the names of their super-prestige champagnes.

Name of producer	Super-prestige champagne
Billecart-Salmon	Cuvée N.F. Billecart
Boizel	Joyau de France
Bollinger	Année Rare or R.D.
Bricout & Koch	Elégance
Canard-Duchêne	Charles VII
Charbaut	Certificate
De Castellane	Commodore and Florens de Castellane
De Venoge	Champagne des Princes
Deutz	Cuvée William Deutz
Gosset	Grande Millésimé
Goulet	Cuvée du Centenaire
Charles Heidsieck	Champagne Charlie
Heidsieck Monopole	Cuvée Diamant Bleu
Henriot	Baccarat
Jacquart	La Grande Cuvée Renommée
Jacquesson	Signature
Krug	Grande Cuvée
Lanson	Special Cuvée
Laurent-Perrier	Cuvée Grand Siècle
Moët & Chandon	Dom Pérignon
Mumm	René Lalou and Mumm de Mumm

Name of producer	*Super-prestige champagne (continued)*
Perrier-Jouët	Fleur de Champagne
Joseph Perrier	Cuvée du Cent-cinquantenaire
Philipponnat	Clos des Goisses
Piper-Heidsieck	Piper Rare
Pol Roger	Cuvée Sir Winston
Pommery	Cuvée Louise Pommery
Louis Roederer	Cristal
Ruinart	Dom Ruinart
Salon-Le-Mesnil	Salon
Taittinger	Comtes de Champagne
Veuve Clicquot	La Grande Dame

Sparkling Wine Producers of the World

The French, it should be noted, do not have the exclusive market on fine sparkling wines; many excellent bubblys are produced throughout the world. These usually command lower prices, however, than those of the prestigious French champagnes. Some well-known French sparkling wine producers are Bouvet, Grandin, Gratien, Kriter, Monmousseau, and Saint Hilaire.

▶ GERMANY

Germany's wine law relative to sparkling wines was amended on September 1, 1986 and affected all wines labeled German Sekt or Deutscher Sekt. The requirements served to bring the labeling for German sparkling wines more in line with German table wine labeling practices. Under the provisions, three categories of German sparkling wines were recognized. All must derive exclusively from grapes harvested in Germany. The three categories are:

Deutscher Sekt b.A.: Sparkling wine made from grapes grown exclusively in one of the 13 specified high-quality wine-producing regions in Germany. The letters b.A. stand for *bestimmter Anbaugebiete,* or *specified growing region,* indicating wines of delimited origin.

Deutscher Sekt: Sparkling wine that derives 100 percent from German-grown grapes whose origin is not, however, limited to one specific region.

Sekt: This term, where it appears alone on the label (not preceded by *Deutscher*), indicates that the sparkling wine was processed and bottled in Germany but contains base wine originating from other Common Market countries. Formerly, these wines could be labeled Deutscher Sekt, but this is no longer allowed under current provisions.

Some well-known German sparkling wine producers are Blue Nun, Deinhard, Fürst von Metternich, and Henkell.

▶ ITALY

On July 9, 1967, four years after the DOC went into effect, Asti (a spumante) was officially granted its DOC designation, and in 1994 it was granted a DOCG status.

Wines (according to DOCG and DOC regulations) used in the process of producing a brut or *secco* spumante must be made from a minimum of 85 percent of the following grape varieties: Pinot Noir, Pinot Grigio, Meunier, and Chardonnay. The remaining 15 percent may be provided by any other variety, with the exception of aromatic types, which are strictly barred. The grapes must be grown in the DOC or DOCG production zones of the Oltrepò Pavese and Franciacorta in Lombardy, the region of Trentino-Alto Adige, and the commune of Serralunga d'Alba in Piedmont. Grapes grown on flat land or valley floors that do not yield suitable wines are excluded.

Nonvintage sparkling wines need to be aged a minimum of one year, and vintage-dated wines, a minimum of two years.

Some *spumante* (sparkling wine) producers who produce Asti and/or brut spumante are:

Antinori	Ca' del Bosco	Fontanafredda
Banfi Vintners	Carpenè-Malvoti	Gancia*
Berlucchi	Càvit	Granduca
Bersano	Collavini	Martini & Rossi
Berrani	Contratto	Monte Rossa
Bosca	Équipe 5	Riccadonna
Burati	Ferrari	Villa Rinaldi

---

*In 1848, Carlo Gancia traveled from Piedmont, Italy to Reims in the Champagne region of France to learn the many techniques behind champagne production at the House of Piper-Heidsieck. Upon his return in 1850, he worked to develop the first Italian sparkling wine. Finally in 1865, the fruits of his labor were rewarded by the release of the first sparkling wine.

▶ SPAIN

Some Spanish sparkling wine producers are:

Borbones	Codorníu	Juvé y Camps
Castellblanch	Dubosc	Lembey
Paul Cheneau	Freixenet	Segura Viudas

▶ UNITED STATES

Almadén, California's oldest producer of sparkling wines, made its first sparkling wine from the *cuvée* of 1888. In 1963, Almadén first bottled its *blanc de blancs* (Cuvée 1959).

FIGURE 5-13 Stainless steel tanks in the Domaine cellars for primary and reserve wine fermentation. (Courtesy Domaine Chandon, Yountville, California)

Domaine Chandon was founded in 1973 in Yountville, California and is owned by Moët-Hennessy of France. The winery also houses a renowned restaurant and a tasting salon that is open to the public. (Figure 5-13 shows the Domaine wine cellars.) Domaine Chandon produces some of the finest nonvintaged *méthode champenoise* sparkling wines, including Chandon Brut, Blanc de Noirs, and Réserve Brut, sold in both traditional 750 milliliter bottles and 1.5 liter magnums.

Gallo Winery of Modesto, California bottled a bulk-fermented sparkling wine in 1966 under the label of The Vintners of Eden Roc. They later changed it to Gallo Champagne, which currently sells under the name of André, the largest-selling sparkling wine in the United States. Gallo also produces three additional sparkling wines—Ballatore Spumante, Tott's, and Eden Roc (recycled name).

Great Western Winery, which began operating on March 15, 1860 in New York, quickly established an international reputation for sparkling wines by winning awards in Paris in 1872 and again in 1873 in Vienna. In March 1871, Charles D. Champlin (then owner) sent a case of sparkling wine to his close friend Colonel Marshall P. Wilder, a well-known Boston horticulturist and connoisseur. After introducing it at a dinner party at the Parker House, Wilder declared "this will be the great champagne of the Western world." The champagne was thus named Great Western.

Korbel Champagne Cellars of Sonoma County, California, the country's oldest producer of *méthode champenoise* sparkling wines, was established in 1882. Since 1954, it has been owned by the Heck family.

Korbel produces a fine line of California champagnes, which include: Blanc de Blancs, Blanc de Noirs, Natural, Rouge, Brut, Extra Dry, Sec, and Brut Rosé.

Schramsberg Champagne Cellars of Napa Valley, California was established in 1862 by Jacob Schram. In 1972 Schramsberg became an overnight success, when former president Richard M. Nixon took 13 cases of its sparkling wines to Peking's emperor, to be served during a televised banquet.

Sterling Vineyards of Napa Valley, California produces *Mumm Cuvée Napa,* an excellent sparkling wine.

Other U.S. sparkling wines are:

S. Anderson	J. Roget
B.V.	Maison Deutz
Chase-Lomogère	Mirassou
Château St. Jean	M. Tribaut
Cook's	Paul Masson
Culbertson	Piper Sonoma
Richard Cuneo	Roederer Estate
Domaine Carneros	Scharffenberger
Domaine Ste. Michelle	Sebastiani
Gloria Ferrer	Shadow Creek
Iron Horse	Wente Brothers

▶ SERVING AND STORING SPARKLING WINES

Contrary to popular belief, sparkling wine and champagne do not improve in the bottle; they are at their best when sold for consumption. A good rule of thumb is if the bottle contains a vintage date, purchase the latest year available, and don't purchase bottles more than ten years past the vintage date. The aging of sparkling wines refers to *en tirage* (on the yeast) in the winery, not in a home or restaurant cellar. Once the sediment is removed by disgorging, beneficial aging of sparkling wine halts and degenerative aging (an oxidative character much appreciated by some palates) begins. If the bottle does not contain a date, it is called a nonvintage (a blend of several years) wine and should be consumed within a six-month to one-year period.

Sparkling wine bottles should be stored standing up, in a cool (50 to 55 degrees Fahrenheit), relatively low-humidity (55 to 65 percent), dark area that is free from vibration. To keep *still wine* corks moist, it is necessary to store the bottle on its side or upside down. However, because of the nature of sparkling wine, the bottle can be stored upright. The reason is simple and this method of storage seems to have added benefits. A bottle of sparkling wine may contain five to six atmospheres of pressure. The air space (called *ullage*) in a sparkling wine bottle contains approximately 100 percent humidity. The high pressure in the sparkling wine drives the moist air into the cork so it maintains moisture and thus its elasticity and resilience. A benefit to storing bottles this way is that without the sparkling wine actually coming in contact with the cork during storage, it is less likely that unwanted odors or flavors will be extracted from the cork. Another benefit is that by upright storage, the incidence of *peg*-shaped corks are kept to a minimum.

To serve sparkling wine, place the bottle in the refrigerator for three to four hours, or use an ice bucket with plenty of ice and cold water to form an "ice bath." Ten to 15 minutes in this bath is sufficient. Sparkling wine can be put into the freezer for chilling, but it will generally take more than twice the time as an ice bucket.

An easy, on-the-spot ice chest can be constructed with an empty cardboard wine case. Remove the inserts, fold the flaps in, line the box with a heavy-duty plastic bag, and fill with ice and water.

The proper procedure for opening sparkling wine is shown in Figure 5-14. To uncork the bottle, carefully remove the foil capsule and then the wire hood by turning it counterclockwise. Next, hold the bottle at a 45-degree angle pointed away from you and anyone around you; while holding the cork firmly in one hand, twist the bottle in a downward motion with the other hand. Allow the cork to slowly ease out until a gentle "pop" is heard. Continue to hold the bottle at this angle for a few more moments to equalize the pressure inside the bottle. Then stand the bottle up; it is ready to pour. If the cork is very tight and difficult to remove, simply place the neck of the bottle under warm running water for a moment. This softens the cork's paraffin coating. If the head of a cork should accidentally break off, first wrap the bottle neck in a towel, then carefully use a corkscrew as in opening a still wine.

a   *b*   *c*

FIGURE 5-14 Step-by-step illustration of the proper method of opening bottles of sparkling wine. (Courtesy Sebastiani Vineyards, Sonoma, California)

Gently pour a small quantity of sparkling wine into each glass, then go back to the first glass and fill each glass until about three-quarters full. This avoids frothing over. Never add ice cubes to sparkling wine; they dilute the taste and cause the bubbles to quickly dissipate.

Correct glassware is most important in serving sparkling wines. During the time of Helen of Troy, milk was served from glasses in the shape of a woman's breast. The popular, flat saucer-shaped or "bird-bath" champagne glass allegedly derives its shape from a mold of Marie-Antoinette's (1755–1793) breasts. However, the saucer-shaped glass or *coupe* was created on June 30, 1663 by Venetian glassmakers at the Duke of Buckingham's glass factory in Greenwich, England. The Queen adored champagne and the glass was viewed as a salute to her good taste. Due to this glass's large surface area, sparkling wines served in it will lose their aroma, send a shower of foam into the mouth, and prematurely go flat. The proper glassware to use is either a fluted or tulip-shaped glass, holding approximately eight to ten ounces. The small-mouthed glass will concentrate the wine's bouquet and flavor as well as conserve its bubbles.

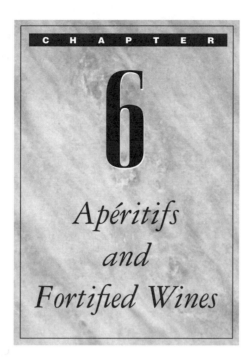

6

Apéritifs
and
Fortified Wines

or centuries aromatized and fortified wines have been savored like champagne; they have virtually no equal among table wines. Fortified wines have always been considered perfect for both beginning and ending elegant dinners. Aromatized and fortified wines have richer bouquets and tastes than table wines and a higher alcoholic content. Fortified wines are table wines to which brandy or other distilled spirits have been added to raise the alcoholic content to somewhere between 16 and 22 percent alcohol by volume. A subdivision of fortified wine is aromatized or aromatic wine.

The names of fortified and aromatized wines such as *vermouth, sherry, port, Madeira*, and *Marsala* are centuries old; however, modern production methods have changed and refined not only the wines, but also their patterns of consumption. Today's consumption levels are lower than those of the eighteenth and nineteenth centuries, but interest in these wines is constantly being generated, making the modern-day consumer considerably more knowledgeable about them than his ancestors.

▶ APÉRITIFS AND BITTERS (DIGESTIVES)

Federal regulations define an apéritif wine as "one with an alcoholic content of not less than 15 percent, made from grape wine containing added brandy or other distilled spirits. These wines are flavored with various herbs and other natural aromatic flavoring materials and possess the aroma, taste, and characteristics generally attributed to an apéritif wine."

Bitters (known as *amaro* in Italy) were originally produced to soothe and relax the stomach after meals and are therefore often referred to as "digestives." Alcoholic products from France that have the letter D stamped on their labels are also digestives.

Aperire, Latin for *to open,* is the origin of the word *apéritif*—a wine that usually "opens" lunch or dinner as a stimulant to the appetite. Most apéritifs have an initial sweet taste with a somewhat bitter aftertaste because of the use of quinine as one of the ingredients. This slight bitterness tends to whet the appetite and cleanse the palate. The French government mandates that apéritifs be produced at least 80 percent from wine with an alcoholic strength of at least ten percent before alcohol is added to raise the strength to between 16 and 19 percent.

Apéritifs are usually grouped into categories depending on the nature of their base ingredient. The following are distilled spirit-based:

Amer Picon	Jägermeister
Angostura	Mercedes Boonekamp
Aperol	Montenegro
Averna	Petrus Boonekamp Amaro
Biancosarti	Peychaud's
Campari	Ramazzotti
China Martini	Suze
CioCiaro	Underberg
Cynar	Unicum
Fernet Branca	

The apéritifs that follow are wine-based (often fortified with brandy or distilled spirits):

Byrrh	Port (white)
Cap Corse	Punt é Mes
Dry Marsala	Ratafia
Dubonnet (red and white)	Rosso Antico
Kir (white wine and Cassis)	Sherry (fino)
Lillet (red and white)	Sparkling wine*
Madeira (sercial)	Spritzer*
Mistelle	St. Raphaël
Panache	Vermouth (red and white)

Some of the more popular brands of apéritifs are:

Amer Picon (France; 80 proof): originally known as *Amer Africain* when produced in 1837 by Gaetan Picon, a sergeant in the French army serving in Algeria. He blended together local African oranges, gentian root, quinine bark, and alcohol. This apéritif is best when served with seltzer water and a twist of lemon.

Angostura Bitters (Trinidad; 90 proof): a concentrated, aromatic bitter flavoring from the island of Trinidad, used in certain cocktails. First sold in 1830 by a German-born medical doctor, Johann Gotlieb Benjamin Siegert. Angostura does not contain Angostura bark, but derives its name from the town of Angostura, Venezuela (renamed Ciudad Bolívar in 1846). Angostura is made from herbs and spices (among them gentian) from the Far East and various Caribbean islands under code names such as "Botanical Number Five." Alcohol is utilized instead of steam for flavor extraction. The extraction takes place for 20 hours and then the flavors sit in tanks for three months where they're allowed to marry. Afterwards it is diluted and allowed to stand for one month prior to bottling.

Aperol (Italy; 22 proof): developed in Italy by Silvio Barbieri in 1919. It has a luminous, distinctive deep orange color and is made from grain neutral distilled spirits with natural flavors.

Averna (Italy; 68 proof): one of Italy's many bittersweet apéritifs or digestives. First introduced in 1868 by Salvatore Averna, who discovered the unusual taste while at the Saint Spirito Abbey near Caltanisetta, Sicily. To honor his generosity to the abbey, the monks in 1854 gave Salvatore the secret recipe for this dark brown spirit. Since that time, a refinement of the product has taken place. Averna is made in stainless steel tanks, along with the traditional copper pots.

The aroma is colalike and taste is bittersweet, with hints of vanilla. It is one of the finest digestives made and is best when served at room temperature after dinner.

Biancosarti (Italy; 56 proof): produced by Luigi Sarti and Sons of Bologna, since

---

*Not fortified.

1885. It is a distilled spirit-based apéritif with a yellow color and a bouquet and initial taste of cloves and cinnamon. Its bittersweet flavor is reminiscent of vermouth. It is best served chilled from the refrigerator.

Byrrh (France): a proprietary *mistelle*-based apéritif first produced in 1866 in the Roussillon region. Byrrh has a ruby red color, hints of cocoa in its taste, and a bittersweet aftertaste. Byrrh is best when served with seltzer, over ice.

Campari (Italy; 48 proof): first developed shortly after 1862 by 14-year-old Gaspare Campari, a native of Cassolnovo in the province of Pavia, southwest of Milan. Campari, who was the proprietor of a cafe, tirelessly pursued distillation experiments in the cafe's basement until his elixir was developed. Campari was originally called *Bitter d'Olanda* (bitter in the fashion of the Dutch), but later he substituted his own name on the label. This ruby-red, bitter beverage is a mixture of aromatic extractions from herbs, roots, plants, and fruits. In 1882 Cordial Campari, a flavorful and sweet, yet not bitter liqueur was invented. In 1932 a premixed Campari and soda was first introduced by Davide Campari, based upon the overwhelming popularity of that beverage. It is currently sold in more than 170 countries. Campari is best when served with seltzer water and a twist of lemon.

Cynar (Italy; 34 proof): a zesty, bittersweet apéritif, made from artichokes. It was conceived in 1950 by Angelo Dalle Molle. A. Charles Castelli, the company's current U.S. president, has stated that Cynar "makes what follows taste softer, taste better." This assertion was based in part on a scientific research paper presented in 1934. Dr. Linda Bartoshuk (Yale Taste Physiologist) found that after eating globe artichokes as a salad course, 60 percent of 250 participants in her study reported that water tasted different—some claimed that it even tasted sweet. Cynar is best when served over ice with a twist of lemon or orange.

Dubonnet (United States; 18 percent alcohol): first formulated by Joseph Dubonnet in 1846 in Chambéry, France. The red and white Dubonnet wines have a semidry taste and a full-bodied flavor. Dubonnet was first introduced into the United States in 1934 and nowadays is produced in the United States under French license. It is best when chilled from the refrigerator or over ice with a twist of lemon.

Fernet Branca (Italy; 80 proof): a dark-brown, extremely bitter beverage, introduced by Maria Scala of Milan, in 1845. Fernet contains more than 40 herbs and spices (myrrh, rhubarb, chamomile, cardamom, and saffron, among others) in a base of grape alcohol. It was the only alcoholic beverage that was allowed to be imported into the United States during Prohibition. It is best when served at room temperature as an apéritif, after dinner as a digestive, or in espresso coffee.

Jägermeister (Germany; 70 proof): a dark red, bitter beverage, made from 56 botanicals, fruits, and herbs including aniseed, citrus peel, ginger, ginseng, juniper berries, licorice, poppy seeds, and saffron, which have been steeped in alcohol.

Kir (France): this drink was named after the late mayor of the City of Dijon, France,

Canon Félix Kir. Kir was the favorite drink of the mayor from the 1940s until his death in 1968 at age 92. Originally, Kir was made by mixing Aligoté wine (a highly acidic white wine from Burgundy) with a tablespoon or so of crème de cassis and served chilled. Nowadays, virtually any white wine is used and mixed with several teaspoons to one-third of a glass of crème de cassis. Cassis is a black currant liqueur; to ensure one is using the best cassis, only those labeled Crème de Cassis should be used. Bottles labeled Liqueur de Cassis refer to a liqueur made from black currants macerated in brandy with added sugar.

Lillet (France): the firm was founded by Paul and Raymond Lillet in 1872, in the small town of Podensac, near Bordeaux. Lillet (both red and white) is a blend of selected aromatic herbs and fruits steeped with a portion of the base wine (which is a white Bordeaux from Graves, Premières Côtes or Entre-Deux-Mers; made from Sauvignon Blanc, Sémillon, Ugni Blanc, and Muscadelle grapes) and quinine for a period of one month. The naturally flavored wine is then mixed in a proportion (known only to the family) with the remaining wine. French brandy is added, then the blend is aged for three years in oak barrels.

Lillet has a fruity bouquet, a trace of citrus essence, and a slightly astringent flavor. It is best when served well chilled on the rocks with a twist of lemon or slice of orange, or with a splash of tonic or seltzer water.

Mistelles (also known as *mutes*): these are sweet wines produced by arresting or preventing fermentation by the addition of distilled spirits. The process is called *mutage.* Some mistelles are used in making apéritifs and vermouths; others stand alone as apéritifs. Some examples are Panache, Pineau de Charentes, and Ratafia de Champagne.

Panache (18 percent alcohol): produced in California by Domaine Chandon, Panache is a Pinot Noir wine-based apéritif, made by selecting Pinot Noir juice that is either too highly colored or too fruity for sparkling winemaking, and blending it with pure distilled spirits (about 192 proof) before the juice ferments. Unlike a *ratafia,* Panache is not wood aged, so it retains a brighter color and fresher, fruitier flavor. This is an apéritif with about 10 percent residual sugar, a sprightly acidity, and a fresh, fruity flavor. It is best when served chilled from the refrigerator or over ice with a twist of lemon. One of the best recipes (called a *Chandon Judy*) using Panache calls for pouring it over ice with a twist of lemon and adding one to two drops of bitters and a splash of Domaine Chandon Brut sparkling wine.

Peychaud's Bitters (United States; 70 proof): a type of bitters produced in New Orleans, used almost exclusively in the Sazerac cocktail. In the early 1800s, Antoine Amedie Peychaud, an apothecary, gained fame in New Orleans not for the drugs he dispensed, but for the compounding of a liquid tonic called bitters.

Pineau de Charentes (France; 17 percent alcohol): similar to Panache, it is produced by adding cognac to the *must,* thus stopping the fermentation of the fresh wine. All of the wine used must be at least 10 percent alcohol by volume and the cognac must be of *three-*

star (minimum of three years old) quality. The combined wine and cognac is placed in barrels and aged for two years in *Limousin* (a type of oak tree from the Limousin forest) oak. The wine is filtered several times before bottling to clear it of any sediment that has developed. Pineau de Charentes has been produced in the Cognac region since the sixteenth century. French law (since 1945) requires that only growers are permitted to produce Pineau and only in years when the sugar content in the grape is sufficient to produce wines of 10 percent alcohol by volume. *Reynac* is the brand name of Pineau supported by the 4,500 growers of Unicoop cooperative.

Ratafia (France): similar to Panache. The first written reference to ratafia appears in the eighteenth-century records of the French champagne house of Veuve Clicquot, although there is speculation that it was produced much earlier. Ratafias are generally aged for one year in wooden barrels, which gives the final product an *oxidized* (darkened color and loss of freshness) color and taste. U.S. federal regulations prohibit use of the name *ratafia* for an American-made product. Hence, Domaine Chandon calls its *ratafia* Panache.

Rosso Antico (Italy): a mixture of wines from Lake Garda, blended with aromatic herbs; first produced in 1820. A brownish-red color, with light chocolate overtones in the taste. A slight bitter finish and aftertaste is characteristic of this beverage. Rosso Antico is best when served chilled from the refrigerator with a lemon or orange peel and a splash of seltzer water.

Spritzers: delightful and refreshing drinks made with white, rosé, or red wines, mixed with seltzer, tonic water, or ginger ale, and garnished with lemon, lime, orange, a sprig of mint, or even a cherry. Spritzers are served on ice.

Underberg (Germany): In 1846, Underberg's founding father, Hubert Underberg, launched his unique product on the market. Underberg's taste derives from a careful selection of natural herbs from 43 countries. It has an intense aroma of aniseed and licorice, with edges of sweetness, followed by a sweet mint flavor with hints of licorice, herbs, and spices. It is available in its distinctive miniature bottle with its strawpaper wrapping and green label. The two-milliliter bottle is the only size Underberg produces.

Unicum (Hungary): a dark brown, distilled spirit-based beverage, first produced in 1790, by Dr. Joseph Swack of Hungary. Unicum is a bittersweet beverage, distilled from a blend of more than 40 herbs, spices, and roots, and aged six months in barrels. It is sold in its familiar round bottle with a white cross on the label.

Serving and Storing Apéritifs

Apéritifs can be served at room temperature or well chilled, either directly from the refrigerator (this is the best way) or with plenty of *fresh* ice. (Fresh ice is important because when ice sits for more than three weeks it starts to absorb odors from frozen foods and actually becomes stale.) Wine-based apéritifs are approximately 18 percent alcohol and do not keep forever once opened. The shelf life (unrefrigerated and opened) is not more than three to four weeks. Therefore, opened bottles should be refrigerated and consumed within six weeks.

▶ VERMOUTH

According to the Bureau of Alcohol, Tobacco, and Firearms (BATF), vermouth is a type of apéritif wine that is made from grape juice and has the taste, aroma, and characteristics generally attributed to vermouth. The BATF regulations also state that apéritif wines fulfilling the characteristics of vermouth shall be so designated.

Vermouth is classified as an *aromatized* or *aromatic* wine, containing 15 to 21 percent alcohol.

Hippocrates (460–377 B.C.), the Greek physician and "father of medicine," can be credited with the "discovery" of vermouth. His flavoring of wine with cinnamon and honey may have not closely resembled present-day vermouth, but it is certainly the earliest record of the production of infused wine. In sixteenth-century Germany, Rhine wines were occasionally flavored with wormwood shrub flowers to give them a rather spicy but pleasant taste. The German word for wormwood is *wermut*; when the Latin countries emerged as the chief producers of this type of wine in the eighteenth century, the word *wermut* was written as *vermouth*.

The wine, as we know it today, originated in Turin, Italy in approximately 1757. Antonio Benedetto Carpano didn't introduce vermouth commercially until 1776, under the name Carpano. The French dry version was first produced in 1800, by Joseph Noilly, who later joined forces with Claudius Prat.

Since that time, both Italy and France have mastered the art of infusing and fortifying wine and are the largest producers of high-quality vermouth.

How Vermouth Is Made

After the basic wines (blend of many) have been fermented and aged separately, they are blended, one of them having been lightly fortified with brandy or other distilled spirits. They are then stored in a large tank or pot still for many months with an infusion of herbs or flavoring agents. The herbs and spices are macerated and steeped in the wine, in a process known as *infusion*, much as tea is infused into boiling water.

When the flavoring agents are sufficiently infused, the wine is carefully separated from the herbs and placed into large glass-lined tanks where the temperature is brought to nearly freezing. This refrigeration allows for the precipitation of excessive potassium tartrate crystals that might show up later in the finished wine. These wines are then agitated constantly with long wooden paddles to ensure proper blending.

After allowing the wine to age, sometimes as long as four years, it is filtered and the color "adjusted." Adjusting means that caramel coloring is added to the wines to make the "red" sweet vermouth, or, if the color in the white vermouth becomes too dark, it is blended with lighter colored vermouths of the same type.

Vermouth's Ingredients

Vermouth, although fortified, is often referred to as an "aromatized" wine, meaning a wine that has been altered by the infusion of *Artemisia absinthium* (any number of related aromatic plants) or bitter herbs. Some of the ingredients used (there are more than 100) are: allspice, angelica, angostura, anise, benzoin, bitter almond, bitter orange, celery, chamomile, cinchona, cinnamon, clove, coca, coriander, elder, fennel, gentian, ginger, hop, marjoram, mace, myrtle, nutmeg, peach, quinine, rhubarb, rosemary, saffron, sage, sandalwood, savory (summer), thyme, vanilla, woodruff (May Wine).

Types of Vermouth

The red vermouths, most notably those from Italy and France, are always sweet and contain approximately 130 to 160 grams of sugar per liter (13 to 16 percent residual sugar per 100 milliliters). The white vermouths, also mainly from Italy and France, can be dry or sweet and contain less than 40 grams of sugar per liter (4 percent or less residual sugar per 100 milliliters).

Vermouth Brand Names

Some of the better-known brands of vermouth are listed below.

Cinzano (Italy): The house of Cinzano of Turin was established in 1757 by two brothers, Carlo Stefano and Giovanni Giacomo Cinzano. Cinzano produces a sweet red, extra dry white, and sweet white vermouth as well as a special formula labeled Antica.

Noilly Prat (France): Noilly Prat was established in 1813, when Claudius Prat joined forces with Louis Noilly, whose father had been making Noilly vermouth since 1800 in Marseilles. Noilly Prat makes a dry white and a sweet red vermouth.

Punt é Mes (Italy): Perhaps the most famous of all vermouths is this one from the Carpano family of Italy. Punt é Mes' history began in 1786, in the Piazza Castello in Turin, where Antonio Benedetto Carpano, a well-respected bar and restaurant owner, tailored his vermouths to fit the individual preferences of his customers—adding a bit more of one herb or another, or a higher proportion of bitters (quinine). This was known as ordering vermouth by "points." It was said that one evening a group of businessmen involved in the stock exchange met at Antonio's bar. One of them, still in conversation about the daily fluctuations of the market, absentmindedly told the barman "Ca'm dag'n *punt é mes*" ("give me a point and a half," in Piemontese dialect), which caused great laughter in the bar. This story is purported to be fact and was confirmed by its last living witness, Maurizio Boeris, a barman, who died in 1944.

St. Raphaël (France; 16 percent alcohol): This vermouth is made in both a red and white version (although solely the red is sold in the United States). St. Raphaël was first produced in 1830 by a young Frenchman, Dr. Pierre Jupet of Lyons, from a mixture of huckleberry, Peruvian bark, cocoa, essences of sweet and bitter orange, bitter orange peels, and vanilla, in a red wine base. St. Raphaël is bittersweet in flavor and when mixed with equal parts of orange juice and poured over ice, makes a wonderful refreshing drink for anytime of the day.

Some other brands of vermouth from Italy are *Berberini, Cora, Duval, Gancia, Martini & Rossi, Mirafiore, Ricadonna, Stock*, and *Boissiere* from France, and *Votrix* from England.

Serving and Storing Vermouth

Vermouth is basically a wine and should be treated as such. Once opened, it should be refrigerated and consumed within six weeks. After six weeks the sweet and especially the dry vermouth takes on a darker color and has a somewhat musty, "off" odor. When serving vermouth, use plenty of ice and fresh citrus fruits. Dry vermouth is the indisputable and essential ingredient for a gin or vodka martini. If a dry vermouth is to be used only for martinis, it is advisable to purchase it in half-bottles (375 milliliters) to maintain freshness.

Vermouth can be served chilled "straight up," or over ice with a twist of lemon. A drink called a "blonde and a redhead" is made with equal parts of dry white and sweet red vermouth.

▶ SHERRY

Sherry is a fortified and blended nonvintage wine (although some vintage-dated sherry is produced) made via the *solera system* and contains 17 to 22 percent alcohol. It is traditionally produced in Spain, although certain other countries produce a similar product that they also call sherry.

Sherry originated in southwest Andalusía, about 90 miles inland from the sea in the region of Jerez. The town of Jerez was founded by the Phoenicians in 1100 B.C., when they brought their sailing ships to an inland city near the Bay of Cádiz off the Atlantic coast and named it *Xera*. After the Roman conquest, Xera was Latinized to *Ceret,* which the Moors pronounced as *Scherris.* This was subsequently Hispanified to *Jerez* and Anglicized (in reference to the beverage) into *sherry.*

The Jerez area is triangular in shape and lies between the Guadalquivir and the Guadalete rivers in southwest Spain, with the Atlantic Ocean on the west. The official sherry-producing zone, known as the *zone de Jerez superiore* or "zone of superior sherry," is bounded by three major towns: Puerto de Santa María, Sanlúcar de Barrameda, and Jerez de la Frontera. The entire Jerez area consists of some 28,325 acres of vineyards (1991).

Laws and Regulations

The Spanish regulatory agency established in 1933 to guarantee the authenticity of sherry is the Consejo Regulador de la Denominación de Origen Jerez-Xérès-Sherry (DO).

The tribunal High Court of England ruled in 1967 that only wine from Jerez may be identified simply as sherry and that imitations must be labeled by their country of origin.

Grape Varieties

Palomino Fino grapes are pale in color, fairly large, and grow primarily in *albariza,* a chalky-type soil, considered by many to produce the very best sherry. This grape, which is used in making 85 percent of all sherry wine, is also known locally by many different names such as *Listán,* in Sanlúcar; *Horgazuela,* in Puerto de Santa María; *Alban, Temprana,* and *Tempranilla* in other areas.

Pedro Ximénez and Moscatel grapes are used to sweeten sherry wine. The Pedro Ximénez grapes grow on the lower slopes of the *albariza* and *barro* soil, while Moscatel grapes grow chiefly on *barro* soil (a heavy, dark soil, with some chalk, but mostly made of clay and sand).

The Sherry Production Process

Grapes destined to be made into sherry are harvested, crushed, and destemmed, and immediately sent to a press, where the first 85 to 90 percent of the liquid obtained is used to produce sherry. The remaining 10 to 15 percent, which is usually of a lower quality, is distilled into brandy, to be used later to fortify the sherry wine.

The *must* is allowed to ferment in large, temperature-controlled stainless steel tanks. After all the sugar has been metabolized by the yeast, resulting in a wine with 11 to 13 percent alcohol, the wine is racked off the *lees*. It is then put into other barrels which are only partially (about 80 percent) filled and loosely "bunged," which helps develop the sherry style.

The wine is then fortified with brandy made from sherry wine, raising its alcoholic content to 15 percent. The high alcohol favors the *flor* action and is sufficiently high enough to prevent acetification (vinegar production). *Flor* is a yeastlike substance *(Saccharomyces cerevisiae)* that forms a whitish film on the surface of certain sherries when the temperature in the cellar is between 60 and 70 degrees Fahrenheit. After a year or so the wine under the *flor* develops a distinctive yeasty taste, which is technically due to a large increase in the aldehyde (a liquid with a distinct odor, which is a by-product of fermentation) content of the wine. The longer the sherry "sits on" the *flor,* the more flavor it extracts and the finer it becomes.

All types of sherry start out the same, but for some unknown reason *flor* forms on the surface of some barrels of sherry and not on others. When the *flor* forms a very thick white blanket, the sherry becomes a *fino*. If a thinner film forms, the sherry becomes an *amontillado*. If no film forms, the sherry becomes an *oloroso*.

After a period of 18 to 24 months of aging undisturbed under the blanket of *flor* (if it forms), the wine is transferred to the winery's *solera* system. A *fino* will be sent to the *fino solera,* an *amontillado* to the *amontillado solera,* and so on.

According to some sherry producers, *solera* comes from the word *suelo,* meaning ground or land, and refers to the butts (barrels) nearest to the ground. Others say that it comes from the Spanish word *solar,* which refers to the tradition that holds a family together. Still others believe it derives from the Latin *solum,* meaning floor, as specifically, it is the bottom-most tier in the aging system.

The *solera* system involves a series of white American oak barrels, generally containing 130 gallons, arranged in rows or tiers, usually four barrels high (Figure 6-1). How-

FIGURE 6-1   Rows of barrels containing *oloroso* sherry in various stages of aging in the solera system. (Courtesy Sherry Wine Institute, New York)

ever, some *soleras* utilize as many as 14 barrels. The arranging of barrels in tiers is not a requirement of the system or the law. The original or bottom row of barrels is called the *solera,* while the upper, or younger rows, which are on the top, are called the *criaderas* (cradles). Each row is known as a scale and moving the wine from tier to tier is often referred to as "playing the scales."

The wine first sold is that on the bottom row, which is then replaced with wine from the second tier, and so on up through as many as 14 tiers. The wine from the most recent vintage is poured into the barrels on the top tier, which were not completely filled, thus the youngest wine is blended with a slightly older wine of the same type, which in turn has been blended with a still older wine, and so on down through the tiers. Wines of a superior quality are created through this "fractional blending."

Wine is not siphoned from tier to tier, but rather is transferred into containers so that wine from various barrels on the same level can be blended for even further standardization. By law, the maximum amount that can be drawn out of a barrel of fully mature sherry is 33 percent. Sherry wines must age a minimum of three years in oak barrels before bottling; some, however, are much older when they are bottled.

One of the reasons for the blending is to "tame" the young, rough wine. The key to the *solera* system is that aged sherries in the bottom "educate" the younger ones by giving them character and taste. The wine is also aerated as it passes from tier to tier and in addition picks up subtle nuances from the oak barrels.

During this entire process, approximately 10 percent of the wine is lost through evaporation, whereas in an aging cellar, where the barrels are tightly bunged, the amount would be only 1.5 to 2 percent.

Blending.   There are basically four types of sherry (in ascending order of sweetness): *fino, amontillado, oloroso,* and *cream.* These are broken down into subgroups, which will be discussed later.

All sherries coming out of the *solera* are bone dry in taste, since during fermentation all sugar was metabolized by the yeast. At this point a determination of the desired degree of sweetness of the final product is made. Sweet sherries, cream (also brown), and *oloroso* are made by blending sweet wines made from the juice of Pedro Ximénez and Moscatel grapes. The Pedro Ximénez grapes are left outside in the sun for 12 to 14 hours to dry after harvesting, which concentrates their sugar levels. They are then placed on *esparto* mats (made of straw) to dry further. So intense is their sweetness that fermentation usually stops at about 14 percent alcohol, resulting in a high degree of residual sugar.

Before final bottling, the sherry is additionally fortified with brandy, raising its alcohol content to 17 to 22 percent. The sherry is then refrigerated for several days to help "stabilize" it, eliminating cloudiness in the final product.

The Major Styles of Sherry

Fino sherries are made entirely from Palomino grapes and are very dry, light, and pale in color, with a distinctive mild nutty-tangy taste.

Amontillado sherries have more color and body than *finos,* with a medium dry taste and nutty flavor. True *amontillado* sherries are the best to use for cooking, for they impart a nutty-tangy flavor to food. *Fino* sherry is too dry for cooking and seems to lack the *amontillado* sherries' charm and depth, while *oloroso* and cream sherries are simply too sweet. Amontillado sherry is also known as *cocktail sherry* or *dry sherry.*

Oloroso sherries are even fuller-bodied and have a deeper color than either *fino* or *amontillado* sherries. *Olorosos* are semisweet and display a more well-rounded flavor than the others.

Cream sherries are a rich, deep amber to a golden brown in color, and usually display an exquisite bouquet. They are very sweet and "creamy" to the taste. (An even sweeter cream sherry, made entirely from Pedro Ximénez grapes, is called a "brown" sherry.)

Other Sherries

Other sherries, which are not as popular or easy to find, are:

Manzanilla.   This is the palest, lightest, and driest *fino*-style sherry made. *Manzanilla* sherries are produced in the town of Sanlúcar de Barrameda, near the coast, at the mouth of the Guadalquivir River, approximately 10 to 15 miles outside of Jerez.

The grape harvest is usually about one week earlier in Sanlúcar than in other parts of the Jerez district. Therefore, the grapes usually come into the winery with slightly lower sugar levels and a higher level of tartaric acid. In many parts of Jerez it is the usual practice to dry the grapes in the sun to concentrate the grape sugars, but this is frequently eliminated in order to make *manzanilla.* These underripe grapes evolve, with the help of the ocean breezes, into fruit from which can be produced a fresh, clean, delicate, and extremely light and dry sherry. *Manzanilla* sherries are also more astringent or "tonic" in taste than *fino* sherries, which is probably due to both the ocean breezes and the unique soil content of the vineyards where the grapes are grown.

The characteristic saltiness or tanginess of this wine has caused writers and winemakers to speculate on its uniqueness. It was originally believed that because of the salty sea breezes, the grapes and resulting wine retained the salty taste. However, it has been demonstrated that when *must* or wine from Jerez is transported to Sanlúcar and allowed to obtain its natural *flor,* the resulting wine acquires the *manzanilla*-type salty taste. Also demonstrated was that when *must* or wine from Sanlúcar was transported to Jerez, it took on the characteristics of a *fino* sherry, but with more saltiness. A reasonable explanation is that Sanlúcar, because of its close proximity to the sea, has an unusually high water table with numerous shallow wells; it is considered the wettest spot in the entire Jerez area. The sherry *flor* yeast *Saccharomyces beticus* thrives on this wetness, thereby imparting the unique salty flavor to the wines, which can be described as "olive brine."

Manzanilla sherry is pale green to gold in color, with a bouquet that is reminiscent of the taste of a ripe apple. It is slightly bitter in taste and should always be served chilled (not over ice); if refrigerated after opening, it will keep for several weeks. *Manzanillas* are usually at their best if consumed within six months of bottling. Unfortunately, *manzanilla* is made in small quantities and therefore has a limited distribution in the United States.

Palo cortado.   This is a true rarity among sherries. Although there is no literal translation for *palo cortado,* these sherries have been described as belonging to an intermediate classification—they are the lightest of the *olorosos. Palo cortado* has a very fresh and clean bouquet, somewhat resembling a well-made *amontillado,* yet its taste is reminiscent of a full-bodied *oloroso.*

Like all fine sherries, the *palo cortados* are produced from Palomino grapes that are grown in the chalky *albariza* soil unique to the Jerez region. They do not develop any type of *flor* and are quite rare. Of a thousand barrels of wine, perhaps only one will develop the distinctive color of brushed gold, the bouquet of almonds, the *amontillado*, nose, and the *oloroso* body, which are characteristic of *palo cortados*. Therefore, a sherry producer cannot produce this style of sherry every year and its production amounts to less than 1 percent of the total. The production of *palo cortado* was greatly cut because of the devastation of *phylloxera* during the 1880s.

Palo cortado is an elegant wine and should be enjoyed as one would a brandy or liqueur. It will keep for many weeks without refrigeration. As with all sherry styles, each *bodega* (winery) strives for individuality in its brand, so that color, bouquet, and flavor will vary from producer to producer.

Pedro Ximénez.   This is the sweetest and most viscous of the sherries. It is a rich, dark brown and liqueurlike in its concentration. It is traditionally served after meals in place of a brandy or liqueur. Pedro Ximénez will keep opened for many weeks without refrigeration.

Serving and Storing Sherry

Sherry is a wine and storage conditions applicable to wine apply to sherry. Most sherries come in either screw-top bottles or bottles with re-corkable tops and can thus be stored standing up. There is really no reason to store sherry for prolonged periods of time because it does not improve to any great degree with age and is usually ready to drink when bottled.

A *fino* or *amontillado* sherry should be refrigerated when opened and is best when consumed at up to three weeks. *Oloroso* and cream sherries are generally kept unrefrigerated and are best when consumed up to six weeks.

When serving a *fino* or *amontillado* (before dinner, as apéritifs), they should be prechilled and at no time should be served over ice, which would dilute their flavor. *Oloroso* and cream sherries are best when served at room temperature (65 to 68 degrees Fahrenheit); traditionally they are after-dinner drinks.

The Spaniards have special "tulip-shaped" glasses for sherry—the six-ounce stemmed glass called *copa* and the four-ounce *copita*. Both glasses allow for a generous serving of sherry with enough space to release the wine's complex bouquet. A four-ounce *whiskey sour* glass, which is similar in shape, is highly preferable to the two-ounce style filled to the brim, as is often seen in bars and restaurants.

The small, stumpy, and cylindrical glass in which *manzanilla* sherry is traditionally drunk is known as a *cañas.*

▶ PORT

Port has been the official drink used for toasts by the English royal family for more than two centuries. And the history of Port in Portugal dates to before the birth of Christ. In fact, the Douro is the world's second legally demarcated wine region (the first, Italy's Chianti Classico region, was demarcated in 1716 by the grand duke of Tuscany). In 1756, during the era of the Marquês of Pombal (almost 200 years before France's *appellation contrôlée* regulations became law), the Douro region was defined to protect the quality and good name of port (known as *Porto,* in Portugal).

The production of port is limited to a strictly defined area of approximately 68,000 acres along the River Douro in the Alto Douro (Upper Douro) region. The slopes of the Douro, which have a very slatelike soil known as *schist,* are cut out and terraced for planting with vineyards. These walled terraces prevent erosion of the precious soil.

Grape Varieties Used

More than 40 grape varieties are planted in the region and used to produce port (red and white); the varieties listed below are those most commonly utilized:

White	*Red*
Códega	Bastardo
Malvasia Fina	Mourisco Tinto
Rabigato	Tinta Amarella
Verdelho	Tinta Barroca
Viosinho	Tinto Cão
	Tinta Francisca
	Tinto Roriz
	Touriga Francesa
	Touriga Nacional

Production

When it is determined that the sugar level in the fermenting *must* is about 10 percent (generally in less than five days), it is poured into barrels that contain a predetermined amount of Portuguese brandy. The brandy utilized for Port contains 77 percent alcohol by volume. Since 1992, the Portuguese government no longer controls the distribution of brandy. The two are then mixed; the proportions being usually 80 percent new wine and 20 percent brandy. At this point, fermentation is arrested by the brandy, leaving a wine with a high degree of sugar and an alcoholic content of approximately 18 to 22 percent. The wine is then barrel aged for a minimum of three years, except for vintage port, which is aged only two.

It wasn't until 1678 that brandy or distilled spirits were first added to the *musts* of port wines made in the Douro region that were destined for export. But this was in order to keep the wines sound during voyage. The process of arresting fermentation by brandy probably became the general rule around 1840.

Quality Controls and Regulations

The production and marketing of port are strictly controlled by the Instituto do Vinho do Porto (Port Wine Institute), set up in June 1933. Stringent laws govern the production of all port from the grapevine to the final product. An official certificate of origin is issued by the Port Wine Institute after careful tasting and examination of each lot. The official seal of guarantee over the neck of the bottle indicates approval by the Port Wine Institute.

The name *Porto* is also specifically protected by law in the United States. Since 1968, the only wine in the United States that can be called *Porto* is the fortified wine produced in Portugal's Douro region. Therefore, if a California wine producer decided to produce a portlike wine, he may not call it *Porto*; it must simply be labeled a port.

Types of Port

White port.   White port tends to run from dry and slightly tangy to medium sweet. Generally, the *must* is allowed to ferment longer (close to dryness) than for wines destined to become red port. Although some white port appears to be slightly oxidized, the drier ones are perfect apéritifs to be served slightly chilled.

Ruby port.   Traditionally, this is the very youngest port, which takes its name from its ruby color. Ruby port, by law, must be aged in wood a minimum of three years or so and bottled while it still retains its deep red color and vigorous taste. It is usually rich and fruity and is best consumed when young. No cellaring is necessary.

Tawny port.   The name is derived from the tawny color of the wine, which comes from long maturing in barrels, causing the wine to lose some of its redness. Much smoother than ruby port, tawny port usually spends a minimum of six to eight years in barrel (which helps round out the fieriness of the alcohol), resulting in a wine with a smooth texture and a touch of sweetness. Some tawny ports are described as having a nutty smell and taste. Tawny port does not improve significantly in the bottle, for it has already matured in the barrel and is ready to consume. Tawny ports that state they are ten, 20, or even 30 years of age are referred to as *Port with an Indication of Age.*

Late-bottled Vintage port.   (Often referred to as LBV, the *V* standing for vintage.) It is a port of a single vintage declared by the shipper from March 1 to September 30 during the fourth year after the vintage. The port is bottled between July 1 of that year and December 31 of the sixth year after harvest. Generally, late-bottled vintage port is made from vintages not declared as vintage ports and is usually ready to drink when released. Late-bottled vintage port replaced what was known as *crusted ports.*

Vintage port. This is by far the greatest of all ports. Vintage port constitutes only about 2 percent of port production and is produced only in years that are declared by the majority of shippers to be the very best (usually only three or four vintages in a decade). A vintage port must be declared by the shipper between January 1 and September 30 of the second year after the harvest. It is aged for two years in wooden barrels, then bottled somewhere between July 1 of the second year and June 30 of the third year after the harvest. Vintage port is very difficult to drink in its youth because it is fiery and peppery, with an almost black color. Its sweetness is masked by concentrated packed fruit, high extract, and dry, mouth-puckering tannins. However, those who are patient enough to wait 15 to 20 years will be rewarded with one of the world's greatest fortified wines. Surprisingly, it was not until 1775 that the first vintage port was produced. Beginning with vintages after 1970, all port must be bottled by the producer, and since 1975, all vintage port must be bottled in Oporto.

Other Terminology

Quinta. A wine estate, equivalent to a French château; or a single-vineyard designation.

Colheita. Basically an aged tawny port, Colheita is another name often used to denote a "port of (year)." Colheita ports must be a minimum of seven years of age prior to bottling.

Port of (Year). A port of a single vintage; this is actually a tawny port, aged in wood, versus bottle-aging.

Serving Port

Due to its high alcohol and sugar levels, port is usually best consumed during cool or cold weather. When it is time to open a bottle of vintage port, the bottle should be stood upright for three to five days, which allows the crusted sediment to settle to the bottom. The bottle should be opened at least one to two hours prior to drinking, which will dissipate any "off" odors or gases that might have developed under the cork. Port need not be chilled and is best when drunk at cellar temperature. (See *The Art of Decanting Wine* in Chapter 14.)

Contrary to popular belief, port has a limited shelf life once opened and should be consumed within several weeks. Vintage port deteriorates eight to 24 hours after opening and should be consumed at one sitting.

▶ MADEIRA

The island of Madeira, in the Atlantic Ocean some 360 miles from the coast of Morocco, was discovered in 1418 by Captain João Gonçalvez, a Portuguese explorer during the rule of Prince Henry the Navigator. Gonçalvez was nicknamed "O Zarco The Squinter" and upon being knighted, took the surname Zarco. The island showed no sign of earlier occupation and because of its dense covering of forest, was given the Portuguese name *Madeira* (island of wood). Before the island could be occupied, huge coast-to-coast forests had to be burned. It was reported that "operation fire" actually lasted some seven years! When the ashes finally blended with the fertile volcanic earth, a unique soil was formed composed of deep deposits of wood ash and humus, which is ideal for the making of Madeira wines.

The wines coming from Madeira were great American favorites in the 1600s, but in 1665, King Charles II of England (who was married to Catherine of Bragança), prohibited all exports of European goods to the West Indies and the American colonies, unless these were transported in British ships from English ports. In a show of defiance against the British Crown, the colonists imported Madeira wine, which was presumed to come from Africa, and therefore not under English control. The wines were generally sold under the grape name, shipper's name, the name of wealthy families that cellared them for years, and occasionally, the name of the ship that the wine came over on, and the year it was imported. Some of the names used were: Success, Charming Martha, Richmond Packet, Charming Nancy, Charming Polly, Hurricane, Earthquake, and Widow 1859. Madeira was cheap and quite long-lived, so spoilage was not a problem.

The Portuguese were doing quite well in the making and shipping of Madeira wine, but as luck may have it, the island of Madeira was struck with two catastrophic disasters. In 1852 *oïdium* (powdery mildew) ravaged the grapevines and the island looked as if someone poured "baby powder" over it. When the growers were just recovering from the *oïdium* disaster, the second and more intense disaster struck; *Phylloxera* in 1872, nearly destroying all the grapevines. A major replanting process took place in the late 1800s, where American rootstocks were grafted onto the grapevines of the island.

The Production of Madeira

Madeira is a fortified wine (beginning in 1753), with an alcoholic content of 17 to 20 percent due to the addition of a 96 proof brandy. The sweeter Madeiras (Bual and Malmsey) are fortified with distilled spirits (while they still contain some residual sugar) before being put through the *estufagem* process. The dry styles (Sercial, Verdelho and Rainwater) are allowed to ferment completely dry and are then put through the *estufagem* process prior to being fortified. Madeira owes its characteristic flavor to the fact that it is kept at high temperatures from 90 days to six months in a special hot room ("hot house") or chambers called *estufa*. These *estufas* heat the wine to a temperature of 104 to 120 degrees Fahrenheit for up to five months, then during the sixth month, the temperature is allowed to drop to 72 degrees Fahrenheit. The *estufa* gives the wine its characteristic cooked and burnt odor and taste. Madeira is uniquely rich in flavor with a sort of nutty, smoky, silky, burnt raisin, caramel taste. Its undertones are unmistakably of burnt wood with a tangy taste.

The origin of the use of *estufas* was an accidental discovery. The original exporters discovered that when Madeira was transported through the tropics in large sailing ships, it was of far better quality when it arrived at its destination than when it left the island. Madeira underwent a transformation from an ordinary table wine to a rich, complex wine with a nutty-tangy flavor. For this reason and because it made wonderful ballast, Madeira was loaded onto ships bound for the East or West Indies and brought back months later for re-export to Europe. This wine would be called East India Madeira, which in fact greatly contributed to its increasing popularity. At that time, Madeira was shipped in large barrels called *pipes,* which contained approximately 110 gallons of wine. In the 1790s, during the Napoleonic wars, it was difficult to find enough ships to make these round-the-world trips; there was also a blockade on all imports to the Americas. The Portuguese producers were therefore forced to find a new way to create the complex Madeiras without the hot voyages. Hence, the *estufagem* system was born.

Types of Madeira

There are five types of Madeira, four of which are named after the grape variety used. From the driest to the sweetest, they are:

Sercial.   The sercial grape variety is viticulturally similar to the German Johannisberg Riesling and was in fact brought to Madeira from Germany. In reality, it bears absolutely no resemblance to the Johannisberg Riesling in taste. Sercial is the driest Madeira; it is similar to a *fino* sherry, although slightly sweeter.

Verdelho.   The Verdelho grape is believed to be a cross between the Spanish Pedro Ximénez and the Greek Verdea grape varieties. The wine is semidry and has a clean taste and a gentle, smooth flavor. It is the perfect Madeira to use when cooking, because it lends just enough flavor to the food.

Rainwater.   This wine was believed to have been created by Mr. William Neyle Habersham, a local Madeira shipper from Savannah, Georgia. Mr. Habersham made very special blends of Sercial and Verdelho that were lighter and quite a bit paler (almost like rainwater) than most of the Madeiras that were consumed during the mid-1800s. However, another account states that wines destined for sale in Savannah, Georgia were accidentally left unbunged overnight during a heavy rain storm. The resulting diluted Madeira was dubbed by wine merchant Andrew Newton "as soft as rainwater." Rainwater is mostly a blend of Negra Mole with at least 15 percent Verdelho grape varieties.

Bual (or *Boal* in Portuguese).   The grape variety is descended from the Pinot Noir of Burgundy, France. The wine is darker in color than either Sercial or Verdelho, with a sort of buttery aroma and definite sweet taste.

Malmsey.   Prince Henry the Navigator transplanted the Malvasia (Malvoisie) grapevines from Crete to Madeira in the 1400s. Malmsey is a luscious, sweet, rich wine, quite dark in color, similar to a cream sherry, but with more character.

Varietal Designation

According to Portuguese law (1985), if a wine is to be labeled as a varietal with one of the noble varieties (Sercial, Verdelho, Bual, or Malmsey), 85 percent of the wine in the bottle must be from that grape.

Vintage Dating

Since 1900, less than 20 vintages have been declared for Madeira wines. It is a striking fact that for Madeiras, the vintage is not declared until the wines have aged (by law) a minimum of 20 years in the barrel and two in the bottle. Some vintages of the 1970s are currently being considered for vintage dating.

Most Madeiras produced nowadays are either a nonvintage blend or are *solera*-dated (produced basically in the same way as sherry wines).

Serving and Storing Madeira

Madeira is a fortified wine and therefore will last a great deal longer than a table wine. It is best to keep bottles of Madeira lying on their sides until several days before serving. The bottles should then be carefully stood up to allow any sediment to settle to the bottom, and then decanted. Once opened, madeira has a shelf life of about six weeks, providing it is not exposed to high temperatures or excessive sunlight and air. In serving Madeira, never use ice, but rather chill the wine in the refrigerator. Sercial, Verdelho, and Rainwater should be chilled and served as apéritifs. Bual and Malmsey should be served at room temperature after dinner in long tulip-shaped glasses that hold five to seven ounces.

Madeira is among the longest-lived wines in the world, some lasting as long as 200 or more years. Madeira can legally be made in the United States, but most are a poor imitation at best, and fortunately very little is produced.

▶ MARSALA

Marsala was first produced in the 1760s, when John and William Woodhouse, English merchants from Liverpool, came to Sicily to purchase *soda ash* to ship back to English soap makers. While in Sicily they tasted the local wines. After noting how similar the wine was to the already popular wines from Jerez and Madeira, they sent back several barrels (60 pipes, or approximately 6,700 gallons) to England. However, they first added alcohol, approximately two gallons of it to each barrel of wine, to ensure that it would survive the long voyage. England was so impressed with the quality of the new-found wine that John decided to stay behind with his sons to help cultivate Marsala wine. In 1773, Woodhouse founded a winery to produce Marsala for export to Great Britain.

Marsala didn't really establish a name for itself until March 19, 1800, when the Very Honorable Rear Admiral Horatio Lord Nelson placed an order with Woodhouse for 500 barrels of Marsala, with the explicit orders to have it shipped to "His Majesty's" ships off Malta, without delay.

The name *Marsala* is believed to have been derived from the Arabic *Marsah-el-Allah,* meaning harbor or port of God.

The Marsala area and rules of production were defined by Law Number 1069, passed on November 4, 1950, which also designated the three provinces of Sicily where Marsala can be produced—Trapani, Palermo, and Agrigento. Marsala was granted its DOC designation on June 10, 1969.

The Production of Marsala

Marsala is both the name of a city in northwest Sicily and the name of a fortified wine, made from a blend of grapes indigenous to Sicily. For Marsala *oro* (gold) and *ambra* (amber), Grillo, Catarratto, Inzolia, and Damaschino grapes are permitted. For Marsala *rubino* (ruby), Perricone (Pignatello), Nero d'Avola (Calabrese), and Nerello Mascalese grapes are permitted.

Like sherry and port, Marsala is a fortified wine; it bears some resemblance to Madeira, in that one or more of its constituents are cooked or heated during the processing. The white wines, rich in extracts and low in acid, are blended and allowed to ferment until dry. The blend is slowly heated for about 24 hours until it has been reduced to about one-third of its original raw volume. During this time the *must* becomes thick, sweet, and caramel-like. This cooked wine, called *cotto,* is then allowed to age. In addition to *cotto,* Marsala producers also make a *sifone,* which is a blend of sweet wine from semidried grapes and neutral distilled spirits. It is the *sifone* that gives Marsala its sweetness and the *cotto,* which imparts the so-called "cooked" taste often referred to as *gusto rancio.*

The *cotto* is added to a base wine in equal proportions of six parts *cotto* and six parts alcohol to 100 parts base wine. This process is used to make the sweet Marsala. The dry Marsala is made in the same way, except that less of the *cotto* is used—sometimes as little as 1 percent.

Marsala is aged in barrels from a minimum of one year to as long as five years and occasionally longer. During this time it takes on a deep brown color, with the original white wine imparting a dry undertaste to the general sweetness, which slowly reduces with age.

Residual Sugar. Dry or *secco* Marsala contains 4 percent residual sugar; for *semisecco* Marsala, 4 to 10 percent residual sugar; and for *dolce* Marsala, more than ten percent residual sugar.

Types of Marsala

The DOC law has set production rules for three versions of Marsala. They are:

Marsala Fine. May be labeled as *oro, ambra,* or *rubino,* and made in the *secco, semisecco,* or *dolce* versions. This Marsala must be aged for a minimum of one year in a barrel and have a minimum alcoholic content of 17 percent. It is the most heavily advertised and consumed of all Marsala in the United States. It is often labeled as I.P., for *Italia Particolare* or *Italia*.

Marsala Superiore.   May be labeled as *oro, ambra*, or *rubino*, and made in the *secco, semi-secco,* or *dolce* versions. This Marsala must be aged a minimum of two years in a barrel (if aged four years, may be labeled *riserva*) and have a minimum alcohol content of 18 percent. It is made in basically two styles, dry and sweet. It is produced with the addition of a heated or cooked *must (cotto),* which gives the wine a delicate bitterness or caramel-like taste. This type of Marsala is occasionally labeled as follows:

L.P.	London Particular
S.O.M.	Superior Old Marsala
G.D.	Garibaldi Dolce

Marsala Vergine or Vergine Soleras.   It may be labeled as *oro, ambra,* or *rubino,* and made in the *secco* version. This is considered to be the finest Marsala and is made by the *solera* system. By law, it cannot contain less than 18 percent alcohol. What makes Marsala *vergine* so special is that it is made from the best wines of the vintage and must be aged a minimum of five years in a barrel before it can be sold by the producer (if aged ten years it may be labeled *riserva* or *stravecchio*). When properly stored, Marsala *vergine* can be cellared for ten to 15 years.

Some of the best Marsala producers are Rallo, Florio, and Pellegrino.

Serving and Storing Marsala

Normal procedures for proper wine storage apply to Marsala, except that most Marsalas come in screw-top bottles so they can be stored upright, increasing storage space. There is really no reason to age Marsala for extended periods of time for it is sufficiently aged prior to bottling. Once opened, Marsala should be refrigerated, which will extend its shelf life to about six weeks.

Dry Marsala is an excellent apéritif served chilled from the refrigerator (not over ice, which dilutes the taste) while sweet Marsala is excellent after dinner, served at room temperature. Marsala is generally bright amber in color with topaz reflections. The odor is clean and well developed with distinct scents of dates, vanilla, and plums. Its taste is full, soft, and velvety, with an elegant background of raisins. The dry version is best to use for cooking, for it imparts a nutty-tangy flavor without a heavy sweetness; cooking with equal parts of dry and sweet Marsala adds an extra dimension in taste.

▶ OTHER FORTIFIED WINES

Commandaria, a fortified dessert wine from Cyprus (originally known as *Nama),* is reputed to be one of the longest-lived of all wines and will often display a *solera*-date on its label.

Málaga, a wine district in the south of Spain, named after the shipping port in the province of Eastern Andalucía, is also a walnut-colored wine, generally sweet or very sweet, made from Pedro Ximénez and Moscatel grapes, in the city after which it is named. There is a sweeter version known as *lágrima,* made only from free-run juice. Málaga was once known as *Mountain* in old English writings.

CHAPTER

7

Brewed Beverages

BEER

Beer is a generic term for all alcoholic beverages that are fermented and brewed from

malted barley, hops, water, and yeast. Other starchy cereals, such as corn and

rice, may also be used where legal.

Beer is known to have existed 7,000 or more years ago. Pottery from Mesopotamia dating back to 4200 B.C. depicts fermentation scenes and shows kings sipping their version of beer through gold tubes. References to brewing have been found in hieroglyphics on walls of ancient caves in Egypt. Archaeological discoveries show that beer was known not only to the Egyptians, but also to the ancient Romans, Greeks, Assyrians, Babylonians, Incas, and Chinese. New York's Metropolitan Museum of Art has on display a wooden model of a circa 2,000 B.C. brewery.

In the third century B.C. in China, beer was known as *Kiu*. Even the Vikings made beer at sea in their war ships and drank it out of the horn of a cow. In the Middle Ages, brewing was done in the home by the women who were known as "brewsters." On February 13, 1602, the father of bottled beer, Dr. Alexander Nowell, died. He was the first to put ale into a glass bottle and seal it with a cork.

In more modern times, Peter Minuit, after purchasing "New Amsterdam," established the first public brewery in 1622. William Penn, the famous American statesman, was probably the first to operate a brewery on a large commercial scale (1638); it was located in Pennsbury, Bucks County, Pennsylvania. Other famous patriots who owned breweries were Samuel Adams, Generals Israel Putnam and Charles Sumner, Ethan Allen, and George Washington. President John Adams (1783–1789) even owned and managed his own tavern.

Fraunces Tavern, the oldest tavern in America still in existence, was founded in 1762 by Samuel Fraunces, a black man. It is located at the corner of Pearl and Broad Streets in Manhattan, where George Washington said farewell to his officers after a victory in 1783.

Federal Regulations: A 1935 federal law prohibited brewers from listing alcohol content or using words that insinuate a product's strength. That law was repealed in 1993.

Beer's Ingredients

Water.   Beer is approximately 90 percent water. Not all water is ideal for beermaking, though it can usually be made so. Since water from any two areas is never exactly the same, breweries continually test samples from each plant location. The water is conditioned or treated when necessary to ensure uniformity of product.

Malt.   Barley that has been steeped (soaked in water) and allowed to germinate (sprout or begin to grow) is called *malt*. Malt is the basic ingredient in brewing and is often referred to as the "soul of beer." It contributes to the color and characteristic flavor. In some parts of the world, malt is the only cereal grain permitted to be used in making beer. This is according to the German brewing purification law called the *Reinheitsgebot,* or The Bavarian Purity Order. It was enacted in 1516 by Bavaria's Duke Wilhelm IV, who decreed that beer could be brewed only from malt, hops, and water, with no other additives except for yeast. This law is also followed in other countries such as Norway and Switzerland.

Corn or Rice.   The primary reason for adding corn grits or rice as *adjuncts* is to produce the milder, lighter beer preferred by most American consumers. Like malt, corn and rice are a source of starch that is converted to sugar in the brewing process.

Hops.   The dried, conelike flowering blossoms from the unfertilized female hop plant called *catkin*, which is a perennial herblike climbing vine *(Humulus lupulus)* of the cannabis family. Hops contain a naturally occurring amount of resin, plus various oils, which are the perfect "bittering" agents for beer. There are many varieties of hops, all of which lend variety to beer bitterness, flavor, and bouquet. The taste of hops is generally characterized by a slight bitterness in some beers, to a distinctive bitter, almost astringent taste in others. Hops also possess antiseptic properties that inhibit the growth of bacteria. This is particularly important in the brewing of the nonpasteurized draft beers.

Brewer's yeast.   This is the agent that transforms *wort* sugars into alcohol and carbon dioxide. It is actually a microscopic cell that multiplies rapidly. At the end of fermentation the yeast population has increased approximately fourfold. It is the enormous quantity of yeast cells that makes possible the rapid conversion of *wort* to beer. While all brewer's yeasts have the ability to ferment sugars to alcohol and carbon dioxide, they can differ considerably in their abilities and hence affect beer flavor in various ways.

Brewing

Brewing is the process of making malt beverages (as beer) by grinding the various grains, then mixing separately with hot water to produce *wort,* flavoring the *wort* with hops, fermenting the hopped *wort* with yeast, and drawing off the fermented *wort* for storage and bottling.

The Three-Step Brewing Process

Brewhouse.   An exact weight of ground malt is mixed with a predetermined amount of corn grits and brewing water in the cooker. The enzymatic action of the malt solubilizes the starches during a precise time and temperature cycle. The solubilized starch is then transferred to the *mash tun,* which contains the main mash. A precisely controlled time and temperature cycle converts the starches to fermentable sugars. The clear liquid, called *wort,* is separated from the grain by straining in the *lauter tun.* The *wort* is transferred to the kettles and boiled. Hops are added in exact amounts to provide the distinctive flavor of beer. At the end of the timed boil period, the hot *wort* is pumped to a tank to allow settling of the unwanted protein.

Fermentation.   The *wort* is converted into beer during this stage. A small amount of brewer's yeast and a quantity of air are injected into the cooled *wort* as it enters the fermentation tanks. The yeast grows, producing enzymes that convert the sugar in the *wort* to alcohol and carbon dioxide gas (CO_2). Some of the CO_2 is collected and saved for later use. Fermentation takes about one week. When complete, the beer is filtered to remove yeast and other solids, then pumped to the aging tanks.

Aging. "Green beer" is allowed to rest for an extended period in the aging tanks. When properly aged, the beer is filtered a final time; if the carbonation level is low, additional CO_2 is added in a process known as *kräusening*. This is a fermentation process where new, actively fermenting beer is added to encourage a complete fermentation and add a natural carbonation. The finished beer is then pumped to the packaging tanks.

Packaging. When the aging process has been completed, the finished beer is then packaged in bottles, cans, or kegs. After packaging, the bottle and can products are pasteurized over a period of approximately one-half hour at a temperature that is allowed to rise to 140 degrees Fahrenheit, then cooled down. Because it is pasteurized, packaged beer may be stored at room temperature without damage to the product (Figure 7-1).

Draft beer, on the other hand, is not pasteurized. It is of a delicate and perishable nature, just like milk, eggs, and other perishables. Its flavor can be changed if it is not kept under constant refrigeration. The ideal storage temperature for draft beer is 38 degrees Fahrenheit. If the temperature is allowed to rise above 45 to 50 degrees Fahrenheit for an extended length of time, secondary fermentation may occur, making the beer unpalatable.

A Beer-Clean Glass

The glass is the last link between a finely brewed beer and your customer. A clean glass is necessary in order to serve beer at its best—it assures your clientele of the best in taste and eye appeal and tells them that you value their business.

To determine if your glasses are *beer-clean,*, take this simple test.*

1. *Sheeting Test.* Dip a clean glass into water. If properly washed, it will shed water evenly in "sheets." If a film exists (visible or invisible), droplets will form on the surface.
2. *Salt Test.* Sprinkle salt on the interior of a wet glass. On a truly clean glass, it will adhere evenly. If salt falls to the bottom or sticks in a random pattern, it is not a "beer-clean" glass and your beverage's flavor may suffer in this improperly cleaned glass.
3. *Head Retention Bubble Test.* Beer poured into a poorly washed glass will have large, loose bubbles that will disappear within ten to 60 seconds, plus bubbles will visibly rise from the bottom and cling to the sides. In a "beer-clean" glass, sparkling, bubble-free beer will form a tight, thick head.

---

* Reprinted from Drackett Company

Product and Handling

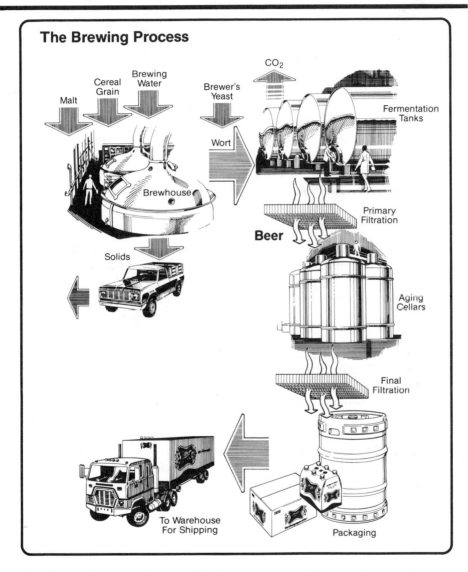

FIGURE 7-1 The brewing process. (Courtesy Miller Brewing Company, Milwaukee, Wisconsin, Copyright 1982)

4. *Lacing Test.* As the beer is consumed, foam adheres to the inside of the glass forming a parallel ring pattern; hence, the glass was properly cleaned. If foam adheres in a loose, random pattern, or not at all, a flavor-damaging film likely exists.

How can you maintain your glassware to keep customers coming back again and again? The most effective system is a three-compartment sink.

Sink number one has an overflow pipe with a funnel strainer in which residue from beer glasses is poured (all sinks have overflow pipes to maintain a constant water level). This sink is filled with warm water and glass cleaner.

Sink number two is the rinsing compartment, filled with cool water. A slow but steady stream of cool water should be allowed to run into this compartment throughout the washing operation.

Sink number three is the sanitizer, filled with clean cool water. Where required or preferred, contains a carefully measured amount of sterilizing compound.

The Five Steps to a Beer-Clean Glass

1. Thoroughly clean your sinks prior to washing glasses, using an odor-free, nonfat, or non-petroleum-based cleaning compound made especially for beer glass cleaning.
2. Empty all contents of the glasses into the funnel located in sink number one. Scrub the glass vigorously using a low-suds nonfat detergent (see above) and wherever possible, motorized brushes.
3. Thoroughly rinse the glasses in the fresh, cool water that should be constantly flowing into sink number two. Always place the glass bottom down in the rinse to eliminate the chance of air pockets forming and/or improper rinsing.
4. Repeat the same rinse operation in the third sink. Remember that many states require the use of sanitizers. If sanitizers are used, measure the amount very carefully to ensure that no odor or taste is left in the glass.
5. Air-dry the glass by placing it upside down on a deeply corrugated drainboard, which allows air to enter the inverted glass and complete the drying operation by evaporation. Never dry glasses with a towel or place them on a towel or on a flat surface such as a bar or countertop.

Important Points to Remember

- DO . . . use specifically manufactured beer glass cleaning detergents only (oil-free and nonfat). Oil-based detergents are the enemy of the beer-clean glass.
- DO . . . use motorized cleaning brushes whenever possible for more sanitary washing than can be obtained with hand brushes, cloths, or sponges.
- DO . . . dry your glasses only by placing them downward on a deeply corrugated drainboard made of plastic or stainless steel.

- DON'T . . . use petroleum- or fat-based detergents, which can leave an oily film on an otherwise clean glass.
- DON'T . . . dry the glass with a towel. The residue from bleaches or detergents in the cloth can impart an odor to the glass and impair the delicate flavor of the beer.
- DON'T . . . place newly-washed glasses on a towel to dry, for the same reasons mentioned above. A truly beer-clean glass is dried by the free flow of air on both the inside and outside surfaces.

Draft Beer: The Retail Market

The impressive gains in draft beer sales during the last several years are positive indicators for 1990s sales. These gains have been in both the on- and off-premise markets. Both are of equal importance—the off-premise market because of its potential volume for bottle and can beer sales, and the on-premise market because that is where consumer brand preference is determined and brands are built.

Draft Beer: Profit Center or Headache?

Beer is very sensitive to temperature and pressure, and foams as a result. If the draft beer is allowed to warm, the liquid and gas will separate and gas bubbles will form in the lines. When beer is drawn, it foams and gases. This wastes beer and profits go down the drain; foam is about 25 percent liquid beer.

Beer is best when served in a perfectly clean glass, with a good head of foam—foam that lasts. A thick, rich, creamy foam should cling to the glass as each sip is taken. The foam releases carbonation, so customers don't get a filled-up feeling. There is also an appearance factor here: The better the beer looks and tastes, the more you'll sell. Beer served in a near-clean glass is less than the best. The head goes flat because of an invisible film from inadequate cleaning methods and incompatible petroleum-based sanitizers; the glass must be filled almost to the top and bubbles stick to its side. The near-clean glass ruins the beer's appearance and your profits.

Beer served in a ten-ounce hourglass with a one-inch head yields 264 glasses from a one-half barrel. The same ten-ounce glass of beer, minus the head, yields only 200 glasses—that's a loss of 64 glasses. At $3.00 per glass, there is $192.00 ($792 for beer-clean glasses versus $600 for non-beer-clean glasses) more gross profit in every half-barrel when beer is properly served (see Figures 7-2 and 7-3).

In addition to brand demand, the profitability of draft beer depends upon:

- Proper temperature
- A balanced system
- Clean lines
- Clean glasses
- Proper glass shape and size
- Drawing the perfect glass of beer

Retailer Profitability

The Draft Beer Profit Story

Profit per ½ barrel

A. Glass size _____ oz.

Glass style _____

Foam head _____

B. Number of glasses per ½ barrel (from Glass Chart) _____

C. Selling price per glass _____

D. Total dollar revenue per ½ barrel _____
(C x B)

E. Cost per ½ barrel _____

F. Gross profit per ½ barrel _____
(D - E)

G. % Margin...Profit on Selling Price _____
(F ÷ D)

H. % Mark-up...Profit on Cost _____
(F ÷ E)

I. Estimated ½ barrel usage (per week, month or year) _____

J. Gross profit (per time period selected) _____
(I x F)

Profit per Glass

K. Cost per glass _____
(E ÷ B)

L. Gross profit per glass _____
(C - K)

Retailer Profitability   *a*

Example:

Profit per ½ barrel

A. Glass size __10__ oz.

Glass style __Hour Glass__

Foam head __¾″__

B. Number of glasses per ½ barrel (from Glass Chart) 248

C. Selling price per glass 75¢

D. Total dollar revenue per ½ barrel $186.00
(C x B)

E. Cost per ½ barrel $35.00

F. Gross profit per ½ barrel $151.00
(D - E)

G. % Margin...Profit on Selling Price 81.2%
(F ÷ D)

H. % Mark-up...Profit on Cost 431.4%
(F ÷ E)

I. Estimated ½ barrel usage (per week, month or year) 315

J. Gross profit (per time period selected) $47,565.00
(I x F)

Profit per Glass

K. Cost per glass 14.1¢
(E ÷ B)

L. Gross profit per glass 60.9¢
(C - K)

b

FIGURE 7-2 (a–b)   The draft beer profit story. (Courtesy Miller Brewing Company, Milwaukee, Wisconsin, Copyright 1982)

 **Here's how many glasses you can expect from a ½ barrel**

TYPE OF GLASS	SIZE	1" HEAD	¾" HEAD	½" HEAD
		APPROXIMATE GLASSES PER ½ BBL.	APPROXIMATE GLASSES PER ½ BBL.	APPROXIMATE GLASSES PER ½ BBL.
SHAM PILSNER	8 oz.	343	325	283
	9 oz.	292	279	260
	10 oz.	265	245	223
	12 oz.	221	204	186
TULIP GOBLET	8 oz.	305	292	275
	10 oz.	248	230	207
	11 oz.	227	209	185
	12 oz.	210	191	167
FOOTED PILSNER	8 oz.	325	292	280
	9 oz.	282	259	245
	10 oz.	250	233	215
SHELL	7 oz.	360	336	315
	8 oz.	315	292	275
	9 oz.	270	255	243
	10 oz.	245	236	220

TYPE OF GLASS	SIZE	1" HEAD	¾" HEAD	½" HEAD
		APPROXIMATE GLASSES PER ½ BBL.	APPROXIMATE GLASSES PER ½ BBL.	APPROXIMATE GLASSES PER ½ BBL.
HOURGLASS	10 oz.	264	248	233
	11 oz.	235	220	205
	12 oz.	220	204	189
	13 oz.	198	184	173
MUG STEIN	10 oz.	248	233	223
	12 oz.	203	189	176
	14 oz.	169	158	153
	16 oz.	149	140	134
HEAVY GOBLET	9 oz.	378	331	294
	10 oz.	330	296	264
	12 oz.	248	220	204
	14 oz.	209	194	172

TYPE OF GLASS	SIZE	1" HEAD	1½" HEAD
		APPROXIMATE PITCHER PER ½ BBL	APPROXIMATE PITCHER PER ½ BBL
PITCHER	54 oz.	47	50
	60 oz.	39	42
	64 oz.	35	38

275053   LA

FIGURE 7-3 How many glasses from a half-barrel. (Courtesy Miller Brewing Company, Milwaukee, Wisconsin, Copyright 1982)

Four Steps in Pouring the Perfect Glass of Beer

1. Start with a sparkling clean glass that has been wetted in cold water. Place glass at an angle, about one inch below the faucet, because foam from the beer can plug up the vent and you might break the glass on the faucet. Open the faucet quickly, all the way.
2. Fill the glass until it is half full, gradually bringing glass to upright position. Let the remaining beer run straight down the middle. This ensures a $3/4$-inch to 1-inch head—your profit center. Do not let the glass touch the faucet.
3. Close the faucet completely and quickly.
4. When using frozen or chilled glasses, pour some cool water on the inside of the glass, otherwise the beer will foam up, giving you an unhappy customer.

Tips on Draft Beer

The following are important to remember for ideal storage and serving conditions for draft beer:

The walk-in cooler in which draft beer is stored should be kept at 36 to 38 degrees Fahrenheit. Trips into the walk-in cooler should be minimized to maintain a constant temperature. The CO_2 pressure valve should not be tampered with; CO_2 pressure should be left constant to match the specifications of the draft system. *Clean* beer glasses should always be used. Finally, for ease of tapping, follow these steps: (1) With the tavern head tapping handle in the up position, align lug locks on the tavern head with the lug housing on the top of the keg (a container of beer with a capacity of 15.5 gallons; also known as a *half-barrel*). Insert tavern head. (2) Give the tavern head a one-quarter clockwise turn so that it is secured to the keg. (3) Pull the tapping handle downward to locking position. This will open the beer and CO_2 valves. The keg is now tapped (see Figures 7-4 and 7-5).

Problems with Draft Beer

The following, according to the Miller Brewing Company, are some common problems that can occur with draft beer equipment, storage, and service. The list indicates problems and their possible causes:

DRAFT BEER PROBLEMS
Flat beer
Greasy glasses
Not enough pressure
Pressure shut off during night
Precooler or coils too cold

Leaky pressure line

Loose tap or vent connections

Sluggish pressure regulator

Obstruction in lines

Wild beer

Beer drawn improperly

Faucets in bad or worn condition

Kinks, dents, twists, or other obstructions in lines

Beer runs are too long or lines are not well insulated

Beer too warm in kegs or lines

Creeping gauge causing too much pressure

False head

Pressure required does not correspond to beer temperature

Coils or direct draw beer lines warmer than beer in keg

Drawing too short a foam collar

Beer drawn improperly

Cloudy beer

Beer was overchilled or frozen

Beer in keg was too warm at some point

Hot spots in beer lines

Beer lines in poor condition or dirty

Bad taste

Dirty faucets

Old or dirty beer lines; foul air in lines

Failure to flush beer lines with water after each keg emptied

Unsanitary conditions at the bar

Oily air; greasy kitchen air

Temperature of keg too warm

Dry glasses

Cooperage and Tapping Equipment

Keg Identification

All Miller Brewing Company kegs are dated and carry plant, shift, strength, and product identification. Information is stamped on the aluminum tap cover and printed with ink on two sides of the keg.

Example:

Brand _____
"Don't sell" date _____
Plant _____
Shift _____
Beer strength _____

Brand _____

Each Miller Brewing Company brand is identified with a two letter brand code. In addition, a color coded brand logo is printed on each foil tap cover.

Brand	Code	Foil Tap Cover
Miller High Life	MR	Gold on White
Lite	XX	Blue on White
Lowenbrau Special	NL	Blue on White
Lowenbrau Dark	ND	Brown on White

XX 07162 1 1 Z

"Don't sell" date _____

A five-digit month/date/year is included in the keg identification. This date is referred to as the "don't sell" date and specifies the last day that the product may be offered for sale in the retail trade.

Example:

07162 would represent the 7th month, 16th day, and 82nd year... or July 16, 1982.

To insure product freshness, the "don't sell" date on all Miller Brewing Company kegs falls 60 days after the keg was racked. All kegs, however, should be sold to the retailer within 45 days. To determine the date, subtract 15 days from the 60-day "don't sell" date. In our example 07162, the keg should be sold to the retailer by July 1, 1982.

July 16, 1982 would be the last day this keg could be sold to the consumer and should be picked up (where legal) and returned to the distributorship any date after July 16, 1982.

XX 07162 1 1 Z

Plant _____

The following one-digit numbers have been assigned to our plants for the purpose of identification:

Milwaukee	1	Irwindale	6
Fulton	3	Albany	7
Fort Worth	4	Trenton	8
Eden	5		

Cooperage and Tapping Equipment

XX 07162 1 1

Shift _____

This information is provided for quality control purposes.

XX 07162 1 1 Z

Beer strength _____

Regular strength beer is designated by the letter "Z".

3.2 beer (maximum 3.2% alcohol by weight) is designated by the letter "A" and two vertical red stripes are printed on aluminum tap cover

Keg Information

Receiving and Storing Draft Beer at the Warehouse

When draft beer arrives, it should be immediately transferred to the draft beer cooler and stored at a temperature of 38° Fahrenheit.

Stock Rotation

Each shipment received should be dated to insure proper stock rotation.

Cooling Time

The kegs should be held in storage for a minimum of two days before delivering to the retail trade.

■ The two days holding period allows the beer time to settle and attain the proper temperature for delivery.

Temperature Check Twice Daily

An accurate thermometer placed in a bottle of water (this ensures that when the cooler door is opened the warm air does not affect the thermometer) should be strategically located in the cooler to insure all locations are at the proper temperature.

■ Check the temperature twice daily (morning and evening) and record on the Miller draft beer cooler temperature record chart.

Delivery and Return of Kegs

All kegs full or empty must be handled with care to avoid damage to the container or product.

■ Rope or rubber bumpers should be used to break the fall when unloading kegs from the draft beer truck.

Cooperage and Tapping Equipment

Ideally the last keg delivered should be as cold as the first.

■ A refrigerated truck assures this kind of delivery. If volume does not warrant a refrigerated truck, a closed insulated truck can be used. The kegs should be kept cold by covering them with an insulated blanket.

■ During hot months, non-refrigerated trucks should return to the warehouse and exchange warm kegs for cold ones. The warm ones should be put back in the cooler and cooled down to the proper temperature prior to delivery.

Empty kegs must be promptly collected from the retail trade and stored in a protected area until they are returned to the brewery.

■ Prompt return of empty kegs to the brewery will insure a smooth flow of product to the trade. It requires four kegs to maintain one keg in a retail account.

Care and Handling by the Retailer

Every retail account can serve a fine glass of draft beer if careful attention is given to draft

beer equipment, storage facilities, dispensing methods and cleanliness. Storage facilities for draft beer should:

■ Be used for draft beer only. Keep doors closed as much as possible to maintain a constant, uniform temperature of 36° to 38°.

■ Be large enough to handle potential as well as present volume.

■ Be properly insulated.

■ Have an accurate thermometer which is located away from pipes, coils and other cooling equipment.

The retailer's stock should be rotated during delivery of draft beer.

■ Always place the most recently delivered kegs in back of any kegs already in the cooler.

■ In replacing kegs in series, always move a partial keg to the CO_2 source (Position 3) and rotate backup stock into the series nearest the faucet (Position 1).

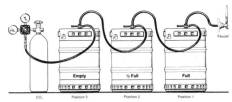

FIGURE 7-4 (a–c) Cooperage and tapping equipment. (Courtesy Miller Brewing Company, Milwaukee, Wisconsin, Copyright 1982)

TAP-O-MATIC Tapping Guide

(for Perlick Tavern Head)

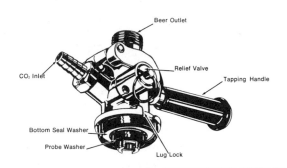

Perlick Tavern Head

This single unit connects both beer and CO₂ lines to the keg.

NOTE:
With the Perlick tavern head, it is not necessary to turn off the CO₂ regulator when changing kegs. CO₂ is automatically cut off at the tavern head by the tapping handle.

Beer Outlet

Relief Valve

Tapping Handle

CO₂ Inlet

Bottom Seal Washer

Probe Washer

Lug Lock

Tapping Procedure

1 With tavern head tapping handle in the UP POSITION; align lug locks on the tavern head with the lug housing on the top of the keg. Insert tavern head.

2 Turn tavern head ¼ turn clockwise; the tavern head is now secured to the keg.

3 Pull tapping handle out and depress downward to locking position. This will open the beer and CO₂ valves. The keg is now tapped.

Twin Gauge Regulator

A twin gauge regulator with separate gauges for cylinder pressure and applied pressure is recommended.

Note: Only low-pressure regulators with approved relief valves should be used.

Applied pressure gauge for this system should be set at _____ lbs.

Gauge Showing Pressure in Cylinder

Gauge Showing Applied Pressure Going To Keg

Regulator Shut-off Valve

Series Tap

NOTE:
When series tapping, CO₂ inlet assembly must be replaced with series adaptors on all tavern heads, except the one closest to the CO₂ tank.

KEG 1   KEG 2   KEG 3

When replenishing the supply of beer: any partially filled keg should be moved to Keg position No. 3.

EXAMPLE: If Keg No. 2 and No. 3 are empty and some beer remains in Keg No. 1, move Keg No. 1 into Keg position No. 3 and full Kegs into positions No. 1 and No. 2.

NOTE: Only tavern head on Keg No. 3 does not require a series adaptor.

FIGURE 7-5 Tap-O-Matic tapping guide. (Courtesy Miller Brewing Company, Milwaukee, Wisconsin, Copyright 1982)

Cans versus Bottles

There are some major differences in the use of canned versus bottled beers. Although cans chill faster than bottles, they also lose their chill faster; bottles take longer to chill but retain the cold longer. Cans are lighter in weight, easier to stack, and are nonbreakable.

Cans, unlike bottles, have an "image problem" in restaurants and bars; this is the main reason why canned beer is rarely served. Contrary to popular belief, there is absolutely no difference in taste between canned and bottled beer. The cans used nowadays do not give off a metallic taste, as they once did.

Beer Classification

The use of a type of yeast *(Saccharomyces uvarum)* that will generally convert sugars to alcohol and CO_2 at lower temperatures is called *bottom fermentation.* Bottom-fermenting yeast is sometimes referred to as *lager yeast* and a slower fermentation is characteristic.

Bottom-Fermented Beers

Bock Beer.   Bock beer is produced from grain that is considerably higher in extracts than the usual grains destined for use in lager beers. *Bock,* in German, means a male goat. Bock beer was originally produced around A.D. 1200 in the town of Einbeck, Germany. Nowadays, Bock beer is produced in virtually every country, in some form or another, on a seasonal basis (mostly during the winter so that it can be consumed in the early spring). Bock beers are usually quite dark in color with an intense, sharp, sweet aroma. They have a full-bodied flavor, followed by a slightly sweet, malty taste. A stronger version produced in very limited quantities in Germany is called double bock *(doppelbock).* Bock beer is ideally served at 45 to 50 degrees Fahrenheit.

Dark Beer.   Dark beer is characterized by a very deep, dark color, a full-bodied flavor, and a creamy taste, with overtones of malt, bitterness, sweetness, and caramel. It is usually produced from the addition of roasted barley during the initial brewing stages. It should be served at approximately 45 to 50 degrees Fahrenheit.

Dortmunder Beer.   A golden-colored beer with a high level of malt and hops, traditionally brewed in Dortmund, Germany.

Dry Beer.   Beer made to be drier to the taste with no aftertaste. Basically, during the cooking process, brewers extract as much sugar as possible from the malted barley and mixing grains (rice, corn, etc.), then allow the fermentation to last an additional seven to ten days. Another method is to allow more of the malt and adjunct cereals (mostly corn and rice) to be converted into fermentable sugars, which are used more efficiently during fermentation. This results in a beer with a higher alcoholic content. Dry beers actually originated in Germany with the brewing of *diat pils,* beers specially produced for people with diabetes.

Festbier.   Beers made for traditional festivals (e.g., Oktoberfest). The styles as well as taste and alcoholic content of these beers vary.

Ice Beer.   It is a beer that has been brewed at a colder-than-usual temperature, then immediately chilled to below freezing (32 degrees Fahrenheit), which forms ice crystals. The crystals are then filtered out of the beer, resulting in a slightly higher alcohol than regular beers. Some brewers claim that this process eliminates bitter-tasting proteins, resulting in a smoother-tasting beer. Contrary to popular belief, this process did not originate in the United States or even Canada, but rather in Germany, where a beer called *eisbock* is brewed utilizing this method.

Kulmbacher Beer.   This beer comes from Kulmbach, Germany. Some Kulmbacher beers are reported to have as much as 14 percent alcohol by weight, but those exported to the United States have far less. Kulmbacher beer is ideally served at 38 to 45 degrees Fahrenheit.

Lager.   Lager was developed in Germany in about the seventh century. It was first introduced into the United States by the Germans in 1840. *Lager* comes from the German word *lagern* (to store) and is applied to bottom-fermented beer in particular because it must be stored at low temperatures for prolonged periods of time. Lagers were traditionally stored in cellars or caves for completion of fermentation. They are bright gold to yellow in color, with a light to medium body, and are usually well carbonated. Unless stated otherwise, virtually every beer made in the United States (more than 90 percent) is a lager. Lager is ideally served at 38 to 45 degrees Fahrenheit.

Light Beer.   Light beer is usually produced by the dilution of regular beers that have been brewed with the use of high-extract grains or barley and have been allowed to ferment dry. Another method of production involves the addition of enzymes, which reduce the number of calories and the beer's alcoholic content; its flavor is also considerably lighter. The purpose of producing light beer is to make a lower-calorie beer. A regular 12-ounce beer has 135 to 170 calories; a light beer usually has under 100 calories. There are no current Bureau of Alcohol, Tobacco, and Firearms rulings on minimum or maximum calorie levels. Light beers are ideally served at 38 to 45 degrees Fahrenheit.

Maibock.   A bock beer brewed in the spring.

Malt Liquor.   This is an American term for a lager beer with a considerably higher level of alcohol (usually above 5 percent) than most lager beers or ales. Tastes vary from brewery to brewery and brand to brand, with some even sweetened with fruit syrup. The name comes from the beer's malty flavor, which has overtones of bitterness. Its color is typically darker than that of regular beers and its taste is correspondingly heavier and fuller-bodied. Malt liquor is ideally served at 38 to 45 degrees Fahrenheit.

Märzenbier.   A medium-strong, amber-colored beer originally brewed in March (hence its name), laid to rest during summer's heat and generally drunk before October, with any remaining beer consumed at Oktoberfest in Germany.

Munich (also *Münchener*).   This type of beer was originally produced in Bavaria, although it is currently brewed in many parts of the world. It is slightly darker in color than Pilsner-type beers, although milder and less bitter than other German types. It also has a more pronounced malty aroma and taste, with a sweet finish and aftertaste. Munich beer is ideally served at 38 to 45 degrees Fahrenheit.

Pilsner (also *Pilsener* and *Pils*).   This is the most popular type or style of beer produced in the world. The word *Pilsner* is taken from the Czech town of Pilsen. Characteristically, these beers are light golden color, with a highly pronounced hops (referred to as *Bohemian*) flavor and a delightfully clean, crispy taste that refreshes and leaves the palate clean. Pilsner-style beers are usually dry to very dry in taste, although there are some slightly sweet pilsners produced. Pilsners are ideally served at 38 to 45 degrees Fahrenheit.

Rauchbier.   An amber to dark-colored beer, brewed with the addition of malt that has been dried over smoking beechwood, mostly found in Bamberg or Hamburg.

Steam Beer.   A highly carbonated, deep brown-gold-colored beer, with an aromatic odor of cloves, orange peels, and peaches, and a tangy-bitter taste with a dry finish. The name *steam* originates from the final *kräusening* stage of fermentation, during which a partially fermented *wort* is added to speed the fermentation; at this point the active head produced by this process releases a *steam*. Steam beer is a bottom-fermented beer, yet with a taste of ale. Steam beer had its origins in San Francisco, California, during the Gold Rush.

Ur-Bock.   A beer that has a darker color and is slightly fuller in body than traditional bock beer.

Vienna Beer.   Amber-colored beers, medium-bodied with pronounced malty flavors. Although this was once a style of beer produced in Vienna, it is now produced worldwide, with the name carrying little meaning.

Top fermentation refers to the use of a type of added yeast *(Saccharomyces cerevisiae)* that floats to the top during fermentation. The yeast converts sugar to alcohol and CO_2

at warmer temperatures, usually between 60 and 70 degrees Fahrenheit. Most top-fermented beers are analogous to red wine, with a richer flavor and more body.

Top-Fermented Beers

Abbey Ale.   Beers made for centuries by Cistercian monks in Belgium, who brewed them for personal consumption and enjoyment with guests. Typically, they are deep golden to coffee in color, with a heavy, pronounced malty bouquet.

Ale.   Ale is a beer with a slightly darker color than lager beer. It usually has more hops in its aroma and taste and is often lower in carbonation than lager-type beers. Ale is usually bitter to the taste, with a slight tanginess, although some ales can be sweet. Ales are usually fermented at warmer temperatures than lager-type beers (60 to 70 degrees Fahrenheit) for from three to five days and generally mature faster. Ale is originally from England, where it is often referred to as *bitters*. Ales should ideally be served at 38 to 45 degrees Fahrenheit.

Alt.   Old, meaning beer brewed in the "old style." A beer popular in Germany prior to the 1800s, when *lager* was first produced. It is often reddish-brown in color with an abundant hop flavor.

Altbier.   An ale with a high barley and hops content, which is quite bitter.

Amber Ale.   An ale with a light amber color.

Bitter.   A term related to amber-colored, well-hopped beers that display a rather strong alcohol content. A strong ale with certain levels of hops or barley will also exhibit levels of bitterness. Also an English term for amber to dark-colored, bitter beers.

Brown Ale.   A dark brown or cocoa-colored beer that has a malty bouquet and bitter-sweet taste. It is light to medium in body, usually rather low in alcohol, and traditionally produced in Great Britain, Belgium, and occasionally Canada. Sometimes called *Nut Brown Ale.*

Copper Ale.   A dark, copper-colored, bitter ale with a distinctive winelike taste and aroma, originally brewed in England.

Cream Ale.   This is a blend of ale and lager beer. Cream ale is highly carbonated, which results in a rich foam and strong effervescence. Cream ale is ideally served at 38 to 45 degrees Fahrenheit.

Dunkel Weissbier. A dark wheat beer.

Faro. A *lambic-type* (see below) beer, often sweetened with fruit or seasoned with spices.

Framboise. A *lambic-type* of wheat beer or sour brown ale to which raspberries have been added; usually brewed in Brussels.

Gueuze. A *lambic-type* beer, made from a blend of various aged *lambics,* which is quite effervescent with aromas of apple or even rhubarb. However, all beers produced from *lambics* are quite sour. It is brewed in Brussels and Berlin, Germany.

Imperial Stout. A very strong dark fruity brew originally made in the Czarist Russian Empire. Nowadays it is brewed mostly in Great Britain, Denmark, and Finland.

India Pale Ale. A very bitter ale with a hoppy aroma and taste. It was the kegged ale that the British sent to their troops serving in India during the 1800s.

Kölsch. A pale, golden-colored beer traditionally brewed in Cologne, Germany.

Kriek. A *lambic-type* beer that has been further fermented by the addition of sour or bitter black cherries to produce a dry brew with an unusual cherry flavor; usually brewed in Brussels.

Lambic. An entire family of wild-fermented beers, generally brewed near Brussels. Some of the added ingredients during the brewing process are cranberries, peaches, raspberries, sour cherries, and wheat. Most of the beers are winelike and somewhat acidic, almost resembling vermouth, rather than beer.

Milk Stout. A low alcoholic, medium-sweet beer with a high lactic acid content and dark color.

Oatmeal Stout. A brewed beverage, rich, flavorful, and quite dark in color, in which oatmeal is added to the roasted malt.

Pale Ale. A copper-colored ale, usually full-bodied, highly hopped, and quite bitter, originally brewed in England.

Porter. This is the predecessor of stout and is characterized by its intense deep dark color, often a smoky or fruity bouquet, and a persistent bittersweet taste. It is lower in alcohol than stout and should ideally be served at 55 degrees Fahrenheit. It was invented in 1722 by Ralph Harwood, a London brewer, who named it after the porters who enjoyed drinking it.

Saison. A sharply refreshing, amber-colored ale that displays a faintly sour taste; originally made in Belgium.

Scotch Ale. A medium-dark, full-bodied ale, with a rich malty taste, generally produced in Scotland.

Stout. Stout evolved from the term *extra stout porter,* a darker and stronger version of porter. This beer obtains its dark (almost black) color from roasted barley, with a very high extract level. It contains mostly roasted barley, which is rendered sterile before germination, and a small amount of malt for added flavor. It is quite thick and malty, with an intense bitterness and underlying sweet taste. Stout is relatively low in carbonation and should be served at 55 degrees Fahrenheit. Specific types of stout are Bitter Stout, Imperial Stout, Irish Stout, Milk Stout, Oatmeal Stout, and Porter.

Trappist. Strong beers brewed by Trappist monks in either Belgium or the Netherlands. The name Trappist is authorized by law for those beers brewed exclusively by the monks. Most of the beers are deeply colored, with high levels of alcohol.

Wheat Beer (also *Weissbier* and *Weizenbier*). This is the German name for a beer made either entirely or predominantly from wheat. It is usually unfiltered and contains some yeast residue, therefore is often cloudy in appearance. It is highly acidic, crisp, and acrid tasting, usually served with a slice of lemon or with about one ounce of nonalcoholic fruit (generally raspberry) syrup. Wheat beer is ideally served at 38 to 45 degrees Fahrenheit. *Hefe weizen* is wheat beer that still has the yeast in the bottle; *Kristall weizen* is wheat beer that has been filtered; *Dunkel weissbier* is a dark wheat beer.

White Beer. A beer first produced in 1543 in Belgium from a combination of barley, wheat, and oats. Also known as *Whitbier.*

Microbrewers and Contract Beers

To some consumers, standard, American-produced beers from the giant brewers just don't offer enough diversity. Many consumers are becoming interested in beers that have a bolder, richer taste and are willing to pay for it. This has opened the door to microbreweries, brew pubs, and the contract-beer business. By definition, *microbreweries* are small breweries of modest size and production, at one time brewing less than 15,000 barrels (one barrel contains 31 gallons). These breweries produce "hand-crafted" small batches of beer. *Brew pubs,* on the other hand, are taverns that brew their own beer for on-premise consumption as well as off-premise sales. Finally, *contract brews* are beers made according to the specific recipes of individual owners by established breweries.

By contracting out for a brewing, a microbrewery's costs are kept low. The major expenses for *contract brews* and *microbreweries* are product packaging, marketing, and advertising.

Some microbrew and contract brew beers are:

Alimony Ale	Pike Place
Boston Beer	Preservation
Brooklyn Lager	Red Brick
Champions Clubhouse Classic	Redhook
Dock Street	Red Mountain
Elk Mountain	Red Seal
Friday's	Red Tail
Full Sail	Rhino
Goat's Breath	R.J.'s Ginseng
Harpoon	Samuel Adams
Helenboch	Sedona Beer
Manhattan	Sierra Nevada
McGuire's	Smith & Reilly
Neuweiler	Spanish Peaks
New Amsterdam	Spirit of St. Louis
Newman's	Stone Mountain
New York Harbor	Vail
Olde Heurich	Widmer
Pecan Street	Wit
Pete's	

Beer Brands from Around the World

Below is a list of well-known brands of beer available in the United States.

United States

Anchor	Carling	Hamm's
Andeker	Champale	Hudepohl
Augsburger	Chesterfield	Iroquois
Ballantine	Cold Spring Export	Jax
Bergheim	Coors	Knickerbocker
Black Horse	Coqui 900	Leinenkugel
Blatz	Erlanger	Lite Beer
Blue Fox	Fort Schuyler	Lone Star
Break Special	Fox Head 400	Löwenbräu
Budweiser	Gablinger	Magnum
Bull's Eye	Genessee	Matt's
Busch	Gibbons	Maximus

McSorley's	Pearl	Schmidt's
Meister-Bräu	Piel's	Schoenling
Michelob	Pike Place	Simon
Mickeys	Primo	Stegmaier
Miller	Prior	Steinbräu
Milwaukee	Rainier	Stroh's
Naragansett	Reading	Tuborg
Natural Light	Red, White & Blue	Utica Club
Old German	Rheingold	Henry Weinhard
Old Milwaukee	Robin Hood	Wiedemann
Olympia	Rolling Rock	Yuengling
Ortlieb's	Schaefer	
Pabst	Schlitz	

Australia

Cooper's	Leopard	Toohey's
Foster's	Swan	Tooth's

Austria

Goldfassl	Steffl	Zipfer Urtyp
Gösser		

Belgium

Duvel	Riva 2000	St. Sixtus
Orval Trappist	Rodenbach	

Brazil

Brahma	Rioco	

Canada

Calgary	Labatt's	Old Vienna
Canadian 55	Molson	Ontario Special
Grizzly	Moosehead	Trilight
Iron Horse	O'Keefe	Yukon Gold

China

Changlee	Tsingtao	Taiwan
Sun Lik		

Czechoslovakia

Pilsner Urquell

Denmark

Carlsberg	Lolland-Falsters	Tuborg
Harboes	Scandia	

Ecuador

Club

England

Bass Ale	Newcastle Brown Ale	Tolly
Cheshire	Old Peculier	Vaux Double Maxim
John Courage	Samuel Smith	Watney
London Pride	Stingo	Whitbread
Mackeson Stout		

Finland

Finlandia	Koff

France

33 Export	Fischer	Kronenbourg

Germany

Altenmünster	Eku	Kulmbacher Kapuziner
Augustiner	Euler	Kulmbacher Mönschof
Beck's	Fürstenberg	Paulaner
Berliner Weisse	Hacker-Pschorr	Pinkus
Bitburger	Henniger	Radenberger
Club-Weisse	Herrenhauser	Reichelbräu
D.A.B.	Holsten	Spaten
Dinkelacker	Isenbeck	St. Pauli Girl
Doppelspaten	Kaiserdom	Stern
Dortmunder	König-Pilsener	Ur-Märzen
Einbecker	Kropf	Würzburger

Greece

Aegean Hellas	Spartan

Holland

Amstel Light	Oranjeboom	Three Horses
Grolsch	Royal Dutch	
Heineken	Skol	

India

Eagle	Kingfisher	Taj Mahal

Ireland

Guinness Stout	Harp

Israel

Maccabee

Italy

Crystal	Nastro Azzurro	Poretti
Moretti	Peroni	Raffo

Jamaica

Red Stripe

Japan

Asahi	Sapporo
Kirin	Suntory

Luxembourg

Diekirch

Martinique

Biere Lorraine

Mexico

Bohemia	Corona Extra	Simpatico
Carta Blanca	Dos Equis	Superior
Chihuahua	Negra Modelo	Tecate

New Zealand		
Steinlager		
Norway		
Aass	Ringnes	Rok
Peru		
Cristall		
Philippines		
Manila	San Miguel	
Poland		
Krakus		
Portugal		
Sagres		
Scotland		
Belhaven	McEwan's	
Lorimer	NewCastle	
Sweden		
Kalback		
Switzerland		
Cardinal	Hopfenperle	
Thailand		
Amarit	Payap	Singha
Venezuela		
Polar		
Yugoslavia		
Union		

▶ SAKÉ

Saké is an ancient fermented beverage known to have been made since about the third century A.D. in China. But it was not until about 600 years ago that saké as we know it today was produced.

In ancient times, the making and serving of saké by experienced brewers called *tōji* was only entrusted to women (who incidentally had to be virgins). *Saké* means "the essence of the spirit of rice"; it is made from rice and legally defined as a rice beer.

The rice used to make saké is "polished," so that the part used for final production is much less than the whole grain, often not much more than the heart of the kernel. The quality of the finished saké is based upon the size (the smaller the better) of the rice kernel after polishing. It is accepted that the finest saké is made from rice that has been polished down to 50 percent of its original size. The polished rice is soaked in cold distilled water for 12 to 18 hours to absorb moisture, then steamed for about 45 minutes in a *koshiki*—a large rice-steaming tub. The rice is then spread out in an area called the *kōji* room, where a mold, *Aspergillus oryzae*, is added. This mold converts the rice starch into sugar in 30 to 35 hours. The rice, now referred to as *kōji*, is mixed with additional steamed rice and water, and instead of depending on traditional wild yeasts, modern saké producers add a pure strain of yeast called *Saccharomyces cerevisiae*. The mash (*moto* in Japanese) is put into large wooden or stainless steel containers for the *moroni*, or fermentation. Saké is generally fermented at 60 degrees Fahrenheit for about two weeks. However, the highest-quality saké is fermented cool, at 50 degrees Fahrenheit, for about three weeks. When fermentation is completed, the liquid, which resembles very thick milk, is drawn off (racked). The rice is gently pressed in a machine that resembles a long accordion. The liquid is allowed to settle, then filtered and run into barrels or stainless steel containers to mature for a short period of time, usually 90 to 100 days. Finally, the saké is pasteurized before being bottled. This eliminates cloudiness, bacteria contamination, and makes it able to withstand ocean voyages and gives an extended shelf life. (Nowadays, molasses alcohol, glucose, or grain alcohol is occasionally added to help offset the rising cost of rice in Japan.)

Saké is produced all over Japan, in parts of China, and in other Asian countries, as well as in Hawaii and California. In China there is a similar rice beer called *samshu,* and in Korea, *suk.* In Japan there is a high-proof spirit distilled from rice called *Awamori* or *Shōchū,* in China it is called *Sochu.* (The ancient Chinese *Alaai* or *Santchoo* were spirits distilled from rice in about 800 B.C.)

Types of Saké

The type and origin of the rice used in saké making determines what the final product will taste like. For example, saké from *Hiroshima* is often quite full-bodied and robust; saké from *Akita* is very heady in its bouquet, often because of its higher alcoholic content. Saké from *Kyoto* is probably the lightest and driest of all and is the most popular type in the United States. More than one dozen types of saké fall roughly into four styles: *mirin* (mi = taste; rin = sweet), for cooking; *toso,* drunk for New Year's celebrations, is aged in Yoshino wooden barrels, giving it a dark color, fullness of body, and a spicy-sweet taste; *nigori*, which is a semirefined saké; and *seishu,* which is also known as *ama-kara-ping* (*ama* = sweet; *kara* = lightly bitter, *ping* = a "delightful effect").

Gekkeikan (meaning *laurel wreath,* the crown that is a symbol of victory in sporting competitions), is Japan's oldest continuously operated saké house, established in 1637 in Fushimi. Some saké brands available on the marketplace are: Chiyoda, Fuki, Fuku-musume, Gekkeikan, Genji, Hakushika, Hakutsuru, Kembishi, Kiku-Masamune, Ni-honsakari, Kizakura, Ozeki, Sawanotsuru, Shirayuki, Sho-Chiku-Bai, and Shogun.

Serving and Storing Saké

The Japanese traditionally serve saké warm, between 100 to 110 degrees Fahrenheit. (James Bond, British Secret Agent, in the movie *You Only Live Twice,* preferred it to be served at 98.4 degrees Fahrenheit.) At this temperature, saké's heady bouquet (which is 12 to 17 percent alcohol) is released. To warm saké, place the opened bottle into a pot of boiling water. Remove it when the saké is 100 to 110 degrees Fahrenheit and immediately replace it with another for later drinking. To serve saké in the Japanese manner, decant the warm saké into the small, beautifully shaped ceramic pitcher called *tokkuri,* or *ochōshi.* Then slowly pour the saké into the tiny porcelain cups or bowls called *sakazuki* or *ochoko,* which hold a little more than one ounce. Saké cups are always filled to the brim. (In ancient Japan, these bowls were made of lacquered wood, were quite large, and often square in shape. Saké was traditionally sipped from these bowls.)

Saké is a versatile beverage and can be served chilled, or on the rocks with a twist of lemon. Saké can be an alternative to dry vermouth in a martini, called a "sakini." Saké is almost colorless, with its color ranging from amber to the palest gold. It is technically considered a *still* beverage because of its lack of effervescence. Its bouquet is somewhat earthy, with subtle undertones; it has a slightly sweet initial taste, followed by a dry after-taste. Saké should be stored in a cool, dark place prior to opening. Saké, unlike wine, does not improve with bottle age and once opened, should be refrigerated and consumed within six weeks.

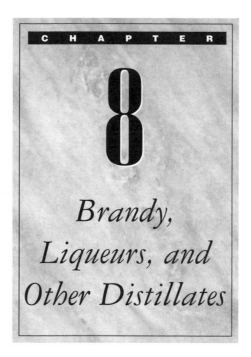

8

Brandy, Liqueurs, and Other Distillates

or many years brandy has been known as the ideal after-dinner beverage or the drink that warms one up on a cold day. The name brandy *originates with the Dutch, who are believed to have been the first great connoisseurs of this drink; they called it* brandewijn, *meaning* burnt wine. *This referred to the process by which brandy was made: Wine was heated and the resulting vapor distilled. This term was carried over into Germany as* branntwein (weinbrand) *and into France as* brandevin. *The English adopted the word as* brandywine, *which was later shortened to* brandy.

In addition to brandy, there are many other high-proof distillates; some are flavored after distillation, while others are flavored by their base ingredients.

The liqueurs we know today (alcoholic beverages made from natural flavorings such as fruits, berries, and juices) have come a long way from the medicinal "magic potions" concocted by medieval monks.

More than 2,300 years ago, Hippocrates, the Greek physician, wrote about a certain liqueur called *Hydromel,* which was made of wine, honey, and aromatic herbs and botanicals. During that era, alchemists strove to develop recipes for use as love potions, cure-alls for man's ailments, guarantees of everlasting life or rejuvenation, and aphrodisiacs.

In 1533, during the High Renaissance of sixteenth-century Italy, Queen Catherine de Medici introduced France to liqueurs when she brought *Rosolio,* an Italian liqueur (as well as many other sweet liqueurs), to France. Thereafter it became fashionable to serve liqueurs at court.

Increased sea trade in the seventeenth century brought new fruits, herbs, and spices to Europe. Many were used in liqueurs, which became more varied.

In the 1700s, when Louis XIV's doctor used an herbal liqueur to cure the king's stomach ailments, liqueurs became even more popular in France. In Victorian times, they became customary at formal dinners.

Bistros all over France were serving exotic, colorful liqueurs to their regulars when the cocktail craze of the 1920s caught on. Liqueurs were used in such cocktails as parfait amour, monkey gland, and forbidden fruit.

► BRANDY

Brandy is a spirit made by distilling wines or the fermented mash of fruit, which is then aged in oak barrels. The varying characteristics of different brandies are the result of differences in fruit and grape varieties used, climate, soil, and production methods, which vary from district to district and country to country.

Generally speaking, the wines used in making brandy are not of drinkable quality; they tend to be rather acidic and harsh.

Brandy is distilled either by the *pot still* (this produces the highest-quality brandy) or by the more common and modern *column still* (also called the *continuous still*). In the pot still method, the distillation process is carried out in single batches, which is laborious, time-consuming, and expensive. Using the column still saves time because the distillation is a continuous process.

The pot still resembles a large copper pot or kettle with a broad rounded base, topped by a long column. The shape of the still, even the way it is fired (flame or steam), the speed of *heating* the liquid, the temperature of the still, and the volume of the *heart* are believed to affect the quality of the brandy. Initially, anywhere from 250 to 2,600 gallons of wine to be distilled (depending on the still's size) are loaded into the base of the pot still. The wine is then heated and kept simmering until the alcohol is vaporized and rises up into the column, taking with it flavors from the wine used; this gives brandy its characteristic aroma and taste. When the vapor rises to a certain point in the column, it comes into contact with a cold condenser, which turns the vapor into liquid alcohol (in this case, brandy).

In the pot still method, there are two distillations. The initial distillation is collected at a strength of 30 percent alcohol; this is then redistilled to approximately 70 to 80 percent alcohol. Only the middle or "heart" of a distillation is collected and the first and last runs, called *heads* and *tails,* are redistilled before they can be used.

After the second distillation, the brandy is colorless and 70 to 80 percent alcohol (140 to 160 proof). It is then aged in charred oak barrels, which softens the fiery, rough liquid. When the distiller feels that the brandy has aged sufficiently, its alcoholic content is cut with the addition of distilled water to a level of not less than 80 proof. At this point, caramel coloring is added to the brandy to "adjust" its color. The brandy is then filtered to remove any suspended particles and finally bottled.

Brandy is expensive simply because ten gallons of wine are needed to produce one gallon of brandy.

Storage of Brandy.   Brandy should be stored upright so that the cork, which will deteriorate, does not come in contact with the brandy. Prolonged contact with the cork can adversely affect the quality of a brandy. Since there are no fermentable materials in brandy, the product is highly tolerant of climate variations. However, brandy should be stored away from direct heat and not be subjected to extreme temperature changes. Once opened, brandy comes in contact with the air, which can begin to alter its quality. It is recommended that a bottle be consumed within one year after opening.

American Brandy

Approximately 95 percent of all American-made brandies come from California; therefore, the following information is based on California production methods and types of brandy.

California brandy was first made by Spanish missionaries after they had produced several successive vintages of wine. Jean Louis Vignes, a Frenchman, is credited with producing California's first brandy (in about 1837). Captain John Sutter later produced brandy at Sutter's Fort in 1841. The brandy industry didn't really develop until about 1867 when Almadén Vineyards of Madera (the oldest producer of brandy in continuous operation in California) began to produce brandy. In 1955, the firm of Fromm & Sichel marketed a premixed cocktail, the Dry Brandini, which was displayed for promotion in a martini stem glass with a twist of lemon peel. It consisted of one part dry vermouth and four parts brandy. In 1889, Korbel produced its first brandy. In 1968, E. & J. Gallo brandy was sold for the first time. In 1945, Christian Brothers introduced their "regular" or mainline brandy, and in 1972, XO Rare Reserve brandy was introduced. Other fine producers are Paul Masson, Coronet, Carneros, Alambics, Assumption Abbey, Hiram Walker, Boilieux, and The Woodbury Winery.

By law, all California brandy must be made from grapes grown and distilled in California. It must be aged a minimum of two years in oak barrels and if aged for less time, must be labeled an "immature brandy." For brandies that are aged more than two years, the age may be stated on the label.

There is no required grape variety for use in brandy making in California; many different varieties are used. Most distillers use the Thompson Seedless or Flame Tokay grapes to make brandy, as they are inexpensive, nondescript, and produce a fairly good product.

Brandies of Other Countries

Chile and Peru.   Pisco brandy is distilled from Muscat of Alexandria and/or Mission grapes. The name Pisco is taken from the name of a port in southern Peru from where the brandy was shipped to the United States prior to Prohibition.

Cyprus.   There are many grape brandies produced, which are sometimes flavored with nut and fruit essences. The most famous brands are Keo, Sodap, and Beristani.

Germany.   Asbach Uralt was first produced in 1907 by Hugo Asbach, who was also the first person to register a brand name of brandy at the Imperial Patent Office in Berlin. Another noteworthy brandy producer is Jacobi "1800."

Greece.   Metaxa distillery was founded in 1888 by Spyros Metaxa. Keo is another brandy producer.

Italy.   Stock Distillery of Trieste is the largest brandy producer in Italy. Its most famous label is *Stock 84.* Vecchia Romagna, originally known as Buton, was first produced in 1820 by a Frenchman, Jean Buton. The name was changed when Buton moved to Emilia-Romagna. Other brandy producers are Branca, Camel, Carpenè-Malvolti, Martini & Rossi, Oro Pilla, Ramazzotti, and Villa Zarri.

Mexico.   Presidente brandy is produced by the Pedro Domecq distillery.

Portugal.   A popular brand is E. Martin, 10-year-old brandy.

Spain.   On August 6, 1987, the world's third brandy appellation (following Armagnac and Cognac) was established by the government of Andalucía, Spain. The Consejo Regulador del Brandy de Jerez officially declared a *DE (denominación específica)* and provided strict regulations for the making of traditional brandy. The *DE* is a guarantee of authenticity for brandy from the Sherry region; the only other category protected with this *DE* status is *Cava,* the *méthode champenoise* sparkling wine.

The regulations require that "Brandy de Jerez" be made from the distillation and low- and medium-strength wines of healthy origin; it must be aged and matured within the same delimited production area as applies to sherry, and is limited to the recognized bodegas already producing sherry.

The production methods for blending and aging must conform to the criadera and solera systems already used for the making of sherry, while the length of maturation is counted by the time the brandy is kept inside the wooden barrels, which must be no larger than 1,000 liters (264 gallons). As in the case of sherry, bulk shipments of "Brandy de Jerez" will be permitted, but only under the control and stamp of the *Consejo Regulador*.

The official minimum aging requirements differentiate three distinct styles of brandy:

- *Brandy de Jerez Solera* has a minimum aging period of six months in wood.
- *Brandy de Jerez, Solera Reserva* has a minimum aging period of at least one year in wood.
- *Brandy de Jerez, Solera Gran Reserva* has a minimum aging period of at least three years in wood.

Brandy de Jerez differs from its competitors by an important technical factor—the solera system or "fractional aging system," as called by the British, which yields a more complex, mellow, elegant, and pleasing product.

Spain is the world's largest brandy-producing country and is the largest domestic market in the world for brandies. Jerez is the largest producer of quality in Spain, which in turn is the world's leading distiller of brandy.

Examples of Brandy de Jerez, Solera Gran Reserva are:

- *Cardenal Mendoza* from Sánchez-Romate
- *Carlos I* (first produced in 1892) and *Fundador* from Pedro Domecq
- *Conde de Osborne* from Osborne
- *Gran Capitán* from Bobadilla
- *Gran Duque de Alba* from Díez-Mérito
- *Gran Garvey* from Garvey
- *Lepanto* from González Byass
- *Terry Primero* from Fernando A. de Terry

Other Spanish brandy producers are Torres, Duff-Gordon, and Sandeman.

Fruit Brandy

Fruit brandies may be produced from almost any kind of fruit. Wild or cultivated fruits containing stones or seeds, and even most berries, will yield a suitable-tasting brandy. The production method is simple: The fruit is thoroughly washed, then chopped or ground until it resembles a *slurry,* known as the *mash.* At this point water and a specially cultivated yeast are added. The mixture is then allowed to ferment until all of the sugar has been metabolized. The mash is then pressed and the liquid collected; the solid mash is discarded or used as animal feed. The liquid is then distilled either in a continuous or pot still until the desired proof is reached. The brandy may also be aged in oak barrels. Fruit brandies are dry, usually colorless, and generally high proof. Fruit brandies state on their labels the name of the fruit used, or use accepted European names such as those listed below:

- *Airelle:* made from the red mountain cranberry.
- *Alisier:* made from rowanberries in Alsace, France.
- *Applejack* or *apple brandy:* made from apples; similar to Calvados. The premier producer of applejack is the Laird's & Co. Distillery, the oldest U.S. distillery, established in 1851.
- *Barack Pálinka:* made from apricots; produced in Austria and Hungary.
- *Calvados:* (see the later section on Calvados).
- *Coing:* made from quince in Alsace, France.
- *Fraise:* made from strawberries in France.
- *Framboise* (called Himbeergeist in Germany and parts of Switzerland): made from raspberries.
- *Houx:* made from holly berries in Alsace, France.
- *Kirsch* (France) *Kirschwasser* (Switzerland or Germany): made from small, semiwild black cherries which generally come from the Black Forest (Germany), the Vosges (France), or parts of Switzerland.
- *Mirabelle:* made from yellow plums in France.
- *Mûre:* made from blackberries.
- *Myrtille:* made from blueberries.
- *Nefle:* made from medlar fruit in Alsace, France.
- *Pêche:* made from peaches.
- *Pflümli:* a prune brandy from Switzerland.
- *Poire:* made from pears, mostly in Switzerland, Austria, Germany, France, and occasionally Canada. The best known is Poire Williams, each bottle of which contains a fully mature pear—not an easy accomplishment. After the pear has flowered and is about the size of a grape, it is placed, still on the branch, in the bottle. When the pear is mature, the branch is cut away, the pear washed, and the bottle filled with pear brandy. It is also known as *Pear Williams* or *pear brandy.*
- *Prunelle:* made from blackthorn or sloe berries. *Prunelle Sauvage* is made from wild plums.
- *Quetsch:* made from blue plums; usually produced in Alsace, France.
- *Schwarzwälder:* made from plums in Germany.
- *Slivovitz:* made from blue plums; usually produced in central Europe and Hungary. Also spelled *slivovice* in Czechoslovakia. Some producers are Jelinek (Czechoslovakia), Dettling (Switzerland), and Brana (France).
- *Sureau:* made from elderberries in Alsace, France.

Calvados

Calvados is made from different varieties of apples that grow in the Normandy, Brittany, and Maine regions of northwest France. Calvados is actually an *eau-de-vie* of cider, or a brandy distilled from either cider or the juice of fresh apples. The Swiss call their apple brandy *Batzi*.

The name *Calvados* is not French, but of Spanish origin. It comes from the name of a Spanish ship, El Calvador, of Phillip II's fleet, which sank off the French coast of Normandy in 1588.

Cider brandy was first distilled in 1553 by Gilles de Gouberville, Norman agronomist and farmer. In 1941, when the French government was instituting regulations to ensure consistent excellence for the region's distilled apple brandy, Calvados was born.

Calvados production is controlled by French law. Those carrying an *appellation contrôlée* designation on their labels must be made from apples grown in the legally established Calvados regions. They must also be pressed into cider and distilled there. They are generally double distilled in pot stills and suitably aged in oak barrels; these are considered the finest Calvados. Calvados labeled *appellation réglementée* is produced by the continuous still method and may use apples from other designated parts of Normandy; it is considered to be of a lower quality than that made in Calvados.

The production process.   Calvados is made by crushing apples into juice, which is fermented in oak barrels until it reaches between four to six degrees of alcohol. This takes approximately one month. The juice is then transferred to a still, in which it is double distilled.

According to a 1971 rule, Calvados must be aged in Limousin oak barrels of varying size (400 to 45,000 liters) for a period of not less than one year before being sold commercially. Generally, Calvados is aged for up to three or four years.

The alcohol content of Calvados ranges between 75 and 84 proof. The color, which is *not* an indication of age or lightness of body, varies among producers.

Younger Calvados are drier and retain an apply taste. The older blends acquire a more refined and subtle taste in aging.

Label designations.   The various designations are as follows:

- Calvados labeled "three-stars" is at least two years old.
- *Réserve* or *vieux* denote three years of aging.
- VO or *vieille réserve* indicates an age of four years.
- VSOP or *grande réserve* indicates an age of five years.
- The terms *extra, Napoléon, hors d'age,* or *age inconnu* apply solely to Calvados that are more than six years old.

A curious practice, referred to as *le trou normand* (literally, the Norman hole), is where, in the middle of a meal, true Normans drink a straight shot of Calvados, to "prepare the stomach" for what is to follow. Calvados actually is a natural aid to digestion, which helps eliminate the feeling one gets when one stuffs oneself. Calvados in this setting is served in "round-bottom" glasses that can't be set down, so diners won't dawdle and throw-off the timing of the next course in the kitchen. Others have stated emphatically that this practice is done so as to have an empty glass for the next drink, generally at the end of the meal.

Brand names.   The following are some of the better-known brands of Calvados:

Boulard	Morice
Busnel	Norois
Chevalier de Brevil	Pere Magliore
Montgommery	

Fruit-Flavored Brandies

These brandies are produced in basically the same manner as fruit brandies, except that a minimum of 2.5 percent sugar is added, along with natural coloring and flavoring derived from the base fruit. In addition to fruits, other ingredients can also be used—coffee beans and anise seeds, for example. According to U.S. federal law (1992), flavored brandies are a mixture of brandy, with a minimum of 2.5 percent sugar, flavored and colored with various types of fruit and/or herbs and that may or may not contain added sugar. It cannot be bottled at less than 60 proof (30 percent alcohol by volume).

Armagnac

Although Armagnac is technically a brandy, it is often confused with its close cousin, Cognac. However, Armagnac's taste is fuller and richer than that of Cognac and is generally described as less "burning," and more mellow.

Armagnac has been distilled in Gascony (in southwest France, 150 miles southeast of Bordeaux and 100 miles south of Cognac) since 1422, making it the world's oldest brandy. However, it was not until the mid-1600s that it was first exported by the Dutch.

The demarcated region of Armagnac comprises approximately 52,000 acres of quite sandy soil, mixed with some limestone, clay, and chalk. It is bounded roughly by the Garonne Valley to the north, Toulouse to the east, Bayonne and Bordeaux to the west, and the Pyrenees to the south. Armagnac's annual production of wine is under 79 million gallons. About one-quarter of this wine is distilled into brandy; the remainder is consumed as table wine.

The Armagnac region is divided into three zones: Upper Armagnac (Haut-Armagnac), the smallest area (3 percent of the total brandy production comes from this zone) to the east and south, which is often called "White Armagnac" because of its chalky, limestone-containing calcareous soil; Lower Armagnac (Bas-Armagnac) to the west (with sandy soil) is by far the largest zone (57 percent of production) and is often called "Black Armagnac," because of its forests; and Ténarèze (40 percent of production), centered on the town of Condom, with a clay-chalk soil. The quality, style, and taste of Armagnac varies from zone to zone, and it is generally agreed that the finest Armagnacs come from the Bas-Armagnac zone.

On May 25, 1909, the French government officially granted the region of Armagnac its own *appellation contrôlée*. Since then the production, viticulture, distillation process, and aging of Armagnac are subject to detailed official inspection and strict controls. These regulations have, since 1909, become more specific with more accurate definitions introduced in 1936, and perfected in 1972.

The production process.   The quality of Armagnac is based on several factors: the grapes, the wine, the distillation process, and the aging and blending processes.

The production of Armagnac involves a multistep process. Major white grape varieties such as the famed St-Emilion, Colombard, Folle Blanche, and Baco Blanc (a cross between the American Noah and Folle Blanche) are used as well as approximately half a dozen minor varieties. These grapes all have two things in common: They yield wines low in alcohol and are high in natural acidity.

After the juice ferments into wine, it is not racked, but instead is left in contact with the *lees* to extract additional flavoring components, which add more complexity. The wine is then transferred to either a pot still or continuous copper stills called *alembic armagnacais* (permitted since 1973), a term that has Moorish origins. The wine is distilled in one continuous, slow process (unlike Cognac production, in which there are two) to produce a colorless brandy with a powerful bouquet and flavor (sometimes described as *eau-de-feu* or fire-water). To accommodate the European Common Market, Armagnac producers may distill the Armagnac as high as 144 proof, without sacrificing odor and flavor characteristics. According to French law, all distillation must be completed by April 30 of the year following the grape harvest.

The brandies made from different varieties of grapes are aged separately for a minimum of three years. During this time there is constant evaporation due to changes in temperature, humidity, and the porosity of the wooden barrels. The amount that evaporates is approximately 3 percent of annual production (15 million bottles) and is known as "the angels' share." In most aging cellars in Armagnac the walls and ceilings are covered with a microscopic grey mold, the *Torula* fungus, which feeds on the alcohol vapors.

Armagnac is traditionally aged in black, sappy, tannic-rich, fine-grained, 400-liter oak barrels from the Monlezun forest of France. The development of Armagnac's complex flavor and deep amber color is dependent on ridges in the wooden barrels: coopers, using axes, shape each stave along the grain to expose more of the wood's surface area (from which the flavor and color is absorbed) to the brandy.

During this aging process, a slow oxidation also takes place, which intensifies the brandy's color and smoothes out its raw flavor. The Armagnac also acquires a musky aroma, reminiscent of hazelnuts, peaches, plums, prunes, and other fruits.

After proper aging, the last and perhaps most important part of the process takes place: blending, the secret to the production of an excellent Armagnac. Armagnac brandies of different origins and ages are skillfully blended under the strictest quality controls. This is an art that has been handed down through the centuries, generation after generation.

After blending, the brandy's alcohol level is adjusted by adding distilled water, and its color corrected by adding caramel. Armagnac is then kept in large barrels for an additional six months to allow for the proper curing, or "marrying," of the blend.

Label designations

- *VS* or *three-star* indicates that the youngest brandy in the blend is at least three years old.
- *VO, VSOP,* or *réserve* indicates that the youngest brandy in the blend is at least five years old.
- *Extra, Napoléon, XO,* or *vieille réserve* indicates that the youngest brandy used in the blend is at least six years old.
- *Hors d'Age* indicates that the youngest brandy used in the blend is at least ten years old.

Generally, the longer an Armagnac remains in wood, the finer and smoother its taste is. But after about 40 years in a barrel, there has been so much evaporation of alcohol and water that the remaining Armagnac starts to become concentrated and viscous.

Legislation enacted by the government rules that if a vintage date appears on the label of a bottle of Armagnac, it signifies the year in which the product was *distilled,* not the year in which the grapes were harvested. Producers must also indicate the date on which the vintage Armagnac came out of wood and went into glass. All Armagnac must come from the year indicated on the label and cannot have been blended with Armagnacs from other years. To guarantee quality, the government has ruled that no single vintage can be sold unless it is at least ten years old.

Brand names.   Some brands of Armagnac that are available in the United States are:

Château de Laubade	Laberdolive
Cles des Ducs	Lafontan
Clos de Moutouguet	Lapostolle
De Montal	Larressingle
Francis Darroze	Loubere
Janneau	Malliac

Maniban   Samalens
Marquis de Caussade   Sempé
Marquis de Monod   St. Vivant
Marquis de Montesquiou

Cognac

Cognac, a small medieval town in southwest France (about 100 miles north of Bordeaux and approximately 315 miles southwest of Paris) originally became known due to its proximity to the town of Angoulême, where the train from Paris once stopped on its way to Bordeaux continuing to Spain. Many foreign buyers of wines and distilled spirits thus found their way to Cognac and, once there, could always be assured of accommodation by the Cognac families.

Cognac is located in the departments of Charente and Charente Maritime (which were established in 1791 by combining the provinces of Aunis, Saintonge, and Angoumois). The Cognac region's stony, chalk-rich soil (probably due to ancient oyster beds), its climate, and the specific grape varieties grown there, as well as the methods used in distilling, blending, and aging the brandy, give that beverage its unique flavor.

Cognac (the brandy) was first produced more or less by accident; until the fifteenth century Charente was strictly a wine-producing area. Its stony chalky soil was mainly suitable for growing varieties of grapes (St-Emilion, Folle Blanche, and Colombard) that made for an exceedingly acidic white wine. These wines did not stand up well on long sea voyages and were far less appealing than the delicious white wines produced by grape growers on the nearby Atlantic coast; and, the fact that these poor, thin, acidic wines were being taxed at the same rate as better-quality wines hardly increased their popularity.

Undaunted, the industrious farmers of the Charente decided to try an experiment. Seamen from Britain and Scandinavia regularly visited the area to obtain salt, which was much sought after by cod and herring preservers. The Cognac vintners realized that they could develop an export market, utilizing these foreign cargo ships, for their rather ordinary wine if they distilled it. (Approximately ten gallons of wine produce one gallon of brandy.) This, they reasoned, would save ship cargo space and reduce export taxes, which at that time were based on bulk. The original idea was that the distilled spirit, which had an alcohol content of 75 percent, would later be reconstituted by adding water. (The region was known as *Cognac* in England as early as 1687, when records offered for sale "Conyack Brandy.")

During this time trade routes were blockaded because of the War of Spanish Succession (1701–1714) and export sales to England and the Netherlands were halted; the distilled wine from Cognac thus had to be stored for a time. When trade resumed, the Limousin oak-aged distilled wine was found to have lost its fiery taste and to have taken on a beautiful golden amber color. Its flavor had also improved and it had acquired a great mellowness.

To accomplish the distillation, the vintners had used an onion-shaped pot still called an *alembic,* which had been brought to the region five centuries earlier by invading Moors, who had used it to distill the nectar of flowers for perfume. (Later, it was used by medieval alchemists in attempts to turn nonprecious metals into gold.) The distillation process, to everyone's astonishment, had resulted in a drink that was delicious in its own right. Since the new drink was as clear as water, the vintners dubbed it *eau-de-vie* (water of life). This "water of life," which was drunk straight, enjoyed tremendous success on the medieval export market.

Word about the discovery spread quickly. Naturally, vintners in other areas tried to copy the production techniques that were fast making the farmers of Cognac the wealthiest in the land, but it seemed that nature had balanced the scales. The vintners of Cognac had struggled unsuccessfully for centuries to produce good wines from grapes grown in their light gray, stony, chalky soil; but when growing grapes for the distilled brandy, they found that the chalkier the soil the better. Other areas simply were not able to produce a comparable product.

Would-be imitators flourished nonetheless, until on May 1, 1909, the French government passed a law proclaiming that only the product made in a sharply defined "delimited area"—250,000 acres surrounding the town of Cognac—could be called Cognac. All other brandies, however good, must be called by some other name.

The Cognac production area.   In 1936, the French government officially divided the delimited Cognac area (see Figure 8-1) into seven sections (the Bois Ordinaires and Bois à Terroir are usually grouped together so there is thus sometimes confusion over whether there are six or seven districts). The seven sections, which (very roughly) describe concentric circles around the town of Cognac, are: Grande Champagne; Petite Champagne; Borderies; Fin Bois; Bon Bois; and Bois Ordinaire and Bois à Terroir (also called Bois à Communs). The highest-quality Cognacs are produced in Grande Champagne and Petite Champagne.

The production process.   Under French law, only these major grape varieties may be used in making Cognac: St-Emilion (known as Ugni Blanc in California, and Trebbiano in Italy), Folle Blanche, and Colombard. The grapes are generally harvested quite early, when sugars barely reach 17 degrees Brix, ensuring a wine with a low alcohol content (about 8 percent) and a very high acid level (usually above 1 percent).

After the juice ferments into wine, it is slowly warmed and transferred into copper pot stills (Figure 8-2), which are heated by gas or coal. The first distillation lasts between eight and 12 hours, producing the *brouillis,* which is a distillate of approximately 50 to 60 proof. This is heated a second time for about 12 hours in an extremely critical process; many years of experience are necessary before one can control temperature and distillate strength—all in the proper balance. The colorless liquid (called the *bonne chauffe*) that is produced by the second distillation is a youthful, strong Cognac which must be matured.

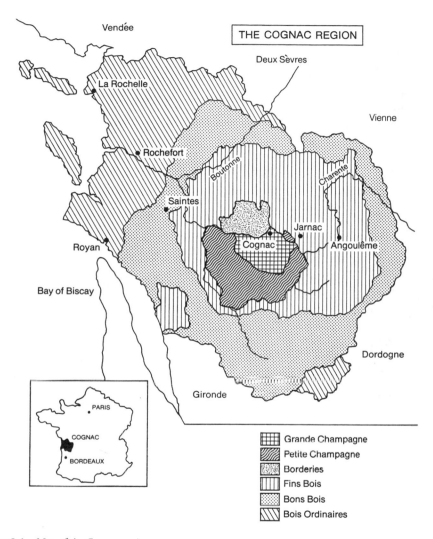

FIGURE 8-1 Map of the Cognac region.

French law states that the final distillate must not have an alcohol content exceeding 72 percent; if it does, it may not be called Cognac. Distillation at this proof allows for the retention of substantial amounts of flavoring congeners.

Under French law, the capacity of these stills may not exceed 793 gallons; this restriction prevents the swift conversion of wine to a distilled spirit. It allows for pinpoint accuracy, however, in restricting or facilitating the flow of the distillate. French law also

FIGURE 8-2   A classic Cognac alembic, or copper pot still, which was used continuously from 1880 through 1973 by the Hennessy Company in France. (Courtesy of Moët-Hennessy, France)

dictates that distillation must be completed by March 31, while the wine is in its bloom of youth, fruity and unoxidized.

Aging.   After Cognac has been distilled for the second time, it is placed into barrels (which hold about 55 gallons) that are made of oak wood from the Limousin and Tronçais forests. The oak used has a considerable influence on the bouquet and taste of the Cognac; it introduces soluble substances such as aromatic aldehydes, lignin derivatives, gum, polyphenols, salts, and sugars. When Cognac is first placed in the barrel it is about 70 percent alcohol and is crystal clear in color. During the aging process, the oak from the barrels imparts its taste, color, and odor to the final product, turning the clear *eau-de-vie* into a mellow, golden drink.

Aging is a critical step in the production process and in conjunction with soil qualities, is a key factor in determining the quality and price of the final distilled spirit. The older a Cognac becomes, the smoother its flavor, the more subtle its aroma, and the more it costs. Most cognacs are ultimately blends that combine distilled spirits from varying sections and vintages into a final product. Currently, in the town of Cognac, there are barrels of distilled spirits that have been aging for a hundred years or more.

Aging barrels of Cognac are stored in warehouses that are usually built on stilts above the ground so that air can circulate freely around the barrels. During this time, there is constant evaporation due to changes in temperature, humidity, and the porosity of the wooden barrels, reducing the alcoholic content of the Cognac to approximately 40 percent. Approximately 3 to 5 percent of annual Cognac production per year is lost through evaporation (this amounts to 22 million bottles, or one-fourth of annual world sales). In order to compensate for this loss, distillers regularly "top off" the barrels with similar Cognacs.

Once bottled, Cognac remains unchanged: unlike wines that age in the bottle, Cognac ages only in barrel. Therefore, a Cognac that has aged three years in oak is a three-year old Cognac, even if it has been sitting in a musty cellar for 100 years.

Aging barrels of Cognac virtually fill the town of Cognac. The stone-walled warehouses of the largest firms often hold as many as 200,000 barrels, stacked in three tiers. A single warehouse may contain 30,000 barrels. Barrels of young, middle-aged, and old Cognacs are stored in each of the warehouses. This way, if there is a fire, a firm will not be left with a shortage of Cognac of a certain year.

Blending.   The last critical phase of Cognac making is the blending of the final distilled spirit. There are currently some 320 Cognac firms, each of which has its own master taster or blender who must reproduce, year after year, the distinctive character and flavor that have become the trademark of the company's product. The possibilities are endless: some firms produce blends that are hefty and full-bodied; others create distilled spirits that are fruity and mellow, or light and smooth. It is the master blender's job to maintain the integrity of the company's signature taste.

His is a difficult job: He must be able to discern, by taste and smell, the year in which the grapes of a certain Cognac were grown and from which sections of the region the grapes came—even from which section within a section. Since the same section may produce quite a different variety of Cognacs in different years, the taster's job is as much an art as a science. He must, in effect, analyze with one sniff the life history of each sample brought to him.

When the tasting is complete, the master selects the Cognacs that he will use to produce this year's blends. He then writes out various formulas and creates samples using the old, middle-aged, and young Cognacs that he has selected. He tastes the samples and sips, smells, and compares them to the established brands he is trying to duplicate. When there is the slightest difference, he revises his formula and has new samples prepared. The process goes on until the precisely correct bouquet and taste have been obtained.

Labels.   The ultimate results of the blender's efforts will be a line of Cognacs that represent a range of average ages and prices. The Cognac drinker can tell a great deal about the particular blend he is purchasing from the label on the bottle.

The following letters are used on Cognac labels in abbreviated designations of various classifications:

E = extra
O = old
P = pale
S = special or superior
V = very
X = extremely

These designations are commonly found:

- *VS* or *three-star:* This means that the average aging period of the Cognac in the blend is five to nine years and the youngest Cognac in the blend is a minimum of three years old.
- *VO, VSOP,* or *réserve:* These means that the average age of the Cognac used in the blend is from 12 to 20 years. The youngest Cognac in this blend is at least four-and-a-half years old.
- *Extra, XO, Napoléon, VVSOP, cordon bleu, vieille réserve, grande réserve, royal,* and *vieux:* These terms apply to Cognacs that contain a very high percentage of Cognac that has been aged for 20, 30, or 40 years or more. The youngest Cognac in this blend is at least six-and-a-half years old.

The following are label designations:

- *Grande Fine Champagne,* or *Grande Champagne:* These terms identify Cognacs made exclusively from grapes grown in the Grande Champagne section of Cognac.
- *Petite Fine Champagne,* or *Petite Champagne:* These terms mean that the Cognac is a blend made from grapes grown in the Grande Champagne and Petite Champagne sections of Cognac; at least 50 percent of it must be from grapes grown in the Grande Champagne section.

The terms *fine Cognac* and *grande fine,* which may also be found on Cognac labels, have no legally defined meaning. The designations *extra old* (EO) and *very old pale* (VOP) are not officially recognized by the Bureau du Cognac.

From 1946 until 1986, French law prohibited a vintage date on a bottle of Cognac. In 1987 this prohibition was lifted.

Serving Cognac.   Cognac can be enjoyed in a variety of ways. It has traditionally been regarded as an after-dinner drink, but in some countries, it is served before or with a meal almost like wine. (The Japanese mix it with seltzer.) Purists prefer to enjoy the older, finer

FIGURE 8-3   Proper glassware for serving Cognac. (Courtesy Cognac Information Bureau)

Cognacs unmixed. A Cognac should be clear in color, but depth of tint is no indication of quality. Traditionally, Cognacs are served in tulip-shaped glasses tall enough to allow a reasonable aroma to build, yet small enough to be cradled entirely in one hand (the hand provides an overall gentle warmth that encourages the aroma). This is the type of glass used by the master blenders (Figure 8-3).

   Since traditional Cognac glasses are not widely available in this country, most people prefer to drink the distilled spirit from classic balloon-shaped brandy snifters. The main consideration is to select a glass that will enhance the beverage's bouquet. The glass should be large enough (ten to 12 ounces) to enable the liquid to move around with ease, spreading the bouquet over a wide surface area. Ideally, the neck should be slightly indented to help the distilled spirit retain its bouquet. Unfortunately, many people choose much larger snifters (some holding as much as 32 fluid ounces), resembling footed aquariums, minus the water and goldfish. The major problem with such glasses is that if a couple of ounces of Cognac are poured and the glass swirled, most of the Cognac adheres to the sides of the enlarged glass. At $40.00 or more per bottle of Cognac, that can be quite expensive.

Another popular item, often sold in specialty stores or catalogs, is a "brandy heater." It features a brandy snifter, perched at a 45-degree angle on a metal holder, above a short candle. The manufacturer suggests that you first pour some Cognac into the glass, light the candle below the bowl of the glass, and allow the candle to gently warm the liquid. In reality, if one follows these directions one will burn one's hands on the glass. And, subjected to an intensified heat, the Cognac's vapors, which are an intrinsic part of its enjoyment, will "burn off."

Although most people prefer not to mix older Cognacs, younger (VS, or three-star) Cognac makes delightful highballs when mixed with soda water, leaving the palate more receptive to wines. Cognac and freshly squeezed orange juice makes an enjoyable cocktail. After dinner, Cognac is the perfect companion to coffee.

Younger Cognacs are also excellent for use in cooking. As the Cognac heats, it releases vapors that impart a subtle and distinctive aroma to the dish. Creating a flambé, in particular, is a dramatic but simple culinary technique that adds excitement and flavor to a variety of plain and fancy fare. The alcoholic content of the distilled spirit is burned off during the process.

Some available brands of Cognac are:

Armand Roux	Hine
Bisquit	Leyrat
Camus	Martell
Casmèze	Monnet
Château de Fontpinot	Odeon
Château Paulet	Otard
Courvoisier	Prince Hubert de Polignac
Delamain	Ragnaud
Denise-Mounié	Rémy Martin
John Exshaw	Renault
Gaston de Lagrange	Salignac
Hardy	M. Tiffon
Hennessy	

▶ OTHER DISTILLED SPIRITS

Akvavit, Aquavit, and Schnapps

Akvavit is a high-proof spirit made from a distillate of caraway seeds, fruits, herbs, and spices; because of its potency, it was nicknamed "Black Death." It is quite popular in the Scandinavian countries where it is known as Akvavit, Aquavit, or, in some locales, Brännvin.

Schnapps is a high-proof distillate flavored with numerous aromatic herbs; it is produced in Germany, Holland, and most Scandinavian countries. (It should not be confused with peppermint schnapps, which is a liqueur.)

Anise-Flavored Distilled Spirits

Anise-based distilled spirits are produced by either infusion or the addition of flavoring and have a high alcoholic content.

Absinthe is an aromatic, yellow-green distilled spirit, flavored with oil of wormwood. The technical name of the main ingredient was *Artemisia absinthium* (wormwood), an Old World plant or herb that grows about three feet high and is botanically related to our southwestern sagebrush. The oil from the leaves, called *absinthol,* contains a rather strong narcotic, *thujone* ($C_{10}H_{16}0$), which is poisonous in large doses. Absinthe was officially banned throughout most of the world on March 16, 1915 (Spain in 1937).

Absinthe, with its dry, bitter, licoricelike flavor and herbal aroma, was resurrected in 1922 under the name Pernod, minus the toxic wormwood. In its place, anise was substituted; the alcohol content was lowered to 86 proof and the drink's popularity was once again on the rise.

The French drink their anise distilled spirits in a tall glass with ice-cold water, one part anise distilled spirit to five parts water. When you drink anise distilled spirits either chilled directly from the refrigerator or over ice, you may notice a cloudiness or opalescence, which adds to the beauty of the drink.

Other anise-based distilled spirits are:

Anesone (Italy)
Chinchon (Spain)
Herbisant (United States)
Masticha (Greece)
Ojen (Spain)
Ouzo (Greece)
Pastis/Pernod/Ricard (France)

Grappa. Grappa is a distillate made primarily from the skins, pulp, and seeds (collectively known as *pomace* or *vinaccia* in Italian) of grapes—the remains from the pressing of the grapes for winemaking. The *pomace* utilized in the production of grappa is generally still quite moist, which adds flavor and varietal character. In Italy grappa is made by distillers collectively known as *grappaioli.*

The origin of the name *grappa* comes from a town called *Bassano del Grappa* in the Veneto region of Italy, where grappa was originally produced. Northern Italy accounts for approximately 90 percent of the grappa sold in Italy.

In Italy, grappa is divided into two types—*pregiate* (premium) and *correnta* (standard or normal). The only *consorzi* in Italy that have developed any type of regulation relative to grappa exists in the region of Trentino-Alto Adige. Elsewhere, the only guarantee of quality a consumer has is the producer's name and reputation.

In the production process, water is added to the pomace (which may be from either red or white grapes), along with yeast and sugar. After the pomace finishes refermenting, the resulting liquid is distilled in either the traditional small *pot still* or the more modern *continuous still.* It is generally removed from the still at between 100 to 130 proof. As with other distilled spirits, only the *heart* or center of the distillate is utilized in the final product.

It is estimated that 225 pounds of pomace yields approximately five liters of pure alcohol. The pomace utilized in making grappa should be fresh and not more than one day old. The pomace of pressed fruit such as apples, apricots, and pears can also be used.

Grappa can be a blend of many different grape varieties or be made from a single grape variety (known as *Grappa di Monovitigno).*

Other types of grappa are *Floral Grappa,* which is infused and often bottled with flower petals. *Fruit Grappa* is infused with or distilled from fresh fruit, similar to an *eau-de-vie. Ùe* is a distillate from a mixture of pomace and wine. *Grappa Aromatizzata* is grappa infused and often bottled with herbs and is also known as *herbal grappa. Grappa Con Ruta* develops its characteristic odor and taste from *rue.* Rue is a strong scented herb from the *ruta graveolens* family, with yellow flowers and bitter-tasting leaves, formerly used for medicinal purposes but now used occasionally as a flavoring for grappa.

The collected distillate is usually stored in ceramic, stainless steel, or glass containers; it is bottled when quite young. However, if it is determined that the distillate should be aged, then oak barrels are used.

Old-style grappa, which was rough or coarse tasting (depending on raw material and production methods utilized) was usually wood aged several years before it smoothed out. Modern-style distillation, which utilizes better raw materials, results in a higher quality grappa that is considerably smoother and more refined. Nowadays, grappa is rarely aged in wooden barrels.

In addition to a considerably higher quality grappa, hand-blown glass bottles and flasks have become an important part of the overall packing of grappa.

Grappa designations. *Grappa Giovane* is young, unaged grappa, generally about six months old. *Grappa Invecchiata* is grappa that has been aged for months or even years, generally in wooden barrels, hence the amber color.

Consumption and Service.   Grappa is usually clear or faintly amber in color, with a fruity bouquet reminiscent of the natural nuances of the different woods occasionally used to age it. Its taste is round, soft, and fruity, with a flavor of dry leaves.

Grappa is traditionally served after dinner as a digestive; it is consumed straight, either at cool room temperature, or well chilled in a small glass or brandy snifter. Grappa is occasionally added to espresso coffee to make *caffè corretto.*

Merchandising Ideas.   For on-premise merchandising, take a wide-mouth, one-gallon glass jar, fill it with any of the following ingredients: Muscat grapes, blueberries, cherries, dried figs, dried candied-fruit, lime, mixed melons, watermelon, mangoes, apricots, peaches, pears, pineapple, raisins, raspberries, strawberries, sun-dried tomatoes, honey, olives, garlic, red onions, or various dried herbs (anise, coriander, cumin, dill, fennel, mint, rosemary, sage, or tarragon). Then add one-third to one-half cup white sugar and fill almost to the top with grappa. Cover jar with lid and allow to age for three to four months. To serve, ladle out several pieces of fruit with some of the liquid into a small glass . . . and enjoy!

A martini can also be made by substituting grappa for either the gin or vodka. Grappa can also be utilized in the making of sorbet.

Grappa is also known as *alcools blancs, eau-de-vie, grape pomace brandy,* or *pomace brandy* (for short). Grappa is produced in many countries around the world and is known as *aguardiente de orujo* (or *orujo*) in Spain; *aguardente de bagaceira* (or *bagaceira*) in Portugal; *dop brandy* in South Africa; *marc* in France; *trester* in Germany; and *tsigouthia* in Greece.

► CORDIALS AND LIQUEURS

The word *cordial* is derived from the Latin word *cor* or *cordis,* meaning *heart* because the earliest cordials were administered to the sick to stimulate the heart and lighten the spirit. *Liqueur* is derived from the Latin word *liquefacere* and means to dissolve or melt, a fitting term since the entire process involves dissolving selected ingredients in a neutral distilled spirit. The words *cordial* and *liqueur* are identical in meaning and are so indistinguishable from the point of view of nomenclature that they are always mentioned together in federal and state laws and regulations. *Liqueur* is generally accepted as the European name and *cordial* as the American, although in practice, this is not quite true. For brevity's sake, liqueur will be utilized in place of the redundant term *cordial.*

Liqueurs sold in the United States, according to federal regulations must contain sugar, dextrose, or levulose, or any combination thereof, equal to a minimum of 2.5 percent by weight of the finished product. In practice, most liqueurs contain large percentages (up to 35 percent) of some sweetening agent. While there is no minimum alcohol level mandated by the federal government, most liqueurs are between 34 to 60 proof, while others are as high as 100 proof.

Production Process

The aromas, flavors, and tastes of liqueurs are produced by the addition of herbs, seeds, barks, roots, plants, flowers, fruit, fruit stones, and peels. The alcohol base can be brandy or neutral distilled spirits.

Liqueurs are made by any of three different methods: *maceration* (also known as infusion); *percolation;* and *distillation.* Maceration and percolation are also known as the *cold methods,* because the flavoring materials are sensitive to heat and would be damaged by it. The cold method is a lengthy process that can take as long as one year.

Maceration is not unlike the brewing of tea. Fruit or other ingredients are placed directly into the distilled spirit or brandy and allowed to steep until sufficient amounts of the aroma and flavor have been extracted into the distilled spirit. Each ingredient has its own unique aroma and taste. After the steeping is complete, the distilled spirit is drawn off and filtered; water is added and the color adjusted, and it is finally blended with sugar syrup or occasionally honey for consistency of taste. It is allowed to age or "marry" from several months to one year, in order to blend the flavors before bottling.

The *percolation* method is similar to the percolation of coffee. Distilled spirits are put into the bottom of a tank and the botanicals (fruits, flowers, and others) are placed in a basketlike container at the top of the tank. The distilled spirits from the bottom of the tank are then pumped to the top where they are sprayed over the botanicals, dripping back to the bottom to be repercolated over and over until the desired flavor has been extracted.

Distillation, also known as the *hot extraction method,* is the process that is usually employed with most seeds, peels, flowers, roots, barks, plants, or some combination. These materials can withstand heat and benefit from a quicker extraction of flavor. The ingredients are first "softened" by soaking in brandy or distilled spirits for several days before being transferred to a pot still.

Since all distillates are colorless, harmless artificial (and natural) colorants are added, along with sugar syrup.

Proprietary and Generic Liqueur

France, Italy, and Holland produce more than 50 percent of all liqueurs currently available; the following table gives information on many of these (asterisks denote proprietary brands).

PROPRIETARY AND GENERIC LIQUEURS

Liqueur	Flavor/Base	Color	Proof	Country
Abisante	anise-herb	yellow-green	120	Many
Abricotine*	apricot	orange-amber	60–70	France
Advokatt/Advocaat	eggnog	creamy yellow	30	Holland, Germany
Aki*	plum	red	49	Japan
Alize*	passion fruit, Cognac	yellow	32	France
Amaretto	almond, apricot	russet	54–56	Many
Amaretto di Saronno*	almond, apricot	russet	56	Italy
Ambrosia*	caramel	amber	56	Canada
Anisette	licorice	clear	42–96	Many
Apricot liqueur	apricot	orange-amber	48–70	Many
Apry*	apricot	orange-amber	60	France
Aurum*	orange	orange	80	Italy
Ashanti Gold*	cacao, Armagnac	chocolate	56	Denmark
Bahia Coffee liqueur*	coffee	brown	53	Brazil
Bailey's Irish Cream*	cream, Irish whiskey	beige	34	Ireland
Banana liqueur	banana	yellow	48–60	Many
Benedictine*	herbs	dark amber	80	France
Blackberry liqueur	blackberry	red-purple	48–70	Many
Black Raspberry liqueur	raspberry	purple	48–56	Many
Boggs Cranberry*	cranberry	red	40	U.S.A.
Café Brizard*	coffee	dark brown	50	France
Café de Love*	coffee	brown	53	Mexico
Café Sport	coffee	brown	48	U.S.A.
Caffe Lolita*	coffee	brown	53	U.S.A.
Carolan's Irish Cream*	cream, Irish whiskey	beige	34	Ireland
Certosa*	citrus	green	80	Italy
Chambord*	raspberry	red	33	France
Chartreuse*	peppermint	yellow or green	80, 110	France

PROPRIETARY AND GENERIC LIQUEURS *(CONTINUED)*

Liqueur	Flavor/Base	Color	Proof	Country
Cheri-Suisse*	chocolate, cherry	dark brown	52	Switzerland
CherriStock*	cherry	red	50	Italy
Cherry Heering*	cherry	dark red	49	Denmark
Cherry liqueur	cherry	red	49–80	Many
Cherry Marnier*	Dalmatian cherry	dark red	48	France
Chococo liqueur*	chocolate, coconut	dark brown	60	U.S.A.
Chocolate Banana liqueur	banana, chocolate	brown	54	Many
Chocolate liqueur	chocolate	dark brown	34–56	Many
Chocolate Mint	chocolate, mint	brown	54	Many
Chocolate Raspberry	chocolate, raspberry	brown	54	Many
CocoRibe*	rum, coconut	clear	60	U.S.A.
Coffee House liqueur*	coffee	dark brown	54	West Indies
Coffee liqueur	coffee	dark brown	48–80	Many
Cointreau*	orange	clear	80	France
Cordial Médoc*	fruit, brandy	dark red	80	France
Cranberry liqueur	cranberry	red	40	Many
Cream of Raspberry liqueur	raspberry	red	60	Many
Crème de Almond	almond	red or clear	54–56	Many
Crème de Ananas	pineapple	clear	48–56	Many
Crème de Banana	banana	yellow	50–60	Many
Crème de Cacao	cocoa, vanilla	dark brown or clear	48–60	Many
Crème de Café	coffee	dark brown	60	Many
Crème de Cassis	black currant	red-brown	30–70	Many
Crème de Celery	celery	yellow or clear	50–60	Many
Crème de Fraise	strawberry	red	50–60	Many
Crème de Framboise	raspberry	red-purple	50–60	Many
Crème de Mandarine	tangerine, orange	orange	50–60	Many
Crème de Menthe	mint	green or clear	48–60	Many
Crème de Moka	coffee	dark brown	50–60	Many

Crème de Noisette	hazelnut	clear	50–60	Many
Crème de Noyaux or Noya	almond	red, pink, or clear	50–60	Many
Crème de Prunelle	plum	brown-purple	50–80	Many
Crème de Rose	rose petal	light red	50–60	Many
Crème de Thé	tea	brown	50–60	Many
Crème de Vanille	vanilla	clear	50–60	Many
Crème de Violet	violet	lavender	50-60	Many
Crème d'Yvette	violet, bubblegum	lavender	50–60	Many
Curaçao	orange	clear, blue, or orange	54–80	Many
Demi-Tasse Coffee Cream liqueur*	cream, Irish whiskey	beige	34	Ireland
Devonshire Cream liqueur*	cream, Scotch whisky	beige	34	Scotland
Drambuie*	honey, herbs, and Scotch whisky	amber	70	Scotland
Dunphy's Original Cream*	cream, Irish whiskey	beige	34	Ireland
Emmet Irish Cream*	cream, Irish whiskey	beige	34	Ireland
Expresso Coffee liqueur†	coffee	brown	60	Italy
Fior d'Alpi*	anise, fruit	yellow	92	Italy
Forbidden Fruit*	shaddock and other fruits	red-brown	64	U.S.A.
Frangelico*	hazelnuts	amber	56	Italy
Galacafé*	coffee, cream	dark red	53	Italy
Galliano*	vanilla, licorice	yellow	70	Italy
Get Peppermint*	mint	green or clear	60	France
Ginger Schnapps	ginger	clear	60	Many
Glayva*	herbs, Scotch whisky	amber	80	Scotland
Goldwasser	orange	clear	60–80	Many
Grand Giffard liqueur*	orange, spices	amber	80	France
Grand Marnier*	orange	amber	80	France
Grasshopper	cacao, mint	green	48–55	Many
Greensleeves Cream*	cream, Irish whiskey	beige	34	Ireland

PROPRIETARY AND GENERIC LIQUEURS *(CONTINUED)*

Liqueur	Flavor/Base	Color	Proof	Country
Grenadine	pomegranate	red	34–50	Many
Häagen-Dazs*	cocoa, Cognac	beige	34	Holland
Halb und Halb*	citrus, cloves	light brown	76	Germany
Honey Dew Melon*	honeydew, lime	lime	30	U.S.A.
Iced Tea	blended tea	dark gold	60	U.S.A.
Irish Coffee liqueur	coffee	brown	70	Ireland
Irish Mist*	honey, Irish whiskey	amber	70	Ireland
Irish Velvet*	coffee, Irish whiskey	amber	46	Ireland
Izarra*	honey, brandy	yellow or green	86, 100	France
Jeremiah Weed*	fruit and Bourbon whiskey	amber	100	U.S.A.
Kahlúa*	coffee	dark brown	53	Mexico
Kirsch liqueur	cherry	clear	90–100	Many
Kona Coffee liqueur*	coffee	brown	53	U.S.A.
Krupnik	honey	amber	80	Poland
Kümmel	caraway	clear	54–70	Many
La Grande Passion*	tropical fruits and Armagnac	orange	48	France
Licor 43 (Cuarenta y Tres*)	vanilla, citrus	yellow	68	Spain
Lochan Ora*	honey, herbs, and Scotch whisky	gold	70	Scotland
Macadamia Nut liqueur	nut	pale yellow	53	U.S.A.
Malibu*	coconut	clear	56	Canada
Mandarine Napoléon*	tangerine	orange	80	France
Maple liqueur	maple, brandy	brown	53	Canada
Maraschino	cherry	clear	50–64	Many
Midori*	melon	green	46	Japan
Mokka Coffee liqueur*	coffee	brown	55	Mexico
Monte Téca*	citrus, tequila	amber	60	Mexico

Nassau Royale*	herbs, fruit	amber	67	Bahamas
Neapolitan liqueur*	vanilla, licorice	yellow	80	Italy
Nocello*	walnut	amber	48	Italy
Nocino	walnut	amber	80	Italy
Opal Nera*	anise	brown	80	Italy
Orange liqueur	orange	orange or clear	50–60	Many
Paradyse*	violets	light blue	80	Italy
Peach liqueur	peach	clear	50–60	Many
Pear liqueur	pear	clear	50–60	Many
Peppermint Schnapps	mint	clear	50–60	Many
Petite liqueur*	honey, citrus	golden	36	France
Pineapple liqueur	pineapples	yellow	53	Many
Pistachio	pistachio	green	50–60	U.S.A.
Praline*	vanilla, pecan	amber	40	U.S.A.
Raspberry liqueur	raspberry	red-purple	50–60	Many
Rock & Rye	fruit, whiskey	gold	48–80	U.S.A.
Roiano*	herbs, spices	yellow	80	Italy
Rosolio*	rose petal, spices	red	48–60	Italy
Rumona*	honey, spices	amber	63	Jamaica
Sabra*	chocolate, orange	brown	60	Israel
Sabroso Coffee liqueur*	coffee	brown	50	Mexico
Sambuca	anise	clear	84	Italy
Samoca Coffee liqueur*	coffee	brown	80	Italy
Sloe Gin	wild plum	red	42–60	Many
Southern Comfort*	citrus, whiskey	amber	80, 100	U.S.A.
Strawberry liqueur	strawberry	red	44–60	Many
Strega*	herbs, spices	yellow	80	Italy
Tia Maria*	coffee	dark brown	53	Jamaica
Tilus*	truffle	amber	70	Italy
Triple Sec	orange	orange or clear	50–80	Many
Tuaca*	caramel, vanilla	golden	84	Italy

PROPRIETARY AND GENERIC LIQUEURS *(CONTINUED)*

Liqueur	Flavor/Base	Color	Proof	Country
Valentino liqueur*	vanilla, licorice	yellow	80	Italy
Vandermint*	chocolate, mint	dark brown	52	Turkey
Venetian Cream*	cream, brandy	beige	40	Italy
Vieille Curé*	herbs, vanilla	green or yellow	86, 100	France
VOV*	eggnog	cream	18	Italy
Waterford Cream*	cream, Irish whiskey	beige	34	Ireland
Wild Turkey liqueur*	fruit and Bourbon whiskey	amber	80	U.S.A.
Wisniak	cherry	dark red	48–60	Many
Wisniowka*	cherry	dark red	80	Poland
Yukon Jack*	fruit, whiskey	amber	100	Canada

Other Liqueurs and Flavorings

Crème liqueurs.   The term means that they are sweet liqueurs generally sugared and not dairy creams. This term could in fact be used to describe most liqueurs.

Falernum.   This is a colorless, slightly alcoholic spiced syrup originating in the Caribbean, used as a flavoring in rum cocktails.

Orgeat.   A sweet-almond-flavored nonalcoholic syrup used in certain cocktails. It is a combination of almond flavoring, orange flower water, and barley water.

Liqueur producers.   Some of the major producers are:

Arrow	Drioli	Morandini
Bols	DuBouchett	Mouquin
Vincente Bosch	Garnier	Old Mr. Boston
Marie Brizard	Peter Hagen	Patrician
Cointreau	Jacquin	Stock
Cusenier	Kord	Hiram Walker
DeKuyper	Leroux	WF
Dolphi	Libarna	

Serving and Storing Liqueurs

There is really no need to refrigerate liqueurs either before or after opening. Due to the alcohol and sugar levels, they have a very long shelf life and will take changes in temperature and humidity quite well. The exception is cream liqueurs, which should be refrigerated after opening and consumed within six weeks. It is advisable to keep all liqueurs out of direct sunlight because the rays could cause a slight color change.

Traditionally, most liqueurs are served after dinner because of their high sugar levels. Liqueurs are also natural digestives, because they contain many different bitter botanicals.

Liqueurs can be served at room temperature, chilled from the refrigerator, or over ice. A liqueur served with crushed or shaved ice is called a *frappé*. Liqueurs are also suitable as "long drinks" (with seltzer water) and in cocktails, and can be used in cooking.

9

Distilled Spirits

ermented alcoholic beverages existed
before distillation was understood or practiced. Fruits and grain were used to produce
wine and beer. The first known documentation of distillation was in 1116 B.C., in
China, using fermented rice. Other important chronological dates in the history of
distilled spirits include the following:

800 B.C.: Distilled spirits made in China from rice and molasses
A.D. 100: Greeks utilized distilling equipment
A.D. 800: Moors learned the art of distilling from the Egyptians
A.D. 1100: Irish whiskey was distilled in Ireland
A.D. 1200: Vodka was distilled in Poland and Russia
A.D. 1422: Armagnac was distilled in France
A.D. 1494: Scotch whisky was distilled in Scotland
A.D. 1530: Cognac was distilled in France
A.D. 1533: Apple brandy was distilled in France
A.D. 1600: Rum was distilled in Barbados
A.D. 1614: Gin was distilled in Holland
A.D. 1750: Rye whiskey was distilled in the United States
A.D. 1789: Bourbon whiskey was distilled in the United States

Alcoholic beverages as defined by law include any beverage in liquid form that contains not less than one-half of 1 percent (0.5 percent) of ethyl alcohol (ethanol) by volume and is intended for human consumption.

These beverages are classified by their method of production:

Fermented beverages.   Produced through fermentation alone, these beverages are of two kinds: malted beverages, brewed principally from cereal grains and malted barley, flavored with hops; and wine, the result of fermentation of grape or other fruit juices.

Distilled spirits.   Produced by distillation of any alcohol-containing mixture—wine or the distiller's beer from a fermentation process. Whiskey, vodka, rum, brandy, gin, and tequila comprise the principal classes of distilled spirits. Another class—liqueurs—is not directly distilled but consists of beverage spirits treated with flavoring materials.

▶ TYPES OF STILLS

Still

An apparatus used to concentrate and produce distilled spirits, which are classified by the method of introducing a fermented mixture.

Coffey Still

A type of still named after Aeneas Coffey, Inspector-General of Irish Excise, who invented the *continuous* still and was granted a patent for it in 1832. Prior to that, all distillations took place in *pot stills*.

Column Still

A still that consists of two cylindrical columns (about 40 to 50 feet high) fitted with a system of interconnecting steam-heated (pot stills utilize a flame) tubes. Steam, which is higher in temperature than fire, allows for different flavor profiles to be obtained. The alcoholic liquid is fed into the tubes, where it is distilled, redistilled, and taken off as highly concentrated and purified alcohol. The vapor goes through a series of plates that have holes with bubbler caps, after which it condenses. The higher up in the still, the cooler the temperature and the higher the alcohol. The liquid condenses on the plates and what does not will continue to vaporize at another temperature. Each plate has a spigot allowing the distiller to select any congeners desired.

Each plate acts like its own condenser; it has its own alcohol concentration and its own composition of congeners.

Continuous Still

There are basically two types of stills used for distilling: the pot still and the continuous still. The continuous still is often referred to as a column still, Coffey still, and even erroneously as a *patent still*. The *continuous still* provides a continuous inflow of distilling liquid, which greatly boosts volume while saving considerable time. It generally does not produce the same high quality as the pot still.

Patent Still

An erroneous name for the "continuously-fed" *column still,* invented by Aeneas Coffey, who was granted a *patent* for it in 1832.

Pot Still

The pot still resembles a large copper pot or kettle with a broad rounded base, topped by a long column. The shape and size of the still, even the way it is fired (flame or steam), the speed of *heating* the liquid, the temperature of the still, and the volume of the *heart* are believed to affect the quality of the distillate. Initially, anywhere from 250 to 2,600 gallons of liquid to be distilled (depending on the still's size) are loaded into the base of the pot still. The liquid is then heated and kept simmering until the alcohol is vaporized and rises up into the column, taking with it flavors from the base liquid used; this gives the distillate its characteristic aroma and taste. When the vapor rises to a certain point in the column, it comes into contact with a cold condenser, which turns the vapor into liquid alcohol.

In the pot still method, there are two distillations. The initial distillation is collected at a strength of 30 percent alcohol; this is then redistilled to approximately 70 to 80 percent alcohol. Only the middle or "heart" of a distillation is collected and the first and last runs, called *heads* and *tails,* are redistilled before they can be used. The distilled spirit, after the second distillation, is colorless and 70 to 80 percent alcohol (140 to 160 proof).

Pot stills produce only single batches of distilled spirits. After each batch has been distilled, the pot still must be refilled again. Pot stills produce the finest quality as well as the highest priced distilled spirits, but the process is laborious and time-consuming.

▶ THE DISTILLATION PROCESS

All distillers go through four or possibly five steps to produce a distilled spirit. They are grain handling and milling, mashing, fermenting, distilling, and maturing.

Grain Handling and Milling

Grain handling involves the selection of barley, corn, rye, wheat, or others according to standards on moisture content, ripeness, and purity. Only the finest grains that are free of odor, available in sufficient quantity, have at least 60 percent starch, and have less than 13 percent moisture (more moisture will cause mold and bacterial contamination) can be used. Once selected, the grains are individually shipped to distillery mills in special rail cars called *hopper cars.* At the mills, the grain is cleaned and sorted, then ground to a meal for cooking, and finally moved to separate containers for weighing and proportioning.

Mashing

Before a fermentation can take place, the starch contained in the grains must be converted into a readily fermentable sugar. This is accomplished by an enzyme called *diastase* that causes the grains, which have been mixed with water, to *malt* or *sprout,* and change the starch into maltose sugars. The various grains are mixed, warmed, and pumped into a sterile fermentation tank and inoculated with a special yeast strain. Fermentation takes three to five days, converting the sugar in the mash to alcohol, which eventually reaches 8 to 9 percent. The distillers call the fermented mash *wash.* Once fermented, the wash is heated in a still until the alcohol, which was produced by the yeast strain digesting the mashed grain sugars, vaporizes. Traces of flavoring components called *congeners* are also produced during the fermenting process. Congeners are fusel oils, esters, tannins, acids, aldehydes, and so on. In proper proportion with other elements, these congeners will eventually help develop and determine the aroma, body, and taste of the final product.

Distillation

Distillation involves the separation of alcohol from the liquid in the fermented mash. Since alcohol boils at 173.1 degrees Fahrenheit and water boils at 212 degrees Fahrenheit, it is relatively easy to separate the alcohol and flavoring components from the mash. The higher the heat, the greater the volume of distilled neutral spirits. The lower the heat, the greater the amount of flavor (from the base grains) that is carried through distillation.

The mash enters near the top of a continuous still or column still, while steam enters near the still's bottom chambers, thus vaporizing the alcohol and flavoring components. When the vapor is drawn off, it condenses into a liquid, known as *low wine,* with an alcohol content of anywhere from 45 to 65 percent. The low wine is redistilled, or further refined, allowing the alcohol to reach an even higher concentration and further remove unwanted impurities and flavors. The resulting liquid is called *high wine* or *new whiskey;* it is crystal clear and ready for maturing.

The double distillation process is expensive, but well worth it if a distiller wants a premium product. Some distillers double distill, some don't.

The spent grains and fluids (called *slop*) which are drawn off from the bottom of the continuous still are dried and used as high-protein feed supplements for both livestock and poultry.

Maturing

The maximum proof at which *American-made whiskey* can leave the still is 160, although most whiskey is actually distilled between 120 to 140 proof. If distilled at 160 proof, the higher-proof whiskey tends to pick up too much of a woody taste during aging. The new whiskey is pumped into a cistern room where it is reduced to a lower proof by the addition of demineralized water prior to aging. This practice, however, is not utilized by all distillers.

The raw whiskey is then put into new or used charred oak barrels (generally white) ranging in capacity from 50 to 66 gallons, which are filled and then stored in large warehouses. Due to heating and cooling in the warehouse, the whiskey both expands and contracts. Higher temperatures cause the whiskey to expand into the wood and as the temperature drops, the whiskey contracts out. With each succeeding cycle, the harsh flavoring components in the new whiskey are further filtered out.

Vital to the flavor, color, and bouquet of whiskey are the uniformity and depth of the two thin charred layers of the barrel's inner surface. The first layer of pure carbon and the second "red layer" of caramelized wood sugars give whiskey its rich, dark color; the deeper layers contribute tannin and vanillin. The carbon layer also removes harshness from the whiskey by absorption, while also neutralizing some of the harshest polyphenols from the wood itself. The barrels are first toasted, then charred; the whiskey thus benefits from consistent char layers and the wood resins that are brought to the barrel surface by the toasting process.

The charring of the barrels takes only about 30 seconds. The proper selection, cutting, and air drying of oak for barrel heads and staves is essential to the proper "breathing" of the barrel, which helps to mature the whiskey.

Throughout the aging period, test samples and periodic inspections of each barrel ensure that the distiller's standards are being met. Occasionally a leak is discovered in one of the barrels. Most leaks are repaired with wood slivers, which are driven into the leak spot, then cut flush with the barrel surface.

A portion of the whiskey volume is lost every year from soakage and evaporation (amounting to as much as 15 percent after four years), but in the end, a unique distilled product is achieved. After aging, the barrels are removed from the warehouse, opened, and the liquid filtered, removing the heavier sediment and solids that have formed on the bottom of the barrel. During bottling, the proof or alcohol content is adjusted usually by the addition of demineralized water.

History of Charred Barrels

Early distillers chose oak barrels for shipping their whiskies. The sturdy cooperage proved strong enough to withstand rough handling aboard the river boats. The use of charred oak barrels for the aging of whiskey first began in the United States in 1850.

The nature of the barrel's role came about accidentally. Supposedly, a nineteenth-century barrel maker was steaming and bending oak staves over an open fire. Through his negligence, the staves began to char. Being a frugal sort, he used them anyway, without bothering to tell the distiller. The distiller who used the barrel found that his whiskey improved in flavor and had picked up a rich color. He then insisted on charred staves for all his barrels.

White oak comes from mostly the central United States, including Arkansas, Kentucky, Minnesota, Missouri, Ohio, Tennessee, Virginia, and Wisconsin.

► BROWN SPIRITS

The term brown spirits or "brown goods" refers to those distillates (generally whiskies) that possess a *brown* color and are generally aged in wood. Examples of brown spirits are blended, Bourbon, Canadian, Irish, light, rye, Scotch, and Tennessee.

Whiskey

It is believed that the word *whiskey* is derived from the Celtic *uisge baugh* or *uisge beatha* (roughly, *water of life*). No one knows for sure which country first used the word, but the Scots and Irish claim rightful ownership of the term. We do know that the English found the word much too difficult to pronounce, so it was shortened and Anglicized to the present *whisky* (English) or *whiskey* (American).

American-Made Whiskey

American-made whiskey was formally defined when the Federal Alcohol Administration Regulations were formulated in 1936. They defined whiskey as an alcoholic distillate made from a fermented mash of grain, distilled at less than 190 proof, in such a manner that the distillate possesses the taste, aroma, and characteristics generally associated with whiskey. The minimum proof at which a whiskey can be bottled is 80; there are no maximum proof standards. American whiskey can only be made from grains specified for each category; potatoes and beets, used in vodka making, cannot be used to make whiskey. Whiskey obtains its characteristic brown color from four sources: coloring matter from the barrel, oxidation, charred barrels, and the addition of caramel for color adjustment.

Flavored whiskey is a mixture of distilled neutral spirits that are flavored and colored with various types of fruit and/or herbs and may or may not contain added sugar. By federal law (1992) flavored whiskey cannot be bottled at less than 60 proof or 30 percent alcohol by volume.

Blended Whiskey

Blended whiskey is a product containing at least 20 percent of straight whiskey that is combined with grain whiskey or neutral spirits and bottled at not less than 80 proof. A blended whiskey containing not less than 51 percent of one of the types of straight whiskey shall be further designated by that specific type of straight whiskey; for example, "blended bourbon whiskey" (bourbon whiskey—a blend).

The blending usually takes place after the whiskies reach full maturity; they are then allowed to rest for further aging. Caramel coloring is usually added prior to bottling.

Blended whiskies made with distilled neutral spirits will carry a label on the back of the bottle showing the percentages of distilled neutral spirits and straight whiskies contained.

Some available brands of blended whiskies are:

Barton Reserve	Four Roses	Seagram's 7 Crown
Calvert Extra	Imperial	Three Feathers
Carstairs	Philadelphia	Tom Burns Reserve
Fleischmann	Schenley Reserve	

Bourbon: Our National Spirit

In 1789 (the year of George Washington's inauguration as first president of the United States), a Baptist minister, Elijah Craig, made a distilled spirit by combining spring water, corn, rye, and barley malt. Craig lived in Bourbon County, Kentucky, where so much of that state's whiskey was produced that within two generations, the name *bourbon* was attached to all Kentucky whiskey, earning the preacher the title of "Father of Bourbon."

At Old Evan Williams Distillery it is argued that in 1783 Evan Williams, an early Kentucky settler and pioneer, earned his permanent role in American history when he built the area's first commercial distillery. Williams also solved pioneer transportation problems by pulverizing about 250 pounds of corn and distilling it into bourbon whiskey. He determined that a single pack horse could easily carry two 20 gallon kegs of the whiskey (the equivalent of approximately 12 bushels, or a quarter-ton of corn) on a riverboat. Williams' transportation methods made the shipment of whiskey much easier: soon after, whiskey was making the long journey to many eastern markets along the Ohio and Mississippi rivers, where it was an immediate success.

The Emergence of the Bourbon Industry.   Distilling remained a rather primitive process, subject to much variation from one batch to another until 1835, when scientific procedures were introduced. Emphasis was then placed on the careful analysis of the ingredients; the use of such precise measuring instruments as the thermometer and the saccharimeter (which gauges the sugar content of the mash), and above all, sanitation. This led to uniformity in appearance and quality between batches among the distillers. Whiskey was shipped in barrels, along with an empty bottle that was refilled and displayed in retail stores. Even though the bottle was marked with the producing distiller's brand name, this was still no guarantee of quality, for many unscrupulous retailers filled popular brand bottles with cheaper or adulterated products. But even with uncertain quality guarantees, consumers continued to enjoy bourbon in ever-increasing quantities.

It was not until 1870, however, that George Garvin Brown, a young wholesale drug salesman in Louisville, Kentucky, introduced whiskey in a clear, sealed bottle, to prevent tampering with the final product. The use of a sealed bottle assured the consumer of the genuineness of the bourbon. The individual bottling of bourbon brands became widely accepted during the late 1800s. It was more expensive for the distillers, but it assured that valued customers were getting the whiskey they paid for. Many distillers quickly capitalized on the idea and soon were bottling, sealing, stamping, and labeling their whiskies at the distillery.

In 1890, there were 1,576 registered distilleries throughout the state. These distilleries were not the corporations we currently recognize, but rather family-owned or partnership operations, each on a relatively small scale, with each one professing to have a premium product. These small distilleries continued production until 1906, when President Theodore Roosevelt signed the Pure Food and Drug Act, which required certain standards of identification for whiskey and imposed greater federal control on the production of distilled spirits. This act marked the turning point in bourbon quality.

In 1933, citizens voted for the repeal of Prohibition by the adoption of the Twenty-First Amendment, thus making the alcoholic beverage industry the only business existing in this country as a result of a vote of the people. After the repeal of Prohibition, Kentucky was in the enviable position of having many medium-sized workable distilleries intact that could begin operating in a short time. But times had changed. The small distiller did not have the capital to start operating on a large scale and many of the smaller companies soon failed or were sold. Most of those who had survived had to seek corporate capital by raising money through the sale of stock and bonds. Thus the high number of family-operated distilleries existing prior to 1920 promptly declined to less than 100 producing distilleries; that number is now substantially smaller. On May 4, 1964, the U.S. Senate passed a resolution recognizing bourbon whiskey as a "distinctive product of the United States," with no other country having authority to call their whiskey products bourbon. And, because consumers associate Kentucky with bourbon whiskey, the U.S. government permits only Kentucky to use its name on the label to identify the product.

Producing bourbon whiskey. The making of Bourbon whiskey is a combination of art and a highly developed science. No two distillers are exactly alike in their operations. And, while the manufacture of bourbon is closely regulated and somewhat standardized by the federal government, the actual process differs from one distiller to the next. Federal regulations require that bourbon be made from a minimum of 51 percent corn; generally 65 to 75 percent is used. When the corn in the mash reaches 80 percent, the product, by government definition, becomes corn whiskey, not bourbon. The higher the corn content and the lower the percentage of other grains, the lighter the whiskey. The blend of the other grains is dictated by the distiller's own private formula; rye, wheat, or barley malt can be used in the grain mix.

Natural, mineral-free limestone water plays an important role in the production of bourbon. Underground alkaline springs act as a perfect filtering agent for fresh water and provide it in almost unlimited quantities, free of minerals and iron deposits.

Federal law specifies that bourbon must be stored at no less than 80 proof and not more than 125 proof in new, charred white oak barrels for a minimum of two years, although most distillers age their bourbon anywhere from four to ten years.

Technically, bourbon can be produced anywhere in the United States, although in practice Indiana, Illinois, and Virginia are the only states besides Kentucky that produce this unique whiskey. Currently, 16 companies produce 80 percent of the world's supply of bourbon, which amounts to approximately 65 million gallons. Some well-known brands of bourbon are:

Ancient Age	Kentucky Gentleman	Old Grand-Dad
Jim Beam	Kentucky Tavern	Old Hickory
Benchmark	Maker's Mark	Old Taylor
Blanton	Old Cabin Still	Rebel Yell
Ezra Brooks	Old Charter	Ten High
Elijah Craig	Old Crow	Wild Turkey
J. W. Dant	Old Fitzgerald	Evan Williams
I. W. Harper	Old Forester	

Bottled-In-Bond

Bottled-In-Bond is whiskey that is mandated by federal regulations to be produced by one distillery in one distilling season, aged a minimum of four years in new charred oak barrels, and bottled at 100 proof. Whiskey that is bottled-in-bond has also been stored and bottled in a Treasury Department bonded warehouse; no excise tax is paid on the whiskey until the beverage is withdrawn or shipped from the warehouse. The term *bonded* on the label therefore does not refer to quality; it means nothing more than that the treasury agent was present to collect the taxes.

Canadian Whisky

Although Canadian whisky (spelled *whisky* in Canada) is a distinctive product of Canada, the Canadian government doesn't set regulations relative to the mixture of the grain blend (providing no one grain exceeds 49 percent), the proof level at which it is distilled, or the type of barrel used. Each distiller is allowed to make his own whisky as he sees fit. Canadian whisky is matured in white oak barrels (mostly used) and for the American market, is bottled at a minimum of 80 proof. Canadian whisky is made only from grains (corn, rye, and barley malt) and may be bottled after three years of age. Canadian whisky sold in the United States is generally four to six years old, and it cannot be designated as a "straight" whisky.

In 1891, a U.S. law required the country of origin to appear predominantly on a product's label. It was at this time that Canadian Club whisky started using the word "Canadian" on its label.

Some better-known brands are:

Black Velvet	Schenley O.F.C. (Old Fine Canadian)
Canadian Club	Seagram's Crown Royal
Canadian Mist	Seagram's V.O. (Very Own)
Lord Calvert	Windsor Supreme

Corn Whiskey

Legally, corn whiskey is distilled at a proof not exceeding 160 and fermented from a mash of at least 80 percent corn. Corn whiskey must be stored in uncharred oak barrels or used charred oak barrels at not more than 125 proof. It must be aged for a minimum of two years—yet there are some corn whiskies on the marketplace that for some unknown reason do not meet this requirement. Because of its dominant corn content, corn whiskey is extremely light in flavor.

Irish Whiskey

Irish whiskey is a distinctive product of Ireland, manufactured in compliance with the guidelines of Irish Distillers, Ltd. It is commonly thought that Irish whiskey is produced from potatoes, mainly because of the general association between the Irish and potatoes; this is not true. Irish whiskey is not a single malt or pure malt whiskey—it is a blend. It is made from a mash of cereal grains, mostly barley (malted and unmalted), wheat, oats, corn, and rye. Most Irish whiskey is produced in pot stills, which help give it a unique taste, although the use of continuous stills is increasing in popularity.

Irish whiskey must be aged a minimum of three years, but is usually aged five to eight years prior to shipping. Aging generally takes place in used Bourbon or sherry barrels or a combination of the two. Irish whiskey has a delicate odor of honey, vanilla, and orange peel, with a light and mild flavor. The two major brands currently available in the United States are Bushmills and Jameson.

Light Whiskey

Light whiskey is a whiskey produced in the United States from various cereal grains. It is distilled at 160 to 189 proof and stored in used or uncharred new oak barrels. If "light whiskey" is mixed with less than 20 percent of straight whiskey on a proof gallon basis, the mixture shall be designated "blended light whiskey" (light whiskey—a blend). It is lighter in flavor, aroma, and taste than other whiskies because the flavor congeners are removed during the distillation at a high proof. This whiskey was first authorized for production after January 26, 1968, and on July 1, 1972, the first bottles were ready for sale.

Rye Whiskey

Rye whiskey is a distilled spirit, distilled at not more than 160 proof from a fermented mash of grain containing at least 51 percent rye. It is stored at not more than 125 proof in charred new oak barrels for a minimum of two years, although four years is the standard. Straight rye whiskey is seldom sold today, although very often American Blended Whiskey or Canadian whisky is incorrectly referred to as "rye." Rye whiskey—real rye— is not to everyone's taste, for it has a strong and distinctive flavor of caraway seeds. Rye whiskey is also known as *Rye Malt Whiskey.*

The top name brands available are: Jim Beam Rye Whiskey, Old Overholt Straight Rye Whiskey, and Wild Turkey Rye Whiskey.

Scotch Whisky

Scotch whisky is a specific product of Scotland (see Figure 9-1), made in compliance with the 1909 laws of Great Britain, as well as the Scotch Whisky Act of 1988. The whisky can legally be called Scotch if it is distilled and matured in Scotland. Technically, however, Scotch can be distilled and matured in Scotland and be bottled in a different country (e.g., the United States). This saves large sums of money, with little or no sacrifice to the product's quality.

Scotch's unique flavor and character come from the water used in its production and the type and amount of malt whisky used. Its distinctive smoky taste comes from the peat fires over which the barley malt is dried.

How Scotch Is Made. The malting of barley is the first stage in making Scotch whisky; this may be done by one of several processes. In the older floor malting method, the barley, after being soaked in water for two to four days, was spread on a kiln floor for germination or sprouting. This process generally took eight to 12 days depending on the season of year, the quality of barley used, and other factors (Figure 9-2). This process has been largely replaced by mechanical maltings of one type or another, but the principle of the process remains the same.

During this malting period, an enzyme called *diastase* is secreted by the barley, converting the starch in it into a readily fermentable sugar. The germination is stopped

FIGURE 9-1 This typical Scotch distillery has a pastoral setting, with swans gliding on the adjacent lake. (Courtesy Scotch Whisky Information Bureau)

by drying and smoking the malted barley over *peat* fires in open malt kilns; this helps to give Scotch its unique smoky taste. Peat is a soft, not fully formed coal in a primary state; it is made up of decomposed and compacted vegetal material often found in swamps (Figure 9-3). During the smoking process, the barley lies above the smoking peat on screens, which allows the burning vapors to permeate the barley, swirling around and under it. This not only dries out the barley but infuses it with a unique smoky aroma and taste.

The barley is then mixed with water and poured into deep vessels and yeast is added. In two or three days, the sugar in the liquid will have been converted by fermentation into alcohol. After this, the liquid is piped into stills, where it is double distilled, until the correct proof is reached (Figure 9-4). Generally speaking, malt Scotches are distilled in the proof range of 120 to 140, whereas the lighter grain whiskies are generally distilled in the 180 to 188 proof range.

Blended Scotch Whisky

Scotch is made from a blend of as many as 50 different malt and grain whiskies. The lighter Scotches are made with greater amounts of grain Scotch whiskies (generally up to 50 percent), distilled in column stills at higher proofs from malted and unmalted barley, corn, wheat, and other cereals.

FIGURE 9-2   Kiln floor: malted barley being dried in kiln. (Courtesy Scotch Whisky Information Bureau)

The blended Scotches, as we now know them, did not really come into existence until about 1860. Prior to that, Scotches were distilled in old-fashioned pot stills at lower proof levels, which produced Scotches with a full body and heavy taste. In 1832, the continuous still was perfected by Aeneas Coffey, for use in the distillation of Scotch whisky. This enabled distillers to produce lighter bodied and flavored Scotch whiskies, which were then blended with the heavier malted Scotches. In 1853, in Edinburgh, Andrew Usher produced the first blended Scotch whisky.

After distillation is completed, Scotch is put into used American oak bourbon whiskey or sherry wine barrels, where it ages for a minimum (by law) of three years (Figure 9-5). However, in practice most whiskies mature for much longer, often five to ten years or even longer, depending on the distiller. Scotch sold in the United States is generally aged a minimum of four years; if it's less than four years old, the bottle must carry an age label. When there is an age stated on the label of a blended Scotch whisky, it identifies the youngest whisky in the blend.

After maturing in wooden barrels, the Scotch is blended and its proof reduced by the addition of distilled water. At this point it is allowed to blend for several months, before being filtered and finally bottled.

It is commonly thought that the longer a Scotch whisky (or any other whiskey, or

Figure 9-3 Peat being dug out from dried-out marsh lands. (Courtesy Scotch Whisky Information Bureau)

even brandy, for that matter) ages, the better or smoother it becomes. Actually, after 12 to 15 years the whisky does not improve significantly and with prolonged barrel aging, could start picking up a woody flavor and start to deteriorate. Whisky does not continue to age or improve after being removed from the barrel—one's 25-year-old Scotch will still be only 25 years old (quality wise) after 50 years.

Some better-known brands of blended Scotch whisky are:

Ambassador	Bell's	Catto
Ballantine	Black Bull	Chairman's Choice
John Begg	Black & White	Chivas Regal

FIGURE 9-4 Huge copper pot stills used for the distillation of Scotch whisky. (Courtesy Scotch Whisky Information Bureau)

Checquers	MacKintosh	Tomatin
Cutty Sark	Ne Plus Ultra	Usher's
Dewar's White Label	Old Rarity	Usquaebach
Grant's	Old Smuggler	Vat 69
John Haig	Park & Tilford	Johnnie Walker
Haig & Haig	Passport	White Heather
Harvey's	Scoresby	White Horse
Inver House	Teacher's	Whyte & Mackay
J & B	The Grand	100 Pipers
McCallum	Macnish	

FIGURE 9-5   Barrels containing Scotch whisky being loaded onto racks for aging. (Courtesy Scotch Whisky Information Bureau)

Malt Scotch.   Malt Scotch, often referred to as single-malt Scotch, is produced by the pot still method from a mash consisting of only malted barley. A *single-malt* whisky means a malt whisky produced by a single distillery. By way of contrast, *blended* Scotch means a blend of pot-stilled malt whiskies with whiskies produced in Scotland by the column still method from a cereal mix that may contain unmalted as well as malted barley and other grains.

Malt Scotches are generally darker in color than blended Scotches, because of increased aging in barrel (by law at least three years); they are traditionally served at room temperature.

The Malt Regions of Scotland are:

- *Lowland:* These Scotches are mild and light in body and flavor, with little smokiness.
- *Highland:* These Scotches are full of body and flavor, sweet oak and intensely smoky, with a great balance.
- *Campbeltown:* These Scotches are very full-bodied and quite smoky, with a pungent, briny and peaty bouquet.
- *Islay:* These Scotches are very full-bodied, peaty, pungent, and salty, with the most distinct flavor.
- *Speyside:* These Scotches are quite mild with a sherrylike odor and flavor.

Some brands of single-malt Scotch whisky are:

Aberlour	Glendronach	Isle of Jura
Auchentoshan	Glenfarclas	Knockando
Aultmore	Glenfiddich	Lagavulin
Balvenie	Glengoyne	Laphroaig
Cardhu	Glenkinchie	Oban
Cragganmore	Glenlivet	Talisker
Dalmore	Glenmorangie	The Edradour
Dalwhinnie	Glenordie	The Macallan

Serving and storing Scotch.   Because of its high alcohol content (minimum 80 proof), Scotch will last almost indefinitely either opened or unopened, unless it is subjected to extremely hot or cold temperatures for prolonged periods of time or constantly exposed to movement or vibrations.

Scotch can be served "neat" (without ice, seltzer, water, and so on); over ice; with water or seltzer; or in a multitude of cocktails. It is best to use blended Scotches under 12 years of age for cocktails that contain sugar, fruit, or lemon flavors. Twelve-year-old single-malt Scotches and well-aged Scotches (often up to 30 years) are best served straight or with a splash of water or seltzer, over ice.

Sour Mash

Federal regulations require that a minimum of 25 percent of the volume of the fermenting mash must be stillage (cooled, screened liquid recovered from the base discharge of the whiskey-separating column) and the fermenting time be at least 72 hours. Sour mash is actually made from a yeast mash "soured" with a lactic acid culture for a minimum of six hours to promote the growth of the yeast and at the same time inhibit the growth of any other organisms. In the sour mash process, spent *wash* from the previous fermentation is added, together with fresh yeast, to the grain mash. This does not change the flavor or taste, but provides continuity of flavor, body, and bouquet in the whiskey, and reinforces the individual characteristics that mark the bourbon or Tennessee whiskey brand. *Sour mash* is a distillers' term and there is nothing actually sour about sour mash bourbon or sour mash Tennessee Whiskey.

Straight Whiskey

Straight Whiskey is an alcoholic distillate from a fermented mash of grain, distilled at 160 proof or less and stored during aging at between 80 and 125 proof. Straight whiskey must be aged for not less than 24 calendar months in new charred white oak barrels. Its proof is reduced to a level of not less than 80 by the addition of distilled water.

Straight whiskies must be made with a minimum of 51 percent of the grain that identifies that particular whiskey. Bourbon, for example, is made with at least 51 percent corn. Other straight whiskies are rye, bottled-in-bond whiskey, straight corn whiskey, and straight whiskey without an identifying grain tag, which simply means it was produced from a mash that contained less than 51 percent of any one grain type (e.g., corn).

A blend of straight rye whiskeys or a blend of straight bourbon whiskeys is a mixture of only straight rye whiskeys or straight bourbon whiskeys, respectively.

Tennessee Whiskey

Tennessee distillers choose to identify their product as Tennessee whiskey, yet it may be technically identified with Bourbon. Tennessee whiskey is leached or filtered through vats of compacted maple charcoal, which eliminates congeners and adds to its flavor prior to bottling. To make the special charcoal filtration system, the distillers of Tennessee whiskey cut down maple trees during the cold winter months when the sap level is minimal so that a resin or sugar taste is not added to the whiskey. Then the hard maple wood is cut lengthwise into long six-foot strips and set on fire. During the burning process, the strips are periodically wet down to slow the burning process and force the wood to become charred rather than disintegrate into ashes. The wood is then pulverized and tightly packed into large tanks at the distillery. When ready, the whiskey is poured in at the top and allowed to run through the charred wood (12 solid feet of it) very slowly, giving a strong maple flavor to the whiskey, which is then filtered and bottled.

The only two brands of Tennessee whiskey currently available are Jack Daniel's (Old No. 7 Black Label, Gentleman Jack) and George Dickel.

▶ WHITE SPIRITS

The term white spirits or "white goods" refers to those distillates that are clear in color and usually not aged in wood. These distilled spirits lack the distinctive flavor generally associated with whiskey and are perceived as being light by most consumers.

Gin

Under federal regulations gin must be bottled at a minimum of 80 proof (except in the case of flavored gins). Gin must have a juniper berry flavor and can be made either by direct distillation or by redistillation. Most gins are not aged and federal regulations do not permit age claims. Distilled gins are allowed to use the word *distilled* on the label, although gins made through the *compound method* (see below) are not.

Gin was invented in about 1650 by Franz De la Boe (1614–1672) whose Latin name was Franciscus Sylvius. Dr. Sylvius was a physician and professor of medicine at Holland's famed University of Leiden. Dr. Sylvius was attempting to produce a therapeutic medicine that was both palatable and inexpensive and could be made by distilling pure alcohol in the presence of juniper berries, which come from evergreen trees. He was aware of medical theory and archaic pharmacology: the Latin *Juniperus communis* literally means *youth-giving.* At that time it was believed that the oils contained in juniper berries offered diuretic properties that could relieve the bladder and also treat kidney ailments. For some reason Dr. Sylvius proposed the use of the French name *genievre* for his juniper berry elixir. The Dutch, however, preferred to use their word for juniper berry and called it *genever.*

England's introduction to gin came when British soldiers, returning from the wars in the Netherlands, sampled the juniper-flavored distilled spirit and nicknamed it "Dutch Courage" or "Hollands." The soldiers found it to their liking and brought back the recipe, along with the name *geneva,* mistakenly thought to be a product from Switzerland. The name was changed to *gen,* which was later Anglicized to *gin.* In no time at all gin became the national drink of England, which still continues.

Gin Production.   The important differences among gins are the result of the type of mash from which the neutral grain spirits are distilled and the quality of the juniper berries and other botanicals used in the redistillation process. U.S. federal law standards of identity permit gin to be produced from any of the following base materials: corn, rye, wheat, barley malt, and sugar cane, among others. Most gins are produced by private formulas, which are the distillers' most closely guarded secret. Known ingredients or botanicals besides juniper berries that are often used in small proportions are: angelica root, anise, bitter almonds, calamus, caraway seeds, cardamom, cassia bark, cinnamon, cocoa nibs, coriander seeds, fennel, ginger, lemons or dried lemon peels, licorice, limes, orange peel, orris root, and other seeds, and almost a limitless number of barks, herbs, and roots. Technically, gin could be called a liqueur, if it were sweetened.

The U.S. federal government acknowledges the existence of different styles of gin; however, it only defines two types. They are *distilled* gin and *compound* gin.

Distilled gin is a distillate obtained from the original distillate of mash or by the redistillation of distilled spirits with juniper berries and other aromatics customarily used in making gin. Gin derives its main characteristic flavor from juniper berries and is reduced at time of bottling to not less than 80 proof.

Compound gin is produced by mixing high-proof neutral distilled spirits with extracts or oils of the juniper berry and other botanicals and flavorings. This gin is of a lower quality than distilled gin and therefore very little gin is produced using this method. This is, however, a federally approved definition that recalls the days of Prohibition, when members of households mixed neutral distilled spirits (often using methyl alcohol or wood alcohol, which is lethal, instead of ethyl alcohol) with juniper or "gin flavoring" to produce a bootleg distilled spirit called "bathtub gin" or "hooch," which was revolting to the taste.

Gin is usually distilled at a high proof, somewhere between 180 and 190, and is therefore clean and free of "off" flavors and undesirable odors. After the initial distillation the producer uses many different methods to produce the characteristic juniper aroma and flavor. One method, often called *original distillation,* is to suspend the cracked and crushed juniper berries on mesh trays, baskets, or perforated racks called *gin heads.* This allows rising vapors to pass from the still through and around the berries, allowing them to pick up essences and become impregnated with the aromatic flavoring oils of the botanicals that remain in the condensed distillate. The proof of the gin is corrected with distilled water and then bottled. Another similar method is to distill the original mash at 190 proof, then redistill it in the presence of the gin head. Although the second method is more common, both methods are acceptable in the United States. The flavoring content of the botanicals used changes from year to year, depending on rainfall, amount of sunshine received, and so on, so the distiller must alter his formula every year in order to achieve the same taste and smell, bottle after bottle.

Types of Gin

British or London dry gin.   In England, gin mash usually contains less corn and more barley because English distillers feel that this produces a distilled spirit of extraordinary smoothness. Their gins are distilled at a high proof, then redistilled in the presence of juniper berries. English gins have a lightly balanced aromatic juniper bouquet and flavor; they are light, dry, crisp, and clean, with the delicate flavoring of the juniper berry, although this is slightly toned down. These gins are ideal for drinking straight, in martinis, or mixed in cocktails. London dry gins, although originally produced only in or near London, are produced all over the world, with the term having little meaning.

American dry gin.   American gins are usually produced by one of two methods, distilling or compounding. They are often labeled "dry" or "extra dry," although these terms have little actual meaning and gins labeled as such are not actually any drier than other gins. American dry gins are ideal for use in cocktails.

Dutch Gin (Holland, Genever, or Schiedam Gin).   The production of Dutch gin is slightly different than that of other gin; the Dutch usually begin with a grain mash of equal parts of barley malt, corn, and rye, distilled in a pot still at around 100 proof. The initial distillate, known as *malt wine,* is then redistilled in the presence of juniper berries in another pot still at a low proof (around 100 to 110 proof), which carries flavoring congeners and produces Dutch gin's full-bodied character. Dutch gins are usually heavy, with very complex, malty aromas and flavors; they have a pungent, full taste of juniper berries. They also have a pronounced grain flavor and, surprisingly, are often slightly sweet. Due

to their heaviness of taste they are usually drunk straight and cold, especially in Holland.
Schiedam Gin is named after one of the Dutch towns where it is produced.

Old Tom gin.   This is a dry gin usually sweetened by the addition of sugar syrup,
which was quite popular during the eighteenth century. It is rarely seen nowadays.

Plymouth gin.   This is actually an *appellation* and is only produced by the Coates
firm of Plymouth, England, which was founded in 1798. It is an aromatic gin, sometimes
pink in color from the addition of angostura bitters. Its taste lies somewhere between that
of Dutch and London dry gin. Plymouth gin was originally associated with the British
Royal Navy which, as legend has it, invented this gin as a tolerable way of drinking bitters, which helped control intestinal disorders. They often mixed it with lime juice; hence
the nickname "limey," a name frequently applied to the British.
Unfortunately, the production of Plymouth gin has dwindled in recent years.

Steinhäger (or Steinhäeger) gin.   This is a German gin produced in Westphalia,
which is similar to London dry types, but with slightly more of a juniper taste.

Golden gins.   These gins are aged in wood for a short period of time and have a
light golden-brown color, extracted from the barrel. Golden gin is quite difficult to find
nowadays.

Sloe gin.   This is not really a gin; it is a liqueur made from sloe berries (small
plums) that give it a rather tart flavor.

Flavored gins.   According to U.S. federal regulations (1992), flavored gins are gins
to which natural flavoring materials (apple, lemon, mint, orange, and pineapple, with or
without the addition of sugar) have been added. They are bottled at not less than 60 proof
(30 percent alcohol by volume) and the name of the predominant flavor must appear as
part of the designation. The famous British Damson Gin, for instance, is flavored with
damson plums.

Some well-known gin brands are:

Beefeater	Doornkaat	Seagram's
Bellows	Fockink	Schlichte
Bombay	Four Roses	Tanqueray
Boodles	Gilbey's	Vlahov
Boord's	Gordon's	Hiram Walker
Booth's	House of Lords	
Burnett's	Old Mr. Boston	

Rum

Rum is a spirit resulting from an alcoholic fermentation and the distillation of sugarcane, sugarcane syrup, molasses, sugar beets, maple sap, or other sugarcane by-products, at less than 190 proof. Rum, by U.S. federal law, should possess the characteristics that are generally attributed to it (aroma, taste, and so on) and cannot be less than 80 proof (40 percent alcohol). The distillation must also occur within the area of production of the sugarcane.

Flavored rum is a mixture of distilled neutral spirits that are flavored and colored with various types of fruit and/or herbs and may or may not contain added sugar. By federal law (1992) it cannot be bottled at less than 60 proof (30 percent alcohol by volume).

Rum production.   Sugarcane, minus the leaves, is cut and shredded by heavy rollers; the juice is collected, strained, decanted, and filtered. Rum, unlike other distilled spirits, has its own natural sugar for fermentation and does not depend on various added enzymes to convert the starch in the cereals to a readily fermentable sugar.

The sugarcane juice is first boiled to evaporate the water, which crystallizes the sugar and separates it from the thick, black molasses. The juice is fermented for one to two days, producing a small amount of alcohol, then double distilled in column stills to about 180 proof. Dark, full-bodied rums are distilled in a pot still at a lower proof, maintaining some of the flavor components in the final distillate.

Both light and dark rums come out of the still almost colorless, although they may taste quite different. The light rums are generally kept in glass or stainless steel vats so they do not acquire color from barrels, while dark rums are kept in lightly charred oak barrels.

Types of rum.   Basically, there are three types of rum; light or amber; dark, full-bodied; and aromatic rums.

Light or amber rums.   Light rum, also labeled "white" or "silver" rum, is clear in color and displays either a very light, molasses flavor or the neutrality of vodka. It must be aged a minimum of one year in either glass or stainless steel containers, but more traditionally is aged in uncharred barrels. If aged in barrels, it is further treated through carbon filtration systems, which eliminate any color that may have been picked up from the barrel.

Amber rum, also labeled "gold" rum, is aged in wooden barrels for a minimum of three years. It contains more flavor than light rum and is darker in color because of the addition of caramel coloring.

Every rum producer also makes a high-quality, well-aged rum, which is often labeled as *añejo* or *muy añejo*.

Light-bodied rums are generally produced in Puerto Rico, the Virgin Islands, Cuba, the Dominican Republic, and Haiti.

Full-bodied rum.   The method of production for the dark, full-bodied, pungent rums of Jamaica, Barbados, Martinique, Trinidad, and Guyana's Demerara is slightly different from that for the light rums, making the resulting product very popular for cocktails.

The skimmings of sugar from previous distillation are added to the sugarcane molasses and allowed to slowly ferment for 12 to 20 days. It is this special fermentation process that gives the dark rums a pungent bouquet and more pronounced flavor of butter and molasses. The mash is distilled twice in pot stills and is run off at between 140 and 160 proof. The rum is then aged and blended. At bottling, the proof is adjusted by the addition of distilled water. Full-bodied rum is aged from five to seven years in oak barrels and at the time of bottling considerably more caramel is added than is the case for lighter rums to give it a deep mahogany color.

Aromatic rum.   The combination of the special quality of the river water on the island of Java in Indonesia and the addition of dried red Javanese rice cakes, which are added to the mash during fermentation, results in a highly aromatic nature and dry taste of this rum. Aromatic rums are generally aged for three to four years in Java, then shipped to the Netherlands where additional aging takes place prior to blending and bottling. One brand available in the United States is Batavia Arak. (It was so named by ancient Arabian seafarers voyaging to the Caribbean islands.)

Some of the more popular brands of rum are:

Appleton	Cruzan	Rhum Saint James
Bacardi	Mount Gay	Ron Castillo
Cockspur	Myers's	Ron Rico

Serving and storing rum.   With the exception of well-aged rum, white, gold, and dark rums are best enjoyed in cocktails, usually containing coconut milk, pineapple juice, or the juice of citrus fruits.

Rum is an extremely versatile beverage that can, in most cases, be substituted in cocktails calling for gin or vodka and occasionally even tequila. Rum, like gin, vodka, and tequila, is a highly stable alcoholic beverage that is not adversely affected by vibrations or changes in temperature; in most cases it will last indefinitely, either opened or unopened.

Well-aged rums should be given the same treatment as brandies or cognacs; they are served in brandy snifters at room temperature.

Tequila

Tequila is distilled from a fermented mash (juice and/or sap) derived primarily from a blue variety of the genus plant *Agave tequilana weber* (so named by Swedish botanist Carolus Linnaeus), with or without additional fermented substances. It is bottled at not less than 80 proof. The Agave species (actually there are more than 400) occasionally called the *maguey* is often confused with cacti. Agave plants are distinguished by the succulence of the leaves rather than the stems. The Agave is known in the United States as the American aloe or century plant, because it was mistakenly believed to bloom only once every 100 years. The Agave plant takes between eight and 12 years to mature before it can be used. Only the heart of the plant, often called the *piña*, or "head," is used.

By government decree (December 9, 1974), tequila can only come from a specific geographic area of Mexico known as Tequila, which is within the state of Jalisco (about 40 miles northwest of Guadalajara) and parts of the states of Michoacan and Nayarit. If produced outside these geographical limits, it is called *mezcal.*

Tequila production.   The heart or base of the agave plant, often weighing between 75 and 150 pounds, contains what the distiller calls the sap or *aguamiel* (honey water). The plant is first split in half, then steamed until the starchy, fibrous pulp turns a mushy brown color. The pulp goes into a shredder which opens up and crushes the fibers, allowing the juice to run off. It is collected in large vats, then mixed with cane sugar or other sugars (up to 49 percent maximum) and yeast, and fermented for two to three days. The liquid is double distilled, sometimes in copper pot stills, between 104 and 106 proof, and filtered through charcoal.

Tequila may be aged or unaged and is usually bottled at 80 to 86 proof for U.S. consumption.

The clear (often described as white or silver) tequila is not aged and is bottled after proofage reduction by distilled water. The brown or gold tequila is aged in oak barrels. *Añejo* is tequila that has been aged for a minimum of one year in oak barrels. If the tequila is aged for from two to five years, it may be called *muy añejo.*

Pulque, a milky-white alcoholic beverage fermented from the juice of agave plants, was enjoyed for centuries before the art of distilling came to Mexico from Spain. Because of its rather low alcoholic content and susceptibility to spoilage, it is consumed locally, and rarely reaches the United States.

A last category of tequila, known as *crema de tequila* or *almendrado,* is a liqueur mixed with almonds, rarely exported to the United States.

Dirección General de Normas (DGN).   In an effort to control the production and quality of tequila, the Mexican government has devised a set of strict regulations. These regulations have since become somewhat more restricted and defined and are currently known as *Norma Oficial Mexicana de Calidad (NOM).*

Tequila's worm?   One will occasionally hear of a person finding a worm at the bottom of a bottle of tequila. In fact the worm is not found in bottles of tequila, only genuine mezcal, which is made from the agave plant in Oaxaca province. The worm has no real significance other than tradition and a shrewd marketing gimmick. However, according to the locals, the worm tastes delicious.

Serving and storing tequila.   Tequila, like other clear or white distilled spirits, has a minimum of 80 proof, which eliminates the possibility of freezing. With the exception of several "super-prestige" brands, there is really no need to chill tequila. It has an extremely long shelf life, either opened or unopened, and reacts quite well to direct sunlight. Although some people enjoy drinking it straight, it is mostly used in cocktails. (Note: In Mexico the fruit utilized to make a Margarita is called *limón,* a light green citrus fruit with a taste quite similar to lemon and lime, with the flavor of lemon predominating. It is indigenous to Mexico and the Southwest United States where it is traditionally served with Tequila drinks. Although limes are the customary citrus fruit used in the United States for Margaritas, a lemon would offer a more authentic taste.)

Tequila has a very unusual and distinctive taste quite different from other clear distilled spirits. Its flavor is somewhat herbaceous, grassy, and vegetal in nature, and has a natural affinity to salt and lemon juice.

There are many brands available in the United States. Among the most popular are:

Jose Cuervo	Gavilan	Monte Alban
Pedro Domecq	Gusano Rojo	Montezuma
El Cuate	Herradura	Sauza
El Toro	Juarez	Torado
Don Emilio	Pepe Lopez	Two Fingers

Vodka

Vodka is an alcoholic distillate from a fermented mash of primarily grain, which is distilled at a high proof, and processed further to extract all congeners with the use of activated charcoal. According to the U.S. federal standards of identity, the final product must be "without *distinctive* character, aroma, taste or color." However, no federal law requires vodka to be *entirely* without aroma or taste; therefore, some vodkas display distinctive characteristics in aroma *and* taste. Federal law governs the production of vodkas in the United States.

Vodka seems to have first appeared in either Russia or Poland around the twelfth century, when it was first known as *zhizenennia voda* (water of life) in the Russian monastery-fort of Viatka. The word *vodka* is a diminutive of the Russian word for water, *voda* (although it has been proved that the Russians took this word from the Poles). By the fourteenth century, vodka began to be used as a beverage; formerly, it was mainly used in perfumes and cosmetics. However, it was primarily employed as the base ingredient of many "wonder drugs" or "cure-all" elixirs. During the fifteenth century, Poland produced many types of vodka as well as several "grades," which varied according to the number of times the vodka was distilled and refined.

Vodka was originally made from the most plentiful and least expensive ingredients available, which in most cases was the potato. Nowadays, grain rules as the main base ingredient for vodka throughout the world. The early vodkas, even if made from grains, were strongly flavored, and therefore it became a common practice to add certain spices to mask the sometimes harsh, raw taste of the grain. It was not discovered until the early 1800s that charcoal could be used to absorb most or all of the aromas and flavors of congeners in the vodka—thus the relatively tasteless, colorless vodka that is produced nowadays.

Vodka production. Vodka can be made from any fermentable material, including rye, wheat, barley, potatoes, corn, beets, grapes, and even sugarcane. Vodkas produced from grain are accepted as the finest; those produced from other materials often display a "distinctive" aroma or taste. To begin with, neutral spirits that are highly refined distillates (with a minimum of 190 proof) are taken from the still and reduced in proof by the addition of pure water. They are slowly and continuously run through tanks containing vegetable charcoal (generally from one and one-half to six pounds for each gallon of spirits) for a period of not less than eight hours. Ten percent of the charcoal is usually replaced after every 40 hours of operation. Filtration systems do not have to use charcoal; in fact, some vodka producers actually use fine sand, which is made from pulverized silicon dioxide. The famed Russian vodka producer Stolichnaya, for example, is proud of its special combination quartz-sand and activated charcoal filtering system.

The type of charcoal used in filtration, what kind of wood it comes from, the duration of the char process, and how long the charcoal was air dried also determines the taste, or lack of distinctive taste, of a vodka. Vodka may be stored in containers of stainless steel, porcelain, concrete, glass, paraffin, or any other neutral material—rarely ever wood. Vodka produced in the United States is never aged, so that no age claim can be made. Vodkas are generally bottled between 80 and 100 proof, although higher-proof vodkas do exist.

Vodka enters the United States. Peter (Pyotr) Smirnoff first began making vodka in Russia in 1818 (actually the Smirnoff family was not Russian, they came from Lvov, Poland). Immediately after World War I, the Bolsheviks gained control of Russia and Vladimir Smirnoff (descendant of Peter) was forced into exile in Paris.

It wasn't until 1934 that vodka was first introduced commercially into the United States by Rudolph Kunett. He was of Ukrainian extraction and his father sold grain and alcohol to the Iron Bridge Distillery of Moscow. Kunett bought the American rights to Smirnoff from Vladimir Smirnoff. Kunett originally set up business in Bethel, Connecticut with the American branch of Societe Pierre (Peter) Smirnoff et Fils, but the venture did not prosper. He then met John G. Martin, the English-born president of the small but long-respected Hartford-based firm of Heublein. Against strong opposition, Martin arranged to retain Kunett and in 1939 Heublein purchased the Smirnoff name and formula for a mere $14,000 (plus some royalties), taking over its production and sales. For many years Smirnoff vodka used the slogan, "It will leave you breathless."

Today's market. Currently, there are more than 200 brands of vodka sold in the United States, including imports from the Baltic countries, Canada, China, Czechoslovakia, England, Finland, France, Germany, Iceland, Israel, Japan, Poland, Russia, Sweden, and Turkey.

Some notable vodka name brands

Absolut (Swedish). The name *Absolut* comes from the phrase *"Absolut renat Brannvin,"* which means "absolutely pure vodka." Absolut vodka, made from wheat, was first produced in Sweden in 1879, but was not introduced into the United States until 1979. In addition to the traditional vodka, Absolut also produces Citron, Kurant, and Peppar (see below).

Finlandia (Finnish). This vodka was first produced in 1888, but was not introduced into the United States until 1970. Its distinctive bottle is the creation of Finland's most famous designer, Tipio Wirkkala. The cracked ice surface of the glass bottle and its classic label portraying two white reindeer in combat under the red midnight sun of Lapland form a unique package.

Stolichnaya (Russian). This vodka was first introduced into the United States in 1973. Stolichnaya also produces a super-premium vodka called *Cristall.* In addition to the traditional vodka, Stolichnaya also produces Limonnaya, Okhotnichya, Ohranj, and Pertsovka (see below).

Other vodka brands are:

Anatevka (Israel)	Moryoskoff (Russia)
Borzoi (England)	Moskovskaya (Russia)
Burrough's (England)	Nikolai (USA)
Carmel (Israel)	Popov (USA)
Cristall (Russia)	Priviet (Russia)
Crown Russe (USA)	Samovar (USA)
Denaka (Finland)	Sermeq (Denmark)
Elduris (Spain)	Silhouette (Canada)
Gilbey's (USA)	Skol (USA)
Gordon's (USA)	Smirnoff (USA)
Great Wall (China)	Suntory (Japan)
Icy (Iceland)	Tanqueray Sterling (England)
Izmira (Turkey)	Tsing Tao (China)
Jarzebiak (Poland)	Wolfschmidt (USA)
Ketel One (Holland)	Wyborowa (Poland)
Luksusowa (Poland)	Zytnia (Poland)
Majorska (USA)	

Flavored vodka. *Flavored vodkas* are a mixture of distilled neutral spirits that are flavored and colored with various types of fruit and/or herbs and may or may not contain added sugar. By federal law (1992) it cannot be bottled at less than 60 proof (30 percent alcohol by volume). The name of the flavoring *must* appear on the label. Some examples of flavored vodkas are:

Chesnochnaya. A vodka infused with a combination of garlic, pepper, and dill.

Citron. A vodka flavored with lemon, lime, mandarin orange, and grapefruit.

Kurant. A vodka flavored with black currants.

Limonnaya. A vodka flavored with the aromatics of fresh lemon peels.

Ohranj. A vodka flavored with orange juice and pulp.

Okhotnichya. This is a 90 proof "hunters vodka," made in Russia, which has a deep straw color and slightly herbal aroma. It is infused with many ingredients including sugar, giving it a honeylike sweetness that makes it ideal for serving with desserts or after dinner. The ingredients are ginger, tormentil (an herb), ash woodroots, cloves, red and black pepper, juniper, coffee, anise, orange and lemon peels, white port, and sugar. The aging process takes several months. (The term "hunter's vodka" originates from the tradition in which the aristocrats of Czarist Russia drank such vodkas to celebrate a successful hunt.)

Peppar. Introduced into the United States in 1986, *Peppar,* which is clear in color, is made from a blend of natural jalapeño pepper and paprika.

Pertsovka. This is a 70 proof vodka made in Russia with an infusion of red, white, and black pepper (capsicum, cayenne, and cubeb, which is another berry from the pepper family). Pertsovka is aged for several months in wood or stainless-steel barrels, then strained and bottled for export. It is brown in color and can be fiery hot.

Starka. This 86 or 100 proof vodka, made in Poland and Russia, is amber in color. Starka is one of the few available aged vodkas (up to ten years) that has hints of brandy, vanilla, honey, and port, and a scent of the leaves of several different types of Crimean apple and pear trees. Starka can also be produced from 100-percent rye grain.

Winiak. This 86 proof, amber-colored vodka from Poland is aged five years in used wine barrels.

Zubrówka. This is a flavored vodka produced in Slavic countries; it has a yellow-green tinge and a distinctive smell and taste, which is derived from various botanicals that have been added. Bottles of it at one time contained a single blade of grass, but these are no longer available in the United States, because U.S. scientists believed that the grass contained *coumarin,* a toxic compound found in some plants, believed to cause liver cancer. The vodka, minus the grass, is currently available in the United States and is free from anything harmful. It is also known as *Bison Vodka* or *Buffalo Vodka.*

Serving and storing vodka. Vodka's taste is that of ethyl alcohol, which is indeed a definite flavor.

Bottles of premium vodka should be stored in the freezer. They won't freeze because of their high alcohol content. They will, however, become somewhat thick and almost syrupy, adding to one's enjoyment of it. Vodka can be drunk neat (straight, without ice), chilled, or even Arctic cold, served in *Y-shaped* glasses and downed in one gulp.

There are many different cocktails that can be made from this most versatile distilled spirit, including Bloody Marys, screwdrivers, Moscow Mules, martinis, vodka and tonics, Black Russians, and White Russians.

Low-Alcohol and Nonalcoholic Beverages

S ince the mid-1980s, there has been a growing trend toward nonalcoholic beverages and "mocktails" (cocktails without alcohol) in the United States. The potential profits they can bring for restaurant and bar owners is limitless. Nonalcoholic beverages have also found favor with such organizations as MADD—Mothers Against Drunk Drivers (among others), which encourages restaurants and bars to serve these beverages to customers who are either "designated drivers" or to those who want "one-for-the-road."

There are many new low-alcohol and nonalcoholic beverages as well as some not so new drinks. Some of the most popular are: sodas (traditional colas and natural fruit-flavored sodas); juices; seltzers; mineral water (both carbonated and still); cocktail mixers; malt beverages, nonalcoholic wines; wine beverages; low-alcohol and nonalcoholic beers; sparkling ciders; and, of course, coolers.

▶ BOTTLED WATERS: MINERAL AND SPRING

With today's health-conscious American consumers, restaurants and bars need to consider carrying one or more brands or flavors of bottled mineral water. Mineral water comes in basically two types—sparkling and still. The most popular version by far is sparkling, which is apparent from the enormous growth in sales of such brands as Perrier and San Pellegrino. Some producers are even flavoring their mineral waters with natural citrus extracts such as mandarin orange, lemon, lime, and raspberry.

Bottled water can also be marketed toward consumers who seek an alternative to alcoholic beverages. Increased awareness of drunk driving laws, coupled with the public's health and fitness consciousness, as well as religious dictates, could actually be used to the advantage of a savvy restaurateur. Consumers also want to be able to choose a beverage that has no artificial coloring or flavors, artificial sweeteners, salt, sugar, other additives, or chemical preservatives. Sparkling mineral water is not only reputed to be a healthy drink; it is a trendy item that is considered chic by many consumers. At present, there are more than 600 different brands of bottled water sold in the United States.

Some Definitions of Water

Bottled Water.   Water that is sealed in bottles or other containers and intended for human consumption.

Carbonated Water.   Ordinary water to which carbon dioxide gas has been injected under pressure. Also known as *carbonated soda water* and *soda water.*

Club Soda.   Ordinary water that has been filtered, artificially carbonated, and has had mineral salts added for flavoring.

Distilled Water.   A process by which minerals are removed from ordinary water by distillation.

Demineralized Water.   Water from which the mineral salts have been removed by passing it over a bed of *ion-exchange resins.*

Drinking Water. Bottled water that comes from a government-approved source (municipal or state), then filtered or treated in some manner before bottling. The water can come from the tap, a well, a lake, and so on. It can also be blended with water from other sources. The water is always processed in some way (e.g., the addition of chlorine or other chemicals, the addition or deletion of mineral salts).

Mineral Water. Natural still or sparkling water that comes from the Earth. All mineral water contains some minerals, but to be classified a "natural mineral water" in Europe, the water must have at least 500 milligrams of minerals (standards set by the European Common Market in 1980, effective 1984) per liter *as it flows from the ground*—minerals that are collected in the water as it travels over great distances through geological formations. The minerals are thus dissolved and become an integral part of the water. Minerals are thought to be more readily absorbed by the body when in solution than as a component of solid food.

In most countries of Western Europe where bottled mineral waters are a common household beverage, no drinking water can be classified as a "natural mineral water" unless it contains dissolved minerals in its natural state. Italian law requires that mineral water be bottled only at its source. In Italy, if the mineral water has a mineral content under 500 milligrams per liter, it is considered to be of low mineral content and must be classified as *oligominerale.*

The U.S. federal government has not established a formal definition for mineral water. In 1979, however, California set a minimum standard of total dissolved solids for mineral water sold in that state at 500 milligrams per liter. This means that a water cannot be called a mineral water unless it has at least 500 milligrams of minerals dissolved in it.

The mineral content of bottled waters varies from state to state, country to country, and producer to producer. In addition to being basically low in sodium and virtually calorie- and carbohydrate-free, mineral water contains many trace elements and minerals, which also vary in their interest to consumers.

Among these elements and minerals are aluminum, ammonia, bicarbonate, boron, bromide, calcium, carbonate, chloride, chromium, cobalt, copper, fluoride, iodine, iron, lithium, magnesium, manganese, nickel, nitrate, phosphorus, potassium, selenium, silica, sodium, strontium, sulfates, zinc, and others.

Natural Water. A term that refers to drinking water that comes either from an underground spring or from a well. No adulteration of the water is permitted; however, filtering may be permissible.

Seltzer. Ordinary water that has been filtered and then artificially carbonated. It contains no added minerals or salts. In most cases, it is salt-free. Seltzer is named after *Niederselters,* a village near Wiesbaden, Germany.

Sparkling Water.   This is a generic term for any carbonated water. It may be naturally carbonated from its *source* and may be labeled *Naturally Sparkling* or carbonation may be added.

Spring Water.   A term used to indicate water from a deep underground source that flows naturally to the surface. If that water remains unprocessed and unchanged—nothing added or taken away—the term "natural" may be added and the product is called "Natural Spring Water."

Mineral and spring waters are best served chilled. It is strongly recommended you do not use ice, as the cubes are usually made from tap water, which can alter the fine, light taste of bottled water.

Nonsparkling bottled water can be served in place of tap water on the table. Have your servers display the bottle's label, then wrap a napkin around the bottle and fill large (ten to 12 ounce) stemmed wine glasses.

Some brands of bottled mineral and spring waters are listed below.

United States

- Aqua Essence Mineral Water (Pennsylvania)
- Arrowhead Spring Water (California)
- Artesia Mineral Water (Texas)
- Bartlett Mineral Springs (California)
- Borassa Spring Water (Arkansas)
- Calistoga Mineral Water (California)
- Crystal Geyser Mineral Water (California)
- Deer Park Spring Water (Maryland)
- Kentwood Spring Water (New Orleans)
- Mendocino Mineral Water (California)
- Mountain Valley Spring Water (Arkansas)
- Poland Springs Mineral Water (Maine)
- A Santé Mineral Water (New York)
- Saratoga Mineral Water (New York)
- Sparkletts Spring Water (California)
- Vittel Mineral Water (California)

Austria

- Vöslau Mineral Water

Belgium

- Spa Light Mineral Water

Canada

- Montclair Mineral Water
- Naya Spring Water
- Sparcal Mineral Water

France

- Évian Spring Water
- Perrier Mineral Water
- Vichy Celestins Naturally Alkaline Mineral Water
- Vittel Mineral Water
- Volvic Spring Water

Germany

- Apollinaris Mineral Water
- Gerolsteiner Sprudel Mineral Water

Ireland

- Ballygowan Spring Water
- Glenpatrick Spring Water
- Tipperary Spring Water

Italy

- Acqua di Nepi Mineral Water
- Boario Mineral Water
- Ferrarelle Mineral Water
- Fiuggi Mineral Water
- FonteSana Mineral Water
- Panna Mineral Water
- Recoaro Mineral Water
- Sangemini Mineral Water
- San Pellegrino Mineral Water
- Surgiva Spring Water
- Terme de Crodo Mineral Water

Portugal

- Pedras Salgadas Mineral Water

Spain

- Cabreiroa Mineral Water

Sweden

- Loka Mineral Water
- Ramlösa Mineral Water

Switzerland

- Alp Water Mineral Water
- Henniez Mineral Water
- Swiss Altima
- Valser Mineral Water

▶ MOCKTAILS

"Mocktails" are well-known cocktails minus the alcohol (often referred to as "virgin" drinks). To help merchandise these drinks, some restaurant and bar owners have come up with fanciful names such as "softtails," "virgin territory," as well as many others.

When creating "mocktails," let your imagination run wild. Develop "signature mocktails," the favorite drink concoction of the bar, which can be called by just about any name you choose. A separate beverage list can be developed to present these drinks, with appropriate descriptive terminology and drink ingredients. They can be served in the same type of glasses used for distilled spirits-based drinks and may include garnishes and plenty of fruit.

There also exist some excellent nonalcoholic "liqueurs" such as crème de cacao, crème de menthe, and triple sec. They are not only ideal to serve to customers but are excellent as ingredients in cocktails, thereby reducing the overall alcoholic content of the drink.

▶ NONALCOHOLIC AND "ALCOHOL-FREE" MALT BEVERAGES

According to the Bureau of Alcohol, Tobacco, and Firearms, effective April 1, 1986, producers of "nonalcoholic" malt beverages must indicate on labels and in advertising that their product "contains less than 0.5 percent alcohol by volume." Malt beverages labeled "alcohol-free" may contain no alcohol whatsoever. "Nonalcoholic" malt beverages cannot be labeled or advertised as beer, lager, ale, porter, stout, or any other designation commonly associated with malt beverages. Instead they shall be designated on labels and in advertising as "malt beverage," "cereal beverage," or "near beer," and *not* "beer." Some available brands of nonalcoholic and alcohol-free beverages are listed below.

Brand names

- Bamberger Hofbräu Alpine (Germany)
- Barbican (England)
- Birell (Pennsylvania)
- Buckler (Heineken, Holland)
- Clausthaler (Germany)
- Coors Cutter (Coors, USA)
- Exel (Molson, Canada)
- Firestone (Firestone Winery, California)
- Goetz Near Beer (Pearl, Texas)
- Haake-Beck (Beck's, Germany)
- Hamm's NA (Pabst, USA)
- Kaliber (Guinness, Ireland)
- Kingsbury Brew Near Beer (G. Heileman, Wisconsin)
- Metbräu Near Beer (New Jersey)
- Moussy (Switzerland)
- Norsk (Norway)
- O'Doul's (Anheuser-Busch)
- Old Milwaukee NA (Stroh, USA)
- Pabst NA (Pabst, USA)
- Patriser Zero
- Pro (Germany)
- Santor (France)
- Schloss Joseph
- Schmidt's Select Malt Beverage (Pennsylvania)
- Sharp's (Miller Brewing)
- Steinbräu Malt Beverage (New Jersey)
- St. Pauli Girl NA (Germany)
- Thaler
- Texas Select (Texas)
- Warteck (Switzerland)

The five most popular brands of "nonalcoholic" brews are (source: *Jobson Handbook* 1995):

1. O'Doul's
2. Sharp's
3. Kingsbury
4. Old Milwaukee
5. Coors Cutter

▶ ALCOHOL-FREE "WINE"

Alcohol-free "wines" are these whose alcohol is removed after fermentation; they are 99.5 percent alcohol-free. Some brands are:

- Ariél (J. Lohr Winery, California)
- Carl Jung sparkling and still wine (Germany)
- Giovane sparkling wine (Italy)
- Marcelino Sangría (Spain)
- Petillion (France)
- Santé sparkling and still wine (California)
- St. Regis red, white, and rosé (Seagram's, California)
- Toselli Spumante (Italy)

▶ LOW-ALCOHOL REFRESHERS

This category, formerly dominated by *coolers,* now includes other beverage types, necessitating the name *low-alcohol refreshers*. Most are simply a blend of fruit juices, carbonated water, and sugar, with an alcohol base of wine, distilled spirits, or malt.

The ten most popular brands of low-alcohol refreshers are (Source: *Impact Databank* 1995):

1. Zima Clearmalt
2. Bartles & Jaymes
3. Seagram's Coolers
4. Bacardi Breezer
5. Jack Daniel's Country Cocktails
6. Jose Cuervo Margaritas
7. Smirnoff Singles
8. Everclean Passion
9. Sun Country
10. White Mountain Cooler

▶ SPARKLING CIDER

Sparkling cider is to cider what champagne is to sparkling wine—its zenith. Soft, fruity, and light, this unfussy yet sophisticated nonalcoholic beverage is a perfect accompaniment to many foods and delicious all by itself. Although most sparkling ciders are nonalcoholic, some ciders contain approximately 5 to 6 percent alcohol, with a few listed as 10 to 12 percent alcohol (the same as table wine). A drink for daily consumption or special occasions, sparkling cider contains no added sugar or preservatives, making it an appealing alternative for today's health-conscious customer. Extremely healthy and loaded with B and C vitamins and essential mineral salts, this festive drink is said to have purifying qualities as well as being uniquely refreshing. The time is right for a fresh alternative to alcohol with an upscale beverage that's festive, with the clean bright taste of cider apples.

Merchandising Cider

Nonalcoholic drinks must be merchandised with flair, pizzazz, and dramatic appeal. Sparkling cider has a fresh, fruity flavor, it provides taste without guilt or unpleasant consequences the morning after. It is not sugary sweet, yet it sparkles. Sold in individual serving-size bottles, it is easy to price and to control. It can also be poured from larger-size bottles during peak periods at a bar or for banquets.

One way of merchandising sparkling cider is offering it during the traditional "happy hour" time slot. Serve it in stemmed glasses or champagne flutes for an appropriately upscale image and garnish it imaginatively with a slice or ring of apple (dipped in lemon juice to prevent discoloration) and a sprig of mint. Or, add a spiral of orange peel studded with a few cloves. Its taste, effervescence, and visual appeal will have customers ordering again and again.

Lunch is the perfect time to feature sparkling cider in your restaurant. Use a blackboard or menu clip-on to alert customers that they can enjoy a beverage that goes well with food yet won't hamper their judgment in their afternoon meetings. Brunch, too, demands something that sparkles, and cider fills the bill. Even children will enjoy its crisp fruit flavor.

Sparkling cider has the qualities that customers are looking for. Print its name on your menu, write it on your blackboard, display bottles near the restaurant entrance, and inspire your staff to do some suggestive selling. To serve it as a special nonalcoholic apéritif, add a splash of nonalcoholic fruit syrup such as cassis or orange. Don't forget the fresh fruit garnish.

Individual serving-size bottles are perfect for room service. Include them in your minibar and use them in VIP set-ups. Another suggestion is to have chilled sparkling cider available on tennis courts or golf courses.

Some available brands are:

Apple Amber	Double Six	Le Duc
Bel Normande	El Gaitero	Le Petite Normand
Bulmer's London Dry	Fleuret	Purpom
Challand	Grand Cru	Richards
Chamay	Grand Real	Santa Ana
Jacques Detoy	Hudson Valley	

Preparing a Beverage List

W ine is one of the great pleasures of the civilized world. Consumer awareness of and demand for wine has grown dramatically during the past ten years. The increase is not just in the quantity of wine drunk, but in the interest in wine, especially fine wines. The savvy restaurateur naturally wants to profit by this wine boom, but to do so he must understand the needs and concerns of his new, more knowledgeable, more demanding customers.

A beverage list (covering wine, beer, and distilled spirits) must be given the same careful thought and attention to detail and market trends that is involved in the planning of a food menu. The beverage list must complement the selections on the menu to satisfy discerning consumers.

A restaurant's wine list should be seen as something valuable in itself—a source of pleasure and information and not simply a catalog of stock. The wine list must also reflect the establishment and its philosophy. If constructed properly, it is one of the most important sales tools available, for it allows the customer to view the list and make a decision with little or no additional questions that need be answered.

Many restaurateurs view the creation of a beverage list as a Herculean task better left to consultants; or, quite frequently, it is ignored. Often, when there is a discussion concerning beverage lists, restaurateurs can rattle off dozens of reasons why their list is mediocre: "No room for storage . . . It won't sell in my restaurant . . . I don't know a thing about the stuff . . . My staff doesn't know one end of a corkscrew or shot glass from another," and so forth. With so many responsibilities and problems to contend with, it may be understandable why restaurateurs often put beverages in last place; but it is important to note the profit potential in a good beverage list.

Beverages make up approximately 35 percent of restaurant check sales and often account for more than 40 percent of its profits. Beverage sales can significantly boost check averages and impact positively on the bottom line. It does not make sense to lose out on those extra dollars by presenting a beverage list that presents incomplete information and a poor selection, or one that is overpriced, misleading, and not matched to menu selections. Careful attention to planning and purchasing of beverages can prevent such a profit loss.

▶ THE WINE LIST

The Preliminaries

Check the competition.   Find out what is and what isn't being done with wine in your area. Visit the restaurants nearby that have the same customer base as yours, as well as restaurants above and below your price range. Study how they merchandise wine and how competent their wine service is and obtain a copy of their wine list if possible. Notice how well it is written, what wines it highlights, and what prices are charged.

Check the availability.   You may decide that you want to feature a rare, old, or hard-to-find wine—but have you checked its availability? Contact the suppliers in your area and explain your objectives to them. Ask them to supply a list of the wines they carry including vintages, prices, and projected availability. Ask for their assistance with your wine list. Many distributors have people who are knowledgeable about wines and whose main job is to work with restaurateurs on their wine lists, merchandising, training, and promotion. It is important to remember, however, that their suggestions are not carved in stone, and you are under no obligation to use them or their products.

Tasting Wines Before Purchasing

One of the biggest mistakes restaurant or bar owners can make is not first tasting the wine they are purchasing, but rather taking the word of a customer, employee, or salesman. There is no way, unless you taste a wine, to determine where it should be placed on the wine list, or what food or foods it will go with. It is foolish to have wines on the list that do not complement your foods. Unfortunately, in some restaurants the quality of the food far outshines the quality of the wine, which makes a poor balance for the consumer.

Before purchasing wines for your list, first determine, with the aid of your chef, the food item you would like to match it to. Let's say that by prior tasting, an Alsatian Riesling would go well with a certain fish dish featured on the menu. But which Alsatian Riesling would you purchase?

Before you place your order, contact all of the distributors from whom you purchase and ask them to drop off a bottle of every Alsatian Riesling they carry. Then, properly chill the wines and taste them blind; either by putting the bottle into a brown paper bag or decanting it into a carafe, making sure that no one, including yourself, is able to see the label. This avoids the possibility of your being influenced by price or label. Have tasting sheets made up so that you will have a written record of the results of the tastings. Evaluate each wine using the criteria of taste; compatibility with menu items; suitability as an apéritif; availability; and, most of all, price. Expect to taste at least three times as many wines as you will actually have on your list.

Taste no more than eight to ten wines at once to avoid palate fatigue and try to plan the tasting for midmorning (10:30–11:00 A.M.); this is when your palate is the keenest.

Have your staff participate in the tastings. They will begin to learn about wines and develop an enthusiasm for your offerings that will translate into increased sales. Taste the wines alone and then with your menu items to make sure you are choosing wines that marry well with the food you serve. This will alert your staff to wine and food combinations they can recommend to customers.

Tally up the results and determine the order in which you have ranked each of the wines. Before you automatically purchase the wine that tasted best, there are many factors to be considered, including price. If your highest-priced entrée is $10.00 and the number-one Alsatian Riesling wholesales for $8.00, that translates to approximately $18.00 per bottle, and will be a tough sale. In this case, the second- or even third-choice wine might have to be considered. Thus, you do not purchase the finest Alsatian Riesling produced, but you *do* purchase the best Alsatian Riesling for your restaurant. Also be certain that there are sufficient quantities of this wine available, now and in the future.

You should, however, take one more thing into consideration before the final purchase order is written: Could this wine be designated a "dual" or "multiuse" type of beverage? A dual or multiuse wine is one that can be merchandised as an apéritif, be sold by the glass, and fit nicely into your wine list.

Dual and Multiuse Wine Brands

Many restaurants have limited storage space and simply lack the shelf area necessary to hold many competing brands. A prime example of a *dual* or *multiuse* wine is dry, white vermouth. Unfortunately, it is usually relegated to the kitchen for cooking or utilized in certain cocktails. Vermouth is the indispensable ingredient for a martini and the way most people drink it nowadays, with a ratio of 16 parts gin or vodka to one part dry vermouth, you will probably get 99 drinks out of a liter. Dry vermouth is an aromatized wine with about 17 percent alcohol and it has an optimum shelf life of six weeks, refrigerated. So if after six weeks a check of the underbar refrigerator shows that there is still two-thirds to three-fourths of the liter remaining, you should consider next time purchasing vermouth in 375 milliliter (12.7 fluid ounces) bottles. How should you merchandise this multiuse drink? Further possibilities are: dry vermouth on the rocks, with a twist of lemon; chilled straight up; mixed with equal parts of sweet vermouth; served as a long drink; a dry Manhattan; a dry Rob Roy; a substitution for white wine in spritzers, Kirs, and so forth. That makes nine different ways to merchandise a brand you *already* have in the bar. By effectively selling the vermouth in larger quantities, you could also lower the A.P. (as purchased) price by volume buying and discounts, usually ranging from 2 to 3 percent on three to five cases, cutting down the beverage cost, thereby increasing the profit margin.

The Wine on the Wine List

Consumers used to judge a restaurant primarily on ambiance, service, and food quality. Now a fourth criteria has been added: wine. Wine selection, service, and pricing are on an equal footing with ambiance, service, and food. Restaurant reviews routinely make mention of the breadth, depth, and price structure of the wine list when rating the restaurant. But what criteria do the reviewers use and what do these terms mean?

Breadth.   *Breadth* refers to the actual number of different selections on the list. (It is important to remember, however, that mere quantity is not enough; reviewers and consumers weigh *quality* just as heavily.) California, Italy, and France produce so many wines that it is easy to offer the customer great breadth; and, when reviewers tout a restaurant because of the scope of its wine list, it increases the volume of business to some degree.

Depth.   *Depth* refers to the extent to which particular regions and/or vintages of certain wines are represented. A list with good depth in Bordeaux would feature five or six classified wines, along with several shippers' or regional wines. A depth of vintages requires offering at least three or more vintages of the same wine, for example Beaulieu Vineyards Cabernet Sauvignon 1990, 1989, and 1986. Restaurants may find it difficult to offer a depth of vintages, as older wines are almost impossible to find and are often quite expensive. Those restaurants with a large range of vintages generally have extensive cellars that have enabled them to lay away wine for future consumption.

Balance. *Balance* refers to the overall range of styles offered and the balance between the different countries and regions represented on the list. California, Italy, and France are the primary producers of fine wines, so it is natural to include a broad selection of these wines on your list. You may choose to balance your list with wines from these major wine-producing countries, or you may specialize in just one region or country. Specialization is not a negative trait on a wine list. By highlighting one region within your list, you might place yourself in a unique marketing position, as you are offering something that your competitors do not.

Some restaurants are including wines from local wineries, setting their restaurant apart from their competitors. Some customers have a sense of pride in their community; by the use of locally produced wines, patronage might be increased. In addition, customers from outside areas might be tempted to try the local "brew" as an alternative to other wines.

Inventory. *Inventory* refers to the approximate number of wines kept on hand. Smaller restaurants often cannot make a capital investment in very large inventories or sacrifice the space necessary for storage. The benefits of a large inventory are in ensuring a continuity of supply and in buying wines for aging and buying large stocks when prices are most favorable.

The customer who has made a reservation at a fine restaurant is prepared to part with hard-earned dollars and will order a better wine to complement their meal than they might drink at home. He or she will experiment and will explore wine selections if the breadth, depth, and pricing of your list encourages them to do so.

How Large a List?

The size of your wine list is in part determined by the size of your storeroom. Wine requires specific storage conditions and storing it improperly jeopardizes your investment. Your capital investment also figures prominently in determining the size of your wine list. The basic reason for a short list could be a matter of dollars and cents, or limited storage space. A distinct advantage of a small list is that it is flexible enough to go with changing menus. An old standby "rule-of-thumb" relative to number of wines on a list is two to three wines per entrée in a restaurant. However, in order to attain any degree of balance and variety in your list, you should have a minimum of 40 to 50 wines. If your restaurant is small, this figure may seem high, but when you consider that these 40 to 50 wines are divided among apéritifs; champagnes and sparkling wines; and white, red, rosé, and dessert wines from different regions or countries, then 40 to 50 begins to sound like a very conservative number. In fact, it could be considered the minimum number that will allow you the flexibility to offer a range of wines appealing to different tastes and ability to pay, suitable for casual drinking or special celebrations.

Some establishments feel that when customers are presented with a list containing 200 or more wines, they tend to order wine with more frequency. It is felt that this communicates the idea that the restaurant specializes in wine, the management is knowledgeable, and the wines will be of excellent quality. Perhaps when customers view this type of list, they will even purchase a better-quality (usually higher-priced) wine.

How Many Wine Lists?

If your wine list contains well over 100 entries, you should consider having two separate and distinct lists. Very few if any of your customers are going to spend an entire evening reading through your wine list. Most customers would certainly be intimidated and overwhelmed by the array of names, types, and prices of wine on such a list. The first list might contain the most popular wines, which have immediate brand name recognition. Brand name recognition has bred loyalty among consumers; and many customers have only a superficial knowledge about wine and do not want to spend large sums of money on a product they generally don't drink at home anyway. They often order wines to be sociable among friends or family, so this list should be merchandised accordingly. Also, this abbreviated list should incorporate low-, medium-, and fairly high-priced items, which will cover most occasions.

If, after looking at this list, the customer decides that he would prefer a better-quality wine, a more comprehensive list should then be made available.

Another reason for having two beverage lists is for increased beverage sales. A good portion of the American public enjoys two things about their beverages; the fact that they are cold and that they are sweet. Most consumers talk dry, but drink sweet, or at least semisweet wines. This can easily be demonstrated by the tremendous sales of Lambrusco and low-alcohol refreshers. As a matter of fact, of the five best-selling imports, two of them are semisweet or sweet wines. If there is room on your menu, list simple wines that are both profitable and popular and that most customers will immediately recognize. Customers feel comfortable with wine names they can pronounce and recognize; and if your customer is more familiar with wines, the second, more extensive list can be asked for and presented.

How to Write a Wine List

Wine lists can come in impressive leather-bound books or on computer printouts, yet they all need to follow a basic structure. Wine lists should be divided into sections on apéritifs, champagnes and sparkling wines, dry white, dry red, rosé, and dessert and fortified wines, in that order.

Under each main category, the wine list can be subdivided. For example, under red wines, you can list Italian red wines, or even list those by region such as red wines of Tuscany. There should be at least three or more wines of a similar type to justify the use of subheadings.

Some restaurateurs attempt to list white wines from the driest to the sweetest, which presents all sorts of problems. First, with the exception of some California wines, you have no idea at all of what the residual sugar or total acidity content of the wine is. Second, most people confuse the taste of fruit in the wine with sugar. Third and most important, the perceived sweetness is in direct relationship to the amount of acidity contained in the wine. Two wines with identical residual sugar contents but different levels of acidity will taste different. A wine with a higher level of acidity will taste far drier than the wine with less acidity. Even professional tasters are occasionally fooled by various acid levels.

After you have established your basic outline, it is time to compile the listing for each individual wine. The following information should appear on your wine list.

Bin number. While not absolutely mandatory, this information simplifies wine storage, inventory, and reordering. It also assists both customers and staff with difficult pronunciations. If the customer can just say, "I'll have number 45," rather than trying to stumble over an unfamiliar name, he will feel more comfortable about ordering. It is a proven fact that people will not order food or drink items they are not familiar with, or can't pronounce. If the customer pronounces the wine's name incorrectly, the waiter does not need to correct him, but can say, for instance, "Yes, sir or madam, bin number 45 is an excellent choice with the steak." However, under no circumstances should the wine list contain a phrase such as "order by the numbers."

Vintage. Never leave out the vintage on your list; it is an insult to your customer's intelligence. Grapes are an agricultural crop and some years are naturally better than others. Also, after a period of time, some reds and most white wines are beyond drinkability and should not be offered to the customer. The customer has a right to choose. If a wine is nonvintage, then the letters *NV* should be used.

Many restaurateurs leave the vintage date off the wine list because they say they cannot be assured of a steady supply of a particular wine or vintage. However, many restaurants have chosen to print wine lists on word processors or by an inexpensive offset process to ensure that the information is accurate and up to date. This also avoids the all-too-common problem of out-of-stock wines and is preferable for the customer who cares more about wine than elegant calligraphy. Leaving out the vintage date creates a lack of wine-buying enthusiasm on the part of your customer, either because he does not want to bother the waiter for specific vintages or does not want to have to ask the vintage dates of several or more wines; and this additional step adds to the amount of time your guest stays in your restaurant without purchasing food or beverage.

If, for one reason or another, you still do not wish to place the vintage date on the list, then on a plain three-by-five index card list each and every wine by bin number and its vintage. This card should be carried by the waiter or sommelier and referred to when asked what vintage a particular wine is. Another suggestion is to have a separate sheet of paper listing the vintages of each wine placed in the rear of the book, with an asterisk or some other means of notification to the customer.

Name of the wine.   The complete name of the wine must appear and be correctly spelled. The wine's name could be varietal (the name of the predominant grape variety used), for example, Chardonnay; generic (the place name), for example, Bordeaux, or even proprietary; (a made-up name), for example, Blue Nun or Creso. An incomplete listing only confuses the customer. Next to (or under) each wine, a description of its style, flavor, food affinities, and food recommendation could be listed. For difficult to pronounce names, consider the use of phonetics, which aids in customer ordering.

The name of the shipper or winery.   This is extremely important for wines that come from the French regions of Burgundy and the Rhône Valley, where many small vineyards operate whose production is bought and bottled by shippers. For wines from regions such as Bordeaux, where the best wine bears the name of an individual château, or California, where the name of the winery is listed on the label, the shipper's name is not needed.

The country or state of origin.   Every wine list should state the country of origin, or if it is an American wine, the state where it was produced. The term *domestic* should be avoided, because it implies inferiority and has the connotation of a cheap replica or imitation. Instead, use the term *American.* H. G. Wells (1866–1946), British novelist, historian, and social reformer, was known to have said, "You Americans have the loveliest wines in the world, you know, but you don't realize it. You call them 'domestic' and that's enough to start trouble anywhere."

Many customers have an allegiance to a certain country or even state. This can translate into increased sales such as when a customer finds a wine that comes from the country or state of his birth.

Bottle size.   The traditional size of bottle in which almost all wines come is the 750-milliliter (25.4 ounces) bottle and unless you are serving a wine that comes in a bottle of a different size, it is unnecessary to list this information. Other bottle sizes that could be brought to the table are 375-milliliter (12.7 ounces) or 1.5-liter (50.8 ounces) bottles (the latter is known as a magnum).

Most customers will order the 750-milliliter size, which will be sufficient for dinner. However, by offering half-bottles (375 milliliter) or splits (187 milliliters), the customer is given an opportunity of trying one, two, or more different wines, while still consuming only as much wine as if he had ordered one 750-milliliter bottle. Half-bottles are ideal for solo diners, business travelers, and perhaps senior citizens. Magnum bottles of wine offer larger parties the opportunity to order one large bottle of a particular wine.

Wine List Design

The obvious purpose of a wine list is to *communicate* the wines (maybe food suggestions) and their prices to the customer. The information contained in the wine list can be given in many formats. The wine list should always be automatically presented with the menu, and because of this, many restaurateurs choose a cover similar in design to their menu cover.

Choose a format that is easily read, with boldface titles (headings, subheads, and special emphasis) and spaces between categories so that customers can easily scan the list. When the list is ready to be printed, assign a minimum of two people as proofreaders to ensure accuracy.

One of the common wine list errors is a wine list too small (physically) to accommodate a large number of wines; the result is crowding or utilizing small typefaces, which makes ordering difficult. Conversely, some wine lists are too large (wines seem to have sufficient room to "swim") for the number of wines listed. Paper quality and type size affect the readability of the list. Colored, textured paper and fancy typefaces are not only expensive, but in the low light of some restaurants, may make the list difficult to read. Avoid using small type, unless the lighting in your dining room is very bright. Bold or uppercase letters are *attention-getting devices*, which strike the eyes, and if used to excess, will actually cause eye fatigue. Avoid using only upper- or lowercase type on the wine list; instead use a combination of both, which is easier on the eyes. Italics or script should be utilized only for accent or special emphasis. If used to excess, italics becomes difficult to follow and tiring to read.

Another common wine list error is *spelling,* which creates anxiety and mistrust with serious wine drinkers. The fanciest of wine lists is of no use if it does not accurately convey basic information.

One of the fastest ways to lose a current or prospective customer is to list incorrect prices or vintages. If a listed wine is out of stock, the sommelier or server should inform the customer of this when the wine list is presented. Avoid having scratched out prices, changes in pencil or ink, or covered up prices on your wine list.

Remember that the wine list should be kept neat, clean, and up to date. Soiled wine lists reflect on the overall cleanliness of the restaurant.

Follow-up.   Once you've written your list, the work is not over. It is important to track wines' popularity to ascertain if the selections you have made are the wines your customers want.

Keep a count of the number of bottles sold per customer (divide the number of covers by the number of bottles sold). If this number is less than 0.5, you need to seriously consider changing your selection and merchandising strategies. Include your staff in discussions.

Figure the proportion of white wine to red wine. If you are selling 60 percent white wine (the national average) and you stock 75 percent red, you may need to adjust your ratio.

Analyze the average price of a bottle of wine sold during a three-month period. If your average check is $16.00, yet most of your wines are $24.00 and over, you need to stock more moderate-priced wines.

Rank the ten most popular wines on the list and analyze what they have in common. This will assist you when you revise your list. If the ten most popular wines are all whites under $20.00, then you may want to focus the bulk of your list on wines such as these.

The Apéritif List

Perhaps the most overlooked part of the wine list is the apéritif list. Very few restaurants effectively merchandise apéritifs, and because of this, loss of revenue runs quite high. In fact, better than 90 percent of all restaurants across the country don't have an apéritif list as part of their wine lists.

It is not enough for your server to ask customers if they would like a "drink from the bar," or "perhaps a glass of white wine." In today's marketplace, everything being equal, why would a customer want to eat, drink, or socialize in your establishment? You must offer the customer something unique or different: an unusual theme or specialized service, for instance.

If you had a listing of various apéritifs that a customer could consult, this would increase beverage sales. If you can sell an apéritif, you have one sale; then, at dinner, if a bottle of wine is sold, that's two sales.

By developing an apéritif list, you can pick up additional sales. Many people are getting tired of a glass of nondescript white wine that costs them as much as a cocktail containing distilled spirits. They may have heard that wine is lighter and contains fewer calories than distilled spirits and want to try some, but are simply afraid to or uneducated in the art of ordering wine. An apéritif list can be placed on the table, awaiting the customers' arrival, showing eight to 12 alternative apéritif drinks besides a martini or glass of white wine.

What is an apéritif? There are many factors that should be considered: The beverage should be dry, light, chillable, and refreshing; it should be relatively acidic, to cleanse the palate; it should perhaps also be slightly bitter.

The popularity of apéritifs lies partly in the fact that they are lighter and lower in alcohol than traditional cocktails such as martinis or Manhattans. They can be more interesting than distilled spirits-based cocktails; most of them are quite flavorful. They also contain fewer calories and stand up to ice better than white wines (which tend to become diluted). They are today's "in" drinks when one is ordering at a bar or restaurant. (See Chapter 6: *Apéritifs and Fortified Wines,* for examples of apéritifs.)

The Wine List and the Menu

Your wine list must relate to your menu offerings. If your menu is primarily seafood, your list should include a larger proportion of white wines that are well matched with seafood. Conversely, if beef and lamb predominate, then a concentration of red wines would be a logical focus.

It is advisable to match wines from your wine list with food offerings on your menu; and foods from the menu with wines on your wine list. Wines-by-the-glass can also be matched with menu food items.

Pricing Wines

Today's customers are well aware of the price of a bottle of wine available in local wine shops and understand that a restaurant must charge additional money for labor and to make a profit. What they do not understand is why some restaurants charge inordinately high prices. Price gouging on wine results in diminished sales and disgruntled customers. Offering good wines at fair prices will sell more wine and keep customers coming back for more. Customers are already intimidated with regard to wine, and astronomically high prices alienate them further; in addition, many may also feel that the restaurateur knows little about marketing and cares little for repeat patronage. Customers are very quick to react unfavorably to overpricing by cutting down or eliminating wine purchases.

Customers are willing to pay a little more for a bottle (or glass) of wine if the following conditions are met:

1. The wine has brand recognition.
2. The wine is of good quality (not necessarily expensive).
3. The wine is served in a generous glassful (often six ounces).
4. The price is right.

For a customer to desire a bottle of wine, it must be within his reach and be fairly priced. The cost of serving an expensive bottle of wine is the same as for an inexpensive one and the total profit is greater when selling more wine at a lesser markup. A pricing suggestion might be to offer a certain group of wines (or the entire wine list) at a set price, for example, 15 wines at $15.00, or perhaps 25 wines at $25.00.

The pricing strategy suggested below guarantees a fair return per bottle for the restaurant, while at the same time encouraging customers to make initial and repeat purchases.

WINE PRICING FORMULA BY THE BOTTLE			
Cost per bottle (750 ml)	Percentage mark-up (%)	Selling price	Gross profit
Up to $4.00	200	$12.00	$8.00
Up to $7.00	150	$17.50	$10.50
Up to $10.00	125	$22.50	$12.50
Up to $15.00	100	$30.00	$15.00
Up to $25.00	75	$43.75	$18.75
Over $25.00	50		

To determine the selling price, take the cost per bottle, multiply by percentage mark-up, then add the two numbers. After the selling price has been established, round it up to the nearest quarter and add $1.00 to cover breakage, spillage, and insurance.

Selling Wines by-the-Glass

More and more restaurants are offering fine wines by the glass. Current estimates are that between 35 and 50 percent of all restaurant wine sales are by-the-glass. Machines that preserve the quality of open bottles are available, allowing you to pour a variety of wines by the glass. With today's sophisticated beverage-dispensing systems, some restaurants can offer just about every wine on their list by the glass. Your restaurant does not have to have an expensive beverage system, or any beverage system, to offer such a program. Just remember that red wines, after opening, generally have a shelf life of two to three days if refrigerated, while whites will last up to five days before serious deterioration takes place. Several types of recorkers are available which are suitable for still or sparkling wines. If you do a very high volume of business and have a fast turnover rate, an expensive system may be unnecessary.

Sparkling wines sold by the glass are continually growing in popularity. Selling wine this way allows a customer to try several different wines while keeping down total alcohol consumption.

Some suggestions for selling wine by-the-glass are:

- If possible, bring the bottle to the table and pour for the customer, so the bottle and label are in full view.
- Consider utilizing 187-milliliter wine bottles for your by-the-glass program; pour only half glass and bring the glass and bottle to the table for the customer's edification.

Some benefits of selling wines by-the-glass:

- Customers can drink one or two glasses, return to work and still function.
- Customers can sample wines they might not be familiar with, prompting them to purchase a bottle.

Pricing methods.   When developing a wine-by-the-glass program, there are two separate and distinct pricing methods, depending on the quality of the wine and the size of the bottles you use. Each portion served should be six ounces, which gives the customer a high level of perceived value.

The pricing formula is similar to that for per-bottle service, but in this case you only round up to the nearest quarter and do not add the $1.00 to cover breakage, spillage, and insurance.

WINE-BY-THE-GLASS PRICING FORMULA	
Cost per bottle (750 ml)	*Percentage mark-up (%)*
Up to $ 4.00	250
Up to $ 7.00	200
Up to $15.00	175
Up to $25.00	100
Over $25.00	75
From bulk	250
(3 or 4 liter or larger)	

Wine-preserving and dispensing systems. Wherever fine wines are served by the glass, by the bottle, or even by the sip, wine-dispensing systems can be found.

Some restaurants have begun to allow customers to taste several wines to determine which they would prefer to drink while dining. This also offers customers an opportunity to select a variety of wines to be enjoyed throughout the meal: sparkling wine before dinner; Chardonnay with the fish; Chianti with the main course; and a Sauternes with dessert, for example.

Wine-preserving and dispensing systems offer numerous avenues of promotion: "awareness advertising," suggestive selling with dinner orders, and wine-tasting events. In addition, these systems are a visual marketing tool: People see and ask about them then generally order a glass of wine. Sales and profits are thus increased.

Consumers may find that where such systems are used, a glass of fine wine is more easily within reach. For the first time, novice wine drinkers can afford to taste the many varieties of wine and discover the differences between them. Wine connoisseurs find themselves able to broaden their expertise of the finest wines and producers find new markets for their premium lines. In addition, with such systems, customers are able to taste truly great wines that they would not otherwise be able to afford.

In short, these systems allow more people to be served a variety of wines, while at the same time increase the profit margin in single-glass sales with virtually no risk of spoilage. Some features of these systems are:

Most systems are designed to keep the contents of opened wine bottles as fresh as when they were uncorked and without spoilage due to oxidation, for up to about six weeks. Inert nitrogen gas, injected under gentle pressure through a sealed stopper, replaces the wine as it is removed from the bottle, and preserves the wine by keeping it oxygen-free. The wine may be quickly dispensed and easily stored after use.

A fast, reliable bottle-changing system is available that generally entails a simple changing of siphon tubes from one bottle to another.

The nitrogen system fits both 750-milliliter and 1.5-liter bottles.

Wines are chilled quickly and proper temperatures of fast-moving wines are electronically controlled and maintained.

Most dispenser systems display temperature, wine pressure, and gas flow, and have open-door signals.

Systems are available to accommodate single bottles or up to 32 bottles; see-through cases are available.

Wine-by-the-glass systems increase your profits dramatically. The profits realized by serving premium wines by the glass will pay for the system, usually within a few months.

The systems increase the sale of premium wines and your per-unit profit rate. Unique or special wines such as dessert wines, Port, or rare red wines that are ordinarily too expensive to stock may be opened and only as much as is desired drawn-off and served. Because a bottle of wine is sold by the portion, more can be charged for it than when selling it by the bottle. Discriminating customers tasting a glass of wine they like may purchase the entire bottle.

PROFITS STRUCTURE THROUGH USE OF A BEVERAGE SYSTEM

Average Bottle Wholesale Price	Average Glass Cost	Average Bottle Price	Average 5 oz Glass	Average Profit 5 oz. Glass	Percentage of Profit (%)
$6.00	$1.20	$18.00	$4.50	$3.30	275

ADDITIONAL PROFITS GENERATED BY THE SYSTEM

Number of Glasses Sold Per Day	Additional Profit Per Day	Additional 30 Days	Profits 60 Days	Each 90 Days
10	$33.00	$ 990	$1,980	$ 2,970
25	$82.50	$2,475	$4,950	$ 7,425
50	$165.00	$4,950	$9,990	$14,850

Above figures according to Cruvinet Wine Dispensing Systems of California.

The wine-dispensing system does not replace your present wine list, but adds to your selection and increases the profitability of your entire wine program.

Some manufacturers of these systems are:

Le Cruvinet	Winekeeper
Vintage Keeper	Wine Systems Int.
Winebar	

BATF ruling. The Bureau of Alcohol, Tobacco, and Firearms permits (1985) the use of carbon dioxide for dispensing wine from original wine containers if the carbon dioxide is not injected into the wine and the carbon dioxide level of the wine is not increased. Advances in modern technology permit many containers to be equipped with dispensing devices that allow carbon dioxide to be added *only* to the headspace of the container. Under federal law (1990), *still wine* (not more than 14 percent alcohol) is taxed at $1.07 per gallon; wine more than 14 percent and not over 21 percent at $1.57 per gallon; wine more than 21 percent and not over 24 percent at $3.15 per gallon; and sparkling wine at $3.40 per gallon. Any addition of carbon dioxide into wine itself is considered a cellar treatment and can be conducted only on the premises of a bonded wine cellar. Distilled spirits are taxed at the rate of $13.50 per proof gallon and beer at $18.00 per barrel (31 gallons).

Wine-on-tap systems. Most of these systems utilize state-of-the-art aluminum canisters, which vary in dimension and capacity from producer to producer. Most are also equipped with inert nitrogen gas systems that replace the wine as it is removed from the keg, which preserves the wine by keeping it oxygen-free. Delicato Winery and Banfi Vintners both use a system that does not utilize nitrogen, but rather uses any gas or compressed air (oxygen included). The principle of its operation is that compressed gas sucks out the wine rather than replacing it with costly nitrogen gas. In both types of systems, the wine may be quickly dispensed and easily stored after use. The systems can be made portable for catering purposes. Paul Masson, for example, uses 30-liter (7.9 gallons or 1,014 ounces) and 58.6-liter (15.5 gallons or 1,981 ounces) canisters which weigh 83.6 pounds and 160.4 pounds full, respectively, and 18.4 pounds and 31.4 pounds, empty, respectively.

The advantages of such systems are listed below.

Eliminates	*Reduces*
Breakage	Inventory carrying costs
Spillage	Refrigeration
Pilferage	Storage space
Trash accumulation	Bar restocking
Leakage	Employee handling
Space needed for empties	
Deposit and return (of bottles)	

Other benefits of the system are: more consistent quality of wines; lower operating costs; greater ease of operation; greater labor efficiency (improved through quicker service); reduced labor costs (through minimum handling); and elimination of waste (virtually all of the wine is deliverable through the system, and there are no disposal costs, and no trash).

Wine sold in kegs is generally generic in nature (Chablis, Rhine, Burgundy, and so forth), but some wineries do offer varietal wines such as Chardonnay, Chenin Blanc, Colombard, Cabernet Sauvignon, Ruby Cabernet, and White Zinfandel, to name a few.

Wine Consumption

Americans generally speak about the per capita consumption of wine in the United States as it compares to that of Europeans. In the late 1960s, some industry experts predicted that the U.S. per capita consumption would be five gallons by 1990 (the consumption was approximately one gallon at the time). However, in 1994, the consumption level was approximately 1.86 gallons.

Major brands of imported wine.   The ten most popular brands of imported wine* are:

1. Riunite "Classics"
2. Bolla
3. Folonari
4. Concha y Toro
5. Marcus James
6. Cella
7. Georges Duboeuf
8. Leonard Kreusch
9. Louis Jadot
10. B & G

Major California varietal table wine brands.   The ten most popular brands* are:

1. Gallo Reserve Cellars
2. Sebastiani
3. Sutter Home
4. Robert Mondavi "Woodbridge"
5. Glen Ellen
6. Inglenook

---

* Source: *Jobson Handbook* 1995.

7. Franzia
8. Beringer
9. Fetzer
10. Blossom-Hill

▶ THE BEER LIST

Beer is steadily growing in popularity: Consumers drink it before, during, and after dinner. This type of consumer might be one who simply refuses to pay for exorbitantly high wine prices and instead drinks beer during dinner; or he may be a true beer lover or someone seeking a beverage low in alcohol. Beer consumption also increases in hot weather. In any case, it is wise to consider having a beer list on hand in those establishments that cater completely or even partially to beer-consuming customers.

Beer drinking nowadays is not only trendy but also sophisticated and most restaurants are taking note of what brands of beer their clientele drink. The annual consumption of beer in the United States was listed as 22.8 gallons per capita in 1994. This is quite high compared to the 1.86 gallons of wine (1994) and 1.29 gallons of distilled spirits (1994) that are consumed (per capita, per year). The U.S. beer-consumption figure is low, however, compared to that of other countries: Germany at 38 gallons, Czechoslovakia at 35 gallons, and Great Britain at 27.1 gallons (all 1994 figures).

In spite of the increasing number of beer drinkers, many restaurateurs do not realize the potentially large revenues to be gained from promoting beer in their establishments.

Major brands of beer.   The ten most popular brands of American beer* are:

1. Budweiser
2. Bud Light
3. Miller Lite
4. Coors Light
5. Busch
6. Natural Light
7. Miller Genuine Draft
8. Milwaukee's Best
9. Miller High Life
10. Old Milwaukee

---

* Source: *Impact Databank* 1995.

The ten most popular brands of American "light beer"* are:

1. Bud Light
2. Miller Light
3. Coors Light
4. Natural Light
5. Busch Light Draft
6. Michelob Light
7. Miller Genuine Draft Light
8. Keystone Light
9. Old Milwaukee Light
10. Milwaukee's Best Light

The ten most popular brands of "imported" beer* are:

1. Heineken (Holland)
2. Corona Extra (Mexico)
3. Molson Ice (Canada)
4. Beck's (Germany)
5. Molson Golden (Canada)
6. Labatt's Blue (Canada)
7. Amstel Light (Holland)
8. Foster's (Australia)
9. Guinness Stout (Ireland)
10. Bass (England)

A good beer list that most restaurants could start with contains a total of 12 beers: five American beers and seven imports, chosen from the above list, with substitutions for local or regional preferences or for locally produced beers. It is extremely important to let your customers know whether the beers are available in bottles or by the draft pump. Avoid selling beer by the can in restaurants because of the image problem associated with cans.

Ethnic restaurants may need a different selection of beer: For example, a German restaurant may need more German beers. Some restaurants across the United States call themselves "American" restaurants; therefore, most or all the beers served should be produced in the United States.

For restaurants with a larger beer-drinking clientele, a list containing 12 imports and six American beers would be proper. Restaurants with an even larger beer-drinking clientele would do well with a minimum of 20 imports and seven American beers.

---

* Source: Impact Databank 1995.

Types of Beer to Include

The most popular type of beer is lager, which is produced worldwide. Other popular types that could be included on a restaurant's beer list are:

Ale	"Light" beer (low in calories)
Dark Beer	Malt Liquor
Dry	Pilsner
Ice	Stout or Porter
Lager	

▶ THE DISTILLED SPIRITS LIST

Although lists containing solely distilled spirits are apparently not in vogue in today's primarily wine-drinking environment, good restaurant profit still lies in the popularity and diversity of distilled spirits. Cocktails are still preferred by some customers over both wine and beer when it comes to cocktail parties, weddings, banquets, and especially before, during, and after dinner. An important adage states that "if you have it at the bar, list it on your *distilled spirits* or *cocktail* list." Most bars and restaurants still play "guess what we have" with customers. By effectively communicating with your customer, additional drink sales will be engendered.

Making up a list that includes only the distilled spirits currently available in your restaurant could very well be off-the-mark when it comes to consumer preferences. For one thing, since the 1970s and through the 1990s, the popularity of "white distilled spirits" (gin, rum, tequila, and vodka) has increased over that of the traditional "brown distilled spirits" (whiskies) that existed before Prohibition. Consumers view white distilled spirits as versatile, mixable with most fruit juices; they taste less of alcohol and not as strong as whiskeys (although their respective alcoholic content is often the same).

The trend toward white distilled spirits shows little sign of weakening. Of the ten best-selling brands of distilled spirits in the United States, Bacardi rum and Smirnoff vodka are clearly at the top of the list. The top-selling brands of distilled spirits are:

Brand name	Category	Cases sold (millions)
Bacardi	Rum	6.25
Smirnoff	Vodka	5.90
Seagram's Gin	Gin	3.95
Jim Beam	Bourbon	3.69
Popov	Vodka	3.43

Brand name	Category	Cases sold (millions) (continued)
Seagram's 7 Crown	Blended	3.19
Jack Daniels Black	Tennessee	3.03
Canadian Mist	Canadian	3.00
Absolut	Vodka	2.90
E & J	Brandy	2.21

Source: *Jobson Handbook* 1995.

The List

Your distilled spirits list is an excellent merchandising tool for selling cocktails. It can be enhanced with color photographs and/or descriptions.

The ten most ordered cocktails in a bar* are:

1. Vodka/ Gin and Tonic
2. Gin/ Vodka Martini
3. Bloody Mary
4. Rum and Cola
5. Margarita
6. Screwdriver
7. Bourbon and Cola
8. Seven and Seven
9. Bourbon and Water
10. Scotch and Soda

The five most ordered cocktails in a bar by region† are:

East

1. Vodka and Tonic
2. Gin and Tonic
3. Screwdriver
4. Gin Martini
5. Vodka Martini

Central

1. Vodka and Tonic
2. Vodka Martini
3. Gin and Tonic
4. Screwdriver
5. Rum and Coke

---

* Source: *Beverage Journal* 1993.
† Source: *Nation's Restaurant News* 1991.

South

1. Margarita
2. Scotch and Water
3. Vodka and Tonic
4. Screwdriver
5. Gin and Tonic

West

1. Vodka and Tonic
2. Gin and Tonic
3. Margarita
4. Screwdriver
5. Rum and Coke

Standard cocktails that are often ordered are listed below, under the name of their main ingredient (the distilled spirit used):

Gin or vodka

Black Russian
Bloody Mary
Gibson
Gimlet
Gin or Vodka and Tonic
Gin Rickey
Godmother
Harvey Wallbanger

Orange Blossom
Martini
Salty Dog
Screwdriver
Singapore Gin Sling
Tom Collins
White Russian

Tequila or rum

Bacardi
Daiquiri
Fruit Daiquiri
Mai Tai
Margarita

Piña Colada
Planter's Punch
Rum and Coke
Tequila Sunrise
Zombie

Scotch

Godfather
Rob Roy
Rusty Nail

Scotch and Soda
Sours

Whiskey

Highball
Jack Rose
Manhattan
Mint Julep

Old-fashioned
Seven and Seven
Sours

Other cocktails

Americano	Long Island Iced Tea
Bee's Knees	Negroni
Bellini	Orgasm
Brandy Alexander	Screaming Orgasm
Cobbler	Sidecar
Copacabana	Slippery Nipple
Glögg	Sloe and Comfortable Screw
Golden Cadillac	Sloe Gin Fizz
Grasshopper	Stinger
Jelly Bean	Swampwater
Kir	Tom and Jerry
Kir Royale	

Name brand and super-premium distilled spirits. The distilled spirits list can contain name brand (also referred to as *call brand*) as well as super-premium (also referred to as *top-shelf* or *super-call*) distilled spirits from each category; some of these are listed below.

Blended whiskey

Barton Reserve	Philadelphia
Calvert Extra	Schenley Reserve
Carstairs	Seagram's 7 Crown
Fleischmann	Three Feathers
Four Roses	Tom Burns Reserve
Imperial	

Bourbon and Tennessee whiskey

Ancient Age	Old Cabin Still
Jim Beam	Old Charter
Benchmark	Old Crow
Blanton	Old Fitzgerald
Ezra Brooks	Old Forester
Elijah Craig	Old Grand-Dad
Jack Daniels Black Label	Old Hickory
J. W. Dant	Old Taylor
George Dickel	Rebel Yell
I. W. Harper	Ten High
Kentucky Gentleman	Wild Turkey
Kentucky Tavern	Evan Williams
Maker's Mark	

Canadian whisky

Black Velvet	Schenley O.F.C. (Old Fine Canadian)
Canadian Club	Seagram's Crown Royal
Canadian Mist	Seagram's V.O. (Very Own)
Lord Calvert	Windsor Supreme

Gin

Beefeater	Gilbey's
Bellows	Gordon's
Bombay	House of Lords
Boodles	Old Mr. Boston
Boord's	Seagram's
Booth's	Schlichte
Burnett's	Tanqueray
Doornkaat	Vlahov
Fockink	Hiram Walker
Four Roses	

Irish whiskey

Bushmills	John Jameson

Rum

Appleton	Myers's
Bacardi	Rhum Saint James
Cockspur	Ron Castillo
Cruzan	Ron Rico
Mount Gay	

Scotch whisky

Ambassador	Cutty Sark
Ballantine	Dewar's White Label
John Begg	Grant's
Bell's	John Haig
Black Bull	Haig & Haig
Black & White	Harvey's
Catto	Inver House
Chairman's Choice	J & B
Chivas Regal	McCallum
Checquers	MacKintosh

Scotch whisky *(continued)*

Ne Plus Ultra
Old Rarity
Old Smuggler
Park & Tilford
Passport
Scoresby
Teacher's
The Grand Macnish
Tomatin

Usher's
Usquaebach
Vat 69
Johnnie Walker
White Heather
White Horse
Whyte & Mackay
100 Pipers

Single-malt Scotch whisky

Aberlour
Auchentoshan
Aultmore
Balvenie
Cardhu
Cragganmore
Dalmore
Dalwhinnie
Glendronach
Glenfarclas
Glenfiddich
Glengoyne

Glenkinchie
Glenlivet
Glenmorangie
Glenordie
Isle of Jura
Knockando
Lagavulin
Laphroaig
Oban
Talisker
The Edradour
The Macallan

Tequila

Jose Cuervo
Pedro Domecq
El Cuate
El Toro
Don Emilio
Gavilan
Gusano Rojo
Herradura
Juarez

Juarez
Pepe Lopez
Monte Alban
Montezuma
Sauza
Torado
Two Fingers

Vodka

Absolut (Sweden)
Anatevka (Israel)

Borzoi (England)
Burrough's (England)

Carmel (Israel)
Cristall (Russia)
Crown Russe (USA)
Denaka (Finland)
Eldurís (Spain)
Finlandia (Finland)
Gilbey's (USA)
Gordon's (USA)
Great Wall (China)
Icy (Iceland)
Izmira (Turkey)
Jarzebiak (Poland)
Ketel One (Holland)
Luksusowa (Poland)
Majorska (USA)
Moryoskoff (Russia)

Moskovskaya (Russia)
Nikolai (USA)
Popov (USA)
Priviet (Russia)
Samovar (USA)
Sermeq (Denmark)
Silhouette (Canada)
Skol (USA)
Smirnoff (USA)
Stolichnaya (Russia)
Suntory (Japan)
Tanqueray Sterling (England)
Tsing Tao (China)
Wolfschmidt (USA)
Wyborowa (Poland)
Zytnia (Poland)

After-dinner liqueurs and brandies.   Some recommended generic and proprietary brands of after-dinner cocktails that can be included on the distilled spirits list (or on a separate list) are listed below.

Amaretto
Anisette
Applejack (apple brandy)
Apricot-flavored brandy
Akvavit (or Aquavit)
Alizé
Armagnac
Asbach Uralt Brandy
Averna
Baileys Irish Cream
Benedictine
Benedictine & Brandy
Blackberry-flavored brandy
Blackberry liqueur
Brandy
Calvados (apple brandy)
Campari
Chambord (raspberry liqueur)
Chartreuse (green or yellow)
Cherry-flavored brandy

Coffee-flavored brandy
Cognac
Cointreau
Crème de Banana
Crème de Cacao (brown and white)
Crème de Cassis
Crème de Menthe (green and white)
Curaçao (orange or blue)
Cynar
Drambuie
Emmets Irish Cream
Fernet Branca
Frangelico
Fraise (strawberry brandy)
Framboise (raspberry brandy)
Galliano
Goldwasser
Grand Marnier
Grappa
Grenadine

Irish Mist
Jägermeister
Kahlúa
Kirsch (cherry brandy)
Kümmel
Lochan Ora
Malibu
Mandarine Napoléon
Maraschino liqueur
Marc
Metaxa (Greek brandy)
Midori
Mirabelle (plum brandy)
Nocello
Ouzo
Peach-flavored brandy
Peppermint Schnapps
Pernod

Peter Heering (cherry liqueur)
Petite Liqueur
Pisco Brandy
Poire (pear brandy)
Ramazzotti
Rock and Rye
Sabra
Sambuca
Slivovitz (plum brandy)
Sloe gin
Southern Comfort
Strawberry liqueur
Strega
Tia Maria
Triple Sec
Tuaca
Vandermint

12

Purchasing, Storage, and Cost Controls

he purchasing function is one of the most overlooked aspects of running an effective beverage business. All alcoholic beverages are not the same and therefore a practice that might pertain to distilled spirits will have little relevance to wine or beer. Distilled spirits, with few exceptions, have an extremely long shelf life and do not require atmospherically controlled storage areas, as do wine and beer. Beer and wine, to some extent, are perishable items and are adversely affected by temperature and humidity fluctuations, exposure to light, and vibrations. Careful ordering, receiving, and storing practices must be strictly adhered to.

Most beverage managers are concerned with the financial running of an operation and rely heavily on beverage controls. Automation has provided the industry with many types of control systems, some costing as little as a few dollars, while other more sophisticated systems may cost well into the tens of thousands of dollars. As the beverage operation moves into hotels, consumer-operated in-room bars have been developed which control each and every purchase. With increasing business from conventions and corporate meetings, banquet managing has also become more sophisticated.

▶ CUTTING COSTS WITHOUT SACRIFICING QUALITY

An important element in the purchasing function is making certain that quality standards remain high, while at the same time seeking out the best possible price.

Be careful in selecting suppliers; find out exactly what they supply for how much money. Also see what other services they might provide for the same money or just a little more. Additionally, if one supplier costs more than another, what are you getting in return, better service, or just higher prices?

Managers with purchasing responsibility and authority must be on the lookout for ways in which costs can be controlled, without ultimately sacrificing quality to the consumer. Some steps to control costs are:

- Put all specifications *in writing* and be certain that they are adhered to.
- Don't allow suppliers to make decisions relative to quality, quantity, and delivery times.
- Conduct negotiations with the suppliers. What determines your negotiating power? Money and the amount you have to spend does. The more you can spend usually determines how much you can save by buying in bulk.
- Get competitive bids from other suppliers in the area.
- Develop *par stock* levels.
- Check inventory levels.
- Evaluate need for all items ordered: Are there any that could be eliminated or replaced at a lower cost without sacrificing quality?
- Consider bulk purchases for items that are not perishable.
- Re-evaluate relative need for high-cost items that have or add little overall value to the customer.
- Don't under-order; you may learn the hard way that your *most popular* beverage on the wine list is sold out.
- Don't over-order; beverage managers find themselves with high inventory levels (especially beer), which ties up money.
- A supplier may be willing to accept a lower price provided he or she receives cash in advance, at the time of delivery, or shortly thereafter. This procedure is sometimes referred to as *cash discounts.*

- Inspect all orders received to ensure that the ordered product, which includes quality and quantity, have been delivered.
- Discontinue unnecessary, wasteful supplier services.

▶ ALCOHOLIC BEVERAGE BOTTLES

The Bureau of Alcohol, Tobacco, and Firearms (BATF) has authorized certain bottle sizes for wine and distilled spirits. Before developing purchasing specifications, determine what size bottles are needed, taking into consideration storage space, space on the back bar, and volume of each bottle.

AUTHORIZED BOTTLE SIZES FOR WINES AND DISTILLED SPIRITS

Wines (all types)

Bottle size	Capacity (oz)
15 liters	507 (Nebuchadnezzar)
12 liters	405.6 (Balthazar)
9 liters	304.2 (Salmanazar)
6 liters	202.8 (Methuselah)
5 liters	169
4.5 liters	152.1 (Rehoboam)
4 liters	135.2
3 liters	101.4 (Jeroboam/ Double Magnum)
1.5 liters	50.8 (Magnum)
1 liter	33.8
750 milliliters	25.4
500 milliliters	16.9
375 milliliters	12.7
187 milliliters	6.3
100 milliliters	3.4

Distilled spirits (all types)

Bottle size	Capacity (oz)
1.75 liters	59.2
1 liter	33.8

Distilled spirits (all types) (continued)

Bottle size	Capacity (oz)
750 milliliters	25.4
200 milliliters	6.8
50 milliliters	1.7

In order to provide the consumer with clearer and more useful information on labels for distilled spirits, BATF issued regulations for labeling: Alcohol content must be indicated by percentage—not just in proof. This is a more readily understood way to convey alcohol content to the purchaser.

Since the repeal of Prohibition, the requirement that labels state alcohol content (formerly expressed in degrees of proof) has remained unchanged. Proof is a traditional term for alcohol content (equal to twice the percentage by volume). Thus, 80 proof means 40 percent alcohol by volume; 100 proof means 50 percent alcohol by volume, and so on.

According to the regulations, labels *must* show percentage by volume of alcohol, but both forms (proof and percentage) may be used. If a proof statement is used, it must be shown in direct conjunction with the percent by volume, emphasizing the fact that both expressions mean the same thing.

▶ SALES REPRESENTATIVES

When it is time to order or reorder, be sure that you are purchasing from a reputable distributor or wholesaler. This could make the difference between prompt service and service that costs you business and money because of delays.

Establish a good rapport with sales representatives. In addition to selling you a product, they can give advice and assistance. If problems arise with deliveries, immediately call the sales representative, inform him or her of the situation, and seek immediate remedies.

Most distributors or wholesalers will not sell you a *broken case* (a case of 12 bottles made up of several brands or types of wine or distilled spirits according to your specifications), but a good working relationship with your sales representatives could result in several broken cases being delivered.

▶ PURCHASE OF ALCOHOLIC BEVERAGES

Purchasing alcoholic beverages is unique in many respects, but, perhaps the most critical issue to contend with is the fact that all alcoholic beverages are tightly controlled by

BATF. Therefore, many of the procedures utilized in the purchase of food, nonalcoholic beverages, supplies, equipment, and so on, do not apply to alcoholic beverages.

Distilled Spirits

The selection and purchasing of distilled spirits generally falls into three distinct areas, which should be understood in order to satisfy customers' needs. The three categories are *premium brands, call brands,* and *well brands.*

Premium brands are top-quality alcoholic beverages that have brand recognition, are positioned well in a customers' mind, and generally command the highest prices. Also known as *premium pour, super call,* and *top shelf.*

Call brands are alcoholic beverages that have brand recognition for which the customer will "call" by name. Also known as *call liquor* or *name brand.*

Well brands are house brands with little name recognition that are generally lower in quality and price. They are used when customers ask for generic drinks. Also known as *bar brands, bar whiskey, house brands, house whiskey,* and *well stock.*

Wine

Wine, both American and imported, basically falls into two distinct categories—*generic* and *varietal.*

Generic wine is a designation of a particular class or type of wine, but such designations also may have geographic significance (the name of a district, commune, or region where the wine originates from). A simpler definition would be a "place-name"—wines that are named after European wine-producing districts such as Burgundy, Chablis, Champagne, Chianti, Port, Rhine, Sauternes, Sherry, and so forth.

Generally, American-made *generic* wines are lower-priced, usually lower-quality, utilized as *house wines*, often private labeled, and generally served when a customer asks for a "glass of wine . . . red, white, or rosé." On the other hand, European-made *generic* wines are the typical wines encountered from most foreign countries.

Varietal is a wine made wholly or predominantly from a single grape variety, named on the label (for example, Cabernet Sauvignon, Chardonnay, Pinot Noir, Zinfandel).

Varietal or varietal-designated wines are most often American produced (although many are available from Chile, South Africa, Australia, and certain European countries) and have great popularity among the American wine-drinking public.

Beer

When purchasing beer, it is imperative to keep in mind that beer (cans or bottles) is semi-perishable and generally has a shelf life of six months. Therefore, do not purchase more beer than will be consumed within six months.

The Miller Brewing Company utilizes a system of code dates, often referred to as *pull dates,* to ensure freshness. A *pull date* is a date by which product should be "pulled" off the shelves, after which time they begin to deteriorate.

Miller's package code-dating system is easy to read and use. It will enable you to maintain a constant quality watch on product age in your establishment.

Here's how the Miller Brewing Company code date works:

Code dates can appear on bottle crowns, back label, bottom of each can, on both side panels of each corrugated carton or tray, and on all 12- and 24-pack can boxes.

The code dates will be the "pull date" for that package. The "pull date" is the date on which *the product should no longer be offered for retail sale.*

As an example, a package stamped 12*31*5*1*2 indicates a "pull date" of December 31, 1995. The last two digits denote plant and shift information. (Reprinted with permission of Miller Brewing Company.)

▶ ORDERING AND PAR STOCK

Prior to ordering, ask yourself these questions:

1. Is ordering done in a haphazard manner with little planning?
2. Is ordering done so that, frequently, too much inventory is on hand?
3. Are you considering only price and neglecting quality, brands, grapes, and other factors?

If your answer to any of the above is yes, you need to improve your ordering procedures.

Ordering effectively can only be accomplished by determining from past inventories what was sold, in what quantities, and how fast. From patterns established over several weeks it is easy to determine how much of a certain product is needed at the bar. The *par stock* is the minimum or maximum specified amount of a product on hand to satisfy customers' needs for a specific period of time. It might be wise to establish different par stocks for seasons, weekends, holidays, parties, and so on. If this is not possible, then plan on those occasions to have on hand one-and-a-half times the needs of your busiest day. Keeping a par stock helps in determining an ordering schedule, since it sets up an inventory level of merchandise. There are several reasons why it is unwise to go above your predetermined inventory level: excess capital will be tied up that could be put to better use; space will be used that could be put to other or better use; and the interest you are paying on your tied-up money may not be regained.

Another point to consider when purchasing is the possible trade-offs involved in certain decisions: Do you want to purchase a particular case of red wine now, when the price is low, although it will not be drinkable or salable for five years, or should you wait five years, when the purchase price is considerably higher, before purchasing? A decision should be based on the following considerations:

- Five years later the wine might not be available.
- How much storage space do you have? Are your storage conditions ideal?
- What is your cash flow?
- What interest rates will be charged against money borrowed for the purchase?
- What dollar amount would you save by purchasing the wine when it first appears, as opposed to buying it at a higher price in five years?
- How secure against theft or fire is your facility?
- If the purchase is made, in what quantity?
- What is the market like: How willing will your clientele be to purchase the wine?
- Does the wine complement any of the food items on your menu?

Reordering must be done before one has completely run out of a product. Many beverage managers have what they call a "reorder point," at which there is sufficient lead time for deliveries yet customers can still be satisfied with what is on hand.

It is suggested that whenever a bottle is ordered from the storeroom, a record of this requisition be made, then sent to the storeroom at the close of the day for inventory and eventual replacement. Another possibility is to use stickers, stamps, or metal-edged numbered tags on bottles, which can be removed as bottles are sold and deposited in a box, from which requisitions for replacements are made up at the close of the day. Some establishments use a "bottle-for-bottle" policy; a practice of requiring an empty bottle be turned in before a replacement bottle is issued. This generally is not for empty wine bottles for they often leave the restaurant with customers.

An inventory system should be set up with adequate space for wines, distilled spirits, and beers. These should be separated if possible. Sometimes a "perpetual inventory" system is utilized: Simply put, this is a bookkeeping system that adds to and subtracts from the inventory as bottles enter and leave the storeroom. In this case, the perpetual inventory should correspond with the actual inventory figures. Beverage managers should check inventory on a weekly basis and report any discrepancies immediately.

▶ RECEIVING

Good receiving practices are necessary if the gains made in good ordering procedures are not to be lost. It doesn't pay to buy good quality merchandise and then lose the quality through improper handling after the goods are delivered.

Assign the manager or bar manager to handle deliveries; insist that they are "rear" delivered (delivered at the service entrance), if possible. When deliveries are received, invoices must be checked against actual merchandise delivered. Simply counting the number of cases received does not ensure that you are getting what was ordered. It is necessary to either open the cases or check labels stamped on the box sides, which indicates their contents. If cases are opened, they should be resealed and initialed and dated for control purposes. This is essential with wines that carry a vintage date, to ensure that you are getting the vintage that was ordered.

Whenever possible, make sure that the contents delivered are not damaged or broken. A simple eye check should immediately pick up such damage, or even missing bottles. Occasionally, through rough handling, boxes are dropped and one or more bottles in the case are broken. This is easy to spot with red wines (due to their staining ability) but difficult with other, noncolored beverages. If the case is left untouched for several months, the cardboard will dry out, and unless the case is shaken, the break will not be detected. This type of breakage is referred to as a "dry break."

Storeroom

All cases of alcoholic beverages should be moved to the storeroom as quickly as possible to guard against pilferage. Storerooms should be locked, with limited access to only a few employees (beverage manager, bartender, food and beverage director). Storerooms should be located in areas void of light, heat, vibration, and high humidity, critical to proper storage of wine and beer.

Racks, generally made out of metal, should be utilized for merchandise that can stand upright (distilled spirits). Once cases are opened, their contents should be completely emptied and stored on appropriate shelves, with the cartons immediately removed.

The use of bin numbers simplifies storage, inventory, and reordering. Each bin card should contain pertinent information about the beverage, including name, vintage (wine), and bottle size. It is easier for a bartender to ask for "bin 23" rather than a "bottle of 1992 B.V. Cabernet Sauvignon 'Rutherford.'"

▶ WINE STORAGE

Wine's enemies are temperature (too high, too low, or widely fluctuating), vibration, light, and excessively high or low humidity. You do not have to spend thousands of dollars building a special cellar, but you do have to use common sense when choosing a storage area.

Storing wine bottles completely upside down often creates problems. The weakest part of the bottle is the neck and if cases are stacked more than six high, pressure could actually cause the necks to snap. Also, sediment collects around the neck, sticking to and becoming embedded in the cork, presenting a problem in decanting or just extracting the cork.

If your bulk wine storage is far away from the dining room, be sure to requisition a day's supply and keep it behind the bar or in another convenient area. If servers have to travel too far to get bottles of wine or can't find a bucket, they will find ways not to sell it.

Light

Strong light, particularly sunlight, can be harmful to wine if a bottle is exposed for long periods. It is not necessary to reproduce sealed darkroom conditions, but wine should be protected from light as much as possible. For this reason most wines are packaged in green or brown bottles.

Temperature and Humidity

Wide and frequent fluctuations in temperature should be avoided. The proper cellar temperature is 52 to 55 degrees Fahrenheit, but a few degrees higher or lower is satisfactory, providing that the temperature is constant. Wines can be safely stored for years in a fairly stable temperature ranging from 55 to 70 degrees Fahrenheit. The cooler the bottle's aging conditions, the more a young wine's character is retained, for a longer period of time. Temperatures are cooler at floor level and on interior walls or closets; exterior walls are affected by sunlight and daily temperature changes. Uninsulated rooms should not be used, as their wide temperature changes damage the wine and shorten its life.

The correct level of humidity for a wine cellar is between 55 and 65 percent. If the humidity begins to rise, reaching 80 percent or more, mold may form around foil, and corks may leak as the wine in the bottle expands. There is also a long-term effect; bottle labels begin to deteriorate and, with long-term exposure, will actually disintegrate. Conversely, if the humidity falls well below 55 percent the corks begin to dry out, as do the wooden wine racks and supports.

Wine racks should be positioned away from water heaters, stoves, and heat ducts. Store white wines and sparkling wines close to the floor, where it is cooler. A room equipped with an air conditioner will help maintain a consistent temperature and humidity, ensuring that the wine your customer orders arrives in the best possible condition.

Vibrations

Wines should rest quietly. Constant vibration can damage their flavor, and storage areas should not be located adjacent to loading docks or dishwashers. Other poor choices are areas near air conditioner or heat exhaust ducts.

Wine bottles should be stored with their labels facing up for easy identification of the type and brand of wine. If the bottle has been stored with the label facing down, chances are that it probably shows abrasions from repeated handling. Since some customers like to save empty bottles or soak off the labels as souvenirs, this could be a problem. (Spraying wine labels of expensive or old bottles of wine with ordinary hair spray will seal the label and protect it from deterioration.) Another and more important reason why labels should face up is so that they can be easily identified in the periodic checks that are made (called *candling*) to determine the amount of sediment (if any) that has formed in the bottle. To candle the bottle, carefully hold it, horizontally, in front of an exposed light bulb (60 to 100 watts) so that light penetrates the glass, displaying any sediment on the bottom side of the bottle. Knowing which wines have started to "throw" sediment aids in serving wines.

Wine Racks

Wine racks should be designed so that wine bottles are stored horizontally, allowing the cork to remain in contact with the wine and ensuring that it will stay moist and pliable. A moist cork provides the best seal for a bottle of wine. If the bottle is allowed to stand upright for prolonged periods of time (two months or longer) the cork will dry out, allowing air to enter the bottle, which eventually causes oxidation, and finally spoilage. When young, corks have more elasticity and stay expanded even if the bottle is allowed to stand. However, when the cork becomes older, it starts to dry out and shrink, and this becomes a problem when wine bottles are stored upright. (An exception to the rule of horizontal storage is for bottles that are sealed with plastic corks or metal screw caps; these may be safely stored upright.) Horizontal rack designs should allow air to circulate and permit, when possible, each bottle to be removed without disturbing its neighbor. Also, several types of shelving are available that absorb vibrations.

There are basically two ways to correctly store cork-finished wine bottles; either horizontally, or with the neck of the bottle tilted slightly upward. (Some wine racks are also designed so that the neck of the bottle is pointed down. This leads to trouble, for it is not uncommon for wine bottles to leak at the neck or through the cork.)

The other problem associated with storing bottles with the necks pointed either slightly up or down is that it wastes cellar space. In an average storage room, whose ceiling is eight feet high, space is at a premium. The diameter of a wine or champagne bottle at its widest point can be up to four inches. If another four inches are allowed for retrieval and two additional inches for movement, a total of ten inches (vertically) is used in horizontal storage. If the neck is pointed upward or downward, another six inches is used, for a total (vertical) space of 16 inches.

▶ PURCHASING NONVINTAGE WINES

Perhaps the biggest problem associated with wines that do not carry a vintage date is that one has no way to determine how long it was stored in the warehouse prior to purchase. It happens quite often that warehouse workers who have little or no knowledge of wines simply place the new merchandise in front of the old; rotation of stock (first in, first out: FIFO), under these circumstances, is rarely accomplished. As the stock is depleted, the older wines start appearing—wines that may have been stored there for several years.

Therefore, it is imperative that you purchase nonvintage wines only from very reputable distributors who have temperature-controlled warehouses and insist on rotation of stock. Do not purchase more nonvintage wine than will be consumed within six months.

It is a good idea to mark cases or even the individual bottles of nonvintage wine with a piece of removable tape showing the date it was received. And always insist that your own stock is rotated.

► PLASTIC BOTTLES

Distilled Spirits

Airlines have been switching to plastic distilled spirits and wine bottles to trim fuel costs. The main reasons why products are packaged in plastic bottles are well documented: they are lightweight, cost-effective, easy to transport and handle, and, most important, they are break-resistant. A nine-gram miniature plastic bottle is approximately 85 percent lighter than glass. A package kit (of 90) of these plastic bottles weighs only 24 pounds, compared to 46 pounds for glass. Safety is also a factor and is another reason why glass is rarely used on airlines.

Wine

Distributors and retailers are receptive to large-size plastic bottles because their reduced weight and their compactness means lower freight cost; there is also no breakage. The use of plastic reduces the overall weight of a filled bottle by at least one-third.

Some California wineries also bottle their wines in plastic jugs, which they report are not only lightweight, but easier for store personnel to move around. Plastic containers also make pouring easier for bartenders. These lightweight wine bottles provide outbound freight savings in excess of 20 percent by increasing the number of cases per truck or rail-car. An empty plastic three liter bottle weighs 3.6 ounces, compared to 38 ounces for equivalent glass containers. An empty four liter plastic bottle weighs 4.5 ounces, versus 42 ounces for a glass jug.

The success of economically priced table wines sold in large, lightweight plastic bottles may prompt more wine producers to eventually switch over to plastic.

► BANQUETS

To effectively sell alcoholic beverages at banquets, bars must be attractive to guests and be stocked with a good assortment of brand-name alcoholic beverages.

For efficient service, a minimum of one bartender is generally needed for every 50 guests, with two being optimum. When one bartender is responsible for 50 guests, speed, efficiency, and organization are extremely important. The bar, which is usually portable, must be entirely set up before the banquet begins; all necessary supplies—alcoholic beverages, ice, glasses, and so on—must be within immediate reach of the bartender. Because of the small size of most catering bars, the number of beverage brands one can supply is limited, and careful selection of the most popular brands is essential.

It is extremely important that the catering staff be instructed on proper pouring of wines at banquets, conventions, meetings, and so on. Stress the importance to your waiters of not filling glasses with wine when the dinner is about to end. As much as 50 percent of what is spent on wine can be saved by insisting on proper pouring. In addition, specify in writing exactly how much wine waiters must pour; six or even eight ounces is more than sufficient. One of the best ways to ensure proper pouring is by using automatic pouring tops that fit all bottle sizes. Proper glassware size is also important as it guarantees the correct distilled spirit-to-mixer ratio.

A complete and total bar inventory must take place prior to and immediately following any and all events.

Pricing Banquets

Prices should be flexible enough to guarantee a sizable profit, while at the same time making your premise accessible to (affordable by) the general public. The pricing structure that follows is a suggested one that can easily be modified to suit individual needs.

Hosted bars, on a per-person basis. This pricing structure provides for unlimited drinks for a minimum of 50 guests and serves name brand distilled spirits. The prices are estimated on a per-person basis and include the cost of employing two bartenders per every 50 guests:

- One hour $11.00 x 50 guests equals $550.00
- Two hours $13.00 x 50 guests equals $650.00
- Three hours $15.00 x 50 guests equals $750.00
- Four hours or more $17.00 x 50 guests equals $850.00

Hosted bars, on a per-drink basis. This pricing structure is based on the service of name brand distilled spirit drinks, but with no minimum set for the number of guests. Either the organization pays the final tab, calculated by each drink, or each guest pays for his or her own individual drinks. When guests pay for individual drinks, fixed prices for drink categories must be standardized to avoid the necessity of committing to memory each individual brand's selling price. These per-drink prices do not include the cost of employing bartenders, which would be covered separately:

- Name brand distilled spirits $4.00
- Premium brand distilled spirits $5.00
- Name brand liqueurs $4.00
- Premium brand liqueurs $5.00
- House wines (white, red, rosé) $3.00
- American beers $3.00
- Imported beers $4.00

Hosted bars, on a per-bottle basis.   This pricing structure is based on the cost of name brand bottles of distilled spirits; it entails no established minimum number of guests. The sponsoring organization pays the final tab, calculated by each bottle opened, regardless of whether the contents have been totally consumed. Some state alcoholic beverage laws permit the organization to claim any opened, unempty bottles (often referred to as "stubs"), while other states prohibit such actions. The drink prices would not reflect a charge of $75.00 per bartender, which would be covered separately.

▶ STANDARDIZATION OF DRINK RECIPES

A standardized drink recipe is defined as a recipe that has been checked and rechecked for all factors and that will consistently produce a known quantity at a desired quality. The standardized drink recipe is consistent in all factors of taste, quantity, quality, appearance, garnish, method of preparation, ingredients, style of service, and, most important, specific "determined" portion served at a specific price.

The standard recipe of a cocktail includes:

- the ingredients (nonalcoholic)
- a garnish
- the generic or proprietary brand of distilled spirit, wine, or even sometimes beer
- the glass size to be used

The following are advantages to having standardized drink recipes.

- easy to make
- consistency of product
- predictable yield
- a system of operation rather than dependency upon an individual
- improved cost control by forecasting and portion control
- predetermined item cost
- easy *par stock* determination
- recognition of deviation from the standard and immediate correction
- provision of a plan of preparation and elimination of employee preparation decisions
- an inventory list and purchase control of nonusable items

Drink recipe testing procedures:

- check the recipe for proper ingredient ratios
- check the preparation procedure for clarity

- check the sequence of work
- check the equipment to make sure it is appropriate for preparation
- give measurements of dry ingredients by weight and liquid ingredients by volume
- have a supervisor work with the production person and record any changes
- prepare a small amount of the item for testing for standard
- increase the amounts and retest for standard if the beverage is satisfactory

When a drink recipe is accepted, implement it as you would in any training program:

1. Explain to the employees why the new recipe has been developed and the advantage of the new recipe.
2. Emphasize and explain any part of the recipe that may affect the final quality or a part where a problem may occur in the preparation process.
3. Work with and assist the employees in preparing the item.
4. Follow up on the item when it appears on the drink menu prepared without your assistance.

Standardization not only maximizes profit per drink, but also provides a consistent product to the most important player in the game—the customer.

▶ BEVERAGE COST FORECASTING

There is no such thing as a perfect cost percentage to be accepted by all beverage managers as an industry standard. Every beverage cost percentage must and should be considered in relation to a particular establishment.

In determining a reasonable beverage cost percentage, you could consider utilizing a "bottom-up approach." In using this method, you first consider an acceptable return on investment out of every dollar, then anticipate controllable and noncontrollable expenses. Other than the cost of the beverage, add these variables and then subtract from $1.00; this will give you a "target" beverage cost. For example:

$.13 represents desired profit from each dollar of sale
.20 represents projected noncontrollable expenses per dollar of sale
.40 represents projected controllable expenses per dollar of sale
$.73 is the gross profit per dollar of sale

You now subtract this $.73 gross profit per dollar of sale from $1.00, arriving at a targeted beverage cost of $.27 per dollar of sale.

To change this figure to a percentage, simply convert all monetary figures to percentages; for example, $1.00 to 100 percent, $.73 to 73 percent, and so on. This $.27 or 27 percent represents the percentage of the dollar that you have targeted to pay for *all* of your beverage costs. It should be noted that you are using the aforementioned figures solely for demonstration purposes; again, they do not represent any type of industry standard.

There are numerous resources available in print that can be used where projected feasibility returns on investments along with payment of expenses can be determined. Armed with this information, the entrepreneur can predict with justifiable accuracy an acceptable beverage cost percentage for his particular establishment.

Every year, the National Restaurant Association publishes a Restaurant Industry Operations Report which is prepared by certified public accountants. At the end of each report the reader is presented with a method by which to analyze his or her existing or future operation. Statistics are presented on national averages for certain types of establishments and which can be compared to our projected sales and expenses, with net income treated as an expense. Once these projections are targeted, you can then target *minimum* selling prices (maximum selling prices are determined solely by what the market will bear).

Determining the Sale Price of a Drink

To determine the price of a single drink, there are several points that must be considered: the size and price of the bottle, and the individual drink size. With today's automatic pourers, bars have a choice of exactly what size drink to pour.

In the following example, a liter bottle of Scotch is used, which costs (wholesale) $10.00. You have determined that a 1.5-ounce drink will be poured to each customer and wish to determine how much each drink will cost. Thus:

$$\frac{\text{Bottle size}}{\text{Drink size}} = \text{number of drinks}$$

(Note: The bottle size is not rounded off, because of the fractions used in the size of the drink.) So, for example:

$$\frac{33.8 \text{ ounces}}{1.50 \text{ (1.5 ounces)}} = 22.5, \text{ or 22 drinks}$$

When rounding off the number of drinks, always round off lower, simply because you cannot divide a drink.

To determine the cost of those 22 drinks, use this formula:

$$\frac{\text{Cost of bottle}}{\text{Number of drinks}} = \text{cost per drink}$$

For example:

$$\frac{\$10.00}{22} = .454, \text{ or } 45 \text{ cents}$$

There are two methods of determining the projected beverage cost:

The divisional method.   To find out the potential selling price, divide the actual beverage cost by the projected beverage cost percentage:

$$\frac{\text{Actual beverage cost}}{\text{Projected cost percentage}} = \text{Potential selling price}$$

For example: A single drink of Scotch costs 45 cents and you are working with a projected 27 percent beverage cost. The selling price would be determined as follows:

$$\frac{45 \text{ cents}}{27 \text{ cents (or 27 percent)}} = \$1.666, \text{ or } \$1.67$$

The price multiplier method.   Continuing our example, to determine a minimum selling price per drink, divide 27 into 100, which will give a price multiplier of 3.70. Take the cost of any drink and multiply it by 3.70 to determine a *minimum selling price.* We will use the cost of 45 cents:

$$45 \text{ cents} \times 3.70 = \$1.665, \text{ or } \$1.67$$

From this point you can establish common prices for each drink category: well, call, and super-premium. Adjustments will be necessary based on clientele and demand. However, you must target all pricing to *average* a 27 percent beverage cost should you want to maintain and *control* this targeted beverage cost.

Determining the Projected Cost Percentage
The formula used to project percentages is the following:

$$\frac{\text{Actual beverage cost}}{\text{Potential selling price}} = \text{Projected cost percentage}$$

Using the same figures as used in determining the selling price, for example:

$$\frac{45 \text{ cents}}{\$1.67} = .269 \text{ (or 27 percent)}$$

Determining the Actual Beverage Cost

If you determine the potential selling price and projected cost percentage of a certain drink, it is easy to determine the actual beverage cost: Multiply the potential selling price by the projected cost percentage. For example:

$$\$1.67 \times .27 = 45 \text{ cents}$$

Determining Gross Profit on a Full Bottle

It has been established that there are 22 drinks in a liter bottle of Scotch (1.5-ounce drinks), which costs $10.00; the potential selling price of each drink is $1.67. To determine total sales from the entire bottle, simply multiply the number of drinks by the potential selling price per drink; for example:

$$22 \text{ (drinks)} \times \$1.67 \text{ (selling price)} = \$36.74 \text{ (total sales)}$$

To determine gross profit, subtract the bottle cost from the total sales. For example:

$$\$36.74 - \$10.00 = \$26.74 \text{ (gross profit per bottle)}$$

Pricing Cocktails

There are many ways to price individual drinks. One method is to take the prime ingredient (distilled spirit) and use that as the base, then add the other ingredients to come up with a total cost.

For example, you would like to make a martini and from your standard recipe determine that two ounces of vodka, $^1/_4$ ounce dry white vermouth, and one green cocktail olive are needed. Olives come in various sizes, with the "small" designation being the correct size for a martini. Depending on the purveyor you choose, the price can vary greatly. Purveyor "A" sells them in the following way:

$11.00 per large #10 can
Contains 51 ounces (drained weight)
Count of 578 olives
Average number of olives per pound = 177–193

If you divide the cost of the can ($11.00) by the number of olives in the can (578), you find out that each olive costs $.0190 cents, or 2 cents. This figure is added to the cost of the vodka.

To determine how much two ounces of vodka costs, divide the cost per bottle by the number of ounces in that bottle; for example:

$$\frac{\$10.00 \text{ (cost of bottle)}}{33 \text{ ounces}} = .303, \text{ or } 30 \text{ cents per ounce}$$

To determine what $\frac{1}{4}$ ounce of dry white vermouth will cost, you first find out the cost per liter. If a liter costs $4.24, how many quarter-ounce drinks will you get, and how much will each of them cost?

$$\frac{33.8 \text{ ounce (size of bottle)}}{\frac{1}{4} \text{ ounce (or .25 ounces)}} = 135.2, \text{ or } 135 \text{ (quarter-ounce) drinks}$$

$$\frac{\$4.24 \text{ (cost of bottle)}}{135 \text{ drinks}} = .031, \text{ or } 3 \text{ cents per drink}$$

To determine the cost of the whole drink, add:

Cost of vodka (2 ounces, at .30 per ounce)	60 cents
Cost of vermouth (.25 ounces)	03 cents
Cost of olive	02 cents
Cost of drink	65 cents

Now, by using your formula for determining a selling price, you find that your drink sells for:

$$\frac{65 \text{ cents (actual beverage cost)}}{27 \text{ cents (projected cost percentage)}} = \$2.407, \text{ or } \$2.41 \text{ (selling price)}$$

Another method for determining this price is to use what is known as a "kicker"— automatically adding five to ten cents to the base cost of the drink, instead of figuring out each and every ingredient. If, for example, Scotch and soda is requested by a customer, the standard recipe might call for 1.25 ounces of Scotch, 6 ounces of seltzer water, and ice cubes. Instead of figuring how much the seltzer water costs, ten cents is added to the base distilled spirit cost of the drink; for example:

Cost of Scotch, per 1.25 ounce	45 cents
Seltzer (10 cents "kicker")	10 cents
Cost of drink	55 cents

Then:

$$\frac{55 \text{ cents (beverage cost)}}{27 \text{ percent (cost percentage)}} = \$2.037, \text{ or } \$2.04$$

Determining Average Beverage Sales

To determine average beverage sales per customer, divide total beverage sales by the number of customers present during that period of time. For example, if the total wine sales (by the bottle) for an evening are $2,350.00, and there were 150 customers present:

$$\frac{\$2,350.00}{150 \text{ customers}} = \$15.666, \text{ or } \$15.67 \text{ (sales per customer)}$$

Making or Buying Beverage Mixes

Occasionally you will be faced with deciding whether to purchase premixed beverage mixes—for a Bloody Mary, piña colada, Margarita, and so on—or make them yourself. The decision should be based not only on the quality of the premix versus homemade blends, but on the relative cost of each. For example: You are able to purchase sour mix at a cost of $23.50 per (12-quart) case; there is a two percent "discount" on three cases. Your bartender makes an equally fine sour mix, but you don't know how much it costs to make. What you do know is that his mix yields two gallons and that the raw ingredients cost you $11.45. In addition, it takes him 25 minutes to make and you pay him $4.85 per hour, with 15 percent in fringe benefits. To determine the cost of the purchased mix:

$$
\begin{array}{rl}
\$23.50 & \text{(case cost)} \\
\times\ 2 & \text{percent (discount)} \\
\hline
47 & \text{cents (discount)}
\end{array}
$$

$$
\begin{array}{rl}
\$23.50 & \text{(cost of case)} \\
-\ 47 & \text{cents (discount)} \\
\hline
\$23.03 & \text{(case cost after discount)}
\end{array}
$$

$$\frac{\$23.03 \text{ (case cost)}}{12 \text{ quarts}} = \$1.919, \text{ or } \$1.92 \text{ per quart}$$

To determine the cost of the homemade mix:

$$\frac{\$11.45 \text{ (2 gallons)}}{8 \text{ quarts (2 gallons)}} = \$1.43 \text{ per quart}$$

4.85 (hourly salary) $\times$ 15 percent (fringe benefit)
= 73 cents

$$
\begin{array}{rl}
\$4.85 & \text{(hourly salary)} \\
+\ 73 & \text{cents (fringe benefit)} \\
\hline
\$5.58 & \text{per hour}
\end{array}
$$

$$\frac{\$5.58 \text{ per hour}}{60 \text{ (minutes in one hour)}} = \$.093 \text{ per minute}$$

$\$.093 \text{ (per minute)} \times 25 \text{ (minutes)} = \$2.325, \text{ or } \$2.33 \text{ for 25 minutes of work}$

$$\frac{\$2.33 \text{ (25 minutes of labor)}}{8 \text{ quarts}} = \$.29 \text{ per quart (labor)}$$

Product cost $1.43 per quart
Labor cost $ .29 per quart
―――――――――――――
                      $1.72 per quart

So, it costs $1.92 per quart to buy the sour mix and $1.72 per quart to make the blend. The difference is 20 cents for two gallons. You must determine how many gallons of sour mix you need per week to find out if it really pays to make your own.

Percentage Increases or Decreases (Mark-ups)

Often a beverage manager wants to determine how much (as percentages) the costs or selling prices of drinks either increased or decreased over a specified period of time. For example, five years ago a bottle of Scotch cost $3.85, it now costs $8.50. To determine how much the cost of the Scotch has increased, the following formula is applied.

$$\frac{DT \text{ (distance traveled)}}{SP \text{ (starting point)}} = \text{Percentage}$$

$8.50 (current cost)
− $3.85 (old cost)
―――――――――――――
$4.65 (difference expressed in dollars)

Now, by using the formula, you have:

$$\frac{\$4.65 \text{ (DT)}}{\$3.85 \text{ (SP)}} = 1.208, \text{ or a 121 percent increase}$$

Another way to use this formula is illustrated in this example: A wine shop owner sells a bottle of Chianti wine for $5.59; he bought it for $3.83. To determine the mark-up percentage in this case, you can utilize the same formula:

$5.59 (current selling price)
− $3.83 (original cost per bottle)
―――――――――――――
$1.76 (difference)

$$\frac{\$1.76 \text{ (DT)}}{\$3.83 \text{ (SP)}} = .46, \text{ or a 46 percent mark-up}$$

Determining a "Better Buy"

When purchasing wines or distilled spirits, you must determine what bottle size or sizes you will need: the traditional 750-milliliter size; the larger liter bottles; a 1.5-liter bottle (wine only); or a 1.75-liter bottle (distilled spirits). Which one is the better buy, or are they priced exactly the same, per ounce?

Let us say that a certain Scotch wholesales per bottle for:

$11.41 for 750 milliliter
$14.62 for 1 liter
$23.20 for 1.75 liters

Which one of these is the better buy? Use the following formula:

$$\frac{\text{Cost per bottle}}{\text{Number of ounces in the bottle}} = \text{Price per ounce}$$

1. 750-milliliter bottle $\dfrac{\$11.41}{25.4 \text{ ounces}} = .449$, or $.45 per ounce

2. 1-liter bottle $\dfrac{\$14.62}{33.8 \text{ ounces}} = .432$, or $.43 per ounce

3. 1.75-liter bottle $\dfrac{\$23.20}{59.2 \text{ ounces}} = .391$, or $.39 per ounce

The better buy in this case is number three; Scotch that wholesales for $23.20 per bottle. Before you purchase this 1.75-liter size, however, determine the size and space of your speed racks, back bar, and underbar, and the frequency with which the brand is chosen by customers. For an extra few cents, it may pay to purchase the 750-milliliter bottle (for size) or the 1-liter bottle (for frequency of drinks).

Happy Hour Two-for-One Drinks

To increase business, many restaurants or bars institute a special "two-for-one" pricing strategy, in hopes of drawing in new customers and thereby increasing not only business, but also profits. It is unfortunate that many owners do not realize that in order to make increased profits (not business), it becomes necessary not to increase the numbers of customers, but to increase the *number of drinks* that each customer consumes. It works this way:

Suppose you regularly charge $3.00 for a cocktail, with a 27 percent Projected Cost Percentage. But during Happy Hours, you reduce the selling price to $1.50 per drink.

Regular Hours
$3.00—Regular Selling Price Per Drink
  .50—Beverage Cost
$2.50—Gross Profit or 83% of Sales

$$\frac{\$2.50 \text{ Gross Profit}}{\$3.00 \text{ Selling Price}} = 83\% \text{ of Sales}$$

Happy Hours
$1.50—Happy Hour Price Per Drink
  .50—Beverage Cost
$1.00 Gross Profit or 67% of Sales

$$\frac{\$1.00 \text{ Gross Profit}}{\$1.50 \text{ Selling Price}} = 67\% \text{ of Sales}$$

If your desired Gross Profit is $2.50 per drink, but because of Happy Hour, it is lowered to $1.00 per drink, it means that 2.5 drinks will have to be consumed by each customer to reach the Gross Profit level of $2.50.

$$\frac{\$2.50 \text{ Gross Profit (Regular Priced Drinks)}}{\$1.00 \text{ Gross Profit (Happy Hour Prices)}} = 2.5 \text{ Drinks}$$

But then, you have only reached the same gross profit had you not lowered the price and customers consumed one drink each.

Are the hours of your Happy Hour long enough to enable each and every customer to consume a minimum of three drinks? With liquor liability laws and emphasis on lowering consumption of alcoholic beverages, is it a good practice to continue "two-for-one" pricing?

Percentages

To determine what percentage (%) one number is of another, use the following formula. The number which follows **OF** goes on the bottom. For example:

What percent is 19 "OF" 38?

$$\frac{19}{38} \text{ Equals .50 or 50\%}$$

To determine a certain percent of a number, say 45% of $2.00, use the following formula:

Multiply 45% (.45) × $2.00 = $ .90

When you know that one number is a certain percent (%) of an *unknown* number, you must find that number.

For example: 38 is 25% of what number?

Divide the whole number (38) by the known percent (25%) to find the unknown number.

$$\frac{38}{25\%} = 142$$

Ratios

Ratios are relationships between two things, expressed as one quantity divided by the other. In a ratio problem you will usually see the question: "What is the ratio of _____ to _____?" The numeral following **OF** is the first number (number compared) and the numeral following **TO** is the second number (number with which it is compared).

The word "TO" always goes on the bottom and the word "OF" goes on the top in the divisional problem.

To find the ratio of the two numbers expressed in a percentage, divide the first number by the second number.

For example, in a bar there are 27 men and 43 women. What is the ratio of men to the total number of customers in the bar?

$$\frac{27 \text{ (OF)}}{70 \text{ (TO)}} = .386 \text{ or } 39 \text{ percent}$$

What would be the ratio of women to the total number of customers in the bar?

$$\frac{43 \text{ (OF)}}{70 \text{ (TO)}} = .614 \text{ or } 62 \text{ percent}$$

The totals of men equals .386
The totals of women equals .614
_____
100 percent or 70 customers

▶ POURING SPOUTS

Constant price increases, rising alcoholic beverage taxes, and tougher liquor liability laws make it essential not to overpour drinks. You could be losing a considerable amount of money by allowing your bartenders to freely pour distilled spirits by using the uncontrollable plastic spouts many bars use. Instead, consider using the portion control pourer, which saves money and increases profits.

For example, if you use a liter bottle of Scotch (33.8 ounces) and pour one-ounce shots, or 33 drinks, charging $4.00 per drink, this totals $132.00 in sales. But, if because of overpouring, spillage, or guesswork when using the free pourer, only 26 drinks are yielded from the bottle ($104.00), that's a loss of $28.00 in sales per liter. If the bartender pours five cases of Scotch per week by the free-pour method, that's a loss of $336.00 per case ($28.00 × 12 bottles), or $1,680.00 per five cases. This is the loss for only one type of distilled spirit served; you could literally be losing tens of thousands of dollars every year.

The national average loss for all types of bars from spillage, overpouring, dead inventory, unauthorized giveaways, dishonesty, and poor recordkeeping is five drinks per bottle. Losses in many bars are actually higher—sometimes six to seven drinks per bottle. By using the portion control pourer, you can guarantee that a controlled amount of distilled spirit is always dispensed. Because a consistent drink is poured every time, service speed is increased (most pourers have a half-second to one full second recycle time), more drinks are sold, and profits are increased. Use of controlled pourers relieves bartender tension and eliminates the cost and constant washing of shot glasses. Cocktail waitresses can also serve more customers in less time.

By using controlled pourers, you can consistently pour whatever size shot you want, without offending your customers. They also guarantee uniformity of drink taste and assure perfectly blended cocktails. Automatic pourers are made for drinks of many sizes, including the following: $1/2$, $5/8$, $3/4$, $7/8$, 1, $1 1/8$, $1 1/4$, $1 1/2$, and 2 ounces. Many manufacturers even color code their pourers for quick recognition. Some manufacturers even offer flip-top caps which protect beverages not only from dust but also from insects, especially fruit flies. Dust caps are required in many areas of the country by government health departments.

In another controlled dispensing system, distilled spirit bottles are placed upside down in a plastic dispenser. To operate, a glass is placed underneath and a lever on the dispenser is pushed up to pour out, with 100-percent accuracy, a measured amount of distilled spirit. At the same time a meter registers and shows in a visible readout each drink and how many drinks per bottle have been dispensed. This simplifies inventory control and gives a full accounting of *all* sales.

Computerized Beverage Control Systems

To effectively cope with rapidly rising costs, bar managers must have access to accurate, timely, and complete information relating to sales, inventory, guest check control, employee productivity, and beverage and labor costs. This vital information should be available on a minute-to-minute basis. Combining the finest in modern technology and management tools, computerized control systems provide the total control of profit and inventory that is essential in today's market.

In the fiercely competitive beverage business it is imperative that you have the full use of all profits, both to satisfy current commitments and to meet capital needs for future growth. Control systems provide the consistency, quality, speed, and total control that you need. It is not enough to partially control products poured at the bar; every distilled spirit, wine, cocktail, soft drink, and even draft beer must be poured accurately, rapidly, and with total accountability.

▶ IN-ROOM BARS

In-room computerized bars offer hotel guests the opportunity to enjoy alcoholic beverages in the privacy of their rooms while the management maintains absolute control over purchases. Upon guest check-in, the room unit is activated, and a key is provided to the registrant. Guests can select from a range of different items in privacy and charges are instantly transferred for addition to the room charge. In such computerized systems printouts are instantaneous and provide a wealth of information, from restocking reports to usage tracked by room type. Computerized in-room systems eliminate the problems associated with "honor" bars. Some of the benefits of such systems are:

- By providing beverages and light snacks, they free room service personnel for larger and more profitable orders.
- They are profitable amenities that differentiate your hotel or resort from others.
- They are virtually pilfer-proof.
- They comply with alcoholic beverage laws through computer controls.
- They promote impulse purchases, which otherwise would not be made.
- They serve the in-room guest, while at the same time not detracting from lounge sales.
- The computerized restocking report saves time and money.
- Detailed statistical printouts provide instant accountability of all sales, tracked through a variety of checkpoints.

Some manufacturers of in-room alcoholic beverage control systems are:

ABC Computer Bar (American Beverage Control; Mogadore, Ohio).
Bar-Vender (Posen, Illinois)
Domestic Mini-Bar (Elkhart, Indiana)
NCR Corporation (Dayton, Ohio)
ServiBar (Tysons Corner, Virginia)

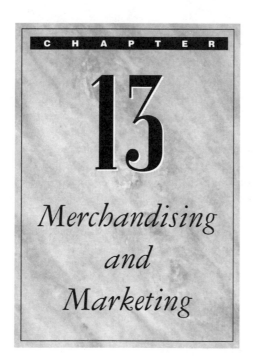

13

Merchandising and Marketing

The marketing phase of a beverage operation is, some experts suggest, the most important one. By researching current consumer likes and dislikes and general trends, long- and short-term goals can be established and plans for reaching these goals developed.

An integral part of any marketing plan is proper merchandising and effective selling. Promotions can make the difference between surviving, or just making ends meet, and financial success. And, in addition to promotions, there are many other ways to increase profits and enlarge the customer base. Some ideas are based solely on intuition, while others incorporate research and experience.

Today's society is moving toward lighter beverages and those that are lower in alcohol. Most people are drinking less, but when they do drink, they demand a high-quality product. Consumer demand for low-alcohol and nonalcoholic beverages has increased of late, due in part to drunk driving legislation. To make up for loss of revenue due to lower drinking levels, marketing and merchandising plans must be developed to alert customers to alternatives to alcoholic beverages.

▶ MARKETING

"Bellyspace"

This concept, introduced more than two decades ago by the late San Francisco-based wine industry consultant Louis Gomberg, is important, because while many beverage industry executives don't appreciate the point, no seller of beverages is competing solely against other sellers of the same category of product. Each beverage, to a greater or lesser degree, is competing against everything else that's potable—beer against soft drinks, soft drinks against milk, milk against fruit juice, fruit juice against wine, wine against distilled spirits, and all of them against all others, as well as against tap water.

Over the past couple of decades, thanks in large part to the marketing skills of sellers of beverages (and thanks also, of course, to the affluence of the American population), tap water has been the big loser. It helps, of course, that tap water in many locales is foul tasting and/or suspected by the citizenry of being contaminated. But that is secondary to the major point, which is that someone is selling millions of liters of nonalcoholic beverages and whoever is selling it is taking business away from whoever is not.

There is only so much bellyspace. The typical human consumes about half a gallon of liquid per day. There is only so much business you can take away from soft drinks and bottled water. Keep in mind that you are *not* selling exclusively or even mainly against other brands in your own category; you are selling against everything else that is potable.*

---

* Source: Paul Gillette, publisher of *The Wine Investor,* Los Angeles, California.

WHO'S DRINKING WHAT?			
Those who drink:	*Total*	*Men*	*Women*
		(in percentages)	
Fruit juices, drinks	93	94	93
Carbonated beverages	91	90	92
Alcoholic beverages	66	77	56
Caffeinated coffee	65	68	61
Decaffeinated coffee	47	47	48
Bottled water	55	56	53

Source: Research Advantage, Inc. Hawthorne, NY, 1991.

BEVERAGE CONSUMPTION		
Type of beverage	*Millions of Gallons*	*Share %*
Soft drinks	12,192	48.9
Beer	5,828	23.4
Bottled water	2,384	9.6
Tea	1,795	7.2
Juice	1,776	7.1
Wine	405	1.6
Distilled spirits	353	1.4
Lemonade	124	0.5
Coolers	87	0.3
Total	24,944	100.0

Source: Jobson Beverage Group, 1991.

► BEER: AMERICA'S DINNERTIME FAVORITE

When Americans drink alcoholic beverages with their dinner, they are more likely to have a beer, rather than wine or distilled spirits, according to a study by *Com-Sci Research*. In terms of beverage alcohol dollar sales, beer contributes 38.9 percent to the bottom line, while distilled spirits bring in 35.7 percent. Consumers' love for light products prevail, as more than 39 percent of total beer sales were light beers. The study contains statistics of on-premise beverage alcohol trends in eight major U.S. markets.

A DRINK WITH A MEAL (1993)	
Beer	38.9%
Distilled spirits	35.7%
House wine	14.9%
Fine wine	10.5%

The data obtained in this and other studies confirm that most Americans drink moderately and responsibly and that beer is far more popular as an accompaniment to meals than is commonly believed. It has been long recommended that the safest policy is to consume food with or prior to drinking since this slows the absorption of alcohol into the bloodstream. It seems clear that many Americans are following this advice.

► MERCHANDISING WINE

It is a fact of life in the restaurant business that a fine establishment cannot survive, much less thrive, without a successful wine program. A well-written wine list is only the first step in realizing the profit potential of wine sales. Three areas of consideration should be:

Wine-of-the-Month

Perhaps your distributor has already alerted you that there is a limited quantity of a special wine. You don't wish to put it on your regular wine list, as the availability is limited. However, you can merchandise it as a "wine-of-the-month." Menu clip-ons make useful beverage recommendations and at the same time remind guests of the wine currently being promoted. A table setting—complete with featured or "special" wines, and perhaps seasonal fruits or vegetables—placed at the front entrance of the restaurant, informs customers what is featured. Blackboards, strategically placed inside the restaurant, along with table "tents," expose customers to special beverage promotions even before they receive the menu and wine list.

Promoting a "wine-of-the-month, -week, or even -day" can be used to draw special attention to a wine on your regular list that doesn't seem to be moving. Make sure that your staff knows the wine; encourage them to actively promote it.

Wine Fact Sheets

Another promotional strategy is to present customers with a card (perhaps 4 × 8 inches) on which pertinent information about the winery, the wine (technical data, e.g., alcohol, total acidity, residual sugar), tasting comments (how it looks, smells, and tastes), selling price by-the-bottle, selling price by-the-glass, and what foods on your menu the wine matches is included. Don't forget to include on the card a label reproduction. Customers are encouraged to keep the fact sheets; this serves as a reminder of the restaurant in which the wine was enjoyed and helps build the customer's bank of wine knowledge. Regular customers are often inspired to experiment with different wines, as they enjoy collecting these fact sheets.

Selling the "Sizzle"

When a restaurant creates an atmosphere centering around good food and fine wine, the perceived image a customer has increases. A suggestion is to display wines in racks that are visible to customers; photos or maps of wine-producing countries, regions, or even wineries can also help to develop this image.

Some restaurants, for example, The Cellar in the Sky, located in the World Trade Center in New York City (re-opened in 1996), displayed their apéritifs by the use of a rolling beverage (or dessert) cart, which conveniently shows off a dozen or more possibilities. Each wine displayed offers its own appeal . . . various shaped bottles, different colored beverages, various names, and even countries of origin. In a restaurant, when a rolling cart full of desserts goes by, most customers' eyes and heads turn (regardless of whether they are choosing an appetizer, enjoying soup, or are ready for dessert). *People eat and drink with their eyes.* When that rolling cart is displayed at a customer's table, it is *not* a matter of saying yes or no, but rather *which one.* Why not put next to each dessert an appropriate dessert wine or after-dinner brandy, liqueur, or so on? Another suggestion for this rolling cart to "catch customers' eyes" is with a display of brandies in decanters, which sits under a spotlight near the restaurant entrance. If your restaurant doesn't have a rolling cart, perhaps offer a small tray of desserts along with recommended beverages.

Price-Fixed Wine Tastings

"What comes around goes around," an often used (and misused) phrase is apropos with *price-fixed* wine tastings. It is another chapter out of the *price-fixed menus* from a couple of years ago. In this new twist, previously selected wines (apéritif through dessert) accompany dinner or even lunch, which is a good technique for selling wines that might otherwise collect dust in the cellar while waiting to be ordered. A side benefit is realized when ordering discontinued, "close-out," or "post-off" wines from suppliers, which often increase profit margins. It also helps sell slow-moving wines that are destined to be discontinued. Another benefit is elimination of the problem of choosing wine for people who are uncomfortable ordering it. It also introduces customers to wine, who will then come back and try new wines from the main wine list.

Table Settings

An often overlooked merchandising strategy is to set a mood by having wine glasses already placed on the table prior to the arrival of your customers, which promotes wine with dinner. An oversized bowl on a wine glass suggests a larger serving and allows the customer to enjoy the fragrance of the wine. This is a positive way of selling a glass or bottle of wine. Remember, when a customer sits down in your restaurant, the first thing he or she sees is your tabletop. Be certain it is clean, has eye appeal, and is not cluttered.

Many wine suppliers include, as part of their merchandising program, corkscrews, champagne buckets, table "tents," and wine list menu clip-ons. These tools can aid in the promotion of your wines, both *still* and sparkling.

Tracking Business

For the future of your business it is very important to "track" sales and if need be divide them demographically to determine subsequent additions to your wine list. First, determine the number of bottles of each type of wine sold by individual category; for example, red, white, rosé, sparkling, sweet, and so on. Then, determine the ratio of sales of one type to another. What was the average price of a bottle of wine sold during a certain period of time (usually three-month intervals)? What are the most profitable and popular wines on your list? Lastly, are there any wines that don't "move" for one reason or another? Base your future wine list on the answers to these questions.

Wine Tastings

Consider holding wine tastings for special customers. Highlight one country, region, or type of wine and encourage guests to discuss these wines while they taste. Then contact your distributor to see if he has a lecturer available. Customers love to be singled out for such special events, and you are not only building good will but are creating knowledgeable customers. The following tips are offered for organizing a successful tasting:*

- Have a large supply of clean glasses on hand. If you would generally plan on using one glass per person (with tasters rinsing glasses between tastes), have two glasses per person on hand for emergencies.
- After removing the glasses from a storage box, put them through a water (no detergent) rinse.
- Make sure you have adequate chilling facilities.
- Make sure that there is adequate drinking water available—ideally at each wine station.
- Avoid bottled club soda, for it contains sodium. Instead, choose an unflavored "still" or carbonated water. Using bottled water will let people know that the water is for drinking, not for rinsing glasses.

---

* These suggestions were provided by Rory P. Callahan, a New York-based wine and food consultant.

- Make sure that you have an adequate supply of spittoons and pour buckets—generally two spittoons or pour buckets at each wine station.
- Always have one staff member circulating at all times to empty the pour buckets.
- Always supply a basic French-type bread or plain crackers (preferably salt-free, matzoh-type crackers). Be certain to have a back-up supply of bread on hand.
- Keep the temperature of the room cooler than usual. People will be moving around or seated in close proximity to each other and consuming alcohol, which is warming.
- Set up the tasting room several hours in advance. The red wines should be set out in the order in which they are to be poured. The whites and sparkling wines should be chilling, so that they are well chilled prior to the event.
- If you have several stations where wines are being poured, vary the number of wines at each station. The first station should have no more than two wines to avoid "traffic jams."
- Provide clean name tags for the staff.
- Don't overcrowd the room. The number of participants should be limited to one-half to two-thirds of the maximum capacity of the room.
- Don't allow smoking.
- Don't overpour: 1 to 1.5 ounces is adequate for tasting.
- Don't give away open bottles of wine at the end of the tasting. You could lose your alcoholic beverage license in certain states and your insurance may not cover any damages that could result.
- Don't let the event last more than two hours. People should not linger at tastings, especially stand-up tastings.

Some Other Suggestions.

- Use tasting note sheets for evaluation of beverage.
- Provide pen and paper.
- Utilize template tasting place mats with circles previously drawn for wine glass placement.

Wine and Food Promotions: How to Organize

Create a Positive Image.   A well-conceived and well-executed "wine and food promotion," perhaps centering around an ethnic promotion (Italian, Chilean, French, or even California), can enhance your reputation for quality, originality, and value.

Increase Cover Counts.   A "wine and food promotion" can significantly boost business during normally slow periods. Therefore, it is suggested that a weekday (Monday, Tuesday, or even Wednesday evening) be selected as the right setting for this event. A special event creates excitement and increases customer cover counts. It can inspire customers who may have never been in the restaurant to try it, and to come back again and order your wines.

Contacts with Co-Sponsors.   If you are trying to secure a partial sponsorship of a "wine and food event," begin to do so at least 90 days before the start of the event. Potential sponsors are airlines, hotels, food and beverage importers and distributors, package stores, and information bureaus, which are public relations arms of major beverage- and food-producing countries. You may receive assistance in paying for the airfare of a guest chef or winemaker, or be promised a trip to be awarded as a prize. Many companies will also provide food and beverage products as prizes. (A listing of *information bureaus, trade organizations,* and *governmental agencies* is contained in Appendix F.)

Time Is of the Essence.   Allow sufficient lead time to plan the "wine and food event" properly. Many important details must be arranged months in advance. Develop a checklist to help you plan a timetable. Be sure to assign deadlines to each task and appoint a specific person to be responsible for its completion.

Increase the Restaurant's Profit.   A successful "wine and food event" should increase average check amounts and in turn increase profits. An increase in beverage sales will be shown as customers experiment with the wines featured at these special events.

Cooking with Wines.   Advise the chef that in addition to pairing food with wines, you would like him or her to incorporate the wine in the recipe. This adds another dimension in which wines can be merchandised.

Secure Written Copies of the Recipes.   Inform the chef that you would like a written copy of each food recipe (which incorporates the wine/s) available for each attendee and, hopefully members of the press.

Publicity.   A well-planned promotion can result in free publicity for wines and also the restaurant in local newspapers and on television and radio. Before you start imagining yourself on the evening news, however, remember that members of the press are looking for a unique story angle. The simple fact that you are holding a "wine and food event" does not make a riveting story. Develop a press kit that includes stories about the restaurant chef, winemaker, background information on the food and wine, and recipes home cooks can recreate. Invite members of the wine and food press to attend the dinner.

Staff Training.   At least one week before the "wine and food event," schedule an intensive staff training session. At this meeting explain the purpose of the event and make sure that the staff is thoroughly trained in proper wine and food service. Present background information on the featured wines and make sure all servers are able to pronounce each wine's name. Finally, give the staff an opportunity to taste the featured wines and foods.

Merchandising.   Decorate the restaurant with posters of the winery or even country of origin (e.g., California, Italy, France, Chile). At each place setting include colorful winery brochures, consider offering a corkscrew, or other appropriate "point-of-sale" items.

Don't Forget.   Be certain that departing guests receive information about the evening, which includes: technical information about the wines tasted, background on the winery, retail selling price of each wine served, perhaps sample wine labels, food recipes utilized during the evening, and, of course, a souvenir program signed by the chef.

Win, Win, Win.   Who wins from "wine and food events"?

1. The restaurateur increases customer count, especially on "off-nights." In addition, publicity is generated in both the food and wine columns, with each of them writing about the event from a different angle.
2. Food writers are primarily interested in writing about food (wine secondary), therefore offer "press kits" with a written copy of the food recipe, as well as which food pairs with which wine.
3. Wine writers are primarily interested in writing about wine (food secondary), therefore offer "press kits" with a written copy of the food recipe, as well as which wine pairs with which food.

▶ DISTILLED SPIRITS PROMOTIONS

One way to increase sales of distilled spirits is to adopt the policy of special theme nights at which the customer purchases a drink whose price includes that of the glass. For example, on "Margarita night," when special 25-ounce frozen margaritas are sold for $8.00, the customer can take home a traditional Margarita glass that is not available in most department stores or specialty glass shops. Not only will customers treasure the glass and enjoy serving Margaritas in it at home, but you will benefit from having your business name, address, and telephone number displayed somewhere on the glass, which increases repeat patronage. The concept illustrated here can be extended to other items, such as ceramic Irish coffee mugs, fluted or tulip-shaped champagne glasses, liqueur glasses, and so on. The list is endless.

Tony May, a well-known New York restaurateur and owner of San Domenico Restaurant, previously utilized printed cards on every table bearing the following message to customers: "Would you like to take home the dishes, the silverware, the salt cellars, the pepper mill? Maybe a teapot. Or a jug of balsamic vinegar. Everything's for sale. Except the chef."

Another method is by offering tasting flights of various categories of distilled spirits, such as Armagnac, Cognac, grappa, single-barrel bourbon, single-malt scotch, or even specialty tequila. Slow-moving brands or brands you wish to close out can be highlighted during these tastings. As an example, offer three or five different types or styles of a distilled spirit, along with appropriate background information.

There are many other ways to increase profits from distilled spirits sales and some of them won't cost you a cent. Many beverage distributors and food purveyors have public relations or promotional budgets which can be tapped. One promotion concept, for example, uses both beverage and food purveyors. It was conceived by Vlasic Foodservice, which took a standard drink recipe and by changing it slightly, converted it into a big seller. Based on the popular Bloody Mary, this drink, called the Pregnant Mary, was created from a flavorful recipe and is, of course, topped off with one of Vlasic's Kosher Pickle Spears to give customers a crunchy, fresh-tasting treat to go along with their drink. Here is the recipe:

4 cups tomato juice
2 tablespoons Vlasic pickle juice
1 teaspoon prepared horseradish
2 teaspoons Worcestershire sauce
2 teaspoons lemon juice
Tabasco sauce, to taste
salt and pepper, to taste
Vlasic Deli Dill or Kosher Spears

Blend all ingredients except pickle spears in a covered container and chill well. To prepare the drink, add 1.5 ounces of vodka to an eight ounce glass with ice and fill with the prepared mix. Blend and garnish with Vlasic Deli Dill or Kosher Spears and serve. The recipe makes approximately six drinks. (Note: Vlasic also offers excellent merchandising tools to help you tell your customers about the Pregnant Mary, including swizzle sticks that feature the trademark Vlasic stork.)

▶ HOLIDAY AND SEASONAL PROMOTIONS

A good idea for sales promotions is to use a calendar to determine what important holidays, events, or celebrations take place each month. It's then a simple task to choose which special event fits within the theme of your restaurant. A plan for its incorporation should then be formulated. A sample calendar might include:

January
New Year's Day (January 1)
Post-holiday blues

National Pizza Week
Super Bowl
The 18th Amendment (Prohibition) took effect

February
Ground Hog Day (February 2)
Lincoln's Birthday (February 12)
Valentine's Day (February 14)
Chinese New Year
Washington's Birthday (February 22)
Mardi Gras
National Cherry Month
President's Day
American Wine Appreciation Week

March
St. Patrick's Day (March 17)
First day of spring (March 21)
National Nutrition Month

April
April Fool's Day (April 1)
Easter and Passover
Post-income-tax-filing celebration (April 15)
National Secretaries Week
National Garden Week
Earth Day
National Humor Month
National Tea Month
Baseball Season Opening Day
Arbor Day

May
May Day (May 1)
Armed Forces Day
Memorial Day (May 30)
Mothers' Day
Kentucky Derby Day
Cinco de Mayo
National Physical Fitness and Sports Month
National Pickle Week
National Tavern Month

National Barbecue Month
National Hamburger Month
National Egg Month
Victoria Day (Canada)

June
Flag Day (June 14)
First day of summer (June 21)
Fathers' Day
National Dairy Month
National Iced Tea Month
Ohio Wine Month

July
Canada Day (July 1)
Independence Day (July 4)
National Ice Cream Day (July 9)
Bastille Day (July 14)
National Hot Dog Month
National Baked Bean Month
National Peach Month

August
Washington State Wine Month
Tailgate parties
Picnics

September
Labor Day
Back-to-school party
NFL Season opens
Grandparents' Day
First day of autumn (September 21)
National Bourbon Month
National Chicken Month
National Honey Month
National Rice Month
National Cholesterol Education & Awareness Month (promotion of red wines)

October
California Wine Appreciation Week
American Beer Week

Columbus Day (October 12)
United Nations Day (October 24)
National Wine Month
National Restaurant Month
National Popcorn Month
World Series
Halloween
New York State Wine and Food Month

November
Election Day
New York State Wine Month
Veteran's Day (November 11)
National Split Pea Soup Week (second week of the month)
Thanksgiving Day

December
Repeal of Prohibition Celebration (December 5, 1933)
Pearl Harbor Day (December 7)
First day of winter (December 21)
Christmas Day (December 25)
Boxing Day (December 26; celebrated in England, Canada, and Australia)

In general, it is extremely important for your servers to make appropriate drink suggestions on the basis of season or climate. For customers who come in during cold weather and want something to warm them up, a brandy or Cognac could be suggested. An alternative suggestion is brandy served with coffee or tea, either mixed or separately, to help eliminate winter's nip. Hot weather demands that servers suggest cold, refreshing drinks that are appealing in appearance, smell, and taste. Suggesting a "frosty cold beer" appeals not only to the thirst, but also to the mind by its simple but powerful description. Most warm-weather drinks can easily be made with fruit juices or a customer's favorite mixes. It is estimated that 60 to 80 percent of the time, customers purchase what has been suggested.

▶ INCREASING BEVERAGE PROFITS THROUGH FOOD SALES

Americans nowadays live mobile, active lives. The traditional three meal periods have been transformed into flexible "on demand" eating occasions. The National Restaurant Association cites five separate meal occasions—breakfast, lunch, mid-afternoon, dinner, and late supper—that have evolved as a result of "on demand" eating patterns. Many of these occasions can be made more profitable by adding creative and exciting alcoholic beverage service.

▶ BRUNCH AS A WAY OF MERCHANDISING DRINKS

Those who eat brunch outside of their homes are predominantly between the ages of 25 and 54. This means that they are well past the 21-year-old-drinking age, generally have more disposable income, and can enjoy a leisurely dining experience. Brunch is a fashionable but casual meal that offers unlimited opportunity for creativity with food and beverage service. In fact, brunch is an excellent occasion for the promotion of specialty drinks. Eye-opener drinks such as Bloody Maries, screwdrivers, mimosas, or Ramos gin fizzes are popular brunch choices, as are fresh fruit daiquiris, Margaritas, piña coladas, Tom Collinses, and of course dry sparkling wines. Many operators successfully promote a free drink with brunch (its cost is built into the price of the meal), which often results in a re-order of the drink at the regular price.

▶ OTHER IDEAS FOR INCREASING PROFITS

Run "white sales" like department stores do, except feature "white goods" like gin, rum, tequila, vodka, grappa, and clear liqueurs instead.

Instead of having a "Happy Hour," take a page from supermarkets and have a *happy minute.* Once, or even several times a day, announce that for the next minute all drinks are "half-price," but must be ordered within 60 seconds. Make certain that you select a different time frame each day, so guests won't expect it at the same time each day. This promotion works especially well on off-days or slow periods during the day. Be certain you advertise it in local newspapers and around business offices.

Another promotional idea is to randomly draw names of patrons present during "Happy Hour," which rewards them with a free lunch or dinner. The patron must be present to win; be certain to advertise it in local newspapers.

Get customers to create and name their own drinks. Then promote them, with full credit to the originator.

When entertaining a convention or business group, consider naming a drink in their honor, or after one of their products, e.g., "The Jailhouse Rock," for Correctional Departments, or "Adam's Apple" for Apple Computers. But don't forget to advertise, price it right, and leave notes in all meeting and guest rooms.

Provide a personal "rain check" for customers who have to leave when someone is offering to buy them a drink.

During slow periods, dust off a slow-moving bottle of distilled spirits and create a drink or even promotion to help move it out. Be certain the price is right and that you inform the servers about the promotion.

During seasonal holidays, such as Valentine's Day, offer specially garnished "red drinks"; on St. Patrick's Day, "green beer"; and "eggnogs" during Christmas season.

"T-shirts" that show a restaurant logo and message can stimulate word-of-mouth advertising. Your servers as well as customers become "walking billboards" when attired in one of your facilities' T-shirts. Offer customers a 10-percent discount, free appetizer, glass of wine, or even dessert if they come in wearing your restaurant's T-shirt. Offer the same deal if they purchase a T-shirt while in the restaurant.

Utilize oversized brandy snifters, fish bowls, or other vessels as a business card drop from customers. After drawing the lucky winner for dinner, take the remaining cards and create a private mailing list for future promotions. Keep the relevant information about your steady customers at the hostess stand, in the manager's office, and behind the bar. Have your servers review it prior to greeting the customer.

Develop a nonvalue credit card for your beverage suppliers and offer them discounts on food and drink simply by displaying the card.

When a customer phones in a reservation, consider placing a small table "tent" on the reserved table with a simple note thanking them for calling in advance, with a small cut-out on the table tent holding a quarter, along with your restaurant's name, address, and telephone number.

Take a promotional tip from the airlines and have a "frequent diners club." Customers receive points for each dollar spent or with the number of persons in their party. Additional points can be earned for wine ordered, or even by offering double or triple points on "off" or slow nights. These points can be redeemed for: free food, drink, cookbooks, cooking classes, special wine dinners, breakfast-in-bed, restaurant discounts, special dinners where the restaurateur cooks in the customer's home, free round-trip limousine service to the restaurant, free theater or concert tickets, amusement park admission, cruise ships, airline purchases, rent-a-cars, business meetings, social events, or even restaurant merchandise like T-shirts, mugs and glasses, pre-packaged nonalcoholic mixes, and so on. Consider "double points" during slow periods, for example, Monday, Tuesday night, or during January and February. However, be certain to collect pertinent database "restaurant" information from each guest, such as anniversary, birthday, children's names, occupation, favorite table, favorite food and drink, and so on for future promotions.

Many business travelers belong to "frequent stay hotel clubs," numbering in excess of three dozen, covering all 50 states. When a guest checks in and presents a "frequent stay" card, offer a complimentary 187-milliliter bottle of red or white wine along with a card informing the guest that additional bottles are available for purchase.

These "frequent buyer's" club can also be extended to purchases from wineries, breweries, and distilleries. It allows customers to accumulate points based on case purchases of alcoholic beverages.

Another often overlooked marketing opportunity is the judicious use of *comment cards*. When customers fill out comment cards, utilize personal information to help build your database mailing list for future promotions and events.

Utilize the local newspaper to generate new and repeat business. Select local heroes (both high school and college), wedding and birth announcements, an outstanding community person, and send them a congratulations card along with a gift certificate to your facility.

"Gift certificates" are an overlooked promotional tool available to bring in additional customers during holidays. They can be developed by utilizing some of the same concepts used for U.S. Savings Bonds; as an example, a $50 certificate costs $40.

If your restaurant is full and there is a long line of waiting customers, have a server pour them some house wine. This eases their wait and stimulates appetites. Very few if any customers will leave and these customers will tell others about "what they got" at your restaurant while standing in line. If you pour each person three ounces of an inexpensive house wine and there are 25 people waiting in line, you will serve a total of 75 ounces and, at a usual cost of less than five cents per ounce, this strategy will at most cost you $2.25.

Cross-merchandise alcoholic beverages with other consumer products, like flowers, foods, or even display bottles in local shops, in or on various pieces of furniture, bath tubs, hot tubs, and so on. Make certain a note is present of where the beverages may be obtained.

Ask suppliers for *large* bottles of wine, generally 3 liters or larger for display purposes, so customers who are waiting in line at your restaurant or perusing in your package store can readily see them.

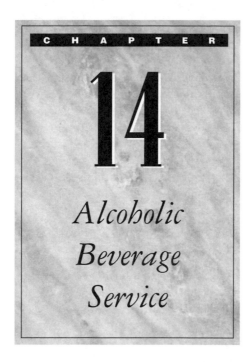

CHAPTER

14

Alcoholic Beverage Service

The bar is an important part of the total concept of a restaurant. In order for the entire restaurant to run smoothly, certain criteria must be addressed. Price must be equal to quality to attract new customers and maintain the current customer base. Customers also want quality—quality drinks, quality food, and quality service. Part of the total concept is staff training in the proper service of alcoholic beverages, both at the bar and tableside. Server and bartender attire must be addressed with the same care given to the food and drink. Decor should also be part of the restaurant's total package. Every aspect of the entire bar and beverage facility is important.

The era of alcoholic beverage liability is upon us in full force and unless we take steps to curb alcohol abuse, more stringent laws will be enacted, further restricting the selling and serving of alcoholic beverages. The National Restaurant Association, in cooperation with local, state, and federal officials, has spearheaded a program to train personnel in the awareness of alcohol abuse. Today's beverage manager must compensate for loss of revenue resulting from alcoholic beverage liability laws and society's trend toward lighter, less alcoholic beverages and develop programs that will provide adequate financial rewards.

▶ BAR OPERATIONS

For the development of a well-run bar, rules must be established pertaining to the duties of each bartender. These rules, along with guidelines and procedures, should be followed up by a training program. Develop a work schedule for the bar that enables it to be run efficiently, with a smooth scheduling of bartender shifts.

Scheduling of Bartenders

Examples of shifts for two bartenders are:

Day shift	Night shift
10:00 A.M.–6:30 P.M.	6:30 P.M.–2:30 A.M.
11:00 A.M.–7:30 P.M.	6:30 P.M.–3:00 A.M.

During weekends, "happy hours," and peak season times, three bartenders might be needed. Examples of work schedules with three bartenders are:

Day shift	Relief shift	Night shift
10:00 A.M.–6:30 P.M.	3:00 P.M.–11:30 P.M.	6:30 P.M.–2:30 A.M.
10:00 A.M.–6:30 P.M.	4:00 P.M.–12 midnight	7:00 P.M.–3:00 A.M.
10:00 A.M.–6:30 P.M.	6:00 P.M.–2:30 A.M.	8:00 P.M.–3:30 A.M.

The productivity of bartenders should be taken into consideration before work schedules are developed. Bartenders can mix and serve up to 125 drinks per hour depending on their experience, their expertise, the difficulty of drink recipe, the efficiency of bar design (the proximity of beverages in the work area and the location of ice machines and the cash register), and the hour of the day or night.

Bartenders should memorize basic drink recipes along with house specials for every drink the bar serves. This cuts down on wasted time searching recipe books and adds professionalism to the operation. Sometimes, if the bartender is not sure of the ingredients of a requested drink, the customer should be asked for the recipe and the suggested way of preparing and serving it.

Duties and Responsibilities of Bartenders

Assigned work sheets outlining each shift's duties and responsibilities need to be developed, handed out, and adhered to.

Day Shift Bartender Duties

- Milk and cream should be smelled daily to ensure that they are not souring.
- Postmix soda guns should be inspected.
- Beer taps should be inspected and cleaned.
- Be certain that backup kegs of beer are available.
- Make sure that an adequate supply of chilled bottled beer is available. Wash tubs can also be filled with plenty of ice and bottled beer for fast chilling and service.
- Ice machines should be inspected and ice troughs adequately filled.
- Bartenders should be responsible for maintaining "par stock" levels and keep a running list of empty bottles that can be checked later against inventory.
- Back bar and speed racks must be cleaned and filled.
- Sinks should be filled with appropriate wash and rinse waters.
- All glassware must be washed and available.
- Beer mugs must be adequately chilled.
- The cash register must be opened for the day.
- When the bartender is ready to open for business, be sure that garbage and other wastes are disposed of. The bar and surrounding areas should be clean and dry.
- Bar stools should be wiped clean and neatly lined up.
- Outside and inside lights should be turned on.
- The daytime bartender should check fruit from the previous day and if necessary throw out spoiled or dried-out fruit and thoroughly wash fruit trays and troughs.

When using fruit for garnishes, select only the freshest and choicest available. To extract more juice from citrus fruits, slightly warm the fruit under warm running water. Then roll the fruit from side to side with the palm of the hand, which separates the juice from the pulp.

Fruits should be cut to proper size with a clean, sharp knife and on a clean cutting board—not the bar top. Citrus fruits such as lemons, limes, and oranges should be cut into three distinct shapes depending on the kind and type of drink served: wheels, peels, and wedges. When cutting for wheels and wedges, the cut piece should contain the outer skin (zest), the inner bitter white surface (pith), and either a little or a lot of the fleshy pulp. A peel contains only the zest and pith. A slice (wheel) of lemon, lime, or orange, cut to an almost transparent thinness, shimmers on the surface of a clear white wine spritzer. Wedges are used in drinks such as vodka and tonic, in which a healthy squeeze of the fruit is a necessary ingredient. Peels are intended for those drinks (martini, for example) in which a "twist" of fruit is desirable. The purpose of the "twist" is to physically crack the skin of the fruit, exposing its oils, which contain both fragrance and flavor. The cracked portion should be rubbed along the rim of the glass, then discarded. Avoid dropping peels into the drink, for the alcohol will absorb some bitterness from the exposed pith.

Cut enough fruit for the entire day and night shifts. The amount will be determined by the number of bartenders, waitress stations, and previously determined needs. Refill trays with the freshly cut fruits (lemons, limes, oranges, pineapples, and others) and cover them immediately to protect them from dust, oxidation, and insects. Cherries, olives, and onions should be covered and stored in their own juices to retain freshness and visual appeal. Be sure to refrigerate the cherries, olives, onions, celery, and possibly bananas.

Punches can be served from large bowls with fresh fruit and sprigs of spearmint or peppermint floating on top. They can even be color coordinated to match tablecloths or party themes.

If juices are called for in drinks, avoid using bottled extracts or reconstituted juices. After opening cans of juice, immediately pour the juice into sanitized containers and store in the refrigerator. Juices left over from the previous day should be checked to ensure that they are still fresh and are not fermenting. Rotate them so that the "first in, first out" policy is adhered to. Shake the juices prior to the start of each shift to counteract settling and separation of contents.

Night Shift Bartender Duties

- When reporting for duty, the day shift bartender should close out his register, and a new "bank" should be established for the night bartender.
- When closing up for the night, the following procedures should be adhered to:
  - Night bartenders should tally up the register, putting all monies into security bags and then into the safe.
  - Inventory sheets should be filled out relative to empty bottles.
  - All fruits, juices, and other perishables should be put into the refrigerator.
  - Bottled beer should be taken out of wash tubs and stored in the refrigerator.
  - The beer tap should be cleaned and hot water poured down the drain to help clean it out.
  - The ice-maker should be wiped down with a damp cloth; check that its door is tightly closed.

- Speed racks should be cleaned out.
- All glassware and bar utensils should be cleaned.
- Blenders should be emptied out and washed.
- Drainboards must be washed down.
- All sinks must be totally drained and scrubbed with steel wool.
- The bar top must be wiped clean.
- All dirty towels should be gathered and placed into a laundry bag.
- The juke box and other machines should be shut down.
- All lights should be turned off.
- The door should be locked and alarm set.

Bar Set-Ups

Each bar and service station should have the following beverages and equipment present.

The basics

- Distilled spirits
- Bottled beer
- Red, white, and rosé wines
- Coolers
- Nonalcoholic malt beverages
- Hot coffee (optional)

Carbonated mixes

- Coke or other cola sodas
- Diet soda
- Ginger ale
- Mineral water (sparkling)
- Seltzer
- Sprite
- Tonic water (quinine water)
- 7-Up or lemon-flavored carbonated mixes
- Flavored sodas such as root beer, Dr. Pepper, orange soda, and so on, depending on geographic location and customer taste preferences

Juices and juice-based mixes

- Apple juice
- Cranberry juice
- Grapefruit juice

- Orange juice
- Pineapple juice
- Tomato juice or V-8

Other liquids for mixing

- Beef bouillon
- Bloody Mary mix
- Coconut milk or cream of coconut
- Falernum or orgeat syrup for rum-based fruit drinks
- Grenadine syrup
- Milk or cream
- Piña colada mix
- Rose's lime juice (brand name)
- Sour mix
- Simple syrup (sugar syrup)
- Tom Collins mix

Miscellaneous bar ingredients

- Fresh lemons and limes
- Green olives
- Cocktail onions
- Cherries
- Eggs, fresh and hard-boiled
- Horseradish
- Mint (spearmint or peppermint)
- Black and cayenne pepper
- Salt (also celery salt and coarse salt)
- Superfine sugar
- Cube sugar
- Brown sugar
- Tabasco sauce or other hot pepper sauce
- Worcestershire sauce
- Bitters (Angostura, orange, Peychaud)
- Nutmeg, vanilla, cloves, cinnamon, and cinnamon sticks

Bar equipment and utensils

- Shaker glass with stainless steel shaker
- Electric blender

- Shot glasses
- Bar spoon and funnel
- Fruit squeezer
- Strainer
- Muddler
- Garnish tray
- Cutting board
- Knife
- Adequate glassware
- Carafes for wine
- Water pitchers
- Sufficient amount of ice
- Plastic ice scoop or tongs
- Toothpicks
- Napkins and straws
- Coasters for beer
- Wine lists
- Food menus
- Corkscrew that contains a knife
- Can or bottle opener
- Automatic pourers or free pourers
- Serving trays
- Guest register checks
- Guest check trays
- Bar towels
- Pens, pencils, and paper
- Matches and ashtrays
- Bar snacks such as pretzels, potato chips, peanuts, and popcorn should also be available.

Glass Rimmers

When serving such drinks as Bloody Maries, Margaritas, Salty Dogs, Gimlets, Pink Squirrels, sours, and so on, it is important to have the correct amount of salt or sugar on the rim of the glass. Too much or too little can ruin an otherwise perfect drink.

There are "rimmers" available on the marketplace that consist of two self-contained circular swing trays. Lemon or lime juice, or a combination of both, is placed in one tray. In the other tray is either coarse salt or superfine sugar. The use of a rimmer guarantees that quick and consistent rims of salt or sugar are effortlessly applied to any of the cocktail glasses. Most glass rimmers manufactured are designed to accommodate all sizes of glasses up to 6.75 inches in diameter. They can easily be fastened under the bar.

To use a rimmer, place the glass upside down in the liquid tray, then immediately into the salt or sugar tray, which leaves a thin layer of either on the rim of the glass.

▶ CORRECT GLASSWARE

Many glass manufacturers used to (and still do today) dictate the kinds, types, and amount of glassware needed at the bar. If one accepted their recommendations the average bar would need as many as 30 different kinds of glasses. Unfortunately, writers, consultants, restaurant and bar owners, and even books continued this exploitation by suggesting that a different glass type is needed for Bordeaux, Burgundy, and Rhine wines; sparkling wines; liqueurs; Port; Sherry; and so on.

Today's restaurants simply don't have the shelf space to accommodate such a multitude of glasses, nor the storage facilities needed for backups and replacements. Confusion is also created for bartenders and service personnel when they have to remember which glass is needed for which drink. Attempting to memorize this list or taking time out to read the restaurant's manual on which type of glass to use for which drink is a waste of valuable time.

Purchasing Glassware

Selecting the right glass can be the key to more profitable beverage service. Plan on purchasing two to four times the number of glasses as the amount of drinks you expect to serve during peak hours of operation. Purchasing or using the wrong glass size can result in a drink being too weak or "burned" (containing too much alcohol).

Glassware can be the most dramatic and least expensive way to create atmosphere or improve the appearance of a table setting. The glassware showcased on the tables and behind the bar should reflect the style and atmosphere of the restaurant's decor. Coordinating the shapes and sizes of the glassware with the decor and ambiance of the dining room will make a positive statement.

Interesting or distinctive glassware can enhance appearance, atmosphere, and/or merchandising appeal while improving service and increasing your business. Durable glassware ensures safety and savings (from decreased breakage). The result is a more profitable beverage service. It might be necessary to upgrade the glassware because of increased volume in your beverage service. Extra durability can be achieved by replacing existing glassware with heat-treated glasses. Their added strength and improved resistance to mechanical and thermal shock lower replacement costs and improve service life.

Upgrading glassware for merchandising appeal will increase sales and profits by increasing the perceived value of service.

Many factors should be considered prior to purchasing glassware. Among them is the washing and sterilizing of equipment needed, initial cost versus replacement costs, future availability, storage space needed, the needs of the restaurant or bar, and the fragility of the glass or its resistance to breakage.

Types of glassware.   For serving wine, champagne, brandy, and liqueurs, stemmed glasses that are crystal clear and free of color and etchings should be used in place of the ordinary water glass or tumbler. The glasses listed below should always be stemware.

- Liqueur, Sherry, and Port glasses   (4–6 ounces)
- White wine glass   (8–10 ounces)
- Red wine glass   (10–12 ounces or larger)
- Flute or tulip-shaped champagne glasses   (8–10 ounces)
- Brandy glasses   (10–12 ounces)

Also needed are the following types and sizes of glasses, which are not necessarily stemware:

- Shot glasses   (1.5 ounces)
- Water goblets   (8–10 ounces)
- Rocks or "old-fashioned" glasses   (6–8 ounces)
- Sour or parfait glasses   (4–6 ounces)
- All-purpose beverage glasses   (8–10 ounces)
- Pilsner beer glasses   (10 ounces)
- Beer steins or mug   (10–12 ounces)
- Highball glasses   (10–12 ounces)
- Margarita glasses   (6 ounces)

Handling Glassware

Libbey Glassware in Toledo, Ohio, offers the following tips on handling glassware for safety and profitability (see Figure 14-1).

Persons handling glassware should be advised of the fine qualities of glassware and how it should be treated and handled. These tips are designed to improve the handling of glassware in your business. Improved handling means less breakage and this means higher productivity and less chance of injury through accident. There are two causes of glass breakage: mechanical impact and thermal shock.

Mechanical impact.   Mechanical impact is contact with another object. It may be a spoon, a beer tap, or another glass. This contact can cause minute abrasions that are invisible to the eye. These abrasions weaken the glass and make it more susceptible to breakage from further impact or thermal shock. Any severely abraded glass must be removed from service.

Thermal shock.   Thermal shock is the result of temperature change. Glass holds temperature and quick temperature changes can cause enough stress in the glass to cause breakage. For example, glass with ice in it cannot be emptied and put directly into the dishwasher. Similarly, glass coming out of the dishwasher cannot be put directly into service. In both cases the glass must be given time to reach room temperature. Never put cold water or ice into a warm or hot glass. Cracks that result from thermal shock usually

Handling Glassware
for safety and profitability

Persons handling glassware should be advised of the fine qualities of glassware and how glassware should be treated and handled. These tips are designed to improve the handling of glassware in your operation. Improved handling means less breakage and this translates into higher productivity and less chance of an injury accident. There are two causes of glass breakage...Mechanical Impact and Thermal Shock.

Mechanical Impact

 is the result of contact with another object. It may be a spoon, a beer tap, or another glass. This contact can cause a minute abrasion, invisible to the eye. These abrasions weaken the glass and make it more susceptible to breakage from impact and thermal shock. Any severely abraded glass must be removed from service.

Thermal Shock

 is the result of temperature change. Glass holds temperature, and quick temperature change can cause enough stress in the glass to cause breakage. For example, glass with ice in it cannot be emptied and put directly into the dishwasher. Similarly, glass coming out of the dishwasher cannot be put directly into service. In both cases the glass must be allowed a few minutes to reach room temperature. Never put cold water or ice into a warm or hot glass. Cracks that result from thermal shock usually form around abrasions caused by mechanical impact. Any severely abraded glass must be removed from service. Remember, the thicker the glass the more time it needs to reach room temperature.

General

- Keep adequate supplies of glass to prevent recently washed glasses from going directly into service.
- Place guides on scrap table for busboys to place glass, china, and silverware in separate areas.
- Check dishwasher temperature twice daily.
- Instruct busboys to "BE QUIET. No one wants to eat in a noisy place." This rule will cut down on breakage of glassware and china, as well as help create atmosphere.
- Always use plastic scoops in ice bins. Metal scoops sometimes chip the glassware. Never scoop ice with the glass.
- Never put cold water or ice into a warm or hot glass.
- Ideally, bus glassware directly into racks, or use divided bus trays with silver baskets.
- Color code your racks for different glassware items.
- Any severely abraded glass must be removed from service.

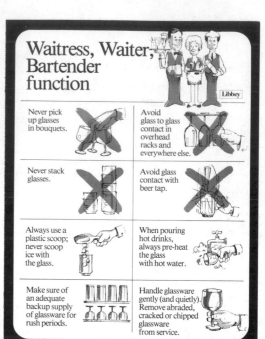

FIGURE 14-1 (a–d) Handling glassware for safety and profitability. (Courtesy Libbey Glassware)

form around abrasions caused by mechanical impact. Remember, the thicker the glass, the more time it needs to reach room temperature.

Other tips

- Keep adequate supplies of glass on hand to prevent recently washed glasses from going directly into service.
- Place guides on scrap tables so that busboys can place glass, china, and silverware in separate areas.
- Check the dishwasher temperature twice daily. Replace worn glass washer brushes.
- Instruct busboys to *be quiet* when clearing tables. No one wants to eat in a noisy place. This rule will cut down on breakage of glassware and china as well as help create atmosphere.
- Always use plastic scoops in ice bins. Metal scoops sometimes chip glassware. Never scoop ice with the glass.
- Ideally, bus glassware directly into racks, or use divided bus trays with silver baskets.
- Color-code racks for different glassware items.

▶ ICE-MAKING MACHINES

A ready supply of ice is always a necessity. One of the most important pieces of equipment that every beverage operation needs, without exception, is a reliable and efficient ice-making machine; one which suits the individual needs of the establishment. The machine should be chosen based on the general needs of the operation, taking into consideration peak and future needs. There are basically two types of machines: one produces cubes; the other, crushed ice.

Some questions to be asked prior to purchasing an ice-making machine are:

- What type and size ice cubes are needed?
- What is the total storage capacity of the machine?
- How many pounds of ice does it produce per hour?
- How large a machine is needed?

The Operating Cycle

Although ice-making machines vary considerably in methods of forming and releasing ice, the operating cycles are similar in most cases. The water-contact or water-container surfaces are chilled to below the freezing point in the ice-making cycle. When the ice reaches a certain thickness, the water-contact or water-container surface is heated briefly to release the ice. This is called the *harvest cycle*. The cycling process is automatic.

The Electrical System

The electrical system consists of a compressor, a condenser, fans, and various thermostats. The elements required for harvesting ice are also part of the electrical system; in certain machines the harvest is controlled by a solenoid valve that transmits hot gas to the copper freezing surfaces.

The Water System

The water system includes a pump and one or more water pans. The water level in the pan(s) is usually controlled by a float-operated valve. The other parts of the water system depend on the type of freezing system used: In certain machines, water is distributed in an even sheet over freezing surfaces; in others, it is sprayed on freezing surfaces or into freezing containers.

Operation and Maintenance

Ice-making machines operate automatically. Kitchen personnel should not adjust the machine except to set the cube-or-chip control. Wash the exterior of the ice-making machine as necessary with a clean cloth dampened in a warm detergent solution. Wipe with a cloth dampened in clear warm water and dry with a clean cloth.

Crushed Ice

Crushed ice is required for cold pans. If a dining facility ice-making machine produces cubes only, an ice-crushing machine may be installed as an attachment to the ice-making machine. If two or more ice-making machines are used, one should provide crushed ice, or both cubes and chips.

Ice Cube Dispensers

Many types and styles of dispensers are available. Among the most popular types are countertop, trigger, push-button-key, and coin-token models.

The Storage Compartment

The ice storage compartment is a large well with a drain. The compartment temperature is controlled by a thermostat. An automatic element in the compartment senses the level of ice in storage. When the compartment is filled with ice, the element activates a switch to interrupt the power supply to the ice-making machinery; as ice is removed from the storage compartment, the element deactivates the switch so that power is restored to the ice-making machinery and the supply of ice is automatically replenished.

Storage capacity can range from 220 to 2,000 pounds and occasionally even more. Some flake ice machines even have the capability of producing from 300 pounds to ten tons per day.

Production

Modern ice-making machines can produce from 100 to 3,300 pounds of ice per hour, depending on the make and model purchased. It is important to note that most ice-making machines give varying production ratings for different temperature levels of the air-cooled or water-cooled condenser unit, as well as for different temperatures of water used. Examples of such varying production are given below.

24-HOUR PRODUCTION (POUNDS OF ICE) IN AN AIR-COOLED UNIT

Air temperature	Water temperature Fahrenheit		
	50 degrees	*70 degrees*	*90 degrees*
70 degrees	100	95	90
80 degrees	90	85	80
90 degrees	80	75	70

24-HOUR PRODUCTION (POUNDS OF ICE) IN A WATER-COOLED UNIT

Air temperature	Water temperature Fahrenheit		
	50 degrees	*70 degrees*	*90 degrees*
70 degrees	100	95	90
80 degrees	95	90	85
90 degrees	90	85	80

Ice Cube Size

Most later-model ice-making machines can be adjusted to produce either ice cubes or ice chips. In these machines, the capillary sheath that governs ice formation is adjusted to be close to the freezing surface for chip ice, or farther from the freezing surfaces for ice cubes.

There are many different sizes of ice cubes produced by various manufactures' ice machines; some of them have been dubbed: "crescent" cubes; "cubelets"; "flake ice"; "flat" cubes; "gourmet" cubes; "full" cubes (also called "dice"); "half-cubes" (also called "half-dice"); "ice nuggets"; "regular" and "square" cubes. Of these, the standard sizes are:

- Regular $1^{1}/_{8}$" × $1^{1}/_{8}$" × $^{7}/_{8}$" (30 cubes per pound)
- Full (also called "dice") $^{7}/_{8}$" × $^{7}/_{8}$" × $^{7}/_{8}$" (48 cubes per pound)
- Half-cubes (also called "half-dice") $^{3}/_{8}$" × $^{7}/_{8}$" × $^{7}/_{8}$" (96 cubes per pound)

Sizing guidelines.   Daily ice needs in any business are rarely stable; there are always minimum and peak ice usage levels. Daily ice needs are usually greater in summer and on weekends. Therefore, size your ice machine and storage bin based on what your peak ice usage needs will be.

Avoid sizing a new ice machine solely on the basis of the performance of your exiting ice-making capability. The age and mechanical condition of an existing ice-making machine may mislead you in determining the quantity of ice needed. Remember, surrounding air and incoming water temperatures affect the quantity of ice a machine produces. Determine what these temperatures will be during peak ice needs and verify your model selection from its ice-production chart.

Use the ice usage guide shown below to calculate your ice usage based on peak ice needs. After calculating how much ice you must have, add to that figure a 20-percent safety factor to accommodate future business growth. Taking time to correctly size ice-making equipment ensures an always adequate ice supply.

ICE USAGE GUIDE	
Hospitality	*Approximate ice cubes/flake ice needs per day*
Restaurant	1.5 pounds ice per person
Cocktail	3 pounds ice per person/seat
Salad Bar	30–40 pounds ice per cubic foot
Fast food	4–5 ounces ice per 7–10 ounce drink
	8 ounces ice per 12–16 ounce drink
	12 ounces ice per 18–24 ounce drink
Guest ice room service	5 pounds ice per room
Catering	1 pound ice per person
Health care	
Hospital	10 pounds ice per bed
Hospital cafeteria	1 pound ice per person
Nursing home	6 pounds ice per bed
Convenience stores	
Beverages	6 ounces ice per 12 ounce drink
	10 ounces ice per 20 ounce drink
	16 ounces ice per 32 ounce drink
Cold plates	50 percent more ice per day
Packaged ice	pounds per bag × bags sold per day

Some manufacturers of ice-making machines are:

Crystal Tips	Manitowoc	Saxony
Hoshizaki	Reynolds/Alco	Scotsman
Ice-O-Matic	Ross Temp	SerVend

► FOOD AND BEVERAGE SERVICE

Is the service in your restaurant or bar perfect? If not, your sales might be considerably lower than expected and unless steps are taken to resolve all problems, sales will continue on a downward trend.

Unfortunately, the level of service in the United States is far from excellent. This statement will certainly ruffle more than a few feathers among those in the industry; nevertheless, it is true. Go out to dinner or even for a drink one evening and carefully make note of the level of service you are receiving. Are all of your questions regarding food and drink answered correctly and with authority, or does the server use these familiar phrases when being asked simple questions? "I don't know; I'll find out; I'll be right back!" Then, do an honest analysis of your own business. You might be surprised by the results. Too many establishments give customers unsatisfactory or even poor service. The majority of customers might accept it once or twice, but not a third time.

Customers look upon servers as if they are looking at you. Servers are an extension of yourself; therefore, steps must be taken to guarantee that customers are receiving the service they deserve and demand.

Personal appearance.   Unless you specify either uniforms or a dress code, you could have a department store syndrome on your hands. Customers will not be able to distinguish your servers from the other customers. Many books and pamphlets are available from purveyors showing uniforms for virtually every type of establishment. Uniforms or approved clothing must be clean, fresh, and pressed. Shabby, torn, worn, undersized, or oversized clothing should be avoided.

Clean hair neatly cut, tied, or covered in a hair net is a necessity, as are trimmed beards and mustaches. Personal hygiene includes general cleanliness as well as clean hands and fingernails and fresh-smelling breath. Some restaurants and bars even make a dish of breath mints available to employees. Colognes and perfumes, as pleasant as they may be, often compete with the subtle aromas of the wines and foods and should be used sparingly, if at all.

Common courtesy.   All too often a server's poor attitude will spoil a customer's dinner, leaving you with one less customer who will certainly not recommend your establishment to others. Therefore, it is important to "screen" all current employees and prospective new ones on their attitudes and use of common courtesy. A simple greeting or good-bye (rarely use the customer's first name) followed by a sincere and pleasant smile can win over new customers and "revive" old ones. Make a game of remembering names of customers. It is estimated that approximately 85 percent of your first-time customers come from word-of-mouth advertising. It costs about five to seven times more money to attract new customers than it does to retain existing ones. It is a proven fact that if a customer is happy with your establishment he is likely to tell three people; but if unhappy, he will tell ten!

The Customer Is Always Right . . . Right?   The often used slogan "The Customer Is Always Right," has been burned forever in the minds and hearts of everyone in the hospitality industry. But we also have an educational job to do with our customers and that sometimes makes a server walk a tightrope between "appeasing a customer" and genuinely expressing concern over a mismatched food and wine order or simply a food or drink suggestion. Several keys to effectively dealing with a potential problem situation are product knowledge, confidence in what you are selling, and finally, an overall comfort level interacting with customers. These keys are developed by training, repetition, and a genuine interest in your business. Be certain that employees who discover unhappy customers are empowered to solve their problem on the spot.

Consider adopting a policy of "allowing guests to send back wine" if they believe it is flawed or spoiled. The bottle sent back can be converted into instant, by-the-glass wine specials; be used as part of staff training; or offered to other customers as a complimentary taste, which may engender an order.

To change a "sad" situation into a "glad" situation, instruct your managers to carry business cards that offer guests a free cocktail, which can make up for slow service or other customer dissatisfaction. It is better to "give away" a free drink than to lose a paying customer.

Salesmanship.   "You can't effectively sell a product you don't know; and the more you know about your product, the easier the sale." This slogan should be the cornerstone of all employee training and be reemphasized periodically. Servers are really salespeople; after all, they are paid a salary, and like a salesperson, work on commission—the tip. The better the service and the higher the check, the larger the commission will be. In some restaurants, it may be advisable to give a *quota* to your servers; if they do not make the quota, they have a problem. Therefore, servers should be completely familiar with all food items in the kitchen, as well as wines appearing on the wine list and the ingredients of the most popular cocktails. This is commonly known as "product knowledge" and its impact on the restaurant's sales can be dramatic. Selling wine is no problem when servers handle merchandise they know and appreciate. You can have the best product in the world, but if you can't sell it, you still have it. Teach your staff to know each and every one of their products. It is better to know the product and not need it than to need it and not know it. Be certain to train your servers and bartenders to be *salespeople, not order-takers*.

Remember, every customer who comes into a restaurant or bar is your *"captive audi-*

ence." The customer is there to *buy,* not window-shop or browse. They don't "try on" food, like clothes, although they do come in for sales. Restaurants are quite different than new car dealers, where customers come in, look around, check the sticker price, maybe sit inside the car, or "kick the tires." Customers come to restaurants *to buy;* they want to be made to feel special. Serve and sell to them. Nobody comes in to *try on* a burger or a cocktail.

It is suggested that all employees, for five or ten minutes prior to the start of their shifts, familiarize themselves with the daily specials and their ingredients, as well as the cooking techniques and so on used for all items on the menu. This is accomplished by insisting that servers communicate with the kitchen staff at the start of each shift. This rule is equally important with regard to the wine list, whose additions and deletions should be brought to the attention of the servers. This should avoid the "I don't know how it tastes . . . management won't let us eat or drink it" routine often heard in restaurants across the United States. Most servers only know three words about wine: Chablis, rosé, and Burgundy. And, most servers also fill wine glasses to the brim so that it's virtually impossible to drink out of them without bringing your mouth to the glass while it's on the table. The phrases "Have you decided on a wine with your dinner this evening?" "Have you decided which wine you would like with dinner?" and "Have you decided yet which wine you'll have for dinner?" carry a powerful punch but they are so subtle the customer would never feel pressured. How about, "Good evening, tonight we feature Chianti, a dry red wine from Tuscany, Italy. It is fruity, with a bouquet of dried plums, and a smooth taste." Try them, or something similar like, "Perhaps you'd like to try our house wine," at every table and see how it brings in the order. It is preferable to the normal "Would you like a glass of wine?" The idea is to think positively about every order and every customer. A very important but often overlooked method of selling more wine is to ask the customer "what he or she likes." Ask "what kind of wine do you enjoy?" (dry, sweet, red, white, and so on); "what type of wine or food are you in the mood for?"; and perhaps "what do you generally drink with this dish or food?" These statements elicit powerful and positive answers from customers, which helps to better serve them. An important issue centers on "reading the customer" (understanding the likes and dislikes of the guest). When a customer comes from outside shivering due to the bitter cold, a light bulb (or perhaps a dollar sign) should flash . . . indicating the guest would like a drink to warm up by. Conversely, when a customer comes in wiping his or her brow from perspiration, a signal is given that a "frosty cold beer," or "chilled glass of white wine," and so forth might be enjoyed.

It is not imperative that servers, including bartenders, know everything there is to know about wines, but they *must* possess at least minimal knowledge of wine names, tastes, grape varieties, and the viticultural growing regions of the world. Teach servers how to *correctly* pronounce each and every wine on the list, including grape variety and the producers' name. If servers can't pronounce the wines, communication with customers breaks down and apathy sets in. Lack of pronunciation also discourages servers from suggesting certain wines. In addition to pronunciation, servers must know the basics of wine service, and especially how to sell the wines on your list. Why is it that servers seem to instinctively know to bring the ketchup to the table when French fries are ordered, but can't be induced to suggest a glass or bottle of wine with an entrée? After all, the ketchup is free!

Service is important, but unfortunately there is usually little emphasis placed on training, discipline, pride, and caring. All too many of us look for the quick sale instead of cultivating new customers and finding innovative ways of keeping old ones. The well-trained, well-motivated employee can make all the difference between an operation that is ordinary and those few that are exceptional. If you do not make an investment of time and training in your employees, you will get back what you put in—nothing.

Staff Training

Training is an extremely vital part of the service of alcoholic beverages. The correct wine served in the correct glass alone will not suffice. Your servers must be thoroughly trained in all aspects of beverage service. Perhaps the most important point of their training is to educate them about beverages and brand names so that they will be able to answer questions posed by customers.

Wine sales have as much to do with your servers as with your wine list. A server who is intimidated by and uncomfortable with wine will do a poor job selling it. Servers must know what they are selling and this can be accomplished through mini-tastings. If there is no one on your staff qualified to conduct such tastings, contact a distributor for assistance. If servers find just one or two wines on the list that they really enjoy, those are the wines they will strive to sell.

Servers' enthusiastic description of special drinks can result in an increase of orders and reorders. You might consider, as part of their training, giving them small samples of these drinks, thereby increasing their ability to sell through the first-hand knowledge they will have acquired. Then, offer appropriate incentives to reach high sales goals.

Customers cringe when wine is presented improperly or the server struggles to open a bottle. Avoid these problems by conducting wine service lessons. Most servers hate to appear inept in front of customers, so teach them proper wine service and have them practice until they feel comfortable. Instead of providing each server a "free" corkscrew, charge them $5.00 or $10.00 (refundable of course), which will automatically ensure that the corkscrew will not become lost or misplaced. Do this even if suppliers provide free corkscrews to your establishment.

Staff Competitions

Many restaurants have been successful in boosting wine sales by holding staff competitions. A goal is set, such as 30 bottles sold per month; anyone who exceeds this goal is "in the running," and the top salesperson receives a prize at the end of the competition. Track wine sales on a large board in the kitchen to create enthusiasm for the competition. The prize does not have to be large to generate excitement and increased wine sales.

Have staff meetings at which you explain that every time a bottle of wine is sold, the check is increased, out of which the staff receive 15 percent. On a $20 bottle of wine a $3.00 tip is received; if five extra bottles are sold, an additional $15 per shift is gained—this amounts to an additional $75 per week, or $300 per month.

Educating Your Staff

One of the most overlooked and underutilized tools for increasing profit is the wine list. Most or all restaurants have at least one and some have two.

How do you effectively sell what's on the wine list to our customers? By educating your servers, that's how. Education and training of servers is a top priority, regardless of how little or how much knowledge they already possess about wine.

It is strongly recommended that on an "off" or slow day, you gather all the servers and present a one-hour lecture (at *your* expense) on how to effectively sell wine. How much will this cost? Let us say that you pay your servers $6 per hour and there are ten servers; that is $60 per hour. During this hour, the servers become a "captive audience." It should be explained that while company profits increase from additional beverage sales, servers' tips also increase. Each and every wine on the list should be identified and ways to properly chill, open, and pour the wine explained; you should also discuss which foods on the menu the wine will complement. It should be instilled in the servers' minds that they are salespeople working on commission; workable quotas that servers *must* meet could be the sale of a certain number of bottles of wine per week or month.

Let us see if that $60 for one hour, or even $120 for two hours that you will spend on the lecture, can be recaptured. If every server, working a five-day week, sells one additional bottle of wine per day, and you have ten servers, you will sell an additional 200 bottles of wine per month. A $6 bottle of wine (wholesale) sold at a 150-percent mark-up sells for $15, or a $9 gross profit per bottle. This $9 times 200 bottles equals an additional $1,800 per month in gross sales, or $21,600 per year: all of this for a simple $60 or $120 investment.

If you can increase an average check by a mere 25 cents per customer, it can pay tremendous dividends over the course of one year. For a restaurant that serves only 100 meals per day, the daily increase is $25, weekly $150 (six day week); or $7,800 per year! Now figure how many meals your facility serves during the course of one year, then determine if beverage training is necessary. The answer will be a resounding yes!

Wine-Selling Tips

Selling wine is fun and it should be done in a manner that is not intimidating to the customer. Though most customers have little trouble selecting food courses, they may occasionally feel uncomfortable in making a wine selection. Helping your customer choose a wine makes you much more important to that customer. In addition to ensuring larger tips, your knowledge of wine selling and service will yield personal and professional satisfaction. Here are some steps to follow for successful wine sales that have been suggested by Sebastiani Vineyards (Sonoma, California):

1. Always assume that your customers will want wine.
2. Present the wine list along with the dinner menu. Do not wait to be asked for it. A comment on the fine wine selection available would be appropriate and could ensure that your customer orders wine.
3. When you return to take the food order, be sure to ask which wine has been selected; this is a positive suggestion and makes the sale. Never ask, "Do you want anything to drink?" This is a negative suggestion that leaves open the possibility of getting "no" for an answer.
4. If you recommend a wine based on the food ordered, give the customer a choice, rather than risking rejection of a single recommendation. Your two recommendations should represent different price categories.
5. If your customers seem hesitant to choose a wine, ask what type of wines they enjoy. From the answer, you can make a suitable recommendation.
6. Do your best to sell wine to your first customers, for as others come into the dining room and observe wine being consumed, they are more likely to order it also.
7. Let the inclusion of bin numbers on your wine list be an aid to your customers, who may have difficulty pronouncing the name of a wine. You should not refer to the wine by the bin number, but rather by its name. Never correct a customer's mispronunciation or disagree with his or her wine selection.
8. When you have taken the wine order, return with the wine without delay.
9. Serve the wine immediately. When the wine is promptly poured the guest has more time to enjoy it; the bottle is finished earlier, and this creates an extra selling opportunity.

Wine Service

Having to wait or ask for a menu seems absurd. But, what about a wine list, doesn't that seem equally absurd? The wine list should always be brought to the table with the food menu. This usually guarantees that the customer is at least aware that wines are available before, during, and even after dinner.

After the customer has selected a wine, instruct your servers that they should promptly present the bottle of wine *unopened* to the customer who ordered the wine for his or her approval. At no time should an opened bottle be brought to the table. The bottle should be opened at the table after the customer has approved it (see Figure 14-2). If a bottle of white wine is selected and was not previously chilled, an ice bucket (a 50/50 mixture of ice and water) filled with ice and water should be brought to the table and the bottle immersed into the ice bath until properly chilled. Everything needed for the proper opening and service of that bottle (corkscrew, napkin, ice bucket, carafe, and so on) should be brought to the table. Stand the bottle on a solid, supportive base, either at the table's edge (on an underliner), a side table, or in the ice bucket. Be certain that the bottle's label faces the customer who ordered it. Avoid attempting to open the bottle in thin air, which resembles more of a carnival side show than the proper method of uncorking a bottle.

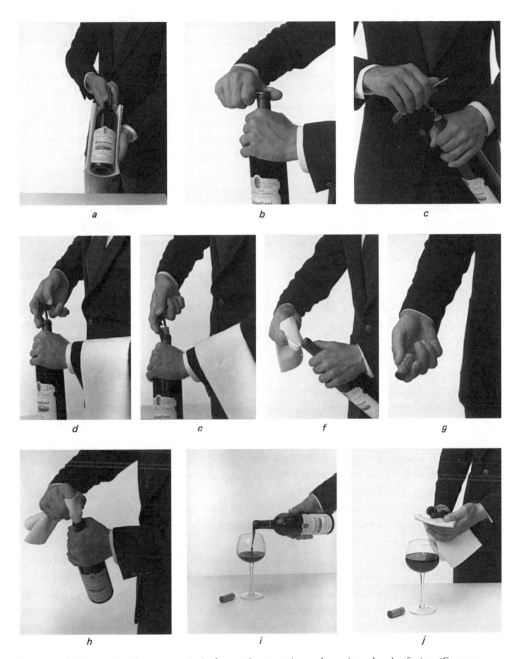

FIGURE 14-2 (a–j)   Step-by-step method of correctly presenting and opening a bottle of wine. (Courtesy Sebastiani Vineyards, Sonoma, California)

To open the bottle, first cut the foil, plastic, or lead capsule at the middle of the bulge, which appears near the bottle's neck, in a neat, clean, and even manner. Remove the capsule carefully using the edge of the knife blade to "peel" the cut edge of the capsule upward to the top of the bottle. Do this in several motions to avoid peeling off little bits and pieces of capsule; once the capsule is pulled back a bit, it should come off in one piece. After removing the capsule, wipe the bottle's top with a damp cloth prior to opening, which will remove any foreign particles or mold that may have gathered beneath the capsule. Using a corkscrew will simplify the uncorking process. Corkscrews should have a helical worm (like wire wrapped around a pencil) instead of a bore or screw, which "drills" a hole in the cork, rather than grasping it for extraction. Insert the point of the corkscrew's worm by lining it up perfectly straight over the cork. Beware of "centering" the point of the worm in the cork, for this will put the entire worm off center. With a gentle downward pressure, screw the worm clockwise until only two notches are showing, for most whites, and a bit further for reds. The goal is to insert the worm far enough to successfully extract the cork without breaking through the bottom end of the cork. Typically, white wine corks are from 1.5 to 2 inches long and red wine corks from 2 to 2.5 inches long. Then, attach the lever to the lip on top of the bottle and while holding it firmly, gently lift up in a straight motion the handle of the corkscrew until the cork comes completely out of the bottle. Do not bend the cork. Immediately wipe the neck of the bottle. Take the cork and place it on the table to the right of the person who selected the wine.

The purpose of the presentation of the cork is *not,* contrary to popular belief, to determine if the cork smells of vinegar, but rather so that its physical condition can be checked. Corks, if stored properly, will maintain pliability, which is easily checked by gently pressing it between the thumb and index finger. While pressing the cork, one should notice moisture at the end that faced the wine. This is the most important thing to check on wine corks. If the cork is not pliable there is a good chance that it is drying out and the wine's storage conditions and thus its own condition might be suspect.

To serve the wine, pour an ounce of it into the host's glass (in a party of customers) and stand back and wait for approval. When approval has been given, gently pour the wine, first for the women, then for the men. Wine glasses should be filled no more than one-third for white wines and one-half to two-thirds for red wines.

When serving wine, the bottle should be held in the right hand in such a way that the person being served can easily see and read the label. Most people like to know what they are drinking. Therefore, do not wrap a napkin around a bottle of wine being served.

Avoid the "down and up" motion of pouring wine, because it increases the chance the bottle will hit the rim of the glass, and it allows wine to drip down the front and sides of the bottle. Instead, after gently pouring wine into a glass with one complete motion, gently twist the wrist with an inward movement, while at the same time tilting the neck of the bottle upward. This avoids dripping wine on the customer, the tablecloth, or the wine's label. Customers may want to take home the empty bottle as a remembrance, perhaps of a birthday, anniversary, or simply a memorable evening. So avoid tarnishing the label with wine stains. It is a good idea to carry a towel in the opposite hand and gently wipe the bottle's lip after each and every pouring.

A very simple way to increase sales of white wine is to instruct your servers to *never* fill a glass (eight to ten ounces) more than one-third full. Most people enjoy white wines because they are chilled. It takes 15 to 20 minutes for a customer to finish four to five ounces of wine. If you fill the glass one-half to two-thirds full, the first, second, and perhaps the third mouthful will be refreshing, but not the fourth and fifth; the wine will have become warm. But if the glass is only one-third filled, each and every mouthful will be chilled, and the customer might even order another bottle of white wine.

Most servers miss a good opportunity to increase the dinner check as well as tips, that is, an after-dinner drink. The standard phrase is "Would you like coffee?" Instead, try "Perhaps you'd like to try an after-dinner drink." This is suggestive selling. Many diet-conscious customers might forgo a dessert because of its caloric content, but would consider a liqueur because of the mistaken belief that it contains less calories.

SERVING TEMPERATURES FOR TABLE WINES (FAHRENHEIT)	
Dry white wines	50–55 degrees
Dry, light-bodied red wines	60–65 degrees
Dry, full-bodied red wines	65–68 degrees
Sparkling wines	42–46 degrees
Sweet red and sweet white wines	42–46 degrees

The proper order of serving wines.   The selection of the wine served should be given the same care and consideration that is given to the choice of the food. If the dinner is a special event and more than one type of wine is to be served, these suggestions might be helpful:

- Light wines should precede heavy or full-bodied wines.
- Dry wines should precede sweet wines.
- Dry white wines should precede dry red wines.
- Dry red wines should precede sweet white wines.
- Dry sparkling wines can be served either before or after dinner, while sweet sparkling wines are best after dinner.

The art of decanting wine.   It is a normal and natural process for any long-lived wine (mostly red) to develop or "throw" sediment as it ages. In red wines, sedimentation is caused by slow reactions in and the eventual precipitation of fruits, tannins, tartrates, pigments, mineral salts, and other compounds as the wine matures in the bottle. A brown deposit settles on the side or bottom of the bottle, depending on how the bottle was stored. Sediment is quite harmless, although aesthetically unpleasant, and tastes like sand.

The purpose of decanting a wine is twofold. First, aeration during the decanting process allows the wine to "breathe," to gain in bouquet, and to dissipate any "off" odors or gases that may have accumulated under the cork. Second, separating the wine from its sediment allows it to be served perfectly bright and clear, thus enhancing its appearance.

Decanting requires little preparation and is extremely simple. Before starting, prepare the following pieces of equipment: a flashlight (or a candle holder and candle); a corkscrew; and a colorless glass decanter or carafe (33 ounce minimum). Be sure that it has been rinsed with a small amount of tepid water and is absolutely free of odor, for certain detergents, if incompletely rinsed away, can ruin a wine's bouquet. Do *not* store your decanters closed with their own stoppers, but instead stuff the necks gently with a bit of tissue paper.

Follow this simple step-by-step procedure:

1. Stand the bottle upright for at least 24 hours before decanting so that the sediment, which is lying along the side of the bottle, can drop gently to the bottle's bottom. If a 24-hour time period is not possible because of immediate ordering, let the bottle rest horizontally for the time being. Decanting should not be done more than one hour before the wine is to be served because the wine may lose its bouquet. Very old wines should be decanted immediately before serving, as the wine fades and oxidizes rapidly. Bottles of vintage Port might have to be stood upright for longer than 24 hours to allow the crusted sediment, known as the dregs, to settle to the bottom.
2. Gently uncork the bottle to avoid disturbing any sediment. If the bottle is lying horizontal, place it into a wicker basket and begin the uncorking process.
3. Stand the flashlight (a candle can be utilized, but its flickering light can distort the view) on end and place next to a clear carafe (between the wine bottle and carafe). Then carefully tilt the wine bottle toward the open mouth of the carafe and allow its contents to trickle in slowly, smoothly, and continuously. While you do this the light of the flashlight should be directly underneath the neck of the wine bottle as to follow the movement of sediment from the bottom of the bottle to the neck, ensuring the decanted wine's clarity. When the sediment reaches the point where the neck and shoulders of the bottle meet, you should be able to see some of the sediment, which is cloudy or hazy, starting to appear. When this starts to happen, you should stop the decanting process. You will find that only one ounce or so of wine will remain in the bottle and you will have a wine that is bright and clear in the decanter.
4. The remaining contents of the bottle should be discarded.
5. When first poured, the color of some older wines is often light orange red, and during a period of about five minutes, the color will deepen to a dark red.

Wine spills.   If for any reason wine, especially red wine, is spilled on a customer's clothing or on the tablecloth, it can be removed by several easy methods.

If white wine is spilled, a little mild soap and water will remove it. If red wine has been spilled, a bit more work is required. Rub some salt or seltzer on the stain, let it sit for a few minutes and most of the stain should be removed. Or, immediately pour white wine over the red wine stain and rub it in until the red disappears. Then simply wash out the white wine with some mild soap and water.

▶ CUSTOMERS' DEMAND FOR QUALITY PRODUCTS

Knowledgeable customers who are brand-name conscious seek labels that they are not only familiar with but have loyalty toward. Stocking identifiable brands establishes a good image for your bar, which increases repeat patronage. This name brand identification is not only applicable to distilled spirits, but also to imported and American beers and wines. Many bars and restaurants utilize the three-tier system of purchasing and serving distilled spirits. The first tier consists of "bar brands" or "off-brands": the second tier consists of "name brand" or "call brands" (the most called for or advertised), and finally "super-premium," often referred to as "top shelf."

A bar stocked with "off" brands or bar brands of distilled spirits immediately gets a reputation for low quality (and high profits for the owner). Today's discriminating consumer demands high quality and is willing to pay for it, especially when it involves brand names and especially super-premium brands. When customers are served beverage brands with which they are familiar, they feel that they are getting a certain perceived value for their dollar. With bar brands, the perceived value is low, and so *should* be the selling price, which unfortunately is usually the same as or only slightly lower than for brand name distilled spirits.

Brown-Forman, Heublein, and Seagram's recommends taking quality one step further—establishing a "premium well." Stocking your well with premium brands and serving them whether or not they are specified can actually increase profits. How? Through higher drink prices. Though a premium brand costs more per bottle than an unknown brand, studies show that people will pay more for a drink made with a brand of distilled spirits they recognize.

Smart beverage managers will capitalize on the fact that people are drinking less alcohol, but are drinking better brands of beer, distilled spirits, and wines. This trend is not confined to the United States alone; the consumption of alcohol has also dropped off significantly in most European countries. If your customers drink better brands, it usually means increased profits for your business.

► ALCOHOLIC BEVERAGE LIABILITY

It is beyond the scope of this book to cover or discuss the laws relating to "alcoholic beverage liability." Instead, we feel that both general and specific questions regarding sections of the law should be addressed to your state alcoholic beverage office or the regional offices of the Bureau of Alcohol, Tobacco and Firearms listed below.

Bureau of Alcohol, Tobacco and Firearms
650 Massachusetts Ave., NW
Washington, DC 20226
202-927-8500

North-Atlantic Regional Office
6 World Trade Center
Room 620
New York, NY 10048
212-264-2328

Southeast Regional Office
2600 Century Park Way, NE
Atlanta, GA 30345
404-679-5010

Midwest Regional Office
300 South Riverside Plaza
Suite 301
Chicago, IL 60606
312-353-3778

Southwest Regional Office
1114 Commerce Street
Room 709
Dallas, TX 75242
214-767-2280

Western Regional Office
221 Main Street
11th Floor
San Francisco, CA 94105
415-744-7013

Methods of Protection from Alcoholic Beverage Liability

Strict drunk driving laws, "alcoholic beverage liability" laws, and the existence of neo-prohibitionist and other citizens' groups all attest to the fact that drunk driving is an extremely serious matter about which all owners of drinking establishments must concern themselves.

To avoid problems with the law, it is suggested that some or all of the following be reduced or eliminated:

- Offering two-for-one drinks during "happy hours." Giving more than two drinks to one person at a time.
- Selling, offering, or delivering to any person an unlimited number of drinks during any set period of time for a fixed price.
- Serving larger-than-normal drinks.
- Allowing "double" drinks to be served.
- Increasing the size of a drink without raising its price.
- Selling, offering, or delivering beer or cocktails by the pitcher.
- Giving free drinks to any person or groups of persons.
- Allowing guests to serve themselves or make their own drinks.
- Announcing last call. This encourages a final drink, doubles, or "one for the road."
- Encouraging or permitting contests on the premises in which drinks are the prizes.

The following practices, instead, should be developed:

- Offer food prior to serving drinks.
- Avoid serving overly salty foods, which increases thirst and therefore beverage consumption.
- Offer a good supply of soft drinks as well as low-alcohol and nonalcoholic beverages.
- Offer hot coffee or tea at the end of a party.
- Serve foods that are high in protein (turkey, chicken, fish, and cheese), which helps slow the absorption of alcohol into the bloodstream. Cheese and bread, for instance, could be served during "happy hours."
- Institute a designated driver program.
- Develop a separate list of nonalcoholic drinks.
- Serve free soda or "mocktails" to designated drivers.
- Guarantee free cab rides home for intoxicated guests.
- Recommend or require your bartenders or waiters to attend a server intervention course, which can be offered by the National Health Education Foundation.
- Train your staff in intervention techniques and general awareness.

There are many inexpensive ways to take the focus off drinking and place it on fun. The National Restaurant Association has suggested several possible tactics.

Make your bartender a celebrity. Since a bartender is often considered the "personality" of a bar, send him out to make presentations for your establishment. Also, make your bartender your spokesperson against drunk driving. Promote guest bartender nights, using local celebrities or regular customers. Hire your staff members based on personality. Once they have been with you for a while, name a drink after them.

Serve dinner at the bar. The National Restaurant Association suggests that singles may be more apt to eat out alone if they are sitting at the bar rather than at a table. The price of the dinner will make up for revenues lost through lowered alcohol consumption; and providing food of any kind helps to ameliorate the effects of alcohol on drinkers.

Another idea is to sponsor contests. Americans love to compete; eating contests, from pretzels to oysters, are always popular.

Bartenders' Responsibilities

According to the National Restaurant Association, bartenders are shouldering more responsibility for customers' alcohol consumption than ever before. Laws in at least 35 states hold establishments liable for accidents caused by intoxicated customers they served. And the number of lawsuits filed against bars and restaurants is increasing each year. You can control excessive drinking in your bar or restaurant by recognizing when a customer has had too much to drink and taking appropriate action.

Note how quickly a customer is drinking. Generally, a 150-pound person consuming four drinks (four ounces of alcohol) in an hour registers a 0.1 percent blood alcohol content and is legally intoxicated (some states). Watch for progressive symptoms of intoxication: lack of inhibition, followed by loss of muscular control, slurred speech, and impaired judgment.

If a customer seems to have reached his or her limit and asks for another cocktail, suggest a "mocktail" or something to eat instead. Encourage intoxicated customers to let a friend drive them home, or offer to call a cab. If you are serving a large group, suggest that someone become the "designated driver." Provide the driver with complimentary "mocktails."

For further information about alcohol server education programs, contact the National Restaurant Association in Washington, D.C., or Intermission, Ltd., a nonprofit "responsible beverage service organization" in Northampton, Massachusetts.

TIPS

Training for Intervention Procedures by Servers of Alcohol (TIPS) is a nationwide program to train servers of alcohol on ways to prevent alcohol abuse in taverns, restaurants, and other businesses where beverages containing alcohol are sold. Through written materials, videotapes, and "role playing," your bartenders, waitresses, and other employees will learn important information on the effects of alcohol; how to identify potentially troublesome drinkers or situations before they become a problem; and how they can deal with intoxicated customers or those who appear to be on the verge of overindulging without creating a scene.

TIPS is a practical, common-sense approach to helping prevent alcohol abuse while at the same time not damaging your business. It can be an important addition to the training your employees already receive in such areas as company procedures and product handling. The program was developed by Dr. Morris E. Chafetz, one of the world's leading authorities on alcohol and the founder and director of the National Institute on Alcohol Abuse and Alcoholism. He is also president of the Health Education Foundation in Washington, D.C., which administers the TIPS program. The basic training takes six hours; employees must pass a written test before they will be certified as having successfully completed the basic training.

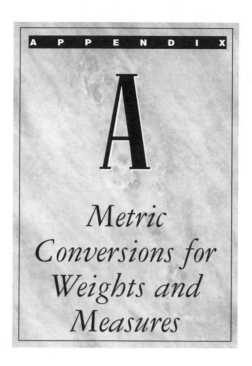

APPENDIX

A

Metric Conversions for Weights and Measures

LITERS TO GALLONS CONVERSION TABLE					
Liters	*Gallons*	*Liters*	*Gallons*	*Liters*	*Gallons*
1	0.3	16	4.2	31	8.2
2	0.5	17	4.5	32	8.5
3	0.8	18	4.8	33	8.7
4	1.1	19	5.0	34	9.0
5	1.3	20	5.3	35	9.2
6	1.6	21	5.5	36	9.5
7	1.8	22	5.8	37	9.8
8	2.1	23	6.1	38	10.0
9	2.4	24	6.3	39	10.3
10	2.6	25	6.6	40	10.6
11	2.9	26	6.9	41	10.8
12	3.2	27	7.1	42	11.1
13	3.4	28	7.4	43	11.4
14	3.7	29	7.7	44	11.6
15	4.0	30	7.9	45	11.9

LITERS TO GALLONS CONVERSION TABLE *(continued)*

Liters	Gallons	Liters	Gallons	Liters	Gallons
46	12.2	65	17.2	83	21.9
47	12.4	66	17.4	84	22.2
48	12.7	67	17.7	85	22.5
49	12.9	68	18.0	86	22.7
50	13.2	69	18.2	87	23.0
51	13.5	70	18.5	88	23.2
52	13.7	71	18.8	89	23.5
53	14.0	72	19.0	90	23.8
54	14.3	73	19.3	91	24.0
55	14.5	74	19.6	92	24.3
56	14.8	75	19.8	93	24.6
57	15.0	76	20.1	94	24.8
58	15.3	77	20.3	95	25.1
59	15.6	78	20.6	96	25.4
60	15.9	79	20.9	97	25.6
61	16.1	80	21.1	98	25.9
62	16.4	81	21.4	99	26.1
63	16.6	81	21.4	100	26.4
64	16.9	82	21.7		

For a more precise conversion: 1 liter = 0.26418 gallons
1 gallon = 3.7854 liters

CAPACITY MEASURE

1 milliliter	= 0.001 liters	=0.0338 fluid ounces	
5 milliliters	= 1 teaspoon		
10 milliliters	= 1 centiliter	= 0.3381 fluid ounces	
15 milliliters	= 1 tablespoon	= 3 teaspoons	
30 milliliters	= $^1/_8$ cup	= 1 fluid ounce	= 2 tablespoons
50 milliliters	= 1.7 fluid ounces		
59 milliliters	= $^1/_4$ cup	= 2 fluid ounces	= 4 tablespoons
79 milliliters	= $^1/_3$ cup	= 16 teaspoons	

100 milliliters	= 10 centiliters	= 3.3814 fluid ounces	
10 centiliters	= 1 deciliter	= 3.3814 fluid ounces	
118 milliliters	= 1/2 cup	= 4 fluid ounces	= 8 tablespoons
158 milliliters	= 2/3 cup	= 32 teaspoons	
167 milliliters	= 6.3 fluid ounces		
177 milliliters	= 3/4 cup	= 6 fluid ounces	= 12 tablespoons
187 milliliters	= 6.76 fluid ounces		
200 milliliters	= 6.8 fluid ounces		
237 milliliters	= 1 cup	= 8 fluid ounces	= 16 tablespoons
375 milliliters	= 12.7 fluid ounces		
474 milliliters	= 2 cups	= 16 fluid ounces	
750 milliliters	= 25.4 fluid ounces		
946 milliliters	= 4 cups	= 32 fluid ounces	
1000 milliliters	= 100 centiliters	= 33.814 fluid ounces *or* (1 liter) *or* (10 deciliters)	
10 deciliters	= 1 liter	= 1.0567 liquid quarts	
1 liter	= 0.26418 gallons		
1.5 liters	= 50.7 fluid ounces		
1.75 liters	= 59.2 fluid ounces		
1.89 liters	= 1/2 gallon	= 64 fluid ounces	
3 liters	= 101.4 fluid ounces		
3.79 liters	= 1 gallon	= 128 fluid ounces	
4 liters	= 135.2 fluid ounces		
10 liters	= 1 decaliter	= 2.64 gallons	
10 decaliters	= 1 hectoliter	= 26.418 gallons *or* [11.111 cases of (12) 750 milliliter bottles]	
10 hectoliters	= 1 kiloliter	= 264.18 gallons	

APPROXIMATE CONVERSION FACTORS

Convert From	To	Multiply by
Acre-feet	Cubic feet	43,560
Acre-feet	Cubic meter	1,233.5
Acre-feet	Gallons	325,851

APPROXIMATE CONVERSION FACTORS *(continued)*

Convert From	To	Multiply by
Acres	Hectares	0.4047
Acres	Square feet	43,560
Acres	Square hectometers	0.405
Acres	Square meters	4,047
Centimeters	Inches	0.3937
Centimeters	Millimeters	10
Cubic feet	Cubic meters	0.02832
Cubic meters	Cubic feet	35.315
Cubic meters	Cubic yards	1.308
Cubic yards	Cubic meters	0.765
Cups	Liters	0.24
Feet	Centimeters	30.48
Feet	Meters	0.3048
Fluid ounces	Liters	0.0296
Fluid ounces	Milliliters	29.573
Gallons	Cubic meter	0.00378
Gallons	Liters	3.785
Grams	Ounces	0.035
Grams	Pounds	0.002
Hectares	Acres	2.471
Inches	Centimeters	2.540
Inches	Millimeters	25.0
Kilograms	Pounds	2.205
Kilometers	Miles	0.6214
Kilometers per liter	Miles per gallon	2.354
Kilometers per hour	Miles per hour	0.621
Liters	Cups	4.2
Liters	Fluid ounces	33.81
Liters	Gallons	0.26418
Liters	Pints	2.113
Liters	Quarts	1.057

Meters	Feet	3.281
Meters	Yards	1.094
Miles per hour	Kilometers per hour	1.609
Miles per gallon	Kilometers per liter	0.425
Milliliters	Fluid ounces	0.034
Milliliters	Tablespoons	0.07
Milliliters	Teaspoons	0.2
Millimeters	Inches	0.04
Ounces	Grams	28.349
Pints	Gallons	8.0
Pints	Liters	0.473
Pints	Quarts	2.0
Pounds	Grams	454
Pounds	Kilograms	0.454
Quarts	Gallons	4
Quarts	Liters	0.9463
Square centimeters	Square inches	0.155
Square feet	Square meters	0.093
Square hectometers	Acres	2.471
Square inches	Square centimeters	6.451
Square kilometers	Square miles	0.386
Square meters	Square feet	10.764
Square meters	Square yards	1.196
Square miles	Acres	640
Square miles	Square kilometers	2.59
Square yards	Square meters	0.836
Tablespoons	Milliliters	15
Teaspoons	Milliliters	5
Teaspoons	Tablespoon	3
Yards	Meters	0.914

LIQUID CONVERSIONS						
	Milliliter(s)	*Ounces(s)*	*Pint(s)*	*Quart(s)*	*Liter(s)*	*Gallon(s)*
1 Ml	= 1	29.6	473.2	946.3	1000	3785
1 Ounce	= 0.0338	1	16	32	33.81	128
1 Pint	= 0.0021	0.0625	1	2	2.1134	8
1 Quart	= 0.0011	0.0312	0.5	1	1.0567	4
1 Liter	= 0.001	0.0296	0.4732	0.9463	1	3.7853
1 Gallon	= 0.0003	0.0078	0.125	0.25	0.264	1

WEIGHT CONVERSIONS				
	Grain(s)	*Gram(s)*	*Ounce(s)**	*Pound(s)**
1 Grain	= 1	15.43	437.5	7000
1 Gram	= 0.0648	1	28.35	453.6
1 Ounce*	= 0.0023	0.0353	1	16
1 Pound*	= 0.00014	0.0021	0.0625	1

* Avoirdupois weight.

WEIGHTS		
1 grain	= 64.79 milligrams	
10 milligrams	= 1 centigram	= 0.1543 grains
10 centigrams	= 1 decigram	= 1.5432 grains
10 decigrams	= 1 gram	= 15.432 grains*
27.34 grains	= 1 dram	= 1.772 grams
5 grams	= 1 teaspoon	
16 drams	= 1 ounce	= 28.3495 grams†
10 grams	= 1 decagram	= 0.3527 ounces
15 grams	= 1 tablespoon	
57 grams	= 2 ounces	= 1/4 cup
10 decagrams	= 1 hectogram	= 3.5274 ounces
114 grams	= 4 ounces	= 1/2 cup
227 grams	= 8 ounces	= 1 cup

10 hectograms	= 1 kilogram	= 2.2046 pounds‡
1 pound	= 16 ounces	= 0.4536 kilograms§
10 kilograms	= 1 myriagram	= 22.046 pounds
10 myriagrams	= 1 quintal	= 220.46 pounds *or* (100 kilograms)
10 quintals	= 1 metric ton	= 2,204.62 pounds‖
1 piece	= 205 liters	= 55 gallons

* Or 0.03527 ounces or 0.001 kilograms or 1000 milligrams
† Or 437.5 grains
‡ Or 35.3 ounces
§ Or 7,000 grains or 453.59 grams
‖ Or 1,000 kilograms

LENGTH AND DISTANCE

1 inch	= 25.4 millimeters	= 2.54 centimeters	= 0.0254 meters
1 foot	= 304.9 millimeters	= 30.49 centimeters	= 0.3049 meters
1 yard	= 0.9144 meters		
1 millimeter	= 0.03937 inches		
1 centimeter	= 0.3937 inches		
1 meter	= 1.0936 yards	= 3.281 feet	= 39.37 inches
1 hectometer	= 328.0833 feet		
1 kilometer	= 0.62137 miles		
1 mile	= 1,609 meters	= 5,280 feet	= 1.6093 kilometers

OTHER MEASUREMENTS

Beer

Alcohol by weight equals alcohol by volume × 0.8

Alcohol by volume equals by weight × 1.25

1 barrel of beer = 31 gallons or (13.8 cases of 12-ounce cans or bottles)

$1/2$ barrel of beer = 15.5 gallons or 1 keg (1,984 fluid ounces; 165.33 12-ounce bottles) or (6.89 cases of 24 12-ounce bottles)

$1/4$ barrel of beer = 7.75 gallons or $1/2$ keg (992 fluid ounces; 82 12-ounce bottles) or (3.4 cases of 24 12-ounce bottles)

$1/8$ barrel of beer = 3.88 gallons or $1/4$ keg (496 fluid ounces; 41 12-ounce bottles) or (1.7 cases of 24 12-ounce bottles)

1 six-pack of beer = 72 ounces or 2.13 liters

OTHER MEASUREMENTS *(continued)*

Still Others

1 case of twelve 750 milliliter bottles = 2.376 gallons; 9 liters; or 3042 ounces

1 four-pack cooler = 48 ounces or 1.42 liters

120 drops of water = 1 teaspoon

60 drops thick fluid = 1 teaspoon

1 dash = $^1/_{48}$ fluid ounces or $^1/_6$ teaspoon = 6 to 8 drops

20 dashes = 1 fluid ounce

1 orange = 6 to 7 tablespoons of juice

1 lemon = 3 tablespoons of juice

1 barrique* = 59.4 gallons of wine

1 tonneau = 4 barriques = 237.8 gallons of wine

* A very common barrel used in Bordeaux, France.

To convert wine grape acreage into potential cases of wine, use this formula:
Tons per acre × gallons per ton divided by 2.38 = cases of 750-milliliter bottles per acre.
For table wines, assume 160 to 165 gallons per ton; for dessert wines, 90.

TEMPERATURE

Celsius	Fahrenheit	Celsius	Fahrenheit
100.0	212.0	72.2	162.0
97.2	207.0	70.0	158.0
95.0	203.0	69.4	157.0
94.4	202.0	66.7	152.0
91.7	197.0	65.0	149.0
90.0	194.0	63.9	147.0
88.9	192.0	61.1	142.0
86.1	187.0	60.0	140.0
85.0	185.0	58.3	137.0
83.3	182.0	55.5	132.0
80.5	177.0	55.0	131.0
80.0	176.0	52.8	127.0
77.8	172.0	50.0	122.0
75.0	167.0	47.2	117.0

45.0	113.0	2.8	37.0
44.4	112.0	0.0	32.0
41.7	107.0	−2.8	27.0
40.0	104.0	−5.0	23.0
38.9	102.0	−5.5	22.0
36.1	97.0	−8.3	17.0
35.0	95.0	−10.0	14.0
33.3	92.0	−11.1	12.0
30.5	87.0	−13.9	7.0
30.0	86.0	−15.0	5.0
27.8	82.0	−16.0	3.0
25.0	77.0	−17.0	2.0
22.2	72.0	−18.0	−1.0
20.0	68.0	−19.0	−3.0
19.4	67.0	−20.0	−4.0
16.7	62.0	−21.0	−6.0
15.0	59.0	−22.0	8.0
13.9	57.0	−23.0	−10.0
11.1	52.0	−24.0	−12.0
10.0	50.0	−25.0	−15.0
8.3	47.0	−26.0	−16.0
5.5	42.0	−27.0	−17.0
5.0	41.0	−28.0	−19.0

To convert Fahrenheit into Celsius, subtract 32 from the Fahrenheit temperature, then divide by 1.8; *or* subtract 32 from Fahrenheit, then multiply by 0.55.

To convert Celsius into Fahrenheit, multiply the Celsius temperature by 1.8 and then add 32; *or* divide Celsius by 0.55, then add 32.

Note: 212 degrees F is equivalent to 100 degrees C.
90 degrees F is equivalent to 32.2 degrees C.
32 degrees F is equivalent to 0 degrees C.

CONVERSION TABLE FOR SUGARS IN GRAPES AND WINE

Baumé is the term used in France to measure the level of unfermented sugar present in the *must*. To determine Brix, take degrees Baumé and multiply by 1.8. To determine Baumé, take degrees Brix and divide by 1.8.

Brix or *Balling* are the terms used in the United States to measure the level of unfermented sugar present in the *must*.

Essenz is the term used in Hungary to measure the level of unfermented sugar present in the *must*.

Gay Lussac. To convert Gay Lussac to Brix, multiply by 2.

Glucometer is the name of the device used to measure the unfermented sugar in the *must* for the production of Portuguese port wine.

Klosterneuburg (KMW for Klosterneuburg Mostwaage Scale) is the term used in Austria to measure the level of unfermented sugar present in the *must*. (One degree KMW = 5 degrees Öechsle.) To determine *Brix*, multiply KMW degrees by 1.25. To determine KMW degrees, divide *Brix* by 1.25.

Öechsle is the term used in Germany and Switzerland to measure the level of unfermented sugar present in the *must*. To determine *Brix*, take Öechsle, divide by 4, then subtract 1. To determine Öechsle, take *Brix*, add 1, then multiply by 4.

APPENDIX

B

Vintage Charts

The purpose of vintage reports, charts, and guides is to give retailers, restaurateurs, and consumers an indication as to how a particular vintage or growing season progressed, and what the final outcome was relative to the quantity and quality of the grapes harvested.

Just saying that the "19—" vintage was very good, great, or poor is not enough and is a general blanket statement, simply because questions that should follow would be: where, and in which country?

As an example, let's pick France. The first logical question would be, in which of the six major regions of France? The next question could be (if we selected the region of Bordeaux), in which district, the Médoc or Saint-Émilion? The following question would be, red or white, sweet, or dry? As you can see in today's wine drinking society, we must be more specific when dealing with vintages.

Vintage charts are actually *generalizations* of a specific grape-growing region and most charts don't take into consideration the region, when the grapes were harvested, climate (the combination of sunshine, temperature, and precipitation), various microclimates, or the expertise of the individual winemaker. Therefore, the numbers used on a vintage chart represent broad-range averages or estimations. Some mediocre wines have been made in great years and excellent wines produced in moderate to poor years.

Another problem inherent in vintage charts is that most of them list vintage years for wines that are well past their prime and even possibly completely undrinkable. The problem that arises when listing older vintages is the lack of availability at either the wholesale or retail level.

A vintage guide is just that—a guide—and should not be accepted as the final word or quoted with biblical authority regarding a particular vintage.

An excellent book on the subject of great wines (which also contains extensive tasting notes back to the 1700s) is written by Michael Broadbent, a master of wine. Mr. Broadbent is perhaps the world's foremost authority on old wines. The book, titled *Great Vintage Wine Book,* was published by Alfred Knopf in 1980 and updated in 1991.

The vintage ratings contained in this book are based on a scale of 1 to 10, with 10 being the highest rating.

9–10 = GREAT 7–8 = VERY GOOD 5–6 = GOOD 3–4 = FAIR 0–2 = POOR

The symbol (————), when appearing in the tables that follow, indicates the wine is probably too old for consumption.

▶ MAJOR WINE-PRODUCING AREAS OF THE WORLD
Australia

Year	Rating
1994	4
1993	4
1992	3

1991	10
1990	9
1989	9
1988	7
1987	8
1986	10
1985	8
1984	8
1983	7
1982	5

France

Alsace.   Most of the wine produced in Alsace is white (90 percent) and with the exception of late-harvested Gewürztraminer or Johannisberg Riesling, should be consumed within four years of the vintage date. The ratings are for white wines only.

Year	Rating
1994	4
1993	4
1992	5
1991	3

Great vintages: 1990, 1989, 1985, 1983, 1976, 1973, 1971, 1970, 1967, 1966, 1961, 1959, 1947, 1945.

Beaujolais.   Beaujolais, which appears on the retail shelves some two months after the vintage, is known as *Beaujolais Nouveau.* It is best enjoyed within one year after harvest.

Other types of Beaujolais, such as Beaujolais-Villages and the *crus,* can be aged for about five to seven years. Older than that, you are taking a chance that the wine is probably "over-the-hill."

Year	Rating
1994	7
1993	7
1992	4
1991	8

Great vintages: 1990, 1989, 1976, 1971, 1969, 1961, 1959, 1949, 1945, 1929, 1928.

Bordeaux.   Generally speaking, in good to great years, these are the red wines of France to lay away. Most of them generally last seven to ten years and the very best will last 25 to 30 years and possibly longer, depending on the vintage. The ratings for the red Bordeaux are from the Médoc, although the wines of Saint-Émilion and Pomerol often mirror the Médoc.

The dry white wines produced nowadays are for current consumption; many receive little or no barrel age. These are best consumed up to four years old.

Sauternes usually do not begin reaching maturity until they are at least ten years old. The better quality Sauternes should easily last 15 to 20 years and if produced in a great year, 30 to 40 years or more is possible.

Year	Red	White dry	White sweet (Sauternes)
1994	4	4	5
1993	4	3	3
1992	3	4	4
1991	2	2	2
1990	8	———	9
1989	9	———	9
1988	7	———	10
1987	6	———	5
1986	8	———	9
1985	9	———	7
1984	5	———	6
1983	9	———	10
1982	9	———	8
1981	8	———	9
1980	6	———	7

Year			
1979	6	———	8
1978	9	———	7
1977	6	———	6
1976	7	———	8
1975	9	———	9
1974	6	———	6
1973	6	———	6
1972	5	———	6
1971	8	———	9
1970	9	———	9

Great vintages (red wine): 1966, 1961, 1959, 1955, 1948, 1947, 1945, 1934, 1929, 1928.

Great vintages (white dry wine): 1982, 1975, 1971, 1970, 1967, 1966, 1964, 1962, 1961, 1959, 1955, 1953, 1952, 1949, 1947, 1945, 1937, 1929, 1928.

Great vintages (white sweet wine—Sauternes): 1967, 1962, 1961, 1959, 1955, 1947, 1945, 1937, 1929, 1928, 1926, 1921, 1919, 1908, 1904, 1901, 1900.

Burgundy.   Most of the red burgundies produced nowadays are *not* vinified for long aging; a smart consumer would be wise not to put away large stocks of these wines. White Burgundies should be consumed within six years after the vintage date.

Year	Red Burgundy	White Burgundy	Chablis
1994	4	4	4
1993	5	4	3
1992	4	9	4
1991	3	4	4
1990	9	9	8
1989	8	———	———
1988	9	———	———
1987	8	———	———
1986	7	———	———
1985	9	———	———
1984	5	———	———

Year	Red Burgundy	White Burgundy	Chablis (continued)
1983	9	——	——
1982	8	——	——

Great vintages (red wines): 1976, 1971, 1969, 1966, 1964, 1961, 1959, 1949, 1947, 1945, 1937, 1934, 1929, 1928, 1926, 1923, 1921, 1900.

Great vintages (white wines): 1978, 1976, 1971, 1969, 1967, 1966, 1962, 1955, 1953, 1952, 1949, 1947, 1928, 1921. White burgundies *do* last longer than other white wines because most of them are barrel-fermented and/or aged.

Champagne. For years, champagne producers, importers, writers, and others have presented vintage charts for various vintages of champagne, informing you of such great vintages as 1921, 1943, 1955, 1965, 1969, etc. Unfortunately, you are not informed that champagne is at its best within ten years of the vintage date. For example, a 1969 Dom Pérignon was at its best until 1979, then it started to slowly decline in quality. Exceptions do occur; however, as a general rule for both consuming and purchasing, stay away from vintage-dated sparkling wines and champagnes more than ten years past their vintage date, and always try to purchase the newest vintage possible.

Loire Valley. The wines of the Loire Valley are predominantly white (75 percent) and with the exception of Pouilly Fumé and some sweet Vouvray, should be consumed within four years of the vintage date. The ratings are for white wines only.

Year	Rating
1994	3
1993	4
1992	5
1991	2

Great vintages: 1989, 1985, 1983, 1978, 1976, 1975, 1973, 1971, 1970, 1969, 1964, 1955, 1953, 1947, 1945.

Rhône Valley. Although some excellent white wines are produced in the Rhône Valley, the majority of wine (95 percent) is red. White Rhône wines appear to have more longevity than whites of either Alsace or the Loire Valley. Your best bet is to avoid white Rhône wines more than four years old.

The reds, on the other hand, will continue to improve for about ten years past their vintage date; of course, there are exceptions to the rule.

Year	Red wines	White wines
1994	4	4
1993	3	3
1992	4	4
1991	2	3
1990	8	———
1989	8	———
1988	9	———
1987	6	———
1986	8	———
1985	10	———
1984	6	———
1983	8	———
1982	8	———
1981	8	———

Great vintages: 1978, 1961, 1949, 1945, 1929.

Germany

With the exception of the late-harvested wines (Auslese, Beerenauslese, Trockenbeerenauslese, and Eiswein), it is best to refrain from purchasing wines more than five years after the vintage. The chart is for white wines only.

Year	Rhine	Mosel
1994	8	7
1993	5	7
1992	8	6
1991	7	7

Great vintages: 1990, 1989, 1985, 1976, 1975, 1971, 1967, 1964, 1959, 1953, 1949, 1945, 1937, 1934, 1921.

Italy

Italy presents the most diversification and also the most problems in attempting to state the quality of each vintage. For starters, there are 20 wine-producing regions and each of them has grapes indigenous to its specific region in addition to grapes shared by other regions.

In an attempt to clarify and present a workable vintage chart, only several of the major red and white wine regions are presented.

With very few exceptions, it is best to consume Italian white wines within three years of their vintage and rarely past five years. During this time they are at their best: fresh, lively, and fruity.

Year	Piedmont		Tuscany		Veneto	
	Red	White	Red	White	Red	White
1994	5	5	8	8	6	6
1993	4	5	3	3	6	6
1992	3	4	2	3	4	5
1991	4	4	3	3	6	6
1990	10	———	10	———	9	———
1989	9	———	6	———	5	———
1988	9	———	9	———	9	———
1987	7	———	6	———	8	———
1986	8	———	8	———	8	———
1985	10	———	10	———	9	———
1984	4	———	4	———	8	———
1983	8	———	8	———	4	———
1982	9	———	9	———	8	———
1981	6	———	8	———	6	———
1980	7	———	7	———	7	———
1979	6	———	8	———	10	———
1978	10	———	9	———	6	———
1977	5	———	8	———	8	———
1976	6	———	6	———	6	———
1975	5	———	9	———	8	———
1974	9	———	9	———	8	———

1973	6	———	6	———	7	———
1972	3	———	5	———	6	———
1971	10	———	10	———	7	———
1970	9	———	9	———	6	———
1969	7	———	8	———	8	———
1968	7	———	9	———	7	———

Great vintages
(Piedmont): 1964, 1961, 1958, 1952, 1947.
(Tuscany): 1964, 1949, 1947, 1945.
(Veneto): 1964, 1959, 1958.

The rating chart above represents the following regions and individual wines from each.

Piedmont (red wines): Barbaresco, Barolo, Gattinara, Ghemme, Nebbiolo, Spanna, and other comparable, full-bodied wines. Other red wines, which include Barbera, Dolcetto, Freisa, and Grignolino, should be consumed within five years of the vintage date.

Piedmont (white wines): Arneis, Gavi, Moscato.

Tuscany (red wines): Brunello di Montalcino, Cabernet Sauvignon, Cabernet Sauvignon/Sangiovese Blends, Chianti, Carmignano, Vino Nobile di Montepulciano, and other comparable full-bodied wines.

Tuscany (white wines): Galestro, Bianco Toscano, Chardonnay, Vernaccia di San Gimignano.

Veneto (red wines): Bardolino and Valpolicella should be consumed within four years of the vintage date. One of the few wines that can be consumed older is Amarone della Valpolicella.

Veneto (white wines): Bianco di Custoza, Soave.

▶ PORT WINE

It may be interesting to list every single year declared, then assign it a numerical rating. However, it is probably better to list those years that in fact a majority of shippers declared a vintage. Years marked with an * (asterisk) are best quality vintages: 1992*, 1991,

1987, 1985*, 1983, 1982, 1980*, 1978, 1977*, 1975, 1970*, 1967, 1966*, 1963*, 1960*, 1959, 1958, 1957, 1955, 1950, 1948, 1947, 1945, 1942, 1935, 1934, 1927.

Spain

Year	Rioja Red	Rioja White
1994	8	8
1993	5	5
1992	5	6
1991	9	9
1990	8	8
1989	7	———
1988	6	———
1987	8	———

Great vintages: 1982, 1970, 1968, 1966, 1964, 1958, 1955, 1952, 1948, 1934, 1924, 1922.

United States

California. California is an extremely large and diversified wine-producing area with many viticultural areas. It would be extremely difficult for anyone to compile a chart showing each viticultural area, then the multitude of grape varieties (both red and white) that grow in each area, and finally normal grape harvest time compared to late-harvested time.

The vintages listed below are for wines produced in Mendocino, Monterey, Napa, and Sonoma Valley.

The red wines are Cabernet Sauvignon, Merlot, Petite Sirah, Pinot Noir, and Zinfandel.

The white wines are Chardonnay, Chenin Blanc, Gewürztraminer, Sauvignon Blanc (Fumé Blanc), and Johannisberg Riesling.

Year	Red wine	White wine
1994	8	5
1993	6	5

1992	5	7
1991	9	9
1990	9	———
1989	5	———
1988	8	———
1987	8	———
1986	9	———

Great vintages: 1985, 1984, 1978, 1976,
1974, 1970, 1968, 1964, 1958, 1955,
1951, 1946, 1935.

New York State

Year	Finger Lakes		Hudson Valley		Long Island	
	Red	White	Red	White	Red	White
1994	6	6	6	6	7	7
1993	6	7	6	6	6	7
1992	3	4	3	3	3	4
1991	10	10	10	10	10	10
1990	7	———	7	———	8	———
1989	5	———	5	———	6	———

Great red wines: 1985, 1983, 1980, 1978.

Washington State
This chart comprises the wines produced in the Columbia and Willamette Valleys.

Year	Red and White wines
1991	8
1990	8
1989	8

Great red wines: 1987, 1985, 1984, 1982, 1980, 1978, 1975, 1972.

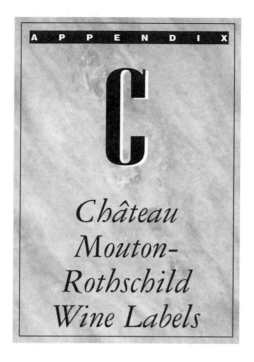

APPENDIX

C

Château Mouton-Rothschild Wine Labels

ne of the most fascinating aspects of *Château Mouton-Rothschild bottles is the art work on the label. Every year Baron Philippe de Rothschild commissions a famous artist to design the upper portion of Mouton's label. The tradition began in 1927 (with the 1924 vintage); but the practice did not become regular until 1945.*

The world-renowned artists who design the labels [see Figure C (a–i)] are not paid in money; rather, they receive five cases of good years of Mouton, ready to drink when the design is delivered, and five cases of the vintage it was created for when the vintage is marketed.

These are the artists who have been commissioned to paint labels for Château Mouton-Rothschild:

- 1924—Jean Carlu
- 1945—Philippe Jullian
- 1946—Jean Hugo
- 1947—Jean Cocteau
- 1948—Marie Laurencin
- 1949—André Dignimont
- 1950—Georges Arnulf
- 1951—Marcel Vertès
- 1952—Léonor Fini
- 1953—No illustrated label
- 1954—Jean Carzou
- 1955—Georges Braque
- 1956—Pavel Tchelitchew
- 1957—André Masson
- 1958—Salvador Dali
- 1959—Richard Lippold
- 1960—Jacques Villon
- 1961—Georges Mathieu
- 1962—Matta
- 1963—Bernard Dufour
- 1964—Henry Moore
- 1965—Dorothea Tanning
- 1966—Pierre Alechinsky
- 1967—César
- 1968—Bona
- 1969—Joan Miró
- 1970—Marc Chagall
- 1971—Wassily Kandinsky
- 1972—Serge Poliakoff
- 1973—Pablo Picasso
- 1974—Robert Motherwell
- 1975—Andy Warhol
- 1976—Pierre Soulages
- 1977—Tribute to Her Majesty Queen Elizabeth (commemorative label)

FIGURE Appendix C (a–i) Mouton Rothschild labels. (Courtesy Baron Philippe de Rothschild, Inc.)

- 1978—Jean-Paul Riopelle
- 1979—Hisao Domoto
- 1980—Hans Hartung
- 1981—Arman
- 1982—John Huston
- 1983—Saul Steinberg
- 1984—Yaacov Agam
- 1985—Paul Delvaux
- 1986—Bernard Sejourne
- 1987—Hans Erni
- 1988—Keith Haring
- 1989—Georg Baselitz
- 1990—Francis Bacon
- 1991—Setsuko
- 1992—Per Kirkeby
- 1993—Balthazar Klossowski de Rola

(No label was commissioned in 1953 because both the wine and label in that year were dedicated to Mouton's first three Rothschild owners to commemorate its centenary.)

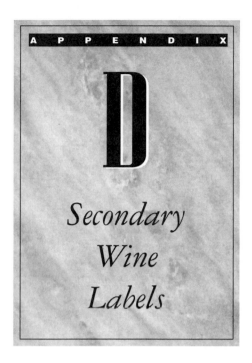

Secondary Wine Labels

Secondary wine labels *are brands or labels created by wineries worldwide for the purpose of marketing and selling additional wine. There are many reasons why many well-known wineries and shippers sometimes bottle wine under a different or second label.*

Some reasons for a secondary label are:

- It is a vehicle frequently utilized by some wineries to raise capital by increasing cash flow.
- It provides an outlet for excess wine not up to quality of regular premium wine.
- To sell lesser quality wines, while not interfering with the sale of premium wines.
- To sell wine from the second or third pressing, which lacks the quality of the regular bottling.
- A method of using up excess inventory.
- Wines made from very young grapevines (usually less than eight years) not considered mature enough for their *regular label.*
- Wines aged in wood for a shorter period of time.
- Grapes, juice, or wine purchased on the open market and finished at the winery.

► AMERICAN WINES

Secondary Label	Well-known Label
Adams Ranch	Adelsheim Vineyard
André Champagne	E & J Gallo
Ariel	J. Lohr
Aries	Robert Sinskey
Armstrong Ridge	Korbel Champagne Cellars
Ballatore Spumante	E & J Gallo
Baron Herzog	Royal Kedem Wine
Bell Canyon Cellars	Burgess Cellars
Black Mountain	J. W. Morris
Bon Marché	Buehler Vineyards
Bonverre	St. Supéry
Breckenridge Cellars	Giumarra Vineyards
Bug Creek	Dry Creek
Buzzard Lagoon	Cook-Ellis Winery
Ca' del Solo	Bonny Doon
Calaveras Cellars	Stevenot Winery
Calistoga Vineyards	Cuvaison Vineyards

Cantebury Cellars	Stratford
Canyon Road	Geyser Peak
Carlo Rossi	E & J Gallo
Carmenet	Chalone Vineyards
Caviste	Acacia Vineyards
Cellar Select	Villa Mt. Eden
Chapen Hill	Ste. Chapelle Winery
Chase Creek	Shafer Vineyards
Château Napoléon	Weibel Champagne Cellars
Christopher Creek	Sotoyome
C. K. Mondavi	Charles Krug
Clairvaux	Rabbit Ridge
Claus Vineyards	Mill Creek Vineyards
Cloverdale Ranch	Pellegrini Family
Consumnes River Vineyards	Story Vineyards
Cook's Champagne	Guild Wineries
Corral de Picdra	Chamisal Vineyards
Counterpoint	Laurel Glen Vineyards
Cranbrook Cellars	Monticello
Creekside Cellars	Colony
Cypress	J. Lohr
Daniel Estate	Dominus
Decoy	Duckhorn
Deer Valley	Smith & Hook
Domaine Breton	Guenoc
Dunnewood	Guild Wineries
Edmeades Estate	Kendall-Jackson
Edna Valley Vineyards	Chalone
Emerald Bay	Château Julien
Eshcol	Trefethen
Estancia	Franciscan
Eye of the Swan	Sebastiani
Felta Springs	Mill Creek Vineyards
Floréal	Flora Springs

Secondary Label	*Well-known Label (continued)*
Fox Mountain	Louis J. Foppiano
Fountain Grove	Martini and Prati
Garland Ranch	Château Julien
Gavilan	Chalone
Glass Mountain	Markham
Gustave Niebaum	Inglenook
Hampton Cellars	Bridgehampton Winery
Haraszthy Cellars	Buena Vista
Hawk Crest	Stag's Leap Wine Cellars
Hibbard-Braden Estate	V. Sattui Winery
Hunter Ashby	Rutherford Hill
Indian Creek	Navarro Vineyards
Innisfree	Joseph Phelps
Jade Wine Company	J. Lohr Winery
LaBelle	Raymond
La Montana	Martin Ray Vineyards
Lang	Granite Springs
Langtry	Guenoc
Le Clos	Clos du Val
Le Fleuron	Joseph Phelps
Liberty School	Caymus Vineyards
Livingston	E & J Gallo
Logan	Robert Talbott Vineyards
Los Hermanos	Beringer
MacKenzie Creek	Roudon-Smith Vineyards
Maddelena	San Antonio
Mariposa	Kendall-Jackson
MEV	Mount Eden
M. G. Vallejo	Glen Ellen
Mirabella	Schramsberg
Mountainside	Château Chevalier
Mt. Madonna	Emilio Guglielmo

Napa Ridge	Beringer
Old Dog Winery	David Bruce Winery
Pedregal	Stags' Leap Vineyard
Pegaso	Clos Pegase
Poplar Vineyards	Bouchaine
Prosperity	Firestone
Proud Country	Brotherhood Winery
Q. C. Fly	Bouchaine
Redwood Valley Cellars	Weibel Champagne Cellars
River Bend Cellars	Davis Bynum Winery
River Oaks Vineyards	Clos du Bois
Riverside Vineyards	Louis J. Foppiano
Russian River Valley Vineyards	Mark West Vineyards
Rutherford River	Round Hill
Saddle Mountain	Snoqualmie Winery
Shadow Creek	Domaine Chandon
Silverado Cellars	Château Montelena
Silver Label	B. R. Cohn
Silverwood	Pine Ridge Winery
Stanford	Weibel Champagne Cellars
St. Carl	Brander Vineyards
Ste. Claire	Kendall-Jackson
St. Dunstans	Sterling
Stephens	Girard Winery
Terra Rosa	Laurel Glen
Thalia	Viansa
Tin Pony	Iron Horse Vineyards
Van Duzer	William Hill
Vendange	Sebastiani Vineyards
VinMark	Markham Vineyards
Vin de Mistral	Joseph Phelps
Windsor Vineyards	Sonoma Vineyards
Woodbridge	Robert Mondavi

▶ FRENCH WINES

Secondary Label	Well-known Label
Abiet	Château Cissac
Admiral	Château Labegorce-Zédé
Amiral de Beychevelle	Château Beychevelle
Arche Lafaurie	Château Arche
Baron Villeneuve du Château Cantemerle	Château Cantemerle
Baury	Château Angludet
B de Belair	Château Belair
Beaumayne	Château Couvent des Jacobins
Beausoleil	Château Villemaurine
Bel Air Marquis de Pomereu	Château Bel-Air Marquis d'Aligre
Bellegarde	Château Siran
Bellevue Laffont	Château Fourcas-Dupré
Cadet de Armande	Château Larmande
Campion (third wine)	Château Prieuré-Lichine
Canteloup	Château Lagorce
Château Canuet	Château Cantenac-Brown
Carillon de L'Angeles	Château L'Angelus
Caroline	Château Lestage
Carruades de Lafite (new label)	Château Lafite-Rothschild
Champs de Faizeau	Château Faizeau
Château Andron Blanquet	Château Cos Labory
Château L'Ariste	Château Voigny
Château Arnaudas	Château de Rolland
Château Artigues-Arnaud	Château Grand-Puy-Ducasse
Château Bahans-Haut-Brion	Château Haut-Brion
Château Barraud	Château Bouyot
Château Beau Mayne	Couvent des Jacobins
Château Beau-Mazerat	Château Grand Mayne
Château Belle Rose	Château Pedesclaux
Château Bon Dieu des Vignes	Château de Chantegrive

Château Brassens-Guiteronde	Château Guiteronde
Château Canon Pourret	Château Franc Pourret
Château Carteau Pindefleurs	Château Carteau Matras
Château Cassevert	Château Grand Mayne
Château Certan-Marzelle	Château Certan-Giraud
Château Chantalouette	Château de Sales
Château Chapelle-des-Tours	Château des Tours
Château Chapelle-Madeleine	Château Ausone
Château Chartreuse	Château St. Amand
Château Clairefont (second wine)	Château Prieuré-Lichine
Château Clos du Roy	Château Certan-Giraud
Château Comte des Cordes	Château Fonrazade
Château Corbin-Vieille-Tour	Château Corbin
Château de Calvimont	Château de Cérons
Château de Candale	Château d'Issan
Château de Délias	Château de Sales
Château de Fontarney	Château Desmirail
Château de Grangeneuve	Château Figeac
Château de L'Ermigré	Château Coulac
Château de Marbuzet	Château Cos d'Estournel
Château de Roquefort	Château Terte Daugay
Château de Roux	Château St-Marc
Château des Ormes	Château d'Armajan-des-Ormes
Château des Rochers	Château du Cross
Château des Roches Blanches	Château Côte Baleau
Château des Templiers	Château Larmande
Château Destieu	Bernard Videau
Château Duluc	Château Branaire-Ducru
Château du Vieux Guinot	Château Fourney
Château Fagouet-Jean-Voisin	Château Jean Voisin
Château Ferrière	Château Laville
Château Grand Giscours	Château Giscours
Château Grand Mayne	Château Lafon
Châteaux Guibeau	Château des Laurets

Secondary Label	Well-known Label (continued)
Château Guinot	Château Lapeyre
Château Haut-Bages-Avérous	Château Lynch-Bages
Château Haut-Beychevelle Gloria	Château Gloria
Château Haut Carteau	Château Carteau Matras
Château Haut-Violet	Château Monteil
Château Hournalas	Château St-Marc
Château Jacques-Le-Haut	Château Mont-Joye
Château La Carte	Château Beau-Séjour Bécot
Château La Caussade	Château La Rame
Château L'Ermitage	Château Partarrieu
Château la Gravette	Château Belair
Château Lamouroux	Grands Enclos du Château de Cérons
Château Latour Corbin	Château Corbin
Château la Tour Fleurus	Château Fouquet
Château les Rochers	Château Voigny
Château les Terres Rouges	Château Napoléon
Château Mahon-Laville	Château Laville
Château Mercier	Château Mont-Joye
Château Monregard-Lacroix	Clos du Clocher
Château Moulin Joli	Château Les Ormes-de-Pez
Château Moulin-Riche	Château Léoville-Poyferré
Château Notton	Château Brane-Cantenac
Château Panet Grand Cru	Château Coudert
Château Petit Val	Château Haut Plantey
Château Pey-Arnaud	Château Perraud
Château Peymartin	Château Gloria
Château Prieurs de la Commanderie	Château Saint André
Château Robin des Moines	Château Cardinal-Villemaurine
Château Roc Blanquant	Château Belair
Château Roquefort	Château La Gaffelière
Château Simon-Carrety	Château Gravas
Château St. Louis du Bosq	Château Saint-Pierre

Château St. Roch	Château Nenin
Château Terfort	Château Loubens
Château Tour Cazelon	Château la Tour-Musset
Château Trintin	Château la Rose Figeac
Chemin Royal	Château Fonréaud
Clos Cordat	Château Monbrison
Clos de la Tonnelle	Château Soutard
Clos de L'Oliviér	Château du Cros
Clos du Marquis	Château Léoville-Las-Cases
Close Renon	Château Millet
Clos J Kanon	Château Canon
Clos Labère	Château Rieussec
Clos La Gaffelière	Château La Gaffelière
Clos la Tonnelle	Château Soutard
Clos Toulifaut	Château Taillefer
Connétable de Talbot	Château Talbot
Conques	Château Ormes-Sorbet
Coste	Château Paveil-de-Luze
Cru de Bruilleau	Domaine de Mayne
Cru Haut-Lagueritte	Domaine de La Gauche
Cru St.-Marc	Château La Tour-Blanche
Cypres de Climens	Château Climens
Dauphin de Guiraud	Château Guiraud
des Gondats	Château Marquis-de-Terme
Domaine Brouillaou	Domaine de Castagnaou
Domaine Chante l' Alouette	Château Chante-Alouette
Domaine de Compostelle	Château la Cabanne
Domaine de Curebourse	Château Durfort-Vivens
Domaine de Fontarney	Château Brane-Cantenac
Domaine de Martialis	Clos Fourtet
Domaine de Montviel	Château Bellevue-Montviel
Domaine des Deux Lions	Château Coulac
Domaine des Douves	Château Beauregard
Domaine de Sainte-Hélene	Château de Malle

Secondary Label	*Well-known Label (continued)*
Domaine du Barrail	Château La Rame
Domaine du Coy	Château Navarro
Domaine du Salut	Château Huradin
Domaine Le Besin	Cru Monteil
Domaine Raymond-Louis	Château Cameron
du Moulin	Château Saint Bonnet
Dupeyron	Château Canuet
Enclos de Moncabon	Château Croizet-Bages
Enclos de Moncabon	Château Rauzan-Gassies
Ermitage de Chasse-Spleen	Château Chasse-Spleen
Fleuron Blanc	Château Loubens
Grand Canyon	Château Colombier-Monpelou
Grand Village Capbern	Château Capbern-Gasqueton
Grangeneuve de Figeac	Château Figeac
Gravieres de Marsac	Château Marsac-Seguineau
Guibeau-la Fourvieille	Château des Laurets
Guibot la Fourvieille	Château des Laurets
Haut Laborde	Château Peyrabon
Haut-Madrac	Château Beausite
Hauts de Smith Haut-Lafitte	Château Smith-Haut-Lafitte
Jaffelin	Joseph Drouhin
Julien	Château Cap Léon Veyrin
La Bastide Dauzac	Château Dauzac
Labat	Château Caronne-Ste-Gemme
L'Abeille de Fieuzal	Château Fieuzal
La Cardonnat	Château Grand Moulin
La Chandeliére	Château Bournac
La Chapelle St. Antoine	La Chapelle-St.-Aubin
La Closerie de Camensac	Château Camensac
Lacoste-Borie	Château Grand-Puy-Lacoste
La Croix	Château Ducru-Beaucaillou
La Croix de Bourseau	Château Bourseau

La Dame de Malescot	Château Malescot-Saint-Exupéry
La Dame de Montrose	Château Montrose
Lady Langoa	Château Léoville-Barton
La Fourvieille	Château des Laurets
La Grave Martillac	Château La Tour Martillac
La Gravette	Vieux-Château-Certan
Laffitte Laujac	Château Laujac
Lalande Robin	Château Vieux Robin
La Parde de Haut-Bailly	Château Haut-Bailly
La Plantey	Château Estruelle
La Réserve du Général	Château Palmer
Larrivaux Hanteillan	Château Hanteillan
Lassalle	Château Potensac
Lartigue de Brochon	Château Sociando-Mallet
La Tour Haut-Brion	Château La Mission-Haut-Brion
La Tour Haut-Vignoble	Château Les Ormes-de-Pez
La Tour l'Aspic	Château Haut-Batailley
La Tour Léognan	Château Carbonnieux
La Vin d'Edouard	Château le Jurat
L de La Louvière	Château La Louvière
Le Baron de Brane	Château Brane-Cantenac
Le Boscq	Château Patache-d'Aux
Le Dauphin	Château Guiraud
Lemoine-Nexon	Château Malleret
Le Petit Cheval	Château Cheval Blanc
Le Priourat	Château la Commanderie
Les Cypress de Climens	Château Climens
Les Fiefs-de-Lagrange	Château Lagrange
Les Forts de Latour	Château Latour
Les-Hauts-de-Pontet	Château Pontet-Canet
Les Hauts Marcieux	Château Lafon
Les Plantes du Mayne	Château Grand-Mayne
Les Tourelles de Longueville	Château Pichon-Baron
Les Traverses	Château Lacombe Noaillac

Secondary Label	*Well-known Label (continued)*
L. P. du Château Lafaurie-Peyraguey	Château Lafaurie-Peyraguey
Ludon-Pomies-Agassac	Château La Lagune
MacCarthy Moula	Château Chambert
Mademoiselle de Saint-Marc	Château LaTour Blanche
Margaux Private Réserve	Château Kirwan
Margaux Réserve	Château Le Terte
Marquis de Cadourne	Château Soudars
Marquis de Ségur	Château Calon-Ségur
Maurinus	Château Villemaurine
Mondot	Château Troplong-Mondot
Moulin d'Arvigny	Château Beaumont
Moulin de Bel Air	Château Les Tuileries
Moulin de Duhart	Château Duhart-Milon Rothschild
Moulin de Noaillac	Château Noaillac
Moulin des Carruades (old label)	Château Lafite-Rothschild
Moulin des Graves	Château Haut-Graves-d'Arthus
Moulin de St. Vincent	Château Moulin-à-Vent
Moulin du Biguey	Château La Gaffelière
Moulin du Biguey	Château Terte Daugay
Moulin du Breuil	Château du Breuil
Moulin du Glana	Château de Glana
Moulin du Jauga	Château Navarro
Moulins-de-Citran	Château Citran
Paul Bouchard	Albert Bichot
Pavillon Rouge	Château Margaux
Petit Rahoul	Château Rahoul
Plantey	Château L'Estruelle
Plantey de la Croix	Château Coufran
Prieuré-de-Meyney	Château Meyney
Réserve de la Comtesse de Lalande	Château Pichon-Lalande
Réserve du Marquis d'Evry	Château Lamarque
Roque de By	Château Tour-de-By

Rose Maréchale	Château Verdignan
Ruat	Château Ruat-Petit-Poujeaux
Salle de Poujeaux	Château Poujeaux
Sarget du Gruaud-Larose	Château Gruaud-Larose
Ségla	Château Rausan-Ségla
Ségonnes	Château Lascombes
Ségur	Château Broustet
St. Roch	Château Andron Blanquet
Thomas Freres	Moillard
Tour Bellevue	Château Arcins
Tour de Capet	Château Capet-Guillier
Tour de Marbuzet	Château Haut-Marbuzet
Tour du Roc Milon	Château Fonbadet
Tourteran	Château Ramage-La-Batisse
Troupian	Château Lestage-Simon
Valoux	Château Bouscaut
Vicomtesse	Château Lafitte-Caracasset
Vieux Montaiguillon	Château Montaiguillon
Vin d'Edouard	Château Haut Corbins

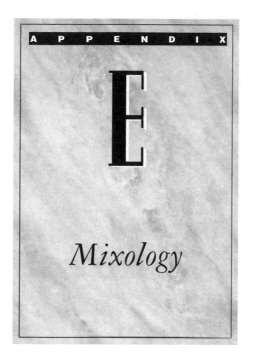

E

Mixology

ixology is the art of following a recipe or formula to produce a standard and consistent drink according to specifications. An experienced mixologist can be compared to a chemist or a chef, producing perfect-tasting, eye-appealing drinks every time. Unfortunately, mixology is slowly becoming a lost art, for most of the mixes are premixed, and the popularity of "standard drinks" is also fading.

One major problem with restaurant bars making their own mix from scratch is consistency of taste. This is why bottled mixes often replace old-fashioned hand-mixed ingredients in popular drinks.

► MIXING METHODS

There are basically three methods of mixing drinks: shaking, blending, and stirring. The reason for these methods is simply to blend the ingredients and properly chill them.

Shaking

In making the shake drink, ice is placed in the shaker, the alcoholic beverage is added, followed by the other ingredients (carbonated beverages are never shaken). The top is placed securely on the shaker and shaken vigorously for about ten seconds. To serve the drink, the top of the shaker is removed and the drink is strained into a cocktail glass. The drink is then garnished and presented to the customer. If the customer has requested that his or her drink be served "on the rocks," a rocks glass is used instead of the customary cocktail glass, and fresh ice is placed in it prior to straining the cocktail. The customary garnish would then be used.

Blending

Blended drinks are made in the same way as shaken drinks, except that drinks containing frozen, partially frozen, or solid ingredients must be blended. By adding shaved ice to the blender, a "frozen" drink will be produced. As in the shaking process, carbonated beverages must *never* be used.

Stirring

The process for making and serving stirred drinks is exactly the same as for shaken drinks, except that they are stirred rather than shaken and carbonated beverages can be added prior to stirring.

Some customers will request their drink be served "neat." They are referring to the drink being served without ice, soda (seltzer), water, etc.—just "straight."

► DRINKS AND NAME ORIGINS

The name of each drink is followed by the key method of mixing (shake, blend, or stir), which refers to the information provided above.

Adonis   *(Shake/Blend)*

Named after the first Broadway musical to run for more than 500 performances. The musical first opened at the Bijou Opera House on September 9, 1884.

1³/4 ounces dry sherry
³/4 ounce sweet vermouth
Dash of bitters (preferably orange)

Alabama Slammer   *(Shake/Blend)*

Equal parts of: Southern Comfort, amaretto, sloe gin, and orange juice.

Alexander   *(Shake/Blend)*

³/4 ounce brandy or gin
¹/2 ounce white crème de cacao
³/4 ounce heavy cream
Garnish: Nutmeg for dusting

Americano   *(Shake/Blend)*

1¹/2 ounces Campari
1¹/2 ounces sweet red vermouth
Splash of seltzer
Garnish: Twist of lemon peel

Bacardi Cocktail   *(Shake/Blend)*

1¹/2 ounces Bacardi light rum
¹/2 teaspoon grenadine syrup
Juice of ¹/2 lime
¹/2 teaspoon sugar
Garnish: Cherry

Bee's Knee's   *(Shake/Blend)*

(This drink is excellent for sore throats.)

1 ounce gin
1 ounce lemon juice
1 ounce honey

Bellini   *(Shake/Blend)*

This drink was created in 1948 by Giuseppe Cipriani at Harry's Bar in Venice, Italy to commemorate the Renaissance artist Giovanni Bellini.

3 medium-sized fully ripened peaches
Juice of 1 lemon
1 chilled bottle of dry Italian spumante or other sparkling wine
2 to 3 teaspoons grenadine syrup (optional)
A carafe

Peel and cut peaches into cubes, then put into a blender, adding the lemon juice at the end (and optional grenadine syrup). Pour the pulp into the carafe, then add the entire bottle of sparkling wine. Stir gently and serve. Serves six persons.

Black Russian *(Shake/Blend)*

3/4 ounce vodka
1/2 ounce Kahlúa

Black Velvet

A mixture of stout and champagne, which was popular in England during the Edwardian days (nineteenth century). It was created when Prince Albert died, an event that sent Queen Victoria (mother of Edward VII, King of England, 1901–1910), along with the entire country into shock. They shrouded everything in black, including champagne, which was mixed with Stout.

The Black Velvet has had a resurgence in popularity. Nowadays, ginger ale is usually substituted because of the high cost of champagne.

Bloody Mary *(Shake/Blend)*

The Bloody Mary, created by Ferdinand Petiot, a bartender at Harry's Bar in Paris in the 1920s, was named after Queen Mary I of England who, because of her persecution of the Protestants, attained the nickname "Bloody Mary." It was later called a "Bucket of Blood," then "Red Snapper," and "Morning Glory." It was introduced into the United States in the 1930s.

1 1/4 ounces vodka
3 to 4 drops Tabasco sauce or other hot pepper sauce
1/2 teaspoon Worcestershire sauce
6 to 8 ounces tomato juice
Juice of 1 lemon
Salt and pepper to taste
Garnish: Stalk of celery
Optional ingredients: celery stick, celery salt,
Horseradish, A-1 Steak Sauce

Blue Hawaii *(Stir)*

1/2 ounce blue curaçao
1 1/2 ounces vodka
3 ounces of sour mix
Seltzer water

Take a ten ounce glass and fill with crushed ice, add blue curaçao, vodka, and sour mix, then add seltzer and mix.

Cape Codder *(Stir)*

1 ounce vodka
Cranberry juice

Champagne Cocktail *(Stir)*

1 sugar cube
Several dashes of bitters (Angostura's)
6 ounces dry champagne or sparkling wine
Lemon peel (optional)

Put the sugar cube into a tulip or fluted-shaped champagne glass and add the bitters. Fill with chilled sparkling wine and gently stir. Garnish with lemon peel.

Chi Chi *(Shake/Blend)*

1 ounce vodka
1 ounce lemon juice
1 ounce coconut milk
3 ounces pineapple juice
1 scoop crushed ice

Blend for 30 seconds and garnish with mint leaves, pineapple chunks, cherry, or orange.

Cobbler

Tall iced drinks with fruit juices, wines, or distilled spirits, decorated with pieces of fruit, and laden generously with ice.

Cocktail

In 1776, Betsy Flanagan invented the American "cocktail." It was in her bar "Halls Corners" in Elmsford, New York, which was decorated with brightly-colored tail feathers of cocks, that she had the notion to add a cock's tail feather as a stirrer to each drink. Hence the name cocktail. During that time, cocktails were often referred to as "roosters."

Collins—Tom/John   *(Stir)*

1 1/4 ounces gin (Tom) or vodka (John)
Juice of 1 lemon
1/2 teaspoon sugar
2 teaspoons grenadine syrup (optional)
Seltzer to fill

Copacabana   *(Shake/Blend)*

1 ounce coffee-flavored brandy
1 ounce light rum
Dash lemon juice
3 drops white crème de menthe
Dash of seltzer

Daiquiri   *(Shake/Blend)*

A cocktail invented in or about 1898 by Jennings S. Cox, an American, who served as chief engineer for the Spanish-American Iron Company, near the village of Daiquiri, in Havana, Cuba.

1 1/2 ounces light rum
1 teaspoon sugar
Juice of 1/2 lime

Fruit daiquiris can be made by cutting back on the amount of sugar, then adding the desired fresh fruit to a blender. Blend for about 30 seconds.

Depth Charge

A Depth Charge is made when you take a shot glass full of whiskey and plunge it (glass and all) into a large glass of beer, then drink the beer!

Frappé

Frappé is a French term for a drink that is super-chilled by the addition of crushed or shaved ice, over which liqueurs are then poured.

Fuzzy Navel   *(Shake/Blend)*

1 1/2 ounces peach schnapps
3 ounces orange juice

Serve over ice.

Gibson   *(Shake/Stir)*

A martini cocktail garnished with a small white onion. The drink was apparently named after the American illustrator Charles Dana Gibson (1867–1944), famous for his drawings of the turn-of-the-century "Gibson Girl." The story goes that Gibson ordered a martini—usually served with an olive—from the bartender Charley Connolly of the Players Club in New York City. Connolly found himself out of olives and instead served the drink with two tiny white onions. The cocktail is first mentioned in print in 1930.

2 ounces gin or vodka
Dash of dry white vermouth
Garnish: A pearl cocktail onion

Gin or Vodka and Tonic   *(Stir)*

$1^1/_4$ ounces gin or vodka
Tonic (quinine water) water
Garnish: Squeeze a wedge of lime into the drink and across the rim of the glass, then drop into the drink.

Gimlet   *(Shake/Blend)*

In the 1890s, a British naval surgeon, Sir T. O. Gimlette, was concerned with the heavy drinking his men were accustomed to. So he diluted the gin with lime juice and although it didn't dissuade them, he unintentionally created a new drink.

3 parts gin
1 part Rose's lime juice

Gin Rickey   *(Shake/Blend)*

Civil War Colonel Joe Rickey had this drink named after him at the St. James Hotel in New York City in 1895.

1 ounce gin
$^1/_2$ ounce lime juice

Glögg

This is a truly Scandinavian drink.

1 bottle (750-milliliter) Akvavit
$^3/_4$ cup raisins
2 bottles (750-milliliter) dry red wine
$^1/_2$ cup blanched almonds
1 tablespoon cardamom seeds, peeled
$^1/_2$ teaspoon whole cloves
$^1/_2$ cup sugar
3 ($^1/_2$-inch) pieces cinnamon stick
1 small piece of a lemon and orange peel

Pour one-half of the Akvavit and all of the wine into a large saucepan. Add raisins, almonds, and sugar. Tie spices in a cheesecloth bag and drop into the mixture. Cover pan. Bring very slowly to the boiling point, but *do not let it boil;* add remaining Akvavit and let simmer 30 minutes. Remove from heat and let steep two hours. When ready to serve, remove the cheesecloth bag, slowly reheat liquid until thoroughly warmed, and then with a long-handled ladle, pour into punch glasses. Serve with raisins and almonds.

Godfather   *(Shake/Blend)*

$^3/_4$ ounce amaretto
$1^1/_2$ ounces Scotch whisky

Godmother   *(Shake/Blend)*

1¹/₂ ounces amaretto
1¹/₂ ounces vodka

Golden Cadillac   *(Shake/Blend)*

1¹/₂ ounces heavy cream
1 ounce Galliano liqueur
³/₄ ounce white crème de cacao

Grasshopper   *(Shake/Blend)*

³/₄ ounce green crème de menthe
³/₄ ounce white crème de cacao
³/₄ ounce heavy cream

Harvey Wallbanger   *(Shake/Stir)*

It seems that in southern California (according to legend), Tom Harvey would arrive at his favorite pub after a day's surfing and order an "Italian Screwdriver"; then after consuming several of them, he would attempt to leave and start "banging" into walls! Hence the name.

6 ounces orange juice
1 ounce vodka
¹/₂ ounce Galliano liqueur

Hawaiian Punch   *(Shake/Blend)*

1 ounce Southern Comfort
1 ounce amaretto
1 ounce crème de noyaux
1 ounce pineapple juice
1 ounce orange juice

Highball   *(Stir)*

In St. Louis in the 1880s, early railroaders used a ball on a high pole as a signal for railroad trains to go ahead or speed up. This signaling device was called a "highball." The trainmen, always on a fast schedule, had time only for a quick drink.

Hence, when bartenders found that ice, whiskey, and water could be mixed speedily into a delightful drink, they called it a "highball."

1¹/₂ ounces blended whiskey
Ginger ale to fill

Hot Buttered Rum   *(Stir)*

1 teaspoon white or brown sugar
1¹/₂ ounces dark rum
2 cloves
1 pat butter
Boiling water

Place sugar, rum, and cloves in a heavy mug or coffee cup. Fill with boiling water. Add butter and stir.

Hot Toddy *(Stir)*

1¹/₂ ounces brandy, rum, or whiskey
1 teaspoon sugar
2 cloves stuck in slice of lemon
Boiling water

Place spoon in old-fashioned glass to prevent cracking. Add ingredients and fill with boiling water.

Irish Coffee

Like many other drinks whose origins are clouded in mystery, Irish Coffee (according to some) was introduced by Joe Sheridan in 1938 to airline passengers who braved cold planes and bumpy flights. Flight attendants would ease the pain by adding a shot of whiskey to hot coffee. The whiskey became Irish when the flights arrived or departed from Shannon Airport in Ireland.

Another story, which takes place in 1952, has the owner of the lounge at Shannon Airport offering customers strong, hot coffee laced with Irish whiskey to ease the long waits in between flights.

1 cube sugar
1¹/₂ to 2 ounces Irish whiskey
Strong coffee
Heaping tablespoon whipped heavy cream

To make Irish coffee, place one cube of sugar into the bottom of a large stem-glass (12 ounces). Pour 1¹/₂ to 2 ounces of a good quality Irish whiskey over the cube. Then put a spoon into the glass and pour in very hot and extremely strong coffee (not espresso). The purpose of the spoon is to absorb the heat so the glass does not break. Then stir gently and add a heaping tablespoon of freshly whipped heavy cream, not one of the dairy creamers or premixed cream from an aerosol can. Serve without stirring.

Jack Rose Cocktail *(Shake/Blend)*

A cocktail named after a gangster who turned states evidence after the killing of Herman Rosenthal in a bar in Times Square in 1912.

1¹/₂ ounces Applejack (apple brandy)
2 ounces lemon juice
1 dash Grenadine syrup

Jelly Bean *(Shake/Blend)*

1¹/₂ ounces anisette
1¹/₂ ounces blackberry-flavored brandy

Kamikazi *(Shake/Blend)*

1¹/₂ ounces vodka
1¹/₂ ounces triple sec
2 ounces lemon juice

Kir *(Stir)*

1 ounce crème de cassis
4 to 5 ounces dry white wine

A popular apéritif drink made with crème de cassis (black currant liqueur) and dry white wine, named after the late mayor of the City of Dijon, France, Canon Félix Kir. Kir was the favorite drink of the mayor from the 1940s until his death in 1968 at age 92. Originally, Kir was made by mixing Aligoté wine (a highly acidic white wine from Burgundy) with a tablespoon or so of crème de cassis, served chilled. Nowadays, just about any white wine is used and mixed with anywhere from several teaspoons to one-third of a glass of crème de cassis.

There are several variations of this drink: the Kir Royale listed below, along with Kir Communist (cassis and red wine), and Kir Imperial (raspberry liqueur instead of cassis and champagne).

Kir Royale *(Stir)*

1 ounce crème de cassis
4 to 5 ounces dry sparkling wine

Long Island Ice Tea *(Shake/Blend/Stir)*

¹/₂ ounce gin
¹/₂ ounce light rum
¹/₂ ounce tequila
¹/₂ ounce vodka
¹/₄ ounce triple sec
3 ounces lemon juice
Splash of Coke or Pepsi

Put into blender for 30 seconds; then pour over ice and add a splash of Coke or Pepsi, and serve with lemon wedge.

Lynchburg Lemonade *(Shake/Blend)*

1 part Jack Daniel's Tennessee Whiskey
1 part triple sec
1 part sweet and sour mix
4 parts Sprite or 7-Up

Garnish with lemon slices and cherries.

Mai Tai *(Shake/Blend)*

This world-famous drink (created in 1944 by Trader Vic) is translated from Polynesian to mean "the best, out of this world."

1¹/₄ ounces light rum
1 ounce dark rum
³/₄ ounce orgeat syrup
¹/₄ ounce triple sec
1 ounce pineapple juice
¹/₂ ounce grenadine syrup
¹/₂ ounce lime juice

Manhattan *(Shake/Stir)*

The former Manhattan Club, a six-story building erected on Madison Avenue in 1859, was originally a residence for Leonard Jerome, the father of Jennie Jerome (1854–1921), a New Yorker (one-sixteenth Iroquois Indian). In 1874, she married Lord Randolph Churchill and two years later she bore a son, Sir Winston, who would later figure quite heavily in English politics. It was this same Lady Churchill who first persuaded a reluctant bartender there to mix bourbon "with a lesser portion of sweet red vermouth and aromatic bitters" to please a guest of honor. As one of New York's leading socialites, she was giving a party in honor of Samuel J. Tilden's election as a reform governor. She named the drink a "Manhattan" after the Club where the celebration was being held—and it is still one of the world's most popular cocktails.

1¹/₄ ounces bourbon or blended whiskey
¹/₂ ounce sweet red vermouth
Dash of bitters
Garnish: Cherry

For a Dry Manhattan, substitute dry white vermouth.

Margarita *(Shake/Blend)*

Purportedly concocted by a Virginia City bartender in memory of his girlfriend who was accidentally shot during a barroom brawl.

Another story has the Margarita Cocktail purportedly created in 1948 in Acapulco, Mexico, by socialite Margarita Sames. Her recipe contained three parts tequila, two parts Cointreau, and one part lime juice.

1¹/₂ ounces tequila
1 ounce triple sec liqueur (minimum 60 proof)
³/₄ ounce freshly squeezed lemon juice
Coarse salt for the rim of the glass
Lots and lots of shaved ice

(Note: In Mexico the fruit utilized is called *limón,* a light green citrus fruit with a taste quite similar to lemon and lime, with the flavor of lemon predominating. Although limes are the customary citrus fruit used in the United States for Margaritas, a lemon would offer a more authentic taste.)

Martini *(Shake/Stir)*

"Martinez" was the original name of this popular drink, first introduced in 1860 by Jerry Thomas in San Francisco's Occidental Hotel. The original recipe was considerably different from what we know today. It consisted of one jigger of gin, one wine glass of sweet red vermouth, a dash of bitters, two dashes maraschino liqueur. It was then shaken well and garnished with lemon slice.

2 ounces gin or vodka
Dash of dry white vermouth
Garnish: Lemon peel or green olive

Use a large stainless steel cocktail shaker. Add plenty of ice cubes, then add the gin or vodka and a dash of vermouth. Now, if you were serving James Bond, shake the ingredients until the shaker becomes coated with ice, or with a long metal stirrer, stir for several minutes. Either strain the martini into a cocktail glass or pour over ice in an old-fashioned glass. Garnish with lemon peel, green olive, or pearl cocktail onion. (If a pearl cocktail onion is substituted for the lemon peel or green olive, the drink then becomes a "Gibson.")

Although the ingredients of today's "Silver Bullet" is considerably different from its original, it did consist of a very dry vodka martini served arctic cold.

The martini was really popularized by James Bond movies in which the super spy requested his "vodka martini" be served to him "shaken, not stirred." Before Bond movies became the "in-thing," television viewers might remember Neil, the alcoholic St. Bernard dog in the television show "Topper," starring Leo G. Carroll, during the 1950s and 1960s.

Mimosa *(Stir)*

3 ounces dry sparkling wine
4 ounces orange juice

Mint Julep

There are probably as many different recipes for the preparation and serving of mint juleps as there are people who drink them on Kentucky Derby Day. To quote from R. B. Harwell in his 1975 drink book, "The julep is part ceremony, tradition, and regional nostalgia; part flavor, taste, and aroma; and only by definition bourbon, simple syrup, mint, and ice."

History and folklore. Kentuckians were awarding silver julep cups at country fairs as long ago as 1816. The word *julep* itself can be traced back more than 600 years and stems from the Arabic *julab* or Persian *jul-ab,* meaning "rose water." The word is cited in English as early as the year 1400 and indicated "a syrup made only of water and sugar." In actuality, the mint and sugar were being blended with distilled spirits before the birth of America. The true "Southern-style" mint julep coincided with the discovery of genuine Kentucky straight bourbon whiskey around the late 1700s.

The receptacle, stirring instrument, quality of water and bourbon, method of crushing, bruising or muddling the mint, and the gentility of the hands preparing it, are among the subjects of lengthy advice to those who would create a perfect mint julep. For instance, Irvin S. Cobb, Kentucky writer, called for crushing the mint with a wooden pestle and using a pewter tankard. He saluted his creation by proclaiming, "Who has not tasted one, has lived in vain."

The mixologist. Following is a free-form combination of prose borrowed from three late but notable julep authorities: Henry Clay, famous Kentucky politician; Judge Soule Smith, a Lexington attorney; and General Simon Bolivar Buckner, grandson of the great Confederate general.

A mint julep is not the product of a formula—it is ceremony and must be performed by a gentleman possessing a true sense of the artist, a deep reverence for the ingredients, and a proper appreciation of the occasion. It is a rite that must not be entrusted to a novice, a statistician, or a Yankee. It is a heritage of the Old South, an emblem of hospitality and a vehicle in which noble minds can travel together upon the flower-strewn paths of a happy and congenial thought.

The Ingredients

Water. Limestone water, preferably hand-drawn from a spring where cool, crystal-clear water bubbles from under a bank of dew-washed ferns. In a consecrated vessel, dip up a little water at the source.

Distilled Spirits. Kentucky Bourbon distilled by a master hand, mellowed with age in oaken barrels yet still vigorous and inspiring.

Mint. Mint leaves, fresh and tender. Follow a stream through its banks of green moss and wild flowers until it broadens and trickles through beds of mint growing in aromatic profusion and waving softly in the wind. Gather the sweetest and tenderest shoots and gently carry them home.

Simple Syrup. Take from the cold spring some water, pure as angels are; mix it with sugar from an ancestral bowl to make a silvery mixture as smooth as some rare Egyptian oil.

Ice. Into a canvas bag, pound twice as much ice as you think you will need. Make it fine as snow, keep it dry, and do not allow it to degenerate into slush. Gather together your finest silver cups and spoons and you are ready to begin.

Combining. Take your glass and crush your mint within it, pressing the fresh mint against the goblet with the back of a silver spoon. Crush it around the borders of the glass and leave no place untouched. Then throw the mint away—it is a sacrifice. Fill the glass with cracked ice; pour in the quantity of bourbon which you want. It trickles slowly through the ice. Let it cool for a moment, then pour your sugared water over it. Let the cup stand until nature, wishing to take a further hand and add another of its beautiful phenomena, encrusts the whole in a glistening coat of white frost.

Around the rim, place sprigs of mint so that the one who drinks may find a taste and odor at one draught.

Fulfillment. When all is ready, assemble your guests on the porch or in the garden where the aroma of the juleps will rise heavenward and make the birds sing. Propose a worthy toast, raise the goblet to your lips, bury your nose in the mint, inhale a deep breath of its fragrance, and sip the nectar of the gods. Sip it and dream.

Colonel Henry Watterson, for 50 years editor of the *Louisville Courier-Journal,* had still another method of making mint juleps:

"Take a silver goblet that holds one pint and dissolve a lump of loaf sugar with not more than a tablespoon of water. Take one mint leaf, no more, and crush it gently between the thumb and forefinger before dropping it into the dissolved sugar. Then fill the goblet nearly full to the brim with shaved ice. Take a few sprigs of mint leaves and use for decorating the top of the mixture, after it has been frapped with a spoon. In a second silver goblet pour in all the bourbon whiskey the goblet will hold. Drink the whiskey and throw away the other ingredients."

Making the mint julep. One of the unfortunate realities of mint juleps is no matter how hard you try, you really can't make a mint julep that tastes authentic, unless it is made in Kentucky. Kentucky is where the ingredients either grow naturally or are produced locally. One of the most important ingredients are delicately scented spearmint leaves (not the peppermint that grows like weeds in home gardens).

For individual mint juleps. Place one teaspoon of superfine sugar into a shallow dish and add three to four sprigs of mint, barely covering this with about $^1/_2$ teaspoon cool water. Lightly bruise the mint leaves and rub them around the rim of a julep glass and discard. Fill the cup $^3/_4$ full of crushed ice and add three to four ounces of bourbon. Then add the bruised mint, sugar and water mixture, and stir gently. On top of this, gently place several sprigs of mint, dusted with powdered sugar. Wait about 30 seconds and all at once the cup or glass will become encrusted with a layer of white frost. Gently sip and enjoy.

For larger batches, one should mull or crush five to six mint leaves in a glass bowl with the aid of a silver spoon until some of the juice is extracted. Then rub the leaves on the inside of the silver mint julep cup or glass before discarding. Add to the mint juice about 5 to 6 tablespoons of superfine sugar and just enough cool water to mix them thoroughly into a sort of slurry, which is known as a simple sugar or syrup. Then place them in the refrigerator. Fill the julep cup or glass with plenty of shaved or crushed ice. Add one to two tablespoons of the simple sugar mixture (according to the desired sweetness) to each cup or glass, then add two jiggers (three to four ounces) bourbon. Stir well and wait for the cup or glass to become frosted. Then place several fresh sprigs of mint around the rim of the cup or glass, dusted lightly with powdered sugar so that one who drinks may find taste and odor at one draft. Place plastic straws into the cup so that they extend about 2 inches above the mint. You might have to cut them slightly to fit the size of the glass.

Mint Julep—Party Batches

58 full fresh mint leaves
1 cup of sugar
$^1/_2$ cup of hot water
48 jiggers (about 80 ounces of bourbon)
Plenty of shaved or crushed ice

In a separate bowl, muddle (bruise with forceful strokes) the mint with the sugar and hot water to make a mint syrup. Then strain mixture and refrigerate overnight. Fill 24 julep cups ³/₄ full of shaved ice. Add two jiggers of bourbon and one teaspoon mint syrup per drink. Stir each drink gently and add additional ice to fill cups. Then garnish with mint sprigs. Serves 24 thirsty people.

Moscow Mule *(Stir)*

A cocktail created and popularized in 1946 at Jack Morgan's Cock N' Bull Restaurant in Los Angeles, California. It consists of vodka and ginger beer, with a wedge of a fresh lime.

Negroni *(Shake/Stir)*

Purportedly conceived by a pub-crawling Count Negroni who demanded that the bartender at his favorite Florentine bar add a shot of gin into his usual Americano cocktail.

1¹/₂ ounces Campari
1 ounce gin
1 ounce sweet red vermouth
Splash of seltzer and twist of lemon (optional)

Old-Fashioned *(Shake/Blend)*

The origin of the old-fashioned is traced back to one Thomas Louis Witcomb, a respected bartender at the Pendennis Club in Louisville, Kentucky, which first opened its doors in 1881. Many older recipes called for a sprig of mint, making it similar to the Mint Julep. Some papers in the 1800s make reference to Juleps made "the old-fashioned way." The drink was first introduced in the East at the original Waldorf bar some time in the 1890s.

1¹/₄ ounces Bourbon whiskey
2 dashes bitters
Splash of water
Simple sugar

Orgasm *(Shake/Blend)*

1¹/₂ ounces Bailey's Irish Cream
1¹/₂ ounces Kahlúa
Splash of cream

Piña Colada *(Shake/Blend)*

Purportedly concocted in 1963 by Don Ramos Portas Mingot, a bartender at the Barrachina Restaurant in San Juan, Puerto Rico. However, one Ramon "Monchito" Marrero of Monchito's Bar in the San Juan Hilton, San Juan Puerto claims he created it in 1954.

1¹/₄ ounces light rum
3 ounces pineapple juice
2 ounces coconut milk
Garnish: Cherry, pineapple wedge, and lime

Pink Squirrel *(Shake/Blend)*

1¹/₂ ounces light cream
¹/₂ ounce white crème de cacao
¹/₂ ounce crème de almond or crème de noyaux

Planter's Punch *(Shake/Blend)*

1 ounce light rum
2 ounces pineapple juice
1 ounce orange juice
1 ounce lemon or lime juice
1/4 ounce grenadine syrup
Orange slice
Float 1/2 ounce Myers's dark rum on top

Presbyterian *(Stir)*

1 1/4 ounces blended whiskey
Seltzer water
Ginger ale

After adding whiskey, fill remainder of glass half with seltzer water and half with ginger ale.

Ramos Gin Fizz *(Shake/Blend)*

Supposedly invented by Henry C. Ramos in 1888, at his famous Imperial Cabinet Bar and Saloon in New Orleans during the Mardi Gras.

1 1/4 ounces gin
1/2 ounce lemon juice
1/2 ounce lime juice
1 teaspoon sugar
1 egg white
1 ounce cream
Seltzer water to fill

Blend or shake all ingredients, then top with seltzer water.

Rob Roy *(Shake/Stir)*

Robert MacGregor, a character immortalized in a novel by Sir Walter Scott (1817), was said to have hidden from the law in an oak tree, where now only a stump remains, 400 yards along the road from the Glengoyne distillery in Scotland. The drink Rob Roy was named after MacGregor because of his "red hair."

1 1/2 ounces Scotch whisky
3/4 ounce sweet red vermouth
Dash of orange bitters

For a Dry Rob Roy, substitute dry white vermouth.

Rum & Coca-Cola *(Stir)*

The Andrew Sisters, a world-famous female singing group, made the song "Rum & Coca-Cola" famous.

1 1/2 ounces light or dark rum
Coca-Cola
Garnish: Twist of lime or lemon

After adding rum, fill remainder of glass with Coca-Cola or other cola-based mixes.

Rusty Nail *(Shake/Stir)*

3/4 ounce Scotch whisky
1/2 ounce Drambuie liqueur

Salty Dog *(Shake/Blend)*

1¹/₂ ounces gin
4 ounces grapefruit juice
Salt for rim of glass

Sangria *(Stir)*

1 (750-milliliter) bottle of dry red, white, or rosé wine
One lemon, lime, orange: cut into quarters, then squeezed
¹/₄ to ¹/₃ cup superfine sugar
Maraschino cherries for garnish

Mix all ingredients together (including the quartered fruit) and allow to chill for several hours before serving.

Sazerac *(Shake)*

A cocktail created in 1859, at 13 Exchange Alley in a bar owned by John B. Schiller. It consists of Bourbon whiskey, Peychaud's bitters, Pernod, and sugar.

Scarlett O'Hara *(Shake/Blend)*

1 ounce Southern Comfort
Juice of ¹/₂ lime
6 ounces cranberry juice

Scotch and Soda *(Stir)*

The Kingston Trio, world-famous singing group from the 1950s, recorded a song entitled, "Scotch N' Soda."

1¹/₂ ounces Scotch whisky
Seltzer water to fill

Screaming Orgasm *(Shake/Blend)*

1¹/₂ ounces Bailey's Irish Cream
1¹/₂ ounces Kahlúa
1¹/₂ ounces vodka
Splash of cream

Screwdriver/Orange Blossom *(Shake/Stir)*

This very popular drink was supposedly created by oilmen or oil riggers, who would use their tools to stir it.

1¹/₄ ounces vodka (screwdriver)
or
1¹/₄ ounces gin (orange blossom)
Orange juice to fill

Sea Breeze *(Stir)*

1¹/₄ ounces vodka
4 ounces grapefruit juice
4 ounces cranberry juice

Pour in a tall glass over ice.

Seven & Seven   (Stir)

1 1/2 ounces Seagram's 7 Crown whiskey
7-Up

Sex on the Beach   (Blend)

3/4 ounce vodka
1/2 ounce Tia Maria, Kahlúa, or other coffee-flavored liqueur
1/2 ounce Chambord or other raspberry-flavored liqueur
Garnish: Orange slice

Shooter

A straight shot of a liqueur called "peppermint schnapps."

Sidecar   (Shake/Blend)

The recipe was first created at Harry's Bar in 1935 from a combination of Cointreau and cognac.

3/4 ounce brandy
1/2 ounce triple sec
1/2 ounce lemon juice

Singapore Gin Sling   (Shake/Blend)

This drink, originally called a "Straits Sling," was created in 1915 by Ngiam Tong Boon, a bartender of the Long Bar at the Raffles Hotel in Singapore.

1 1/2 ounces gin
3/4 ounce cherry-flavored brandy
1 ounce consisting of lemon and orange juice
Top with a squirt of seltzer
Garnish: Cherry, orange slice, or sprig of mint

Pimm's Cup

A "gin sling," flavored with various herbs, spices, and sweeteners, was invented in 1841 by James Pimm at the Oyster Bar in London. Years back, Pimm's Cup was produced in six different versions, each with a different base ingredient, and identified by a number of the label, for instance: Pimm's Cup #1, #2, #3, #4, #5, #6. But because the gin version (number 1) comprised 99 percent of total sales, the other variations were dropped, along with the "No. 1" on the label.

Slippery Nipple   (Shake/Blend)

1 1/2 ounces sambuca
1 1/2 ounces Bailey's Irish Cream

Sloe Gin Fizz   (Stir)

1 1/2 ounces sloe gin
3/4 ounce lemon juice
1 teaspoon sugar
Top with seltzer

Sloe and Comfortable Screw
(Shake/Blend)

1¹/₂ *ounces vodka*
1¹/₂ *ounces Southern Comfort*
³/₄ *ounce sloe gin*
Orange juice to fill

Sour   *(Shake/Blend)*

1¹/₄ *ounces of any type of whiskey*
³/₄ *ounce lemon juice*
1 teaspoon sugar
Garnish: Cherry, orange slice.

Note: Instead of using whiskey, basically any other distilled spirit, along with liqueurs and fruit-flavored brandies, may also be used.

Stinger   *(Shake/Blend)*

1³/₄ *ounces brandy*
³/₄ *ounce white crème de menthe*

Swampwater   *(Shake/Stir)*

1¹/₂ *ounces green Chartreuse*
Juice ¹/₂ lime
6 ounces pineapple juice

Must be drunk from a Mason jar.

Tequila   *(Shot)*

When drinking tequila straight, first wet the fleshy area between your thumb and index finger, sprinkle salt on the wet spot, and then "lick" the salt with your tongue. Immediately follow with a straight shot of tequila, downed in one gulp. Then put a lemon wedge into your mouth and suck deeply. This ritual is known in Mexico as "Los Tres Cuates"—"The Three Chums."

Tequila Sunrise   *(Shake/Stir)*

A drink purportedly served as a "dawn pick-me-up" at the Agua Caliente racetrack in Mexico, where the bars never closed.

1¹/₂ *ounces tequila*
6 ounces orange juice

Float 1/4 ounce grenadine syrup on top

Tom and Jerry   *(Shake/Blend)*

The "Tom and Jerry" was created from Edan's *Life in London*, also known as *Days and Nights of Jerry Hawthorne and his Elegant Friend, Corinthian Tom*, in 1928.

1 egg yolk, beaten
1 egg white, beaten
1 teaspoon sugar
¹/₄ *teaspoon allspice*
1 ounce white rum
Milk
Dusting of nutmeg

Beat egg white until fluffy. Then beat egg yolk with sugar, allspice, and rum until smooth and thick.

Add egg white and pour into heated mug. Fill with hot milk and dust with nutmeg.

Watermelon   *(Shake/Blend)*

1 ounce Southern Comfort
1 ounce vodka
2 ounces pineapple juice
Dash of grenadine syrup

White Russian   *(Shake/Blend)*

³/₄ ounce vodka
¹/₂ ounce Kahlúa
1 ounce cream

Zombie   *(Shake/Blend)*

A cocktail developed by Los Angeles restaurateur Don the Beachcomber which featured perhaps every type of rum he had on hand at his bar. This drink boasted a challenge that many simply could not pass up: "Only one to a customer."

1 ounce light rum
1 ounce dark rum
³/₄ ounce gold rum
³/₄ ounce pineapple juice
³/₄ ounce papaya juice
³/₄ ounce lime juice
2 teaspoons Falernum or simple sugar
¹/₂ ounce apricot-flavored brandy
¹/₂ ounce orange curaçao or passion fruit syrup
¹/₂ ounce 151 proof Demerara rum
Garnish: Orange wheels and several sprigs of mint.

Shake all ingredients with cracked ice and either strain into a cocktail glass or pour over ice in an old-fashioned glass. Float 151-proof rum on top.

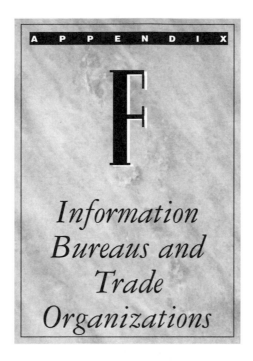

APPENDIX

F

Information Bureaus and Trade Organizations

Alabama Grape Growers & Winemakers
1926 Hwy 31 South
Suite 117
Birmingham, AL 35244-1141
Phone: 205-664-5583

Amador Vintners Association
P.O. Box 667
Plymouth, CA 95669
Phone: 209-245-6942
Fax: 209-245-6617

American Bartenders' Assn.
P.O. Box 11447
Braden, FL 34262

American Beverage Institute
607 14th Street, NW
Suite 1110
Washington, DC 20005
Phone: 800-843-8877
Fax: 202-347-5250

American Brandy Assn.
1 Market Street
Suite 1111
San Francisco, CA 94105
Phone: 415-546-6810
Fax: 415-546-6813

American Dairy Assn.
6300 North River Road
Rosemount, IL 60018
Phone: 312-696-1880

American Soc. for Enology & Viticulture
P.O. Box 1855
Davis, CA 95617
Phone: 916-753-3142

American Vintners Assn.
1301 Pennsylvania Ave., NW
Suite 500
Washington, DC 20004
Phone: 800-879-4637
Fax: 202-347-4637

American Wine Society
3006 Latta Road
Rochester, NY 14612
Phone: 716-225-7613

Arizona Winegrowers' Assn.
P.O. Box 726
Sonoita, AZ 85637
Phone: 602-455-5369

Arkansas Wine Producers Assn.
Wiederkehr Wine Cellars
Route #1; Box 392
Ozark, AR 72949
Phone: 501-667-3841
Fax: 501-468-4791

Armagnac Information Bureau
c/o Food and Wines From France
215 Park Avenue South
New York, NY 10003
Phone: 212-477-9800

Assn. of Maryland Wineries
8535 Bradford Road
Silver Springs, MD 20901
Phone: 800-237-9463

Assn. of Tequila Producers
147 World Trade Center Hall
Box 58083
Dallas, TX 75258
Phone: 214-744-5711

Assn. of Wisconsin Wineries
321 Mill Street
Algoma, WI 54201

Association of Brewers
P.O. Box 1679
Boulder, CO 80306-1679
Phone: 303-447-0816
Fax: 303-447-2825

Association Winery Suppliers
21 Tamal Vista Blvd.
Suite 196
Corte Madera, CA 94925
Phone: 415-924-1021

Australian Trade Commission
636 Fifth Avenue
New York, NY 10111
Phone: 212-245-4000

Austrian Trade Commission
845 Third Avenue
New York, NY 10022
Phone: 212-605-0370

Austrian Wine Info. Service
Cornerstone Communications
575 Madison Ave, Ste. 1006
New York, NY 10022
Phone: 212-605-0370
Fax: 212-605-0371

AWARE
244 California Street
Suite 300
San Francisco, CA 94111
Phone: 415-291-9113
Fax: 415-291-8212

Beef Industry Council
444 North Michigan Avenue
Chicago, IL 60611
Phone: 301-467-5520

Bordeaux Wine Information Bureau
c/o Food and Wines From France
215 Park Avenue South
New York, NY 10003
Phone: 212-477-9800

Brotherhood of the Knights of the Vine
P.O. Box 2212
Fair Oaks, CA 95813
Phone: 916-966-8141

California Assn. of Winegrape Growers
225 30th Street
Suite 306
Sacramento, CA 95816-3354
Phone 916-448-2676
Fax: 916-448-0475

California Beef Council
551 City Boulevard
Suite A
Foster City, CA 94404
Phone: 415-571-7000

California North Coast Grape Growers
P.O. Box 213
Ukiah, CA 95482
Phone: 707-462-1361

California Raisin Advisory Board
P.O. Box 5335
3445 N. First Street; Ste 101
Fresno, CA 93755
Phone: 209-224-7010
Fax: 209-224-7016

California Table Grape Commission
2975 N. Maroa Avenue
Fresno, CA 93704
Phone: 209-224-4997

Canadian Soc. of Enology & Viticulture
P.O. Box 38
Vineland Station
Ontario, Canada LOR 2EO
Phone: 905-562-4141
Ext: 142
Fax: 905-562-3413

Canadian Wine Institute
50 Burnhamthorpe Rd West
Suite 401
Mississaugua, Ontario, Canada L5B 3C2
Phone: 905-949-8463
Fax: 905-949-8465

Champagne News & Information Bureau
355 Lexington Avenue
New York, NY 10017
Phone: 212-949-8475
Fax: 212-370-9047

Club Managers Assn. of America
1733 King Street
Alexandria, VA 22314
Phone: 703-739-9500
Fax: 703-739-0124

Cognac Information Bureau
11 E. 47th Street
New York, NY 10017
Phone: 212-308-1874

Colorado Wine Industry Devel. Board
155 S. Madison
Suite 330
Denver, CO 80209-3014
Phone: 303-399-8033
Fax: 303-399-8037

Concord Grape Assn.
5775 Peachtree-Dunwoody Rd.
Suite 500G
Atlanta, GA 30342
Phone: 404-252-3663
Fax: 404-252-0774

Connecticut Grape Growers & Winemakers
RFD 1
North Grosvenor Dale, CT 06255

Cork Quality Council
1200 Jefferson Street
Napa, CA 94559
Phone: 707-255-7667
Fax: 707-255-1119

Cyprus Trade Center
13 E. 40th Street
New York, NY 10016
Phone: 212-686-6016

DISCUS
1250 Eye Street, NW
Suite 900
Washington, DC 20005
Phone: 202-628-3544
Fax: 202-682-8888

El Dorado Wine Grape Growers Assn.
P.O. Box 248
Placerville, CA 95667

Finger Lakes Wine Growers Assn.
Canandaigua Wine Co., Inc.
116 Buffalo Street
Canandaigua, NY 14424
Phone: 716-394-7900

Florida Department of Citrus
P.O. Box 148
Lakeland, FL 33802
Phone: 813-682-0171

Florida Grape Growers Assn.
2521 13th Street
Suite D2
St. Cloud, FL 34769
Phone: 407-892-9008
Fax: 407-931-0036

Food and Beverage Assn. of America
140 Manhattan Avenue
New York, NY 10025
Phone: 212-864-3764

Food and Wines From France
215 Park Avenue South
16th Floor
New York, NY 10003
Phone: 212-477-9800

Georgia Grape Growers Assn.
c/o Habersham Vineyards Winery
Highway 365
Alto, GA 30510
Phone: 404-239-9463

German Wine Information Bureau
79 Madison Avenue
New York, NY 10016
Phone: 212-213-7036
Fax: 212-213-7042

Greek Food and Wine Institute
1114 Avenue of the Americas
16th Floor
New York, NY 10036
Phone: 212-221-0572
Fax: 212-221-8011

Hudson River Region Wine Council
c/o Brimstone Hill Vineyards
Brimstone Hill Rd; RD 2
Pine Bush, NY 12566
Phone: 914-744-2231

Idaho Potato Commission
P.O. Box 1068
Boise, ID 83701
Phone: 208-334-2350

Indiana Wine Grape Council
Merchants Plaza; Suite 1320E
101 W. Washington Street
Indianapolis, IN 46204
Phone: 317-264-9648

Inflight Food Service Association
304 West Liberty Street
Suite 301
Louisville, KY 40204
Phone: 502-583-3783

International Assoc. Culinary Professionals
304 Liberty Street
Suite 201
Louisville, KY 40202
Phone: 502-581-9786
Fax: 502-589-3602

International Chili Society
P.O. Box 2966
Newport Beach, CA 92663

Irish Distillers International
156 East 46th Street
New York, NY 10017
Phone: 212-697-8676

Israel Food & Wine Exporters
350 Fifth Avenue
New York, NY 10118
Phone: 212-560-0600, ext. 425
Fax: 212-564-8964

Italian Trade Center, Inc.
One World Trade Center
Suite 8949
New York, NY 10048-0202
Phone: 212-432-2000
Fax: 212-938-8317

Italian Trade Commission
499 Park Avenue
New York, NY 10022
Phone: 212-980-1500
Fax: 212-758-1050

Jeffersonian Wine Grape Growers Soc.
Rt 5, Box 429
Charlottesville, VA 22901
Phone: 804-296-4188
Fax: 804-293-6631

Kansas Grape Growers & Winemakers
R.R. #1
Box 25
Strong City, KS 66869
Phone: 316-273-8416

Kentucky Distillers Association
110 West Main Street
Springfield, KY 40069
Phone: 606-336-9612
Fax: 606-336-9613

Lake County Grape Growers Assn.
65 Soda Bay Road
Lakeport, CA 95453
Phone: 707-263-0911

Lake County Wine Grape Commission
P.O. Box 877
Lakesport, CA 95453
Phone: 707-995-3421
Fax: 707-995-3618

Lawyer Friends of Wine of San Francisco
P.O. Box 190458
San Francisco, CA 94119-0458

Licensed Beverage Info. Council
1225 Eye Street, NW
Suite 500
Washington, DC 20005
Phone: 202-682-4776
Fax: 202-682-4707

Livermore Valley Winegrowers Assn.
P.O. Box 2052
Livermore, CA 94551
Phone: 510-447-9463

Lodi District Vintners Assn.
P.O. Box 1398
Woodbridge, CA 95258
Phone 209-239-1215
Fax: 209-239-8031

Lodi-Woodbridge Winegrape Comm.
1330 S. Ham Lane
Suite 102
Lodi, CA 95242
Phone: 209-367-4742
Fax: 209-367-0737

Long Island Grape Growers Assn.
246 Griffing Avenue
Riverhead, NY 11901

Maryland Grape Growers Assn.
James L. Russell, Communications
18517 Kingshill Road
Germantown, MD 20874-2211
Phone: 301-972-1325

Mendocino County Vintners Assn.
P.O. Box 1409
Ukiah CA 95482
Phone: 707-468-1343

Mexican Food & Beverage Board
575 Madison Avenue
New York, NY 10022

Michigan Grape & Wine Industry Counc.
P.O. Box 30017
Lansing, MI 48909
Phone: 517-373-1058

Michigan Wine Institute
116 W. Ottowa Street
Suite 401
Lansing, MI 48933
Phone: 517-485-5536

Minnesota Grape Growers Assn.
318 Agriculture Science Bldg
River Falls, MI 54022
Phone: 715-425-3851
Fax: 715-425-3785

Mississippi Muscadine Assn.
P.O. Box 5034
Meridian, MS 39301
Phone: 800-233-1736

Missouri Grape Growers Assn.
P.O. Box 30
Dutzow, MO 63342
Phone: 314-433-2245

Missouri Wine & Grape Advisory Bd.
MO Dept. of Agriculture
P.O. Box 630
Jefferson City, MO 65102
Phone: 314-751-6807

Monterey Wine Country Assn.
P.O. Box 1793
Monterey, CA 93942
Phone: 408-375-9400

Napa Valley Grape Growers Assn.
4075 Solano Avenue
Napa, CA 94558
Phone: 707-944-8311

Napa Valley Vintners Assn.
Box 41
900 Meadowood Lane
Napa, CA 94574
Phone: 707-963-0148

Napa Valley Wine Library Assn.
St. Helena Public Library
1492 Library Lane
St. Helena, CA 94574
Phone: 707-963-5244

National Alcohol Bev. Control Assn.
4216 King Street West
Alexandria, VA 22302
Phone: 703-578-4200
Fax: 703-820-3551

National Assn. of Beverage Importers
1025 Vermont Avenue, NW
Suite 1205
Washington, DC 20005
Phone: 202-638-1617
Fax: 202-638-3122

National Assoc of Catering Exec.
304 West Liberty Street
Suite 201
Louisville, KY 40202
Phone: 502-583-3783
Fax: 502-589-3602

National Beer Wholesalers' Assn.
1100 South Washington St.
Alexandria, VA 22314
Phone: 703-683-4300
Fax: 703-683-8965

National Coffee Assn.
P.O. Box 4060
Westbury, NY 11590

National Fisheries Institute
2000 M Street, NW
Suite 580
Washington, DC 20036
Phone: 202-296-5090

National Licensed Bever. Assn.
4214 King Street
Alexandria, VA 22302-1507
Phone: 703-671-7575
Fax: 703-845-0310

National Livestock & Meat Board
444 Michigan Avenue
Chicago, IL 60611
Phone: 312-467-5520

National Pork Producers Council
P.O. Box 10383
Des Moines, IA 50306
Phone: 800-937-7675

National Restaurant Assn.
Educational Foundation
250 So. Wacker Dr; Ste 1400
Chicago, IL 60606-5834
Phone: 800-765-2122

National Restaurant Assn.
1200 Seventeenth St., NW
Washington, DC 20036-3097
Phone: 202-331-5900
Fax: 202-331-2429

Nat'l Assn. of Beverage Retailers
5101 River Road
Suite 108
Bethesda, MD 20816-1508
Phone: 301-656-1494
Fax: 301-656-7539

Nat'l United Merchants Bev. Assn.
609 Ann Street
Homestead, PA 15120
Phone: 412-521-0723
Fax: 412-521-0171

New Mexico Vine & Wine Society
P.O. Box 26751
Alburquerque, NM 87125
Phone: 505-294-6217

New York Assn. of Wine Producers
Canandaigua Wine Co.
116 Buffalo Street
Canandaigua, NY 14424
Phone: 716-394-7900
Fax: 716-394-6017

New York State Wine Grape Growers
350 Elm Street
Penn Yan, NY 14527
Phone: 315-536-2853
Fax: 315-536-0719

New York Wine & Grape Foundation
350 Elm Street
Penn Yan, NY 14527
Phone: 315-536-7442
Fax: 315-536-0719

Ohio Wine Producers Assn.
822 North Tote Road
Austinburg, OH 44010
Phone: 216-466-4417
Fax: 216-466-4447

Ontario Grape Growers Mark. Board
P.O. Box 100
Vineland Station, Ontario, Canada L0R 2E0
Phone: 905-688-0990
Fax: 905-688-3211

Orange County Wine Society
P.O. Box 11059
Costa Mesa, CA 92627
Phone: 714-546-8664
Fax: 714-546-5002

Oregon Wine Advisory Board
1200 NW Front Avenue
Suite 400
Portland, OR 97209
Phone: 503-228-8336
Fax: 503-228-8337

Oregon Winegrowers' Assn.
1200 NW Front Avenue
Suite 400
Portland, OR 97209
Phone: 503-228-8403
Fax: 503-228-8337

Paso Robles Vintners & Growers Assn.
1225 Park Street
Paso Robles, CA 93446
Phone: 805-238-0506
Fax: 805-238-0527

Pennsylvania Grape Industry Assn.
Rd 4
Box 4660
Glen Rock, PA 17327
Phone: 717-235-6281

Pennsylvania Wine Assn.
Rt. 413
Box 371
Buckingham, PA 18912
Phone: 215-794-7188

Pinot Noir America
1202 East Pike Street
Suite 644
Seattle, WA 98122

Portuguese Trade Commission
590 Fifth Avenue
3rd Floor
New York, NY 10036
Phone: 212-354-4610
Fax: 212-575-4737

Rice Council of America
P.O. Box 740121
Houston, TX 77274
Phone: 713-270-6699

Rioja Wine Information Bureau
220 E. 42nd Street
New York, NY 10017

Roundtable for Women in Foodservice
3022 W. Eastwood Ave.
Chicago, IL 60625
Phone: 312-463-3396
Fax: 312-463-3397

Santa Barbara Co. Vintners Assn.
P.O. Box 1558
Santa Ynez, CA 93460
Phone: 805-688-0881
Fax: 805-686-5881

Santa Clara Valley Wine Growers Assn.
P.O. Box 1192
Morgan Hill, CA 95037

Santa Cruz Mountains Winegrowers
P.O. Box 3000
Santa Cruz, CA 95063
Phone: 408-479-9463

Silverado Trail Wineries Assn.
P.O. Box 453
Deer Park, CA 94576
Phone: 707-257-0130
Fax: 707-257-3311

Society of Medical Friends of Wine
P.O. Box 218
Sausalito, CA 94966
Phone: 415-383-5057
Fax: 415-381-8185

Sommelier Society of America, Inc.
435 Fifth Avenue
New York, NY 10016

Sonoma County Grape Growers Assn.
850 Second Street
Suite C
Santa Rosa, CA 95404
Phone: 707-576-3110

Sonoma County Wineries Assn.
5000 Roberts Lake Road
Rohnert Park, CA 94928
Phone: 707-586-3795
Fax: 707-586-1383

So. San Joaquin Valley Winegrape Grow
4358 Laval Road
Arvin, CA 93203
Phone: 805-858-2291

S/E Grape Industry Assn. of Penn.
P.O. Box 229
Chadds Ford, PA 19317
Phone: 215-388-6221
Fax: 215-388-0360

Tasters Guild
1451 West Cypress Creek Rd.
Suite 300
Ft. Lauderdale, FL 33309
Phone: 305-928-2823
Fax: 305-928-2824

Tea Assn. of the USA, Inc.
230 Park Avenue
New York, NY 10169
Phone: 212-986-9415

Tennessee Viticultural & Enolog. Soc.
Beachaven Winery
1100 Dunlop Lane
Clarksville, TN 37040
Phone: 615-645-8867

Texas Dept. of Ag. Marketing Div.
P.O. Box 12847
Austin, TX 78711
Phone: 512-475-1663

Texas Wine Market. Research Inst.
Texas Tech University
P.O. Box 41162
Lubbock, TX 79409-1162
Phone: 806-742-3077
Fax: 806-742-0125

Texas Wine & Grape Growers Assn.
One Liberty Park Plaza
Grapevine, TX 76051
Phone: 817-424-0570
Fax: 817-488-0148

The Alcohol Policy Council
P.O. Box 148
Waterford, VA 22190
Phone: 703-882-3933

The American Institute of Wine & Food
1550 Bryant Street
7th Floor
San Francisco, CA 94103
Phone: 415-255-3000
Fax: 415-255-2874

The Beer Institute
1225 Eye Street, NW
Suite 825
Washington, DC 20005
Phone: 202-737-2337
Fax: 202-737-7004

The Century Council
550 South Hope Street
Suite 1950
Los Angeles, CA 90071-2604
Phone: 213-624-9898
Fax: 213-624-9012

The Coastal Wine Group
Sakonnet Vineyards
P.O. Box 197
Little Compton, RI 02837
Phone: 401-635-8486
Fax: 401-635-2101

The Concord Council
P.O. Box 88
Forestville, NY 14062
Phone: 716-965-4800

The National Wine Coalition
1703 Rhode Island Ave., NW
Suite 402
Washington, DC 20036
Phone: 202-785-9510
Fax: 202-785-9402

The Organic Grapes into Wine Alliance
54 Genoa Place
San Francisco, CA 94133
Phone: 800-477-0167

The Scotch Whisky Info. Bureau
415 Madison Avenue
New York, NY 10017
Phone: 800-274-7942

The Wine Council of Argentina
7540 Fullerton Ct.
Springfield, VA 22153
Phone: 703-644-6344
Fax: 703-644-6837

TIPS Health Communications, Inc.
600 New Hampshire Ave., NW
Suite 100
Washington, DC 20037
Phone: 202-333-8267

Vinifera Wine Growers Assn.
P.O. Box 10045
Alexandria, VA 22310
Phone: 703-922-7049
Fax: 202-785-9402

Virginia Wineries Assn.
P.O. Box 96
Barboursville, VA 22923-0096

Washington State Grape Society
P.O. Box 722
Prosser, WA 99350-0722
Phone: 509-786-1000
Fax: 509-786-7110

Washington Wine Institute
1932 First Avenue
Suite 510
Seattle, WA 98101
Phone: 206-441-1892
Fax: 206-441-3130

Washington Wine Institute
P.O. Box 61217
Seattle, WA 98121
Phone: 206-728-2252
Fax: 206-441-3130

West VA Grape Growers Assn.
101 Piterra Place
Purgitsville, WV 26852
Phone: 304-289-3493
Fax: 304-289-3900

Wholesale Beer & Wine Assn. of Ohio
37 W. Broad Street
Suite 730
Columbus, OH 43215
Phone: 614-224-3500
Fax: 614-221-6944

Wine Council of Ontario
5 Maywood Avenue
2nd Floor
St. Catharines, Ontario, Canada L2R 1C5
Phone: 905-684-8070
Fax: 905-684-2993

Wine Institute of California
425 Market Street
Suite 1000
San Francisco, CA 94105
Phone: 415-512-0151
Fax: 415-442-0742

Wine & Spirits Guild of America
1766 Dupont Ave. South
Minneapolis, MN 55403
Phone: 612-377-6459
Fax: 612-377-6211

Wine & Spirits Wholesalers of America
1023 Fifteenth Street, NW
Fourth Floor
Washington, DC 20005-2602
Phone: 202-371-9792
Fax: 202-789-2405

Winegrape Growers Coun. of Australia
P.O. Box 503
1 Gawler Street
Nuriootpa, South Australia 5355
Phone: 085-622-088

Winegrape Growers of America
4519 Salem Lane NW
Washington, DC 20007
Phone: 202-337-2434

Wines From Spain
Commercial Office of Spain
405 Lexington Ave; 44 Floor
New York, NY 10174-0331
Phone: 212-661-4814

Women for New York State Wine
350 Elm Street
Penn Yan, NY 14527
Phone: 315-536-3696
Fax: 315-536-0719

Women For WineSense
1925 Vintner Court
Yountville, CA 94599
Phone: 800-204-1616
Fax: 707-944-1492

World Assn. of the Alcohol Bev. Indus.
1250 Eye Street, NW
Suite 900
Washington, DC 20005
Phone: 202-628-3544
Phone: 202-682-8888

Yakima Valley Wine Growers Assn.
P.O. Box 39
Grandview, WA 98930
Phone: 509-786-2163

Bibliography

Abel, Bob. *The Book of Beer.* Chicago: Henry Regnery, 1976.

Adams, Leon. *The Wines of America.* 4th ed. New York: McGraw-Hill, 1990.

Allen, H. Warner. *Sherry and Port.* London: Constable and Company, 1952.

Ambrosi, Hans. *Where the Great German Wines Grow.* New York: Hastings House, 1976.

Amerine, Maynard A., *Wine Production Technology in the United States.* Washington, DC: American Chemical Society, 1981.

Amerine, Maynard A., H. W. Berg, Ralph E. Kunkee, Cornelius S. Ough, Vernon L. Singleton, and Dinsmoor A. Webb. *Technology of Wine Making.* 4th ed. Connecticut: AVI, 1980.

Amerine, Maynard A., and Cornelius S. Ough. *Methods for Analysis of Musts and Wines.* 2d ed. New York: John Wiley & Sons, 1988.

Amerine, Maynard A., and Edward B. Roessler. *Wines: Their Sensory Evaluation.* 2d ed. New York: W. H. Freeman, 1983.

Amerine, Maynard A., and Vernon L. Singleton. *Wine: An Introduction.* 2d ed. Berkeley: University of California Press, 1977.

Anderson, Burton. *The Wine Atlas of Italy.* New York: Simon & Schuster, 1990.

Anderson, Burton. *Vino: The Wines & Winemakers of Italy.* Boston: Little, Brown, 1980.

Anderson, Burton. *The Pocket Guide to Italian Wines.* New York: Simon & Schuster, 1987.

Ashley, Maureen. *Encyclopedia of Italian Wines.* New York: Fireside Books, 1990.

Baldy, Marian W. Ph.D. *The University Wine Course.* California: The Wine Appreciation Guild, 1993.

Balzer, Robert Lawrence. *Wines of California.* New York: Harry N. Abrams, 1978.

Barr, Andrew. *Pinot Noir.* New York: Penguin Books, 1992.

Baxevanis, John J. *The Wines of Bordeaux and Western France.* New Jersey: Rowman & Littlefield, 1987.

Baxevanis, John J. *The Wine Regions of America.* Pennsylvania: Vinifera Wine Growers Journal, 1992.

Benson, Jeffrey, and Alistair MacKensie. *Sauternes: A Study of the Great Sweet Wines of Bordeaux.* London: Sotheby Publications, 1990.

Benson, Jeffrey, and Alistair MacKensie. 2d ed. *The Wines of Saint-Émilion and Pomerol.* London: Sotheby Publications, 1983.

Berberoglu, H. *The World of Wines, Spirits and Beers.* 2d ed. Dubuque, Iowa: Kendall/Hunt, 1984.

Bergmann, John F. *Tips For You.* New York: CBI, 1979.

Berry, Liz, MW. *The Wines of Languedoc-Roussillon.* London: Edbury Press, 1992.

Bespaloff, Alexis. *New Signet Book of Wine.* 3d ed. New York: Signet, 1985.

Bespaloff, Alexis. *The New Frank Schoonmaker Encyclopedia of Wine.* New York: William Morrow, 1988.

Bezzant, Norman. *The Book of Wine.* NJ: Quarto Books, 1985.

Birmingham, Frederic. *Falstaff's Complete Beer Book.* New York: Award Books, 1970.

Boulton, Roger B., Vernon L. Singleton, Linda F. Bisson, and Ralph E. Kunkee. *Principles and Practices of Winemaking.* New York: Chapman and Hall, 1996.

Bradford, Sarah. *The Story of Port.* London: Christie's Wine Publications, 1978.

Brander, Michael. *Scotch Whisky.* London: Canongate, 1990.

Braun, Lionel, and Marion Gorman. *The Drink Directory.* New York: Bobbs-Merrill, 1982.

Broadbent, Michael. *Wine Tasting: Enjoying Understanding.* 5th ed. London: Christie's Wine Publications, 1977.

Broadbent, Michael. *The Pocket Guide to Wine Tasting.* New York: Simon & Schuster, 1989.

Broadbent, Michael. *The Pocket Guide to Wine Vintages.* New York: Simon & Schuster, 1992.

Broadbent, Michael. *The Great Vintage Wine Book.* 2d ed. New York: Alfred A. Knopf, 1991.

Brook, Stephen. *Sauvignon Blanc and Sémillon.* New York: Penguin Books, 1992.

Brown, Gordon. *Handbook of Fine Brandies.* New York: Macmillan, 1990.

Cadiau, Paul. *Lexiwine: French-English Wine Dictionary.* France: Self-published, 1987.

Casas, Penelope. *The Foods & Wines of Spain.* New York: Alfred A. Knopf, 1982.

Cattell, Hudson, and Lee Miller. *The Wines of the East: The Hybrids.* Lancaster, PA: L & H Photojournalism, 1978.

Cattell, Hudson, and Lee Miller. *The Wines of the East: The Vinifera.* Lancaster, PA: L & H Photojournalism, 1979.

Cattell, Hudson, and Lee Miller. *The Wines of the East: Native American Grapes.* Lancaster, PA: L & H Photojournalism, 1980.

Chidgey, Graham. *Guide to the Wines of Burgundy.* London: Monarch, 1977.

Clark, Corbet. *American Wines of the Northwest.* New York: William Morrow, 1989.

Clarke, Oz. *New Encyclopedia of French Wines.* New York: Simon & Schuster, 1990.

Clarke, Oz. *New Classic Wines.* New York: Simon & Schuster, 1991.

Coates, Clive, MW. *The Wines of France.* California: The Wine Appreciation Guild, 1990.

Coltman, Michael M. *Cost Control for the Hospitality Industry: Second Edition.* New York: Van Nostrand Reinhold, 1989.

Cooper, Derek, and Dione Pattullo. *Enjoying Scotch.* London: Johnston and Bacon, 1980.

Cossart, Neil. *Madeira: The Island Vineyard.* London: Christie's Wine Publications, 1984.

Dahmer, Sondra J., and Kurt W. Kahl. *The Waiter and Waitress Training Manual: Third Edition.* New York: Van Nostrand Reinhold, 1988.

Dallas, Philip. *Italian Wines.* 3d ed. London: Faber and Faber, 1989.

De Blij, Harm Jan. *Wine: A Geographic Appreciation.* Totowa, NJ: Rowman & Allanheld, 1983.

De Blij, Harm Jan. *Wine Regions of the Southern Hemisphere.* Totowa, NJ: Rowman & Allanheld, 1985.

Delaforce, John. *The Factory House at Oporto.* London: Christie's Wine Publications, 1979.

Dittmer, Paul R., and Gerald Griffin. *Principles of Food, Beverage and Labor Cost Controls: Fifth Edition.* New York: Van Nostrand Reinhold, 1994.

Duffy, Patrick Gavin. *The Official Mixers Manual for Home and Professional Use.* 7th ed. New York: Doubleday, 1983.

Duijker, Hubrecht. *The Wine Atlas of Spain.* New York: Simon & Schuster, 1992.

Evaluating Beer. Colorado: Brewers Publications, 1993.

Eyres, Harry. *Cabernet Sauvignon.* New York: Penguin Books, 1991.

Faith, Nicholas. *The Winemasters.* New York: Harper & Row, 1978.

Faith, Nicholas. *The Pocket Guide to Cognac and Other Brandies.* New York: Simon & Schuster, 1987.

Faith, Nicholas. *The Story of Champagne.* New York: Facts On File, 1989.

Faith, Nicholas. *Château Margaux.* London: Christie's Wine Publications, 1991.

Féret. *Bordeaux and Its Wines.* 11th ed. Bordeaux, France, 1986.

Fielden, Christopher. *White Burgundy.* California: Wine Appreciation Guild, 1988.

Finch, Christopher. *A Connoisseur's Guide to the World's Best Beer.* New York: Abbeville Press, 1989.

Flower, Raymond. *Chianti: The Land, the People and the Wine.* 2d ed. New York: Universe Books, 1988.

Forbes, Patrick. *Champagne: The Wine, the Land and the People.* New York: William Morrow, 1967.

Ford, Gene. *Wines, Brews and Spirits.* Dubuque, Iowa: William C. Brown, 1983.

Gaertner, Pierre, and Robert Frederick. *The Cuisine of Alsace.* New York: Barron's, 1981.

Galet, Pierre, and Lucie T. Morton. *A Practical Ampelography: Grapevine Identification.* Ithaca, NY: Cornell University Press, 1979.

Garner, Michael, and Paul Merritt. *Barolo: Tar and Roses.* California: The Wine Appreciation Guild, 1990.

George, Rosemary. *The Wines of Chablis.* Pennsylvania: Harper and Row, 1984.

George, Rosemary. *The Wine Dictionary.* London: Longman, 1989.

George, Rosemary. *Wine Label Decoder.* New York: Simon & Schuster, 1989.

George, Rosemary. *French Country Wines.* London: Faber and Faber, 1990.

George, Rosemary. *Chianti and the Wines of Tuscany.* California: The Wine Appreciation Guild, 1990.

German Wine Atlas and Vineyard Register. New York: Hastings House, 1977.

Getz, Oscar. *Whiskey: An American Pictorial History.* New York: David McKay, 1978.

Gillette, Paul. *The Wine Investor.* Los Angeles: PAG Publications, 1995.

Ginestet, Bernard. *Margaux.* New York: Holt, Rinehart and Winston, 1984.

Ginestet, Bernard. *Saint-Julien.* New York: Holt, Rinehart and Winston, 1984.

Gold, Alec. *Wines and Spirits of the World.* Chicago: Follett, 1972.

Goolden, Jill. *Armagnac.* London: Christie's Wine Publications, 1980.

Gorman, Marion, and Felipe P. de Alba. *The Tequila Book.* Chicago: Contemporary, 1978.

Grapes and the Grapevines of California. Harcourt Brace Jovanovich. 1981.

Green, Maureen and Timothy Green. *The Best Bottled Waters in the World.* New York: Fireside Books, 1985.

Greenberg, Emanuel, and Madeline Greenberg. *The Pocket Guide to Spirits and Liqueurs.* New York: Putnam, 1983.

Grimes, William. *Straight Up Or On the Rocks.* New York: Simon & Schuster, 1993.

Grossman, Harold J. *Grossman's Guide to Wines, Beers and Spirits.* 7th ed. New York: Scribner's, 1983.

Grudzinski, Ted. *Winequest: The Wine Dictionary.* New York: Winequest, 1985.

Halász, Zoltán. *The Book of Hungarian Wines.* Hungary: Corvina Press, 1981.

Hallgarten, Peter. *Spirits and Liqueurs.* 2d ed. London: Faber and Faber, 1983.

Hallgarten, S. F. *German Wines.* London, 1981.

Halliday, James. *The Australian Wine Compendium.* London: Angus & Robertson, 1985.

Hanson, Anthony. *Burgundy.* 2nd ed. London: Faber and Faber, 1994.

Hayes, David. *Bar and Beverage Management and Operations.* New York: Chain Store Publishing, 1987.

Heath, Henry B. *Source Book of Flavors.* Connecticut: AVI, 1981.

Heath, Henry B., and Gary Reineccius. *Flavor Chemistry and Technology.* New York: Van Nostrand Reinhold, 1986.

Henriques, E. Frank. *The Signet Encyclopedia of Whiskey, Brandy and All Other Spirits.* New York: Signet, 1979.

Hobley, Stephen. *Travelers Wine Guide to Italy.* New York: Sterling, 1990.

Italian Wines & Spirits Magazine (Civiltà del Bere), New York.

Jackson, David, and Danny Schuster. *The Production of Grapes & Wine In Cool Climates.* New Zealand: Butterworths, 1987.

Jackson, Michael. *The Pocket Bartender's Guide.* New York: Simon & Schuster, 1979.

Jackson, Michael. *The Pocket Guide to Beer: A Discriminating Guide to the World's Finest Brews.* New York: Pedigree, 1982.

Jackson, Michael. *The New World Guide to Beer.* Philadephia, PA: Running Press, 1988.

Jackson, Michael. *Simon & Schuster Pocket Guide to Beer.* 2d ed. New York: Simon & Schuster, 1988.

Jackson, Michael. *Complete Guide to Single Malt Scotch.* Philadephia, PA: Running Press, 1990.

Jackson, Ron S. *Wine Science: Principles and Applications.* San Diego, CA: Academic Press, 1994.

Jeffold, Andrew. *Port: An Essential Guide to the Classic Drink.* New York: Exeter Books, 1988.

Jeffs, Julian. *Sherry.* 3d ed. London: Faber and Faber, 1982.

Johnson, Hugh. *Wine.* New York: Simon & Schuster, 1966.

Johnson, Hugh. *Modern Encyclopedia of Wine.* New York: Simon & Schuster, 1983.

Johnson, Hugh. *The World Atlas of Wine.* 3d ed. New York: Simon & Schuster, 1985.

Johnson, Hugh. *The Atlas of German Wines.* New York: Simon & Schuster, 1986.

Johnson, Hugh. *Vintage: The Story of Wine.* New York: Simon & Schuster, 1989.

Johnson, Hugh, and Hubrecht Duijker. *The Wine Atlas of France.* New York: Simon & Schuster, 1987.

Johnson, Hugh, and James Halliday. *Vintners Art: How Great Wines Are Made.* New York: Simon & Schuster, 1992.

Johnson, Frank. *The Professional Wine Reference.* 3d ed. New York: Harper & Row, 1983.

Johnson, Robert, and Richard Pasichnyk. *The Consumer's Guide to Organic Wine.* Lanham. MD: Rowman & Littlefield, 1993.

Jones, Stan. *Jones' Complete Bar Guide.* Los Angeles, CA: Barguide Enterprises, 1977.

Katsigris, Costas, and Mary Porter. *The Bar and Beverage Book: Basics of Profitable Management.* New York: John Wiley & Sons, 1983.

Kaufman, William I. *Champagne.* New York: Viking, 1973.

Kaufman, William I. *Pocket Encyclopedia of American Wines—Northwest.* California: The Wine Appreciation Guild, 1992.

Keister, Douglas C. *Food and Beverage Control.* 2d ed. Englewood Cliffs, NJ: Prentice Hall, 1990.

Kondo, Hiroshi. *Saké: A Drinker's Guide.* Tokyo, Japan: Kondansha, 1984.

Kramer, Matt. *Making Sense of Burgundy.* New York: William Morrow, 1990.

Kramer, Matt. *Making Sense of California Wine.* New York: William Morrow, 1992.

Lambert-Gócs, Miles. *The Wines of Greece.* London: Faber and Faber, 1990.

Larousse. *Wines and Vineyards of France.* New York: Little, Brown, 1990.

Laube, James. *California's Great Cabernets.* San Francisco, CA: Wine Spectator Press, 1989.

Lausanne, Edita. *The Great Wine Book.* Lucerne, Switzerland: World Publishers, 1970.

Learmonth-Livingstone, John, and Melvyn C. H. Master. *The Wines of the Rhône.* London: Faber and Faber, 1978.

Levinson, Charles. *Food and Beverage Operations.* 2nd ed. Englewood Cliffs, NJ: Prentice Hall, 1989.

Lichine, Alexis. *New Encyclopedia of Wines and Spirits.* 3d ed. New York: Alfred A. Knopf, 1981.

Lichine, Alexis. *Alexis Lichine's Guide to the Wines and Vineyards of France.* New York: Alfred A. Knopf, 1982.

Lipinski, Bob, and Kathie Lipinski. *The Complete Beverage Dictionary: Second Edition.* New York: Van Nostrand Reinhold, 1996.

Lord, Tony. *The New Wines of Spain.* California: Wine Appreciation Guild, 1988.

MacQuitty, Jane. *The Simon & Schuster Pocket Guide to Australian and New Zealand Wines.* New York: Simon & Schuster, 1990.

Magee, Malachy. *1000 Years of Irish Whiskey.* Dublin, Ireland: The O'Brien Press, 1980.

Marcus, Irving H. *How to Test and Improve your Wine Judging Ability.* Berkeley, CA: Wine Publications, 1974.

Margalit, Dr. Yair *Winery Technology & Operations.* California: The Wine Appreciation Guild, 1990.

Mariani, John F. *The Dictionary of American Food and Drink.* New York: Ticknor and Fields, 1983.

Martells, Jack. *The Beer Can Collector's Bible.* New York: Ballantine Books, 1976.

Mayberry, Robert W. *Wines of the Rhône Valley.* NJ: Rowman & Littlefield, 1987.

Mayo, Oliver. *The Wines of Australia.* London: Faber and Faber, 1986.

McGee, Harold. *On Food and Cooking: The Science and Lore of the Kitchen.* New York: Scribner's, 1984.

McWhirter, Kathryn, and Charles Metcalfe. *Encyclopedia of Spanish and Portuguese Wines.* New York: Fireside Books, 1991.

Meinhard, Heinrich. *The Wines of Germany,* 2d ed. New York: Stein and Day, 1980.

Meredith, Ted Jordan. *Northwest Wine.* Washington: Nexus Press, 1990.

Miller, Jack E. *Menu Pricing and Strategy: Third Edition.* New York: Van Nostrand Reinhold, 1992.

Morgan, William J., Jr. *Food and Beverage Management and Service.* Lansing, MI: Educational Institute of the American Hotel and Motel Association, 1981.

Morton, Lucie T. *Winegrowing in Eastern America.* Ithaca, NY: Cornell University Press, 1985.

Mouton-Rothschild: Paintings for the Labels. Boston: Little, Brown, 1983.

Mr. Boston Official Bartender's Guide. 49th ed. New York: Warner Books, 1984.

Ninemeier, Jack D. *Principles of Food and Beverage Operations.* Lansing, MI: Educational Institute of the American Hotel and Motel Association, 1984.

Nykiel, Ronald A. *Marketing in the Hospitality Industry.* 2d ed. New York: Van Nostrand Reinhold, 1989.

Osterland, Edmund. *Wine & the Bottom Line.* Washington, DC: National Restaurant Association, 1980.

Ough, Cornelius S. DSc, MS. *Winemaking Basics.* New York: Haworth Press, 1992.

Parker, Robert M., Jr. *Burgundy.* New York: Simon & Schuster, 1990.

Parker, Robert M., Jr. *Bordeaux.* 2d ed. New York: Simon & Schuster, 1991.

Penning-Rowsell, Edmund. *The Wines of Bordeaux.* 2d ed. New York: Scribner's, 1981.

Peppercorn, David. *Bordeaux.* London: Faber and Faber, 1982.

Peynaud, Emile. *Knowing and Making Wine.* New York: John Wiley & Sons, 1984.

Peynaud, Emile. *The Taste of Wine.* California: Wine Appreciation Guild, 1987.

Pieroth, Kuno F. *The Great German Wine Book.* New York: Sterling, 1973.

Pigott, Stuart. *Riesling.* New York: Penguin Books, 1991.

Pinney, Thomas. *A History of Wine in America.* Los Angeles, CA: University of California Press, 1989.

Platter, John. *John Platter's 1992 South African Wine Guide.* Somerset West, South Africa: The Natural Corporation, 1992.

Plotkin, Robert. *The Professional Guide to Bartending.* 2d ed. Tucson, AZ: PSD Publishing, 1991.

Pogash, Jeffrey M. *How to Read a Wine Label.* New York: Hawthorn Books, 1978.

Poister, John J. *The New American Bartender's Guide.* New York: Signet Books, 1989.

Pomerol, Charles. *The Wines and Winelands of France.* Bordeaux, France: 1986.

Poupon, Pierre, and Pierre Forgeot. *The Wines of Burgundy.* 5th ed. Paris: Presses Universitaires de France, 1974.

Powers, Tom. *Marketing Hospitality.* New York: John Wiley & Sons, 1990.

Preston, William A. *Cork Wine.* St. Helena, CA: Illuminations Press, 1983.

Ratti, Renato. *Asti.* Italy: 1985.

Ramey, Bern C. *The Great Wine Grapes.* Berkeley, CA: Great Wine Grapes, 1977.

Ray, Cyril. *The Wines of Italy.* New York: Octopus, 1966.

Ray, Cyril. *Bollinger: The Story of a World-Famous Champagne.* New York: Pyramid, 1971.

Ray, Cyril. *Cognac.* New York: Stein and Day, 1973.

Ray, Cyril. *Lafite.* 2d ed. London: Christie's Wine Publications, 1978.

Ray, Cyril. *Mouton-Rothschild.* London: Christie's Wine Publications, 1980.

Read, Jan. *Spain and Portugal.* New York: Simon & Schuster, 1977.

Read, Jan. *The Wines of Spain.* London: Faber and Faber, 1982.

Read, Jan. *The Wines of Portugal.* London: Faber and Faber, 1982.

Read, Jan. *Chilean Wines.* London: Sotheby's, 1988.

Read, Jan. *Sherry and the Sherry Bodegas.* California: The Wine Appreciation Guild, 1988.

Reid, Robert D. *Foodservice and Restaurant Marketing.* New York: CBI, 1983.

Ribéreau-Gayon, Pascal. *The Wines and Vineyards of France.* New York: Penguin Books, 1990.

Ries, Al, and Jack Trout. *Positioning: The Battle For Your Mind.* New York: McGraw-Hill, 1986.

Ries, Al, and Jack Trout. *Marketing Warfare.* New York: McGraw-Hill, 1986.

Ries, Al, and Jack Trout. *Bottom-Up Marketing.* New York: McGraw-Hill, 1989.

Robards, Terry. *Terry Robard's New Book of Wine.* 2d ed. New York: Putnam, 1984.

Robards, Terry. *California Wine Label Album.* New York: Workman, 1986.

Robertson, George. *Port.* London: Faber and Faber, 1987.

Robertson, James D. *The Great American Beer Book.* Thornwood, NY: Caroline House, 1978.

Robinson, Jancis. *Vintage Timecharts.* New York: Weidenfeld & Nicolson, 1989.

Robinson, Jancis. *Vines, Grapes, and Wines.* New York: Alfred A. Knopf, 1986.

Roncarati, Bruno. *Viva Vino 200+ DOC + DOCG Wines & Wine Roads of Italy.* London: Wine and Spirit Publications, 1987.

Roycroft, Roy, and Ben Turner. *The Winemaker's Encyclopedia.* London: Faber and Faber, 1979.

Sandeman, George G. *Port and Sherry: The Story of Two Fine Wines.* Self-published, 1955.

Sarles, John D. *ABCs of Italian Wine.* San Marcos, CA: Wine Books, 1981.

Schreiner, John. *The World of Canadian Wine.* British Columbia, Canada: Douglas & McIntyre, 1984.

Seaberg, Albin. *Menu Design: Merchandising and Marketing: Fourth Edition.* New York: Van Nostrand Reinhold, 1990.

Seldon, Philip. *The Great Wine Châteaux Bordeaux.* New York: Vintage Magazine Press Books, 1975.

Sharp, Andrew. *Winetaster's Secrets.* New York: Sterling, 1981.

Sichel, Peter. *The Wines of Germany.* 4th ed. New York: Hastings House, 1980.

Simon, André. *The History of Champagne.* London: Octopus, 1971.

Sommelier Executive Council. *Vintage Wine Book.* 2d ed. New York: Haworth, 1992.

Splaver, Bernard. Edited by William Reynolds and Michael Roman. *Successful Catering: Third Edition.* New York: Van Nostrand Reinhold, 1991.

Spurrier, Steven, and Michel Dovaz. *Académie du Vin: Wine Course.* New York: Macmillan, 1990.

Steadman, Dave. *Restaurant Biz Is Showbiz!.* New York: Whittier Green, 1991.

Stefanelli, John. *Purchasing: Selection and Procurement for the Hospitality Industry.* 2d ed. New York: John Wiley & Sons, 1985.

Stevenson, Tom. *Sotheby's World Wine Encyclopedia.* London: Sotheby's, 1988.

Stevenson, Tom. *Champagne.* London: Sotheby's, 1986.

Stornello, Gianni. *Il Vino è Piemonte, Italy.* Asti, Italy, 1988.

Sutcliffe, Serena. *André Simon's Wines of the World.* 2d ed. New York: McGraw-Hill, 1981.

Sutcliffe, Serena. *Champagne.* New York: Simon & Schuster, 1988.

Tartt, Gene. *The Vineyard Almanac and Wine Gazetteer.* Self-published from Saratoga, CA, 1984.

Torres, Marimar. *The Spanish Table: The Cuisines and Wines of Spain.* New York: Doubleday, 1986.

Torres, Miguel A. *Wines and Vineyards of Spain.* Penedés, Spain: 1982.

Vandyke Price, Pamela. *The Taste of Wine.* New York: Random House, 1975.

Vandyke Price, Pamela. *Guide to the Wines of Bordeaux.* London: Monarch, 1978.

Vandyke Price, Pamela. *Alsace Wines & Spirits.* London: Sotheby's, 1984.

Vandyke Price, Pamela. *Dictionary of Wines and Spirits.* London: Peerage Books, 1986.

Vandyke Price, Pamela. *Wines of the Graves.* California: The Wine Appreciation Guild, 1988.

Van Kleek, Peter E. *Beverage Management and Bartendering.* New York: CBI, 1981.

Vine, Richard P. *Commercial Winemaking: Processing & Controls.* New York: Chapman and Hall, 1981.

Vine, Richard P. *Wine Appreciation.* New York: Facts On File, 1988.

Voss, Roger. *The Pocket Guide to Fortified and Dessert Wines.* New York: Simon & Schuster, 1989.

Wagner, Philip. *A Wine-Grower's Guide.* 2d ed. New York: Alfred A. Knopf, 1976.

Wagner, Philip. *Grapes Into Wine.* 2d ed. New York: Alfred A. Knopf, 1972.

Wasserman, Sheldon. *The Wines of the Côtes du Rhône.* New York: Stein and Day, 1977.

Wasserman, Sheldon, and Pauline Wasserman. *White Wines of the World.* Piscataway, NJ: Scarborough, 1978.

Wasserman, Sheldon, and Pauline Wasserman. *Guide to Fortified Wines.* Piscataway, NJ: Scarborough, 1983.

Wasserman, Sheldon, and Pauline Wasserman. *Sparkling Wine.* Piscataway, NJ: New Century, 1984.

Wasserman, Sheldon, and Pauline Wasserman. *Italy's Noble Red Wines.* 2d ed. New York: Macmillan, 1991.

Weaver, Robert J. *Grape Growing.* New York: John Wiley & Sons, 1976.

Webb, A. Dinsmoor. *Chemistry of Winemaking.* Washington, DC: American Chemical Society, 1974.

Winkler, Albert J., J. A. Cook, W. M. Kliewer, and L. A. Lider. *General Viticulture.* 2d ed. Berkeley: University of California Press, 1974.

Young, Alan. *Australian Wines & Wineries.* Melbourne, Australia: Castle Books, 1983.

Young, Alan. *Making Sense of Wine.* Richmond, Australia: Greenhouse Publications, 1986.

Young, Alan. *Chardonnay.* Napa, CA: International Wine Academy, 1988.

Yoxall, Harry W. *The Wines of Burgundy.* 2d ed. (International Wine and Food Society Guide.) New York: Stein and Day, 1978.

Zoecklein, Bruce W., Kenneth C. Fugelsang, Barry H. Gump, and Fred S. Nury. *Wine Analysis and Production.* New York: Chapman and Hall, 1995.

Zraly, Kevin. *Windows on the World Complete Wine Course.* 2d ed. New York: Sterling, 1992.

Index